Preble's Boys

Commodore Preble and the
Birth of American Sea Power

FLETCHER PRATT

PREBLE'S BOYS
Commodore Preble and the
Birth of American Sea Power

ISAAC HULL · JACOB JONES · STEPHEN DECATUR
WILLIAM BAINBRIDGE · JAMES LAWRENCE
ISAAC CHAUNCEY · DAVID PORTER · WILLIAM
BURROWS · JOHNSTON BLAKELY · LEWIS WAR-
RINGTON · JAMES BIDDLE · CHARLES STEWART
THOMAS MACDONOUGH · STEPHEN CASSIN
DANIEL TODD PATTERSON

WILLIAM SLOANE ASSOCIATES
Publishers   *New York*

DEDICATION

This is contrary to union rules, as it is well known that all publishers are detestable creatures who live on caviar and champagne purchased with the blood and tears of starving authors. Nevertheless, I take the opportunity of this dedication to testify to the friendship, encouragement, generosity, and intelligence of Bill Sloane.

Acknowledgment and Apologia

The author of this book believes that the place for a bibliography is in a library; and besides, when it is put into a book, it runs up the production costs, which is a matter of importance these days. But it would be unfair and ungrateful not to acknowledge indebtedness to the admirable books of Howard I. Chapelle—*The History of American Sailing Ships* (Norton, New York, 1935), and *The History of the American Sailing Navy* (Norton, New York, 1949)—so carefully researched, which have done so much to clear away misconceptions about the wooden walls of Columbia. It would be equally unfair not to mention Theodore Roosevelt's *Naval War of 1812* (Putnam, New York, 1882), in which weights of metal, tactics, and the details of the combats were for the first time subjected to critical examination; Commodore Dudley W. Knox's *History of the United States Navy* (Putnam, New York, 1936), which performs the same office for strategy; and Henry Adams' *History of the United States, 1801–1817* (Scribner, New York, 1891), where the political and diplomatic background is examined.

Of course, this brings up a question. If all these books do so well by the War of 1812, why produce another one? Well, none of them, except incidentally, looks at the personal and emotional side of the war, and in the long run wars are not fought by politics, strategy, tactics, or even by ships, but by men. The sea captains of 1812—and the real decisions of the war were taken on water—have received surprisingly little attention, considering that they did important things at a decisive moment in American history. There have been a couple of biographies of Decatur, there was recently one of Isaac Hull, and a monograph on Macdonough was published in 1909. Beyond that, one must go back to the 1840s, when people had a somewhat livelier sense of what had been accomplished in 1812–15.

In the interval a good deal has been lost. We are in the dark on some of the springs that actuated these men, and even as to some details of their careers. This is a pity, for they belong—most of them—to a vanished pattern. Many of the ideas they held, and even some of the terms they used, no longer have the same meaning today. Yet these were the men who, at a critical period in our history, determined that the United States should take one direction and not another. They did it as a group, and an examination of them as a group should not be altogether valueless.

Contents

Battle Diagrams

PREBLE'S BOYS

Before the Curtain

THIS IS A BOOK ABOUT SOME LITTLE-KNOWN AND RATHER PECULIAR people.

Hardly any of the events narrated in it are more than 150 years old, and the main actors are Americans. But they differ widely from to-day's Americans—not merely by the lack of gasoline engines and names from the midcentury immigrant nationalities, but also in habits, ideas, and methods of thinking about ideas. The difference is as great as though they were Romans of the republic or Chinese of the Ming Dynasty, and perhaps greater for literary purposes; for in the two latter cases, the whole setting is so far away and long ago that the resemblances between Romans, Chinese, and ourselves can safely be stressed. But everyone makes the tacit assumption that a Pennsylvanian of the Jefferson administration was driven by much the same compulsions and desires as a Pennsylvanian in the administration of Harry Truman.

It isn't true. "Jefferson Man" (to use the anthropological term) was the product of quite another environment, and it affected him in many nonphysical ways. He lived in a world where the Philadelphia papers carried ads about runaway slaves; where a mechanic was a man who joined one piece of wood to another by means of iron; where it was indelicate to mention any woman's name, orally or in writing, unless she was being born, married, or dying; where one had to demonstrate the ownership of property in order to vote; and where the Chief Justice of the United States came to court with his thumb in the neck of a jug of whiskey and borrowed a cork from one of the tipstaves.

These are perhaps minutiae, and it is perhaps also a detail to record that Jefferson Man was supposed to be through with college at 17, to

· 3 ·

be well set up in business by 20, and ready to retire as an old man at 40. It is not quite so much of a detail that if he wanted to go from Philadelphia to New York, he made the trip by water because it was quicker and cheaper than the land route; and it is hardly a detail at all that if Jefferson Man got a bad break in business, he could always strike out for himself into the limitless forests of the West. He never had an unemployment problem.

More important, as far as this book is concerned, is the fact that Truman Man is a citizen of one of the largest nations on earth, and, on the whole, a member of its most successful and progressive society; while Jefferson Man lived in a highly experimental commonwealth, one which had not yet settled upon its dominant patterns in government, politics, foreign relations, economics, or even morals.

It was not yet decided (for instance) that when Congress passed a law in conflict with the Constitution, that law had no force. President Jefferson doubted whether he had the authority to purchase Louisiana for the national account, and did believe that it would be impossible for a central government to control so huge an area as that of the 13 states. Changes might take place in the experimental commonwealth over which he presided, but Jefferson Man essentially lived in a world where the very thought of progressive development had not been invented. The whole idea of making changes was to find a favorable point for stasis. Even Mr. Jefferson's expressed wish to see a revolution in the United States every so often at regular intervals meant only that he perceived the need of development if the organism were to live, but could not conceive of its coming about except as overturn.

The Americans of his period believed they had achieved a stasis highly favorable to their best interests as human beings. No doubt because their commonwealth was the only one of its kind, and few non-Americans believed that it would succeed, they were wildly patriotic in a way few people are today. They did not talk about these things; the ideas formed part of the intellectual climate. They were accepted as points of reference; and, precisely because they were, it is necessary to restate them today, when the points of reference have changed.

Even so, it is difficult for anyone now to understand some of the emotions that made Jefferson Man tick. When the news of the Battle of Lake Erie came through, everybody who could afford it from New Hampshire to Georgia put candles in all his windows. This is more or less the equivalent of hanging out flags and letting off strings of firecrackers (though Americans no longer have many means of expressing personal satisfaction over a national achievement); but I do not recall anyone's behaving that way over the tremendous news from Midway in June, 1942. A naval captain who said he lived for glory would sound theatrical and a trifle silly now; but in 1812 it was a perfectly proper remark, and indeed a conventional one.

If one is to understand the men in this book, men who did so much to make the American navy, and through it the American nation, under the hard conditions of the War of 1812, one must begin with their frame of reference. In fact, one must almost end there; so much of what it would be most desirable to know about that lost world and its inhabitants has disappeared. The little world of the navy, that is. The life of A. A. Gallatin is elaborately documented; so are the motives of Aaron Burr and the boyhood of Henry Clay. But these men were in politics, and to Jefferson Man politics was not only a subject fascinating in itself, but one of the leading diversions in a period which had few others. People are always interested in the private lives of public figures, and those of Gallatin, Burr, and Clay received much the same attention that would today be given to the divorces of a movie star.

With the sea-captains it was different. They were men of action, and to the ideas of their own age, indeed to their own ideas, were interesting only when in action. Why should anyone take down the table-talk of Edward Preble, or ask whether the home life of Lewis Warrington was happy? They were military men under orders, visible to the general public only when some outstanding act of valor made them shine; it was hardly granted that they had mental processes.

It was hardly granted, because everything they did, except that outstanding act of valor, was commonplace. One of the ruling, formative facts about Jefferson Man was that he lived in the shadow of the greatest war the world had seen; a war whose effects were produced not by the intensity of the struggle, but by its duration. That war went on so long that there were men of business, diplomats, editors, and ship-captains who could not remember when there was not war—except for the unreal 13-month interval of the Peace of Amiens.

Suppose a man were a midshipman in 1793, when the war began; by 1813 he was ready for flag-rank or retirement without ever having seen a time when danger and violence were not his daily bread. Suppose he were a clerk in a counting-house in the earlier year; in the latter he would be ready to turn over his business to his sons without having known what a peacetime economy was like. During that shock of the empires whole countries had come into being and disappeared, and alliances shifted feverishly around the one fixed point of the long-continued struggle between England and France.

It followed that the commercial world and the world of social intercourse were filled with a strange kind of internationalism, almost a hangover from the Middle Ages, when two men could fight each other all day and sit down to dinner together in the evening. Thus the officers of British frigates, putting into Norfolk for water, were entertained by Captain Isaac Hull or Captain Stephen Decatur as members of the trade-union of fighting men, one of the most commonly practiced professions in that age of perpetual war.

They might be blowing each other's brains out next fortnight—indeed, they might be doing it next morning, for the *code duello* was in force—but that would not last either. As a normal small nation of the period, the expectancy was that the United States would not fight long on either side of the big quarrel—unless the nation were whipped off the board in some fit of imperial petulance, as had happened to Parma, the Venetian Republic, and even Poland.

The officers who thus met and thus dined were debarred by good manners from discussing politics; they sang songs together, made a few comments on personalities, and turned with pleasure to the safe common ground of the technique of their profession. They talked out such matters as the utility of lime-juice, whether heavy chase-guns on the forecastle did not make a ship work when on a following wind, and the relative qualities of the ships they commanded, which might soon be in combat with each other.

The conversations were abetted by the fact that British and Ameri-

Before the Curtain

cans spoke the same language, wore almost identical uniforms (during the war John Rodgers captured a small British cruiser whose captain came aboard in the most friendly manner to have a glass of wine with someone he took to be the commander of a British frigate), and had the same standards of social contact—by which is meant that a British officer visiting Norfolk did not swoon over his hostess' hand, like one of those dancing Froggies, or attempt to seduce her, like one of those damned Austrians. Yet in the general disappearance of the information we would like to have, enough has survived to indicate that British extended to Americans a degree of condescension only one stage removed from contempt.

It never became overt, because to make it so would be not only bad manners, but also an invitation to a duel. The British, out of their wide knowledge and vast experience, merely addressed Americans as American officers today might speak to a group of lieutenants from Peru or Thailand. The relationship was somewhat closer, since the American was a kind of bastard Englishman, and there was a deep-seated conviction in the Royal Navy that the only good seamen in the American service were renegade Britishers. But there was no mistaking the general tone.

It will perhaps surprise moderns to learn that this tone, this attitude of British toward Americans, had sound reasons behind it. It had nothing to do with the fact that the United States was a small nation, but was based on the exhibited characteristics of the Americans themselves. The British liked and appreciated other small nations. The adjective they commonly used before the word "Swiss" was "heroic." The greatest of British admirals referred to "the brave Danes" as "the brothers of Englishmen," and a somewhat lesser naval worthy expressed satisfaction at having some Portuguese ships under his command. But no Britisher ever referred to Americans in such terms, and the low estimate in which they were held, in which the American navy in particular was held, was based strictly on the record.

First of all, there was the general, quasi-political record. It appeared to bespeak a high degree of national spinelessness to an age in which corporate entities as well as individuals were expected to reply to an insult with a blow. There was something wrong with the ex-Britishers who had "fled" (this was the term in which the thought was cast) beyond the Atlantic, and that something was specifically poltroonery. The idea of general American cowardice was so firmly embedded in the British consciousness that not even the War of 1812 dislodged it at once; some of the strangest passages in the classic British naval history of James are those in which he narrates the events of the war with that American characteristic as a primary assumption—his general line of argument being that Americans put big guns and big crews aboard their ships because they were afraid to fight on an honest, even basis.

The fact that American merchant ships, and later even some American warships, allowed British officers to come aboard and take out members of their crews as British deserters would be in the minds of the visitors at Norfolk. It was proper that Americans should behave in this way, and the British would have used force to compel submission if they had not. But the heroic Swiss, the brave Danes, and the Portuguese had given examples of resistance against hopeless odds and thereby enhanced the dignity of the human spirit.

There was also the matter of American relations with the powers of North Africa. The four Barbary states, Morocco, Algiers, Tunis, and Tripoli, lived on a combination of piracy and tribute paid by Christian states to prevent their ships' being pirated. The usual arrangement was that the amount of tribute was in inverse proportion to the force of the assessed nation and in direct proportion to the amount of its sea commerce.

The British themselves sent "gratifications" to these Barbary powers, but they had a special reason; as a noble lord once remarked, if the Barbary powers had not existed, it would have been necessary for England to invent them. They fulfilled a function in British economics. The prosperity of the island empire was based on the carrying trade; the long war, like previous maritime wars, exposed British ships to enemy attack, boosted insurance rates, and tended to drive the trade into neutral bottoms. By subjecting these neutrals to some of the same disabilities, the Barbaries equalized matters and made it possible for the British to compete, even in wartime.

After Independence, the United States emerged as the most formidable competitor for the carrying trade that England had ever had. The new nation was itself a great exporter of food and raw materials. It occupied an extremely favorable position with relation to the richest trade route of all, that from the West Indies to Europe, which in sailing-ship days ran right up the American coast to near Newfoundland before striking across the Atlantic because the best winds were found along this line. The country was inhabited by people whose normal method of travel was seafaring, and finally, the abundant supplies of timber made shipbuilding costs in America far lower than anywhere else in the world.

Another nation would have given so great and vital a commerce some naval protection, for the Barbaries were not the only pirates and the British not the only people who restricted others' commerce. But the Americans had no navy at all. The very reverse, in fact. During the administration of George Washington, Algiers declared war on the young republic and began to take American ships, whereupon Congress authorized the construction of six frigates, or cruisers, as they would be called now. But when the Algerines offered to settle, the ships were cancelled, and instead the United States built a very fine warship which was delivered to the Dey of Algiers as a present in recognition of his kindness in permitting Americans to be at peace with him on the payment of increased tribute.

Now President Washington was dealing with an extremely complex internal situation in a nation that was not yet a nation, one of whose characteristics was the violent prejudice against any form of permanent armed force which came down from the days before the Revolution. Jefferson Man considered a standing army as the hallmark of a coercive state, and a standing navy as very little better. Jefferson himself held this opinion, though he later modified it with regard to the navy. The members of the 4th Congress of the United States were not very happy about paying tribute to the Algerines, but they believed themselves faced with a choice of evils, and tribute was a cheap price to pay for the preservation of their liberties from a military caste.

Of course, the British were profoundly unaware of this. They had had a standing navy for a long time and did not regard their government as a coercive state. To them, American conduct vis-a-vis Algiers was another example of the national cowardice at sea. It was a confirmation of the record of the Continental navy during the War of the Revolution.

For without arguing the matter out, even with themselves, the British officers, Britons generally, were thoroughly aware that in the sea service, tradition transcends all rationalizations to make its own heroes and poltroons; and, once established, is almost impossible to break. The outstanding tradition of the British navy was one of fighting at every opportunity and with absolutely indomitable courage. It was the tradition of Grenville and *Revenge*; that made Commodore King, assailed by triple odds in the battle off Madras in 1782, wipe the blood from his face and say, "There is nothing to do but fight the ship until she sinks"; that sent Hawke whirling through night and a wild gale onto a lee shore to fight the French among the rocks of Quiberon Bay; the tradition that led the captains of three British ships, in the presence of six French, to agree that "They seem to want a fight and it would be a pity to deprive them of it."

Of course, any fighting service must have some tradition of bravery; but it does not necessarily extend so far in the direction of offensive action as the British tradition did. Nobody called the French cowards, though their sea tradition, in the words of its leading exponent, Ramatuelle (*La Tactique Navale*), ran: "The French navy has always preferred the glory of assuring or preserving a conquest to that more brilliant perhaps, but actually less real, of taking some ships." Mahan says (correctly) that such a doctrine leads to strategic futility. It may also be noted that the French tradition produced a concern with maneuver that made them the best tacticians in the world, and, as a by-product, produced an interest in finely-maneuvering ships that gave the French the reputation of the best naval architects in the world.

The important point here is that the French tradition at sea did not set a low value on courage; it merely defined the ends to which courage was to be applied. But the American naval tradition, as it developed during the Revolution, was not a fighting tradition at all. It was one of avoiding battle for any purpose and of conducting attacks on the enemy's commerce: the tradition of gangsters engaged in smash-and-grab raids.

Before the Curtain

John Paul Jones was an American naval captain of the Revolution, but the British considered him a pirate (they used that very word) who had found the rebel flag a convenient one with which to cover operations that might as well have been conducted under the skull and crossbones. In any case he was an exceptional figure. The typical American captain of the Revolution was John Joyner who, in command of *South Carolina,* 40, one of the most powerful frigates of her time, ran below when she fell into action with a British ship, and only came back on deck to surrender. He was not the only one who behaved that way. The first commodore of the American navy was Esek Hopkins, removed for acts which could be interpreted as either cowardice or incompetence. Captain Thomas Thompson, in command of a fine 32-gun frigate, ran away from a 24-gun consort which had been attacked by a British 20 and a 16, both of which he should have captured single-handed. Commodore Saltonstall burned his squadron in the Penobscot rather than face the smaller British force that came in after him. Captain Hector McNeill was dismissed from the service for cowardice.

In fact, of the 35 warships built or purchased by the American navy during the Revolution, only one remained in American hands at the end of the war. All the rest had been captured by the British or burnt to avoid capture. There were some 15 or 20 warships fitted out for the navies of the several states, and they all went in similar fashion.

In return, there had been inflicted upon the British navy the loss of exactly five ships. Two of these were *Drake* and *Serapis,* taken in memorable actions by John Paul Jones. The remainder were small brigs of 12, 14, and 16 guns respectively, two of which were early recaptured, and the third sent in as a cartel for prisoners.

It was a thoroughly miserable record; an actually discreditable record; the kind of record one would expect from a service ridden with greed for big money out of merchant-ship captures, with quarrels, backbiting, personal and sectional jealousies. Or as the British would put it, the kind of record one would expect from Americans.

Commodore D. W. Knox once wrote a book called *The Naval Genius of George Washington,* and it is quite clear that our first President, who had one of the better military minds of record, did not do all his strategic thinking with regard to operations ashore. In the circumstances, it seems not unlikely that one of the subsidiary reasons behind the cancellation of the six frigates was a certain doubt as to whether the British might not be partly right; whether Americans, who were such bold and adroit seamen, might not have—as a defect of the very qualities that had given them freedom—an inherent inability to conduct warfare at sea; whether the disciplines of the naval profession were such as they could submit to and remain Americans.

If so, Washington was not the only one who regarded American naval inefficiency as one of the permanent facts of an unprogressive world. John Randolph of Roanoke, a kind of triple-distilled Jefferson Man, thought it would be no disgrace for the great mammoth of the American forest to turn his back on the sea and abandon any contest with the shark. The only disagreement came from some of the people in this book.

Chapter 1

Edward Preble

O<small>N WEDNESDAY, JUNE</small> 6, 1798, <small>MR. STEPHEN HIGGINSON OF BOSTON</small> sat down to write a letter. He should have been happy and cheerful. The day was bright with New England spring, the form of the new Massachusetts State House with whose construction he had been connected rose gracefully on Beacon Hill, he was successful and prosperous, one of those substantial Boston businessmen who delighted British visitors by appearing in church in red cloak, powdered wig, and dignity, thereby alleviating fears that America was entirely given over to the noxious French doctrines of equality. But Mr. Higginson was in a mood that would be described as acidulous if Boston Brahmins ever had any other kind of mood. He was little pleased with the current aspect of the business before him.

That business was the preparation for sea of the United States frigate *Constitution,* of 44 guns, now lying at Mr. Edmund Hartt's wharf, with her lower shrouds rattled down and workmen shouting "Yo-hee!" as they hove on ropes to sway up the topmasts. As Navy agent at Boston, Mr. Higginson was responsible for sending her out in good condition, and he was concerned with a concern far more than official. He had contributed $3,000 out of his own pocket and another $2,000 in the name of his son toward the building of that ship because, like every Federalist and nearly every Bostonian, he believed that the naval defenselessness of the United States (which had possessed no warships whatever for 15 years) was a national disgrace that would lead to ruin. Like other Bostonians he had been very far from approving the highly experimental design for the ship which had been sent on from the capital at Philadelphia. But sound New England workmanship had gone into her; she was a noble ship, and disapproval was yielding to pride in the facts that she had the heavy

· 13 ·

planking of a battleship and taller spars than had ever before been seen on a vessel of her class.

Neither was Mr. Higginson disturbed by the tavern gossip that the ship was doomed to misfortune because she had stuck going down the ways, and was only reluctantly persuaded to enter the water, weeks after the guests at the launching had gone home, so disappointed they did not even eat the collation provided for the occasion. Mr. Higginson thought such superstitions unworthy a rational man with a firm trust in almighty Providence.

What disturbed him was the fact that two days ago there had arrived in Boston copies of President Adams's proclamation authorizing public ships of the United States to take and bring into port armed vessels "acting under the authority or pretence of authority" of the French Republic. That proclamation had been received with shouts of "Adams and Liberty!" at the Boston Theatre, and the whole audience rose to sing:

> "Immortal patriots, rise once more!
> Defend your homes, defend your shore!"

to the air of "The President's March"; an affecting scene.

That was war; and Mr. Higginson, old enough to remember other affecting and martial scenes, such as the day when the great Massachusetts expedition set out for the Penobscot in 1779, was not comforted by certain detectable resemblances. For that Penobscot expedition had been led to disaster by officers whose good intentions and high political recommendation failed to compensate for their utter lack of military experience and capacity. Now, of the officers appointed to the splendid new *Constitution*, only one had any record of naval service, the captain, to wit.

His name was Samuel Nicholson; he was a foreigner from what Boston thought of as the West—that is, from Maryland, where he was known as "The Duke of Queen Anne County" and was prodigiously influential in politics. This was doubtless the reason Mr. Adams had been persuaded to appoint him, for there could be little other. Even the Continental navy found reason to send Captain Nicholson before a court-martial, and, though he was acquitted, never employed him at sea again. But Mr. Higginson was a just man, who confined himself strictly to current and personal observation as he wrote:

"Capt N: is in my estimation a rough blustering Tar merely, he is a good Seaman probably & is no doubt acquainted with many or most parts of his duty, So far as relates to practical seamanship, but he wants much more as a Commander in my view, prudence judgement & reflection are no traits in his character, nor will he ever improve. his noise & vanity is disgusting to the Sailors; but a belief that he wants courage goes much farther to render him unpopular with them, for Sailors love to have brave Commanders. This opinion or belief however may not be well founded, I suspect it is not, it may have arisen from another opinion which is indeed often true, that blusterers are not apt to fight. Mr. Cordis the second L^t is a young man, who possesses none of the requisites, he is deficient in every point, essential to a good Officer, he is said to be intemperate and he looks it.—the Surgeon, Read, is the opposite of what he ought to be in Morals, in politics & in his profession. there is not a man in this Town who would trust the life of a dog in his hands. His second, Blake, is of the same cast of character as Read, but not so highly finished.—Mr Prebble the first L^t is a smart active popular man, judicious & well qualified for his station, or for the first command. I should tremble for the issue should She meet a french Cruiser of equal force, though I am sure we have a great national superiority over them for naval operations."

Stephen Higginson was not the only person in Boston to wish "Mr. Prebble" had command of the frigate, or to think him a cut above the other men leaving the cabins of merchant ships to take commissions in the experimental navy. The town, which was "like a large family party," knew him well as a friend of the Sturgises, Russells, and other merchants in the China trade, and Trumbull the painter took off his likeness in his first naval uniform—a tall man of 36, with heavy, powerful shoulders and a commanding presence; a long face, with tight lips; red hair curling heavily around a balding forehead. People who saw him say he was free and nimble in all his movements, and this is easy to believe, for he was seldom quiet except when asleep; a great hunter in the woods, an athlete who could outdo most younger men in any contest. Socially popular as well; he had a strong voice, a seaman's baritone, and he could "render a patriotic song or nautical ballad" with much effect. He had traveled widely, especially in Spain, where contacts with people of the upper orders placed a veneer of genuine courtliness over manners made naturally good by an upbringing in the best New England tradition.

Edward Preble was the full and correct name. He came originally from the outlying Maine District of Massachusetts, being born at Falmouth, son to Jedediah Preble, who was locally known as "the Brigadier" because he had been one in the old French wars. The Brigadier was an active man of imposing figure and mercantile pursuits, the first person to climb Mt. Washington, unless some unrecorded Indian got there before him. He belonged to the Church of England, therefore kept a household less strait-laced than those of the surrounding Congregationalists, with twelve children, as lively and gay as a zoo in the springtime, with the father always roaring with laughter and playing practical jokes. The first remembered incident in the life of young Edward grew out of one.

The occasion was the arrival at Falmouth of a ship which numbered a rather grisly-looking Turk among her crew. On inquiring about this turbaned whiskerado, Edward, *aetat* 10, was informed that he was a son of black Mahound, one of those villains with a habit of carrying little boys off to their own country in big, smelly bags. That evening the Brigadier arranged it that Edward and one of his younger brothers should be left alone in a house lighted only by the fireplace, whereupon the terrible Turk climbed through the window, bag in hand, as advertised. Edward promptly seized a brand from the hearth and thrust it into the intruder's face, scorching him considerably and procuring from the Brigadier the remark that the lad had the right stuff in him.

Another sidelight on the distinctly unusual household in which the naval officer spent his formative years is afforded by the tale of the day Jedediah Preble set out in a boat with some friends to row to an island off Portland. Edward wanted to join the party and was refused permission; so he took the direct action of following the boat alongshore, pelting its occupants with stones. That would have been worth a pluperfect caning in most families, but not in Preble's; the Brigadier beached the boat and took his son aboard, laughing heartily and remarking that Edward would be a general some day.

But these are anecdotes, tantalizingly brief glimpses from an age which believed that environment had nothing to do with the formation of character, and that men of action were worth talking about only when in action. Any personal letters there were have not survived, and the only matters recorded by Lorenzo Sabine (the sole biographer who talked to people who knew the young Preble) are generalizations. The boy was sent to Dummer Academy in "the home state," where he was too much interested in outdoor sports to obtain more than fair grades except in the arts of writing and speaking, in which he was to excel all his life. This is the sum of it. Where did he acquire the sense of discipline, of self and others, so marked in his later life? Nobody bothered to ask. Did he have any of his father's sense of humor? In Edward Preble's intense nature it seems to have been transmuted to a wit that could become nasty, but there are no data on the process. The convention of the age required that something like those two anecdotes should be attached to a hero's childhood; for the rest, Edward Preble's life is a blank until he comes on stage at the age of 15, about as fully formed as he will be.

II

In the first naval action of the Revolution, the British schooners *Margaretta* and *Diligent* were taken by "about 40 men, armed with guns and pitchforks," acting under the orders of an entirely unofficial committee of patriots from Machias. The prizes were carried to Falmouth, whence they were later translated to Boston. This was in the summer of 1775; a few weeks later Lieutenant Henry Mouatt, R.N., arrived on the station with a squadron of four small vessels and a determination to punish the rebels who had made free with His Majesty's property. The affair of the two schooners was apparently related to him in a garbled version, for he went to Falmouth instead of Machias, burned the place to the ground, and placed the coast under blockade.

The inhabitants were turned out to build such huts as they could, with winter fast approaching. The event dropped the Preble family, who had been so gay in their big house, from easy affluence down to the subsistence level, for the customary exchange of local lumber and fish against the products of the Boston markets was cut off. With spring, young Edward was brought home from his schooling to join the other boys of the family in the job of grubbing a living from the ground with hoe and potato-fork. The lad stood it for one season, one can imagine with what developing internal stresses as tales of adventure and battle on the high seas floated in along that coast of mariners. But when the school year of 1776-77 came to a close, instead of returning to Falmouth young Preble went to Newburyport and entered as cabin-boy of the privateer *Neptune* of 24 guns, Captain William Friend. The old Brigadier took it philosophically, as one might expect, only remarking that this would cure the runaway of any nonsense about wishing to make the sea his profession.

There would be no story if the elder Preble had not been wrong, but the manner in which the error developed has some importance. Young Edward found a cabin-boy's existence boresome and spent all his time on deck or running about the rigging and was permitted to do so by the indulgent Friend, who changed the articles to give him an ordinary seaman's status. There is a hiatus in the story at the close of *Neptune's* cruise; the next record of Edward Preble is that he is receiving a midshipman's warrant in the new Massachusetts State ship *Protector*, commissioned during the winter of 1779. She was a heavy corvette or light frigate of 26 guns, an unhandy, in-between size of warship which seems to have been intended as a raider. After one brief and fruitless cruise the General Court of the colony sent her to lie off the Banks of Newfoundland, in the track of the rich traffic bound from the West Indies across the Atlantic.

There, on the morning of June 9, 1780, a fog lifted to show a "large ship to windward under English colours, standing down before the wind for us, we being to leeward. Looked as large as a 74"; and though apparently not a warship (one could tell by the set of the yards) she seemed willing enough for action, as all British vessels were against Continental ships in those days. The Americans offered

Edward Preble

just enough fighting to make things interesting for the better-disciplined ships of the mother country, then good prize money at the end of it, because of the fine design of their ships.

Protector stood on under cruising sail, piping the hands to quarters. The stranger hove to under fighting canvas, jibs and topsails. *Protector* came down on the run, luffed under her lee quarter, and a broadside was ordered; the British replied with three cheers and a broadside of their own, and both ships ran down a reach, wind abeam, firing at pistol range, each gun perhaps once in seven or eight minutes, for these were amateur warriors, and even from their slow fire there were not many hits. No more were there from the Britisher; her size and lofty decks made most of her shot go high, which in the rolling smoke the gunners failed to notice.

But the marines in the American's tops were not amateurs. They were backwoods marksmen who cleared the enemy's tops and then turned attention to his decks where, after about an hour of these exchanges, one of them killed the man at the wheel. Before he could be replaced, the Britisher fell off, jabbing her bowsprit over *Protector's* quarter. It was lashed fast; the Americans crowded aft to board, firing into the enemy's ports to kill men at the guns.

Before they could mount, a tug of the swell broke the lashings. *Protector* fired a raking broadside as her opponent swung, and a deadly broadside it was, for it brought down the enemy's mizzenmast and set her afire in the main-topgallant. The blaze ran down her rigging with the American marines bringing down everyone who sought to quench it, and dropped sparks in a hogshead of cartridges; there was a violent explosion which blew off the enemy's whole quarter-deck. Now she began to sink rapidly by the stern, her people leaping overboard to escape the spreading flames. *Protector's* boats were much damaged, but she got away such as she could and saved 55 of the enemy's people, half of them wounded. They said the lost ship was *Admiral Duff*, 36, a big West India letter-of-marque from St. Eustatius to London with sugar, tobacco, and a desire to increase profits by capturing an American; they had never seen anything so deadly as the fire of the Yankee small-arms.

Thus the account, which makes no mention of Midshipman Edward Preble, in command of a division of main-deck guns. He certainly did well enough, because he was promoted to a lieutenancy at the age of 19, but this is hardly so important as the fact that he had acquired a piece of information whose precise nature did not become evident for some time.

But *Admiral Duff* had carried the West India fever aboard. In a few weeks *Protector* had 60 sick and was lucky to escape after a running action with H.M.S. *Thames*, 32. After an interval of refit and recruiting she cruised to the West Indies, where she captured several prizes before May of 1781, when she fell in with two British frigates, one slightly more than her own force, the other a 50-gunner, and so was easily taken.

The British sent Mr. Lieutenant Preble to the horrible prison ship *Jersey* in New York harbor, the Buchenwald of the American Revolution, from which few men escaped alive. The young man contracted a fever there (it was probably typhus) and might have died of it but for the kindness of a British colonel named Tyng, who had known his father during the old wars. He nursed young Edward through the worst of the disease and then arranged his exchange, but it took a full year of open-air living to restore him to the point of going to sea again.

III

By this time Edward Preble was 21 and had acquired the habit of command, as well as a reputation for sudden gusts of temper that "did not last long enough for him to take a turn of the quarterdeck" but were nevertheless somewhat feared by those under his orders. He now had plenty of men under orders, for at the end of his year of recuperation he was given the First Lieutenancy of the new Massachusetts State ship *Winthrop*, under that very thorough seaman, George Little. In view of Preble's age the appointment probably owed more to family connections than to reputation.

Lord Fisher's dictum that favoritism is the basis of military efficiency is no doubt a dangerous one; but it is one which the cruise of

Edward Preble

Winthrop did nothing to disprove. She was only a sloop—that is, a rather large one-sticker—with 12 guns, but she conducted one of the best minor operations of the war, cruising off the coast of Maine all through the summer of 1782 and taking two good-sized privateers and another vessel of unspecified character before her most important exploit.

Toward the end of the summer Captain Little learned that the British brig *Allegiance,* 14,* was searching for him, operating out of Castine on the Penobscot and lying over each night under the guns of the fort the British had built at that place. Little decided to cut her out by a night attack; forty men, the better part of his crew, were dressed in white smocks for mutual identification and Lieutenant Preble was placed in charge of the storming party.

Winthrop slid into Castine under darkness and, as the ships touched sides, Preble launched himself into *Allegiance's* main chains with a shout. But either *Winthrop* had too much way on or her helmsman made an error; she was loose and away before more than 14 Continentals could follow their leader.

"Do you need more men?" cried Captain Little.

"No," shouted Preble, his trumpetlike voice rising over the confusion of pistol shot, cutlass clang, and snarling. "We already have too many; they stand in each other's way."

The British lost heart and broke across the deck, some leaping overboard, some throwing down their arms. Followed by his few, Preble burst into the main cabin, where he told startled officers just beginning to turn-to that resistance was in vain. Before the fort ashore was waked enough to fire a shot he got way on the prize and was taking her out without a man lost after as bold and skillful a deed as any done in the war.

Winthrop made two more cruises, of which nothing is recorded except that she took prizes and was judged a successful ship; then was sold out of service, since the men of Massachusetts, like those of other colonies, had grown weary of maintaining a war. Edward Preble was

* She is called *Meriam* in American accounts; this was probably her name before being taken into the Royal Navy.

on the beach, but a young man of his reputation and connections need not stay there long, and he was speedily appointed a resident commercial agent in Spain.

Letters, mostly now lost except for digests of the information they contained, show him at the busy life of a New England seafarer during the next 15 years. A voyage to the West Indies; a voyage to Bordeaux in charge of a ship; a trading voyage to the Guinea coast as captain of the brig *Polly*, which turned out a commercial failure when Preble refused to embark slaves as part of his return cargo. Later he is sailing to Spain as captain of another ship and Biscay gales blow him into Bilbao, from where he notifies his owners that the place is a "king's port," which means that merchandise may be landed only for the account of His Most Catholic Majesty. After "a great deal of trouble and some trifling presents to the king's officers" he secures an exemption. Later still he is at Bordeaux again, selling ship and cargo both, investing the proceeds in pipes of brandy and bones of wine, and handling some £2,000, a transaction of no mean importance.

There was also record of a public document advising all men that "whereas Edward Preble in the city of Cumberland in the month of March dealt James Lamb a violent blow on the head with a gun, the said Preble" has given Lamb $245 and received a quit-claim— which indicates that the volcano was still active under an exterior more and more noted for being frozen except on social occasions. A French cruiser intercepted him on another voyage and carried him into port, where the admiralty court ordered the ship and all she contained confiscated and Preble placed in house arrest, on the ground that he had been carrying some goods of English origin.

IV

The same thing had been happening rather frequently in various parts of the world, thanks to an ingenious decree of the Directory of the French Republic, which hoped to cripple British commerce by attaching guilt to goods. It was a doctrine which Mr. President Adams would never admit as valid. His theory, the American theory generally, was that the flag covered all goods; that is, they were safe aboard a neutral ship in time of war, no matter where they had been produced or how obtained. That in addition to being themselves confiscable, British articles should so pollute the accompanying American goods and the holds in which both lay as to make them subject to seizure was simply monstrous. Mr. Adams asked for and received from Congress authority to complete the three big frigates which had been laid down four years before, when the Algerine pirates started taking American ships, and on which construction had been abandoned when the Algerines agreed to take tribute instead. A few weeks later some smaller warships were authorized; to the six captains borne on the list since construction began, lieutenants were added. Preble was one of these—the second-ranking lieutenant of the service by virtue of Captain Nicholson's being the second-ranking ship commander.

Mr. Higginson thought the new First Lieutenant would refuse to go in *Constitution* when he had made the acquaintance of his fellow officers, and the Navy agent was perfectly right. The reason does not appear in the record, but Nicholson sailed in July of '98, while Preble remained in Boston, handling commercial affairs, until December. At that date the revenue cutter *Pickering*, a brig of 14 guns and 70 men, came in from a cruise off the New England coast, where she had been covering commerce against small French privateers. She was taken into the naval service and Preble was made her skipper, with the title of Lieutenant Commandant.

In *Pickering* he did a six months' cruise to the West Indies, main seat of the war, taking one big convoy down and bringing back another, and in the interim operating out of Prince Rupert's Bay at Dominica, where the British had rendered their facilities available to our ships. It was an uneventful service, filled with chasing vessels that were not caught, or that, when run down, proved to be innocent merchants too lazy to answer signals; with urging commercial captains to make more sail or to keep station; with accounts of gallons of water expended and signals from the commodore. Preble did recapture one ship that had been taken by the French; he found her badly mauled and with her foremast down. When her papers were brought it was discovered that she had been commanded by his brother Joshua, who was now a prisoner.

Preble's Boys

What chiefly impresses one about *Pickering's* log-books for the cruise is the advanced state of readiness in which Preble kept his ship. Of the whole squadron only Captain Truxtun's *Constellation* offers anything like the constant repetition of "Gave chace.—Beat to quarters, furnished the men in the tops with a pair of pistols & a sharpened cutlass apiece." This was something altogether new in naval practice and not without its importance, for it was a new service. The captains, largely from the merchant marine, ran their ships pretty much as they pleased; procedure had hardly appeared, much less crystallized into custom.

John Barry was the squadron commodore under whose general orders *Pickering* sailed. He returned to the States somewhat earlier than the little brig, taking home a report on Preble as one of the ablest officers in his command, but also a worry lest so good a man resign the service. Preble had spoken of it; he was troubled by stomach ulcers, and seems to have had an agreement with his commercial firm that after one cruise for the navy he would return to them. The consequence was that when he reached New York in June of 1799, a letter was waiting from Mr. Benjamin Stoddert, the newly appointed Secretary of the Navy. President Adams had been pleased to promote Lieutenant Preble to the grade of captain and would give him a good ship if he remained in the service. For the present he was to await orders at Boston.

That the orders did not come until October can be charged only to the somewhat leisurely pace of affairs at the time. They sent Preble up to Salem to take charge of the new frigate *Essex*, 32, gift of the city. She was destined for Batavia in the East Indies, taking out a small convoy and bringing home a big one, worth several millions, to sail in company with *Congress*, 38.

Captain James Sever of the latter ship was the senior officer and therefore commodore, but the two warships were not three days out of port when they ran into a warm gale in the Gulf Stream. The rigging, set up in a New England winter, went slack, and the intricate system of bracing that it represented no longer held the spars in place. *Congress* pitched out all three masts and had to crawl in under a jury rig. Preble was a better ship handler than Sever and saved his ship a similar misfortune, then pushed on with his convoy to carry the American flag east of Good Hope for the first time. The cruise was notable only in that Preble kept his crew so healthy that he returned with none dead and only nine men sick of the dreaded tropical fevers. The Secretary advised another captain taking a ship out east to copy his methods.

Unfortunately one of the nine sick men was Preble himself. He had hardly brought his ship home before he had a dreadful bout with a fever impossible to identify at this distance, from which he was never fully to recover. Matters were not helped by the fact that while he was still convalescing orders came to fit *Essex* for sea again as part of a squadron of three frigates sailing against the pirates of Barbary under Commodore Truxtun, and Preble insisted upon carrying out the orders. When the ship was ready he broke down and asked for relief. It was granted; he bought a house in Norfolk, married an heiress from his native state named Margaret Deering, and settled down to make a recovery.

v

In the meanwhile, the world moved. Truxtun, the hero of the French War, was exceedingly touchy about rank. He desired a flag-captain for the Mediterranean command, someone to skipper his ship while he was acting as commodore of the squadron. To men who were so nervous about European antirepublican leanings that they refused to name an admiral or even a commodore (save as a courtesy title) this had a hint of aristocratical tendencies. The request was refused and Truxtun resigned the service. Richard Dale took the little fleet to the Mediterranean instead, an old man now, who had been a lieutenant under John Paul Jones in the Revolution; too old to conduct operations with much energy. He set up a partial blockade of Tripoli, the leading offender among the Barbary powers, and the presence of his vessels no doubt did something to keep the other African states from making one of their peculiar "wars" on American shipping, but nothing real was accomplished.

In the following year Captain Richard V. Morris took out three of the heavy frigates and two light ones, but one of his ships was badly damaged by an explosion and he handled the rest so weakly that Tripoli was unblockaded for most of the summer and felt no real pressure. The department ordered him home and, after a court of inquiry, dismissed him from the service.

The sentence was harsh to the point of injustice, but it can be explained by the fact that both the country and the navy itself had reasonable grounds for believing that there was something so decidedly wrong with the whole structure of the service that shock treatment was indicated. The performance in the French War was, on the whole, good, but not especially significant, since everyone was beating the French at sea in those days. After the war ended morale was certainly not improved by the bill reducing the navy to a peace establishment through the dismissal of 19 of the 28 captains, all the masters-commandant, and two-thirds of the lieutenants. The manner in which the act was administered was still less encouraging, for among the first to go were Silas Talbot, James Sever, and George Little, officers with outstanding service records, but whose preferment by President Adams was the reverse of a recommendation to President Jefferson. Salaries had been reduced and there was no longer any prospect of prize-money, while the government had given an indefinable impression of caprice and inconsistency by the way it handled ships and accounts.

Of the captains at the head of the service, John Barry, the senior, was too old for work and would die within the year. Nicholson, the rough, blustering tar, stood next, but had not been allowed to take a ship to sea since his first cruise. Truxtun's resignation had been followed by those of Dale and Thomas Tingey. Even Preble himself had tried to resign when appointed to one of the light frigates for the Morris cruise, enclosing a doctor's certificate that he was too ill for the task along with a letter which said he was honored at having been chosen as one of the nine captains, but preferred that the place should go to "a better man."

That is, the whole service was one of amateurs, on a somewhat shaky foundation, and in need of some integrating force if it was to perform even the limited duty of protecting American commerce against the corsairs of the Mediterranean. In a happy hour President Jefferson declined to follow the example of his predecessors by buying a peace from the Tripolitans; in one still happier, Secretary of the Navy Robert Smith, who never did anything else of importance in his life, refused the resignation of Edward Preble, sixth ranking captain of the nine, and appointed him to command the squadron that should go to the Mediterranean in the fall of 1803.

It was not done with any idea of pulling the service together. At the time nobody thought the service needed any such thing. In fact, Jefferson and his Secretary believed they had traced the cause of the poor performances of Dale and Morris to the jealousies arising from too-close mutual acquaintance among the captains. They simply went down the list and chose a commander who knew and was known by very few in the service. On semidetached service in *Pickering*, off to the East on the long, lonely cruise of *Essex*, Preble had had little opportunity to meet any of them, and since the French War had lived almost in retirement.

For the Mediterranean enterprise, he would be in command of *Constitution*, 44, which was regarded as having fairly well justified the omen of misfortune at her launching, for in the French War she had not taken one prize. Under Preble's orders would be a second heavy frigate, *Philadelphia*, 38, commanded by one of the junior captains, William Bainbridge; three schooners, *Enterprise,* 12, *Nautilus,* 12, *Vixen,* 12, the two latter newly built; and two brigs, *Argus,* 16 and *Siren,* 16. *Argus* and *Siren* were also new ships, built when the reports of the previous commodores showed the need of light vessels to work inshore among the reefs that beset the African coast. Preble himself had superintended the construction of *Argus*.

They would be a help in enforcing the blockade against the small coasters of felucca rig which the Tripolitans used in considerable numbers to import their grain in. (Preble informed himself elaborately about such matters; there is among his papers a memorandum he requested from one of his midshipmen, a précis listing the number, location, and state of readiness of all the guns in the citadel at Tunis, which was on quite friendly terms with the United States.) But from the very beginning the new Commodore demonstrated that he was not thinking in terms of anything so passive as the blockade he had been ordered to set up. Almost his first letter to the Secretary asks that each of the light vessels going out shall carry one or more big mortars in her hold. He thinks that small vessels in which to mount this artillery can be procured in Italy, and that they will be "serviceable" in the kind of campaign he proposes to make. Three weeks later he wants authorization to buy light craft of the type the Tripolitans themselves use, man them from the squadron, and push them right into the enemy harbor, perhaps under disguise. Two weeks later still he inquires what is the American view of international law with respect to keeping all neutral shipping out of a port under "siege."

That is, he is preparing to act offensively: not merely to prevent the Tripolitans from taking American ships, as his instructions bid him do, but to hit them so hard with everything he has that they will be unable to think of anything but their wounds. It was a doctrine calculated to sit well with the spirit of the lieutenants and midshipmen in the squadron. They were nearly all young, so young that Preble raged he had been given "nothing but a pack of boys" for officers when he saw them. Only one of the lieutenants was anywhere near the Commodore's own age, the average was nearly twenty years below it, and Bainbridge, the officer next senior to himself, was twelve years younger than he.

Nearly all of them were southerners or middle-states men, children of a tradition, a way of life, and even a speech more alien to his own than one can readily realize in these days of a nearly homogeneous nation. He was precise as a clock; they were given to duels; excitable, ardent, adventurous. They had to be in order to stay in the navy, in that period of the peace establishment, when so many officers had been dismissed and so many more were resigning. Whatever sea service they had—and there were veterans among them, in spite of their age—had taken place in the free-wheeling days of the French War, when the navy was like a well-run commercial venture, with a strong flavor of individualism. Except for two or three who had been with Truxtun in *Constellation*, they were inclined to regard Preble's taut discipline as tyranny, and the old man himself as possessing the kind of character Mr. Higginson had given to Captain N:. *Constitution* was anything but a happy ship on the voyage out.

At least until the incident of the midnight encounter. It fell close under Gibraltar, in the midst of night. A large ship loomed through the dark, running parallel with the American frigate in a heaving seaway. There was a confusion of hails and hails again, each vessel seeking to learn the other's identity without revealing his own. Preble's temper took charge; he seized the speaking trumpet from the officer of the deck.

"I now hail for the last time," he shouted. "If you do not answer me, I'll fire a shot into you."

"If you fire, I'll return a broadside," came the reply.

"I should like to see you try that!" said Preble. "I now hail for an answer. What ship is that?"

"This is H.M.S. *Donegal*, 84, Sir Richard Strachan, an English commodore. Send a boat aboard."

"This is U.S.S. *Constitution*, 44, Edward Preble, an American commodore, and I'll be damned if I'll send a boat aboard any ship. Blow your matches, boys!"

The Englishman sent the boat and she proved to be only a 32-gun frigate; from which incident the delighted junior officers gathered the conclusion that an old man willing to take his ship into action with an opponent of something like three times her force had the right stuff in him; were willing to take a little hardness from a man who was so clearly a fighter. It would perhaps be somewhat later that they arrived at the rather more important point that the reason the Britisher sent the boat was that *Constitution* had been ready for action, with matches burning and cartridges laid out, while her vis-à-vis had not.

VI

In Gibraltar bay Preble found *Philadelphia* and a problem. His instructions authorized him to shift the squadron base from that place, which had been used by the earlier Mediterranean commands, forward to Malta, and this was precisely what he expected to do. But the news from Bainbridge was that this might expose him to having his communications cut; for Morocco, which held the key of the straits, had decided to make war on the Americans.

There was no doubt about it. Bainbridge had heard that a couple of Tripolitan corsairs were cruising off Cape de Gat, and, running down, he found an unmistakable Barbary warship in company with a brig whose lines pronounced her American. The latter had a prize-crew of Moors from the warship, which was only a 22 and could make no defense against the powerful frigate. When ordered aboard, the Barbary captain refused to show any authority for the capture of American ships, saying he had taken the brig "in anticipation of war"; but changed his mind when Bainbridge said that in such a case he was a common pirate, subject to being instantly hanged from a yardarm. There was the commission in black and white, orders from the Governor of Tangier to make war. At the same time Spanish sources said that another American ship had been taken to Mogador and her crew imprisoned.

"Cringing to these fellows," remarked Preble, "will never do," and issued orders to capture all Moorish ships, while a letter of explanation went to the Secretary of State. *Nautilus* had joined by this time; *New York*, 36, and *John Adams,* 28, of last year's squadron, were in Gibraltar, homeward bound. The two latter were under John Rodgers, who was superior to Preble on the list, and not a little mortified to see the latter fly a broad pennant in his presence. Preble wrote him a pacifying letter and invited him to dinner; Rodgers agreed to waive his rank for the time being, and while *Philadelphia* was sent up to maintain the blockade of Tripoli, the other three frigates and the Moorish prize sailed into Tangier, cleared for action and quite ready to blow the place to bits unless they obtained satisfaction.

His Majesty the Emperor of Morocco was at home. Preble went ashore and found him "a very positive and strong-headed gentleman," who asked the Commodore whether he was not worried over being detained. "No, sir," said Preble, waving his hand toward the harbor, where the squadron was visible, with ports triced up and guns grinning merrily through the portholes; "for if you do my squadron will lay your batteries, your castle, and your city in ruins in an hour."

Edward Preble

There are times when a temper is not altogether a drawback. Negotiations proceeded with a celerity strictly abnormal in Barbary affairs, resulting in the disavowal of the Governor of Tangier's orders and a treaty which gave the Moor back his ship, released the Americans at Mogador, and promised amity in the future without the payment of any tribute whatever.

Constitution went on up to Cadiz, where Preble made the required formal proclamation that Tripoli was under blockade, then sailed for Malta. En route a stranger came over the horizon, signaling to speak; she was the British frigate *Amazon*, and she bore the appalling news that *Philadelphia* had been captured by the Tripolitans.

No one ever blamed Bainbridge or ever called it anything but an accident. *Vixen* had gone through the straits to keep company with the larger ship to prevent just the sort of thing that happened; but on October 31, 1803, the day of ill omen, the schooner had been sent westward on report of a corsair in the strait of Sicily, while *Philadelphia* pursued another, close off Tripoli harbor and well inshore. As she made a turn the wind and tide were just right to drive her hard onto a flat uncharted reef. Bainbridge hauled all his guns aft and braced his yards hard aback—no use; he cut away his anchors and hove over most of his artillery—no use again; cut away the foremast. By this time gunboats out of Tripoli were swarming around, growing bolder every minute, and firing steadily if not with a great deal of accuracy. The frigate had canted over so badly that no pieces would bear from her broadside, and the Tripolitans speedily discovered how to keep out of range of the one or two that were manhandled round to shoot out emergency ports cut in the stern. Bainbridge had holes bored in *Philadelphia's* bottom and hauled down his flag.

The worst part of the disaster was that two days later a strong wind from the north piled up so much water on the reef that the ship floated free, whereupon the Turks weighed up her guns and anchors, patched the holes, and took her into Tripoli harbor. The strategic situation was now completely altered. It was merely the simplest aspect of the new problem that a good two-fifths of Preble's force had been subtracted from him and added to the enemy. The other Tripolitan corsairs were small, but the captured frigate was too strong a ship to be kept in port by any ship Preble had, save *Constitution* herself, which would have meant no relief for her, with winter coming on, when the seas damage ships so much that they must have relief. Many weary months would be needed before messages could go and reinforcements come from across the Atlantic. Moreover, the Bashaw of Tripoli now had prisoners, which were assets of immense financial and diplomatic value in the world where he moved. He sent word that he would take $1,000 a head for them, as a preliminary to any negotiation of other points.

This was not all. Malta would clearly never do as a base; not so much from lack of facilities, as because a row had grown up with the British authorities there over seamen. There were certainly some foreigners aboard Preble's ships, since he had found it difficult to enlist native seamen because the pay offered under the peace establishment had fallen below that offered by the booming merchant marine. But the trouble was that every malcontent, every man who had been punished, would slip overboard as soon as he found himself in a British harbor, report himself to the local authorities as a British subject, and claim the protection of the flag—which he inevitably received without further inquiry. At Gibraltar it had been necessary to moor the whole squadron over toward the Algeciras side of the bay to prevent such losses, and a midshipman had been caught in correspondence with the British on the subject of what he could gain by deserting to them.

From the confined nature of the harbor, Malta was worse than Gibraltar. Preble perceived that if he wished to keep any morale in his squadron he would have to base at Syracuse in the Kingdom of the Two Sicilies, in spite of its greater distance. At the same time it was clear that *Philadelphia* must somehow be destroyed before the Tripolitans could fit her for sea. Bainbridge had the same idea and communicated it from his prison in a ciphered correspondence conducted through the good offices of the Danish consul.

The Commodore took his flagship down to see the pirate stronghold with his own eyes, then ran back to Syracuse, where he left *Constitution*, lest his remaining big ship be damaged by the freaks of the winter gales, which at Tripoli blow onshore with great force. The flag was shifted to *Vixen*; in her he joined his pack of boys on a blockade which, to the incredulity of the British, was maintained throughout one of the severest winters in Mediterranean record.

One of those boys was Lieutenant Stephen Decatur, commander of *Enterprise,* 12, a young man full of ardor, already well known in the service, who frequently ate at the Commodore's table. He was the first to hear of Preble's project against the captured frigate; they developed the plan together, along the lines of the cutting-out expedition against *Allegiance* in the Penobscot during the old war. Decatur wanted to take his own ship in for the job, but Preble said no to that, pointing out that courage would not carry the day unless aided by skill; even at night the schooner might be recognized as American and all surprise lost. However, the squadron possessed a ketch that had been captured while trying to run the blockade, a local vessel. She was renamed *Intrepid* and packed with 74 volunteers, mainly from Decatur's command.

The story of that expedition belongs to the young lieutenant and will be told later; enough here to say that they did burn *Philadelphia* where she lay, and so took an enormous load off the Commodore's shoulders. At this point he would have been justified in settling down to a straight blockade until more ships should come out; but it is not three weeks from the wild night when the frigate blew up in Tripoli harbor that he is writing home about a plan for attack. When spring breaks, he expects to borrow light-draft gunboats and mortar vessels from the King of the Two Sicilies for a close-in assault; he wants 100 barrels of powder at once, as he expects to spend a large quantity "in fireships and infernals to blow up the Bashaw's works." The letter also has a reference to another project, the pet scheme of one William Eaton, consul at Tunis. The Bashaw Yusuf Karamanli, had a brother named Hamet who claimed to be the rightful ruler of Tripoli. Preble agrees with Eaton that even the force present in the Mediterranean is adequate to place this individual in command of the secondary cities of Derna and Benghazi and so light a fire in the Bashaw's rear.

Spring came; the mortar-boats and gunboats were borrowed, two of the former and six of the latter. All were in bad shape, requiring extensive refits before they would operate to American satisfaction, and Preble had to take three of his ships to Tunis for a show of force, since the Bey of that regency was turning very shirty, with threats of war unless he obtained more tribute. Moreover, Preble kept hoping for reinforcements that did not come. He was determined on attack, but "Having no vessel in the Squadron excepting this ship *Constitution* whose cannon can make any Impression on the Bashaw's Walls I expect we may suffer much."

During that winter and spring the young lieutenants and mids learned a good deal more about the frozen-faced old man from Maine. He made them write letters of apology for every infraction of discipline and came down sternly on anything that looked like dissension; but he was as quick with praise when things were well done, not only direct to the doer, but in letters home. The situation must have been a painful trial to the old man, for he had not only the ordinary labors of handling a big ship and supervising the movements of a squadron, but also the whole diplomatic business of the Mediterranean, letters to the U.S. consuls, negotiations perpetual with the other Barbary powers, efforts to resolve the Tripolitan trouble by peaceful means, a long correspondence with Spain, where some clerk had forged Preble's name to drafts of account on London. Moreover the commodore was by this time a sick man; in April the stomach ulcers became so bad that he began to make arrangements for a passage home.

Summer weather and the prospect of action worked a rally in his physical condition. In late July of 1804 the squadron sailed, adequate or no, and on the 28th was before Tripoli, where the mortars worked close enough to throw some shells into the town before a freshening onshore wind made it unsafe to stay. For three days it grew to a storm of hurricane proportions, not dying out till August 3, when all the fleet moved in on Tripoli again.

The harbor there is formed by a long tongue of land from which a line of reefs and shoals juts eastward. The town is behind the spit, on which stood the main defenses, though there was another big castle, Fort English, southeast on the shore. Some 16 of the Turks' lateen-rigged gunboats, with one heavy gun and a light one apiece, stood ready to operate through the gaps in the reefs. Preble took *Constitution* into point-blank range of the big castle, with the lighter ships in line behind, while the mortars fired over the batteries into the town and the borrowed gunboats dashed round the tail of his line and locked with the Tripolitan gunboats in a desperate hand-to-hand combat. Whenever the frigate could bring her guns to bear, the enemy were driven from theirs, and she had only one man wounded; but the pirates had always thought highly of themselves as deck fighters and stood up fiercely to the gunboats.

The story of that combat is also Decatur's, who led the light craft; what belongs to Preble is the tale of how his ardent subordinate mounted to *Constitution's* deck when the battle was over, streaked with blood and powder, his face sad over the loss of a brother, mortally wounded in the fight.

"I have brought you three of the enemy's gunboats, sir," he reported.

Preble, his face working, seized Decatur furiously by the lapels, almost shaking him as he cried; "Three, sir! Where are the rest of them? Why have you not brought me more, sir?"

The other officers stared in dumb horror as Decatur's hand clapped to the hip where he usually wore his dirk, his face going red and white, as Preble turned his back and disappeared. Two long minutes, more perhaps; a messenger appeared to say that the Commodore wished to see Captain Decatur in his cabin.

For a long time no sounds emerged. One of the lieutenants, fearing or hoping, or merely curious, at last tapped on the door and then flung it open. The two men were seated side by side on a cabin bench and both were in tears.

Three days were spent in refitting the captured gunboats; on the morning of August 7, Preble sent them in for a new form of attack, all vessels close to the fort at the base of the spit, while the fast schooners stood by to cut off the Tripolitan gunboats, should they venture beyond the reef line. The wind was onshore that day. *Constitution* accordingly had to keep room to wear round, and could give only distant support, so the lighter craft had a rough time of it, all of them being knocked about a good deal, and one of the gunboats blown up, with the loss of half her crew. Yet they gave better than they took; the outer walls of the sea-battery were virtually destroyed,

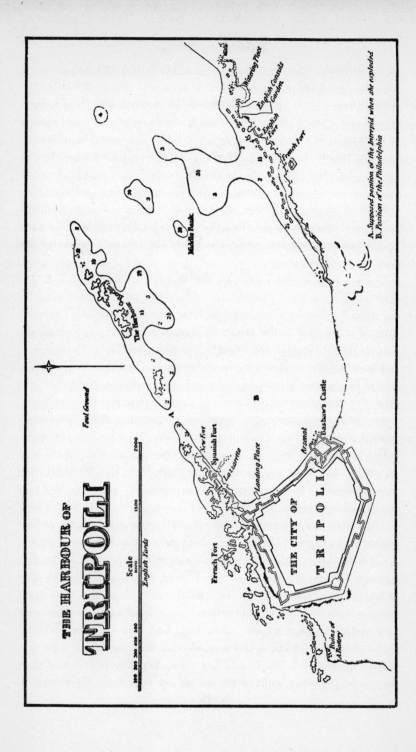

THE HARBOUR OF

TRIPOLI

Scale

100 200 300 400 500   1000   1500   2000

English Yards

Foul Ground

The Harbour

Middle Rock

New Fort
Spanish Fort
Lazzaretto
Landing Place

French Fort

Ruins of A Battery

Arsenal
Bashaw's Castle

THE CITY OF
TRIPOLI

English Consuls
Gardens
Watering Place
English Fort
French Fort

A. Supposed position of the Intrepid when she exploded
B. Position of the Philadelphia

some of its guns dismounted, a good many Turks killed, and not a little damage done to the town.

There was a pause at this point for more refitting and another gale, during which the Bashaw tried for peace by offering to forgo tribute in the future and to cut the ransom for his prisoners. Preble's reaction was that he would not pay a cent, and he towed his mortars in for a night bombardment on the 24th. It was not a success because the mortars themselves and the powder in their shells were so bad.

But four days later the Commodore tried a new variation, by sending all his gunboats close up to the gaps in the reef at three o'clock in the morning. Here they anchored and began firing slowly at the town and the shipping on its waterfront; in the dark the batteries lacked points of aim for any effective reply. This bombardment was very good; the town took a heavy battering, a big ketch was sunk at her quay, and a good many people ran out into the fields. Toward dawn the Bashaw ordered his own gunboats out to drive off the Americans by gunnery, but three of them were sunk in the attempt, and with the day *Constitution* came sliding in to musket-shot range, exchanging fire with the batteries and covering the retreat of the light ships.

The hot young lieutenants were getting as much fighting as their stomachs called for and, in the intervals, working 18 hours a day— toiling on the unsatisfactory mortar-boats, for instance, in consequence of a letter from the French consul in town, who reported that the Bashaw was not much worried about the battering his town was taking from solid shot, but greatly feared that it would be burned up by mortar shells. The two boats were ready for another attack on September 3, by which date the steady onshore swells were enough relaxed to permit a daylight bombardment, with the whole squadron participating. As the ships moved in, it was perceived that the Tripolitans had worked out a new scheme of defense, their gunboats moving to the far side of the harbor, firing from under the batteries of Fort English. Preble had to detach his light forces to engage them, since an opponent not under fire becomes very accurate. This left *Constitution* alone against the town and castle, 26 guns in broadside against over 70, but the big frigate moved in so close and fired so fast that her own gunnery was a protection. She lost not a man and, as before, the enemy were driven from their pieces with damage.

That night a new note was struck. Observing how the Tripolitan gunboats bunched near the shore at dark, Preble filled the hold of the ketch *Intrepid* with explosives, and sent her in under a valiant lieutenant named Richard Somers to blow them up; *Constitution's* green cutter being towed astern as a getaway craft. But in spite of elaborate precautions with slow-matches something went wrong in a way that could not later be ascertained; there was a shattering explosion in the dark harbor, and no one came out of it alive.

VII

And that ended the Tripoli story, with the full tide of war suddenly piling to a stop. The weather turned foul; before it cleared there arrived the powerful reinforcement that had begun fitting out as soon as the news of *Philadelphia's* loss reached the United States—*President,* 44, *Congress,* 38, *Constellation,* 38, *Essex,* 32. But the senior officer was Captain Samuel Barron, who ranked Preble and therefore automatically took command. To complete this part of the tale, Barron went back to the system of blockade that Dale and Morris had used, while backing Eaton's expedition to Derna which took the place—whereupon that unpleasant political officer, Tobias Lear, negotiated a treaty under which ransoms were paid after all.

Old Preble went home aboard *John Adams,* setting down in his journal that "this supercedure lacerates my heart." The words were written before a little scene on *Constitution's* quarterdeck, when young Decatur, promoted captain for gallantry, stepped proudly forward in his new uniform and presented the Commodore with a scroll signed by every surviving member of the pack of boys: "We, the undersigned officers of the squadron late under your command, cannot, in justice, suffer you to depart without giving you some small testimony of the very high esteem in which we hold you as an officer and a commander."

There is hardly anything else like it in all naval history, and there is very little else like the avenue of cheering along which Edward Preble went home. The Pope wrote to President Jefferson that the little force off Tripoli "in forty days has done more for the cause of Christianity than the most powerful nations in ages." There were dinners at Malta and Gibraltar and New York, a sword and a gold medal voted by Congress, and a special reception on inauguration day in the temporary White House. Even more, to those who understood, was the fact that Admiral Lord Nelson looked from his flagship at *Constitution's* neatly crossed yards and slick maneuvers and remarked that in the handling of those transatlantic ships lay a nucleus of trouble for the navy of Britain.

But that statement was for private ears, quickly forgotten and not called up till another day. What mattered at the moment was that the man who made it true was going home, very ill. The ulcers had turned to cancer of the stomach. He had to spend long periods in bed and could no longer sing an ode at social gatherings. President Jefferson wanted to make him Secretary of the Navy, and when word of the plan got abroad, several of the young lieutenants wrote of how the appointment would please them, signing themselves his *"boys of the infant squadron."* His health clearly would not stand it and the tender was never formally made. In the meanwhile, the Commodore shuttled between Boston and Portland, superintending the construction of some of the miserable defense gunboats, of whose value Jefferson held so exaggerated an opinion.

In June of 1807 the British frigate *Leopard* halted our *Chesapeake* on the high seas, fired into her, causing 21 casualties, then seized four of her crew as deserters from the Royal Navy. Preble fell back in his bed when he heard the news, staring in astonishment and without saying a word. A week later a letter arrived asking if he could take a command for war. "I am very low," he wrote in reply, "but will obey if I am obliged to be carried on board. The occasion will soon restore me."

It was his last recorded action. In August he died.

THE FIGHTING MEN

Chapter 2

The Steadfast Farmer: Isaac Hull

A crash,—as when some swollen cloud
  Cracks o'er the tangled trees!
With side to side, and spar to spar,
  Whose smoking decks are these?
I know Saint George's blood-red cross,
  Thou Mistress of the Seas,—
But what is she, whose streaming bars
  Roll out before the breeze?

Ah, well her iron ribs are knit,
  Whose thunders strive to quell
The bellowing throats, the blazing lips,
  That pealed the Armada's knell!
The mist was cleared,—a wreath of stars
  Rose o'er the crimsoned swell,
And, wavering from its haughty peak,
  The cross of England fell!
        —OLIVER WENDELL HOLMES: *The Pilgrim's Vision*

SELDOM HAS THERE BEEN A MILITARY ENTERPRISE THAT IN THE LIGHT of the surrounding circumstances was much madder than the sailing of the frigate *Constitution* from Boston on August 2, 1812; and seldom has any action without immediate strategic importance produced a wider or more permanent effect.

It all seems simple today, when we have read the last pages of the story. But in the summer of 1812, the book had been opened only to the introduction, and the emotion that could be expected from any

American over what he read there was dread. For *Constitution* was sailing against England, truly the ruler of the seas, which had over 600 warships afloat, while *Constitution* was one of a navy of 17, mostly small ships. It was a contest at odds more severe than those between Russia and Finland in modern times. The weaker party in such a combat may have courage and address, but he will nearly always be destroyed in the end.

Nor was arithmetic the only factor. The Spartans of Thermopylae were held to have acquitted themselves not dishonorably against odds as ponderous. But of *Constitution's* sailing, it is to be said that the balance against her was moral as well as material. The British Royal Navy was at the peak of its glory, universally acknowledged to be not only the most numerous in the world, but composed of the best seamen and sea-fighters. Since the quickly retrieved, minor defeat at Algeciras, 12 years before, it had been engaged in over 200 battles, great and small. Only three single-ship actions were lost, all against considerable odds, and British ships had often triumphed over forces as disproportionate as when their *Speedy*, of 14 guns and 28 pounds weight of metal in the broadside, captured the Spanish *Gamo*, of 32 guns and 190 pounds weight of broadside. In the Revolution the British navy had reduced the American to a single ship, at the cost of only one important defeat, at least as memorable for having occurred at all as for the manner in which John Paul Jones inflicted it.

In 1812 nothing visible to the public offered any assurance that the American navy could improve on its Revolutionary record. A few years previously one of its captains had tamely submitted to having his crew mustered and one of his men impressed into a British ship. Another had been faced with a similar demand for seamen; was found in a state of such shameful unreadiness that he could fire only a single shot in reply to the cannon that supported the order; and saw four Americans taken off his ship, one of them to be delivered to the gallows. The first two American ships to put to sea in the war had been captured without either firing a gun; three of our frigates had brought a British 38 into range without accomplishing anything but damage to themselves from exploding artillery; and *Constitution* herself had barely escaped a British squadron. It was allowed to be a masterly escape, a splendid piece of seamanship, but such luck could not last forever.

Moreover, the frigate sailed to try these odds from a mutinous city, flatly against the wishes of a government which had no confidence in its navy or in this ship's captain. There was open talk of secession from the Union in Boston that summer. Press and pulpit were loud against those who supported the "abominable and unnatural war" with their money or their bodies. *Constitution* could not even have been provisioned for sea but for the generosity of a private citizen, who was roundly abused for his pains. The orders that brought her to Boston forbade her to fight unless attacked, and her captain had every reason to believe that new orders were on the way, directing him not to leave port for any reason. Therefore, in a moment of insubordination as sublime as that when Nelson clapped his glass to his sightless eye, he sailed without any orders whatever.

The subsequent event at large from Halifax thus turned the world upside down quite as thoroughly, though in a different way, as the somewhat more elaborate one which had earlier taken place under the rampart of Yorktown. It provided the necessary impetus for our victory—none the less real for want of formal recognition—in the second War of Independence, and in thirty minutes it changed the character of an age. For Americans there is a certain appropriateness in the fact that the event should have arisen, not from a high romantic defiance of reason, but out of the level-headed calculation of a hardscrabble Yankee.

Isaac Hull was from Connecticut (born Derby, 1773), a man who never did anything more romantic in his life than to run away to sea at the age of 14—a common crotchet among lads of his age and geographical background. He had been neglecting his schooling at the time, which was also part of the normal pattern. After two years in the coasting traffic and one which he spent with an uncle at Newton, Mass., who tried to prepare him for Yale and the law, he was allowed to make one deep-water voyage in the hope that it would cure him of his passion for the sea. The journey ended in shipwreck on the coast of Ireland, and it will surprise no one who knows the literature of the period to learn that young Isaac Hull returned from it more determined than ever to be a sailor.

The only difference from the norm was that he resolved not to do his seafaring before the mast. From this time forth his voyages were interspersed with long sessions at night school, where he succeeded in acquiring the mathematics he needed for navigation, but never in overcoming the difficulties of the English language, whose grammar and spelling remained a mystery to him.

This period of on-job education lasted till 1798, which year found Hull back at Derby and penniless, as a result of his shipowner's having gone bankrupt while the young man was enjoying a bout with yellow fever in the West Indies. While he was looking for a new billet there arrived a communication from the government. In 1794, when three frigates were laid down to deal with the pirate Algerines, the young man had applied for a commission in the new navy, but nothing ever came of it. The letter now in hand said that a navy was being equipped in view of the current difficulty with France. The President had been pleased to grant his request of four years previous. Mr. Hull would report aboard the frigate *Constitution*, then fitting out at Boston, to be her Fourth Lieutenant. He accepted and went on the ship's first cruise, which was remarkable only for the end of it. *Constitution's* record was so unsatisfactory that the captain and all three lieutenants senior to Hull were permanently set ashore or shifted elsewhere. Under the then custom of the service, this made him First Lieutenant by inheritance when the ship put to sea again.

Her captain on this occasion was Silas Talbot, quite a different order of fish from the previous captain, Nicholson—an active, enterprising man who had led a famous cutting-out expedition during the Revolution, and as soon as he arrived in the West Indies found an opportunity to repeat the operation. A very fast French privateer named *Sandwich* was discovered under the guns of a fort at Porto Plata, Santo Domingo; Spanish fort, but Spain and France being such close allies, Captain Talbot decided he need not be too nice about international law, and would send the boats in after her. As First Lieutenant and executive officer, Hull naturally had charge of the business. His instrument was a small sloop well known on the coast, which had been captured with a load of contraband.

He packed this little craft with 80 men and ghosted into the harbor through a night in which she was halted by a British man-o'-war, whose boarding officer was astounded to find himself in a circle of armed men. But he let them go with a handshake and good wishes, only remarking that his own captain would be disappointed; he was planning precisely this expedition, but for a few days later. At high noon, as the orders bade him, the sloop slid into the harbor, bumped sides with *Sandwich,* and Hull and his 80 burst from the hold, brandishing weapons and "yelling like devils." They caught the French at their siesta and captured them without a blow being struck, while a force of marines swarmed through water up to their necks, took the fort, and spiked its guns.

The privateer had been stripped to her lower masts and must be rigged complete. The whole population of the place boiled out to watch, headed by some soldiers and officers, who began to growl. Hull double-shotted the inshore guns of his prize and warned the interferers off; his men labored like beavers, running ropes and getting spars aloft, and at two in the morning he was sliding out of the harbor with his prize, after as crisp and well-planned an action as any done in that war.

Sandwich had to be given up later after a legal argle-bargle over the sovereignty of Porto Plata, so there was no prize-money, but his exploit made Hull a marked man among the young lieutenants. There was never any question about retaining him when so many officers were dismissed under the peace establishment of 1801. In the service itself his reputation stood even higher, as the result of an event which shoregoers would not perhaps completely understand.

This happened after the cutting-out, when *Constitution* met a British frigate, whose skipper was an old acquaintance of Talbot's and came aboard for a pipe and a look at the ship. A small argument developed. The Britisher admired the American frigate's structural strength, her big guns and massive scantling, but (he said) all this would make her a dull sailor, especially to windward. The result was the bet of a cask of Madeira on a race which was sailed as soon as the British ship had her bottom scraped and her rigging overhauled.

It was an all-day beat to windward. Talbot, who had originally come from the army, thought a captain should be military head of his ship while the exec handled her propulsion, and left everything to Hull; and Hull handled the frigate so well that when sunset gun was fired, he had left his opponent hull-down astern. Of course, the ship herself had a good deal to do with it, but in the minds of those present the skill of the young lieutenant had more, and the Madeira was drunk in his honor.

II

Early in the Barbary war, Hull went out to the Mediterranean as First Lieutenant of the corvette *Adams*, 24, in Richard V. Morris's squadron. He was now very senior to be under a captain and received the first independent command available—the famous "lucky little *Enterprise*," the single light ship of the French War to be retained in service. She was a schooner, mounting 12 guns and very fast, exactly the vessel in which Hull could get the most out of his uncommon skill in seamanship.

His chance to show it came on June 21, 1803, when Commodore Morris, after an abortive and badly managed attempt to bombard Tripoli, and a still less successful effort at negotiation, had left Hull's ship with *Adams* and *John Adams,* 28, to blockade the port. There was a good deal of movement among the harbor gunboats, which led Captain John Rodgers of *John Adams*, who was senior officer present, to suspect an attempt to push a corsair through the blockade in one direction or another. He therefore split his force—*Adams* well out to the west of the harbor, *Enterprise* well out to the east, while he remained at the center of the line with his own ship.

Hull made the contact next morning at dawn—on the largest ship belonging to the Tripolitan regency, the polacre-rigged corvette *Meshouda,* 22, trying to work her way in. She was powerful enough to have blown *Enterprise* to pieces, for in addition to having more guns, she had heavier ones. But Hull outmaneuvered her; the Tripolitan captain found he could not close without either sweeping wide out to sea, which would bring a frigate down on him, or taking a raking fire, which is very dangerous for a polacre, since a single hit could bring down all the sails on a mast.*

Meshouda therefore turned into a deep, narrow bay; and, while Hull ran down to pick up the frigate, sent for help overland. When *Enterprise* returned with *John Adams,* the corsair was moored with springs on her cables so that her broadside would bear in any direction; a troop of cavalry was covering the shore against any attempt at a boat assault, and 9 gunboats were beating through the shoal water along the coast to support. Rodgers worked his frigate in carefully, chose a good range, and opened fire. The Tripolitans could not match *John Adams* in range or accuracy; after 40 minutes of it, they abandoned ship, and Rodgers signaled *Enterprise* in "to amuse the enemy," while he wore round, away from some dangerous reefs, and lowered his boats to take possession. Seeing they had only the schooner to deal with, the Turks began to come out and climb aboard their ship again, but *Enterprise* was now close in, firing fast from the 6 little guns of her broadside. By the time Rodgers had his boats back and brought the frigate in to join the cannonade, smoke and flame were spurting from *Meshouda's* portholes. A few minutes later she blew up.

A week after this the ships on blockade were recalled; they made a periplus (coast pilot's chart) of the Western Mediterranean; and then, under Morris's languid leadership, drifted down to Gibraltar, where for the first time in his life Isaac Hull met Edward Preble. The thin man and the chubby one—already Hull's figure showed a tendency to squat and his cheeks held more than a hint of apple—were almost the only officers in the squadron who spoke and thought New England. They became fast friends at once, though somewhat uncommunicative ones, developing a relation of mutual confidence and

---

* The masts of a polacre come in one piece, and there are no crosstrees or caps. The upper yards can thus be dropped down close together in a group and the sailors stand on the lower yards in furling or setting sail, which makes for quick and easy handling, but with the disadvantage noted.

respect. When the new brig *Argus,* 16, arrived, Preble promptly placed the young man in command of her. There was rather more in this than meets the eye, for the Commodore had personally supervised every plank that went into the little ship and she was the darling of his heart, as sweet a vessel as had ever been seen in the inland sea, which even the grumpy British praised for her neatness, fine lines, and great speed.

Her first cruise was on detached orders, Preble leaving her to work off Cape de Gat to intercept any Tripolitan corsairs that might slip through the blockade. There was also the duty of holding at Gibraltar American merchants entering the Mediterranean until they could be convoyed in a group to their destination. This lasted until mid-April, when Hull was ordered up to Tripoli to help maintain the blockade. With some help from *Siren* and *Enterprise, Argus* held the line there until the August attacks, capturing a few ships and now and then exchanging a few shots with the batteries. There was nothing particularly remarkable about this service, or about Hull's conduct during the battles, though the latter was good enough twice to bring him a letter in which Captain Hull was advised that he "would please accept the Commodore's thanks for the Gallant Manner in which he brought his vessel into action."

Soon after the arrival of the relief squadron, Hull was summoned to *President's* cabin. The new commander, Samuel Barron, was waiting, and so was a short, tanned, and heavy-faced man with intense eyes, who was introduced as Mr. William Eaton. Hull knew of him as a rather queer character, a self-styled general, sometime American consul at Tunis, who had cooked up the project of putting pressure on the Bashaw of Tripoli by placing part of the regency in possession of his brother and rival, Hamet Karamanli. The idea had at last borne fruit in the form of money and letters from President Jefferson; Hull and his little cruiser were to supply naval support for the adventure.

That was the beginning of as romantic a campaign as any in American history, but it was Eaton's campaign. Hull managed to remain aloof from the attendant troubles and to render naval support in the quantity and at the times desired; the only letter he writes home complains of his purser, who has cheated an Englishman at cards and bilked an Egyptian courtesan. The naval support consisted in carrying supplies to Eaton's polyglot and amazing "army," helping in the capture of Derna, and beating off two counterattacks by the Bashaw's people with naval gunfire. When Tobias Lear's peace with Tripoli closed out the Derna business, Isaac Hull sailed for home—after four consecutive years at sea in the Mediterranean, more than any other man in the squadron had served.

III

Hull cannot have regarded this long sea service as a hardship, for it brought him promotion to a captaincy; he was an unmarried man and one to whom the old love of the sea still clung strongly. But he returned to an America which must have seemed to hold little future for any naval officer. The British-French restrictions on our commerce were at their height; the English were daily impressing men out of American ships. The best answer the administration could think of was to abolish seagoing commerce through the Embargo, and prepare for defense by laying up all the cruising warships and laying down over 200 of the wretched one-gun gunboats, which capsized on the slightest provocation and rocked so badly that the only weather in which they could fire their guns more than once in half an hour was a flat calm.

Hull in his new captain's uniform went up to Middletown, Connecticut, to build four of these impossible wooden pots, and then to Newport to build more. (All were laid up in shady creeks as soon as built, and most of them never hoisted a sail.) While he was about this task the *Leopard-Chesapeake* affair occurred; Hull was appointed with Captain Isaac Chauncey to a board of inquiry under the presidency of Captain Alexander Murray, to get at the facts of the case.

The evidence showed that U.S.S. *Chesapeake*, 38, had put to sea under command of Captain James Barron in June 1807, after dropping down from Washington to Hampton Roads. While she was at the capital the British Minister had made a demand on the American government for the persons of three men of her crew, claimed to be deserters from the Royal Navy. No extradition treaty or international law covered deserters from the armed services, but an investigation was ordered. It established that all three men had indeed run from a British ship, but that earlier they had been forcibly impressed into this ship out of an American merchant. They were Americans; *Chesapeake's* captain knew one of them personally, and another was a Negro.

Now as *Chesapeake* began to rock to the Atlantic swells on the way out, there slid up to her H.M.S. *Leopard,* 50, which had been following all day, after lying inside the capes (itself an illegal act) to blockade a couple of French privateers that had taken refuge in the bay. The Britisher backed a topsail, sign of a social call; Captain Barron put on his best uniform and doubtless ordered out the sherry. But instead of *Leopard's* captain, the boat contained a lieutenant, who demanded that the American frigate's crew be mustered so the British deserters could be picked out. When Captain Barron refused, *Leopard* closed in and opened a fire which killed 3 and wounded 18 of *Chesapeake's* men, only ceasing when the American flag was hauled down; then sent another boat, mustered our frigate's crew and took not three but four men out of her. Only one shot had been fired by Barron's ship and that was a protest—set off by a lieutenant who carried a hot coal from the galley stove to fire it.

Why had *Chesapeake* taken this dreadful abuse so meekly? Well, she was but newly put to sea and not properly shaken down. The gundeck was cluttered with lumber, many of the cannon had not been fitted to their carriages, powder-boxes were unfilled, matches were not primed. The marines lacked cartridges for their rifles. Whose fault was this? Well, it was the captain's place to give orders, but it did not appear that he had given any except as to housekeeping details. Even when the British lieutenant presented his outrageous demand, he had said nothing about clearing for action, though the fact that *Leopard* had been following his cruiser out into the ocean had made it evident for several hours that something more than a game of cat's cradle was on the way.

At this point in the testimony, we may picture the two junior members of the court clearing their throats and looking at each other. They were a pair of Preble's boys, and things had never been so done in any ship under the old man's command. In fact, the tale that never grew thin among them was that of the midnight encounter off Gibraltar, with *Constitution* ready for instant action before hail was given or answered, matches burning and gun-crews poised like cats. The inquiring body drew up a report which caused Barron to be translated before a court-martial—which found him as guilty as Judas Iscariot—which resulted in his being suspended from the service for five years without pay.

The punishment seems to fall far short of being adequate, and the oddity is increased by the fact that after Barron had worn out his exile he returned to the navy list and was treated by the powers as though nothing had happened. But the background must be taken into account: the two Barrons—Samuel and James—were Virginians, were in a sense the representatives of that proud state in the naval service, and thus were somewhat under the special protection of the Virginia presidents, Jefferson, Madison, and (later) Monroe. In the still incompletely welded nation there was more of this type of particularism than moderns conceive; Adams had shown a similar preference for the New Englanders, Talbot and Christopher Perry.

But the effect of the James Barron case was to accentuate the contrast between Samuel Barron's conduct before Tripoli and that of Preble, and to split the service into two parties. The break remained at the level of opinion and personal conversation for the most part, and produced few readily visible results. It is impossible to trace it in detail or with finality; it shows up only in small things: methods of operation, the emphasis placed on one or another part of training. But it was there; and for some years at least, the veterans of the forty days before Tripoli were the weaker party.

They were strong enough, however, to obtain a change of naval policy when Madison came in with a new Secretary, Paul Hamilton, who had no record of commitment to the gunboat program. All the craft of that type save those at New Orleans were put away in pickle and the frigates were brought out of it to go for practice cruises along the coast. In the fullness of time, in the summer of 1810, this brought Hull orders to fit out the frigate *President*, 44. He never took her to sea because John Rodgers, who was his senior and in command of *Constitution*, reported that his ship was so sluggish a sailer that he wished to exchange.

This seemed very odd to the man who had handled that ship in the race for the Madeira, but when the shift had been made and he took his old ship from Hampton Roads up to Boston, he found that it was perfectly true: by no seaman's trick or alteration of rigging could he make *Constitution* behave like anything but a perfect tortoise. The difference between Hull and another commander is that he reasoned there could only be one cause behind such an effect. After his return to the Roads, he sent divers down, who reported that the frigate's bottom was hung with oysters, mussels, and barnacles to a quantity which he estimated at 10 wagonloads. As the ship was wanted in service, she could not be hove down for scraping, but he took her up the Chesapeake into fresh water to kill the oysters and attacked the growths with an iron drag of his own invention. It produced some result; the exchange of the 42-pound carronades on the ship's upper deck for 32s did even more; and then Hull was ordered to Europe to deliver $28,-000 in cash to Holland, due on a loan of the Revolution, and to carry out Joel Barlow, the new minister to France.

IV

By sailing day it was August of 1811; *President* had shot H.M.S. *Little Belt* to pieces when the latter fired into her during the night; H.M.S. *Guerrière*, on sentry duty along our northeast coast, had pressed a man out of an American brig-of-war and several more from merchant ships in the very mouths of our harbors; the total of Americans dragooned into the Royal Navy had reached 914. The commercial Orders in Council bore hard on our commerce, and tempers were short everywhere—American against British arrogance. British against American presumption in questioning their rule of everything that floated on blue water.

As *Constitution* arrived off Cherbourg, the sails of the blockading squadron hove over the skyline. Hull cleared for action, beat to quarters and had his matches already alight when one of His Majesty's frigates hailed him to back a topsail so that a boat could be sent. It contained a lieutenant who brought word that Hull was to go aboard the flagship before proceeding farther. The Captain answered that he was taking a diplomat to France and proposed to complete his mission; would obey no orders but those of his own government. The lieutenant bowed and departed; half an hour later he was back with an order that *Constitution* must delay her entry to the port. Hull replied stiffly that he would delay for nothing but the weather and sailed right on in the next morning.

There was no immediate repercussion, but word of such occurrences gets around, and when the American frigate reached Portsmouth to prepare for the voyage home the British had an opportunity to pay this colonial out for his truculence. A seaman from *Constitution* slipped overside during the night and swam to the British frigate *Havanna* as she lay in a nearby berth. He was too exhausted to explain his purpose of desertion immediately and the British sent word they had picked him up. Next morning, when Hull's gig called for the man, it was explained that the fellow was a British subject and now under protection of the national flag. Hull called on the port admiral with a protest and was told that no, there was no proof of English citizenship except the man's bare assertion, but since he had made that assertion, the admiral was obliged to believe it and would not yield him. "The aspect and language of our Commander on that occasion can never be forgotten," wrote one of *Constitution's* people; double sentries were posted all round the ship, with orders to fire on anything in the water.

Something was in the water that very night. Hull leaped from his cabin at the sound of muskets in the dark, to find a man just being fished aboard, who said he was from the frigate *Havanna,* but was an impressed American. Next morning came a demand for the man; the port admiral's compliment was returned in precisely the same words in which it had been delivered. Friends ashore told Hull they thought an attempt would be made to take the man out when the frigate put to sea. He mustered his crew at the gangway and told them the whole story, ending with: "Are you ready to fight?"

There was a hurricane of cheering, even the men in irons for offenses begging to be released to take their places at the guns. Next morning two British frigates entered the harbor and anchored so near *Constitution* that it seemed she must foul them when she moved. Hull was too good a ship-handler to be caught that way; in the face of probability he slipped past them, hoisted sail, and rode out into the Channel. One Britisher and then the other followed him into a gathering dusk, but as they caught the winds it became apparent that one of the pair was much faster than the other, for she opened a long gap on her consort. Hull hung out his battle-lanterns, cleared for action and tacked round, remarking: "Now if that fellow wants a fight, let's give it to him."

"The people took hold of the tackles as if they were about to jerk the guns through the ship's side," and the Englishman thought better of making trouble. But it was clear to anyone afloat that those guns would be shooting some day soon, and on reaching Washington early in 1812 Hull asked permission to have his frigate hove down and thoroughly cleaned. The job was well done under charge of the famous "Jumping Billy" Haraden, and had hardly been completed when word came of the declaration of war on June 18. Hull dropped down the Chesapeake early in July, after having received some of the most extraordinary orders ever issued to a military officer.

"Sir," wrote Secretary of the Navy Hamilton in a first instruction: "You are not to understand me as impelling you to battle unless attacked"; and in a supplement to it: "You will weigh anchor and proceed to New York. If, on your way thither, you should fall in with an enemy's vessel, you will be guided by your own judgment, bearing in mind, however, that you are not, voluntarily, to encounter a force superior to your own. On your arrival at New York, you will report yourself to Commodore Rodgers. If he should not be in that port you will remain there till further orders."

This fairly reflects the state of mind in which official Washington regarded naval war against Great Britain. It was only with the greatest difficulty that Madison had been persuaded to let any of the ships go to sea at all, and the result of the first sailing seemed to justify the croakers. Rodgers had put out with *President*, 44, *United States*, 44,

Congress, 38, *Hornet,* 18, and *Argus,* 16; sighted the British frigate *Belvidera* and gave her a long chase, only to see her slip away and to have his own leg broken by the explosion of one of his main-deck guns.

Rodgers's squadron swung wide out into the Atlantic and made a success of his cruise in the objective for which a navy is maintained—the protection of commerce—by forcing the British commodore from the Halifax station to keep his own ships together lest they be picked up singly by the American squadron. He—the British commodore—thus failed to set up patrols off the American ports, and some hundreds of American merchant ships came winging home freely at the outbreak of war. But points like this are established only by subsequent analysis, while decisions are made and orders given on the basis of immediate appearance and emotional reaction.

Three days after dropping the capes of Virginia astern, in light airs from the north and east, several strange sail were sighted from *Constitution's* masthead. Hull thought them Rodgers's squadron at first, but, not being close enough to get a signal, cleared for action as he bore toward the nearest. When it fell dark, night signals were put out; the stranger not only failed to answer them, but began making incomprehensible signals of her own, therefore was probably enemy. Dawn confirmed this in an appalling manner, for it brought into clear view four heavy frigates, a line-of-battleship, and a brig, all under British colors. (The last was on the ex-U.S.S. *Nautilus,* 12, which had sailed right into their squadron and been taken, a couple of days before.) The nearest group, consisting of three frigates, was only five miles away, and the air where *Constitution* lay was so near a flat calm that the ship's head could not be kept up.

Hull had some of his stern-work cut away and pushed four guns through newly made ports there, meanwhile ordering out the boats and beginning to tow. The Britishers imitated the latter action and, having rather better airs to help their boats, began to close in fast, so that by seven in the morning one of them thought herself close enough to open fire. Short. At this juncture Hull tried a seaman's trick, by having an anchor carried out ahead and the ship pulled up to it—each man along the deck gripping the anchor cable where it came through the bows and walking aft with it, then dropping it at the stern to run forward and latch on again.

The method is known as kedging; *Constitution* gained on her pursuers with it for a couple of hours, or until the British spied through their glasses what was going on, and repeated it themselves. At noon Hull started out* most of his water and made another gain, but lost all this back and more too when the enemy had the inspiration of putting all the boats in their squadron to pull one frigate, which now came walking up rapidly. On *Constitution's* deck there was gloom and grim; Hull turned to his First Lieutenant: "Let's lay a broadside on them, Mr. Morris, and fight the whole. If they sink us, at least we'll go down like men."

It was not necessary to make the sacrifice; before the Briton could work into range a series of light puffs touched the surface. *Constitution* took in her boats on the run, thanks to Hull's careful preparation for just this, while the British had to abandon many of theirs as they jockeyed down the narrow corridors of the breeze. The men stayed on deck all night; a somewhat gloomy company, for if the old aristocratic tradition of war still permitted officers to be exchanged for those of equal rank, the common sailor could expect only to rot in some stinking lightless hulk till the fight was over. Hull sent those not actually handling ropes to the windward side of the vessel to stiffen her a trifle against the faint airs and so gain maybe a foot or two.

All through the next day and second night it was the same tale of drifting from capful to capful of tiny gust. *Constitution* footed so well and was so sharply handled that little by little she pulled ahead on her pursuers at this game, with men wetting the sails and answering orders in growing enthusiasm as it became clear they were winning. The end came in a squall of rain from eastward and ahead. Hull, being nearer than the enemy, could see that it was only a gust and quite thin, but he gave a convincing demonstration of a man caught unexpectedly, by sending all hands into the rigging to cast loose the light sails in frantic haste. The British all promptly cut down to storm canvas to be ready for the gale; as soon as the curtain of rain

* That is, he pumped the fresh water overboard.

hid *Constitution*, she got all her kites out again and went booming. When they next sighted her, she was hull down, too far away to be caught.

This was the background of the frigate's arrival at Boston, to which she went because the British squadron lay between her and New York. In the old seafaring town her escape was recognized as an almost incredible piece of seamanship, certainly not dimmed by the fact that Hull published a card in the papers giving all the credit to his crew.

But it was an escape; and if the ship, Boston's own, and her captain, a New Englander, gained a certain popularity in Massachusetts by it, the war itself had not. The peace party had triumphed in the election, and New England big pots of Federalist persuasion even boycotted the purchase of government bonds for the duration. Secession was openly discussed.

The navy agent at Boston even lacked the money to provision and equip the frigate for another cruise; that came from the pocket of a private citizen, one William Gray, who was read out of the Federalist party for making the loan. For that matter, Hull had no orders to sail on another cruise. He had reached a port which, if not the one intended, was an acceptable substitute, and by custom should have awaited an advice from Washington. The trouble was that, having been in the capital when war was declared, having received a set of orders that were a counsel to cowardice, he had a fairly clear idea that his new orders would be to lay the ship up. As a matter of fact, he did not guess the half of it; the order already on the way bade him in the coldest official terms to turn *Constitution* over to Captain William Bainbridge and betake himself to Washington at once. Therefore, the boy who had run away to sea at 14 did it again at 39. On August 2, he sailed from Boston without orders of any kind.

A disaster would certainly have placed him before a court-martial harder than the one James Barron had faced. Yet it is to be noted that it was no act of bravado that took the frigate to sea. Hull had now been in command of his ship for nearly two years, and the crew were his men, trained in his style. In Portsmouth harbor, and later during the great chase, they had given every evidence that they were heartily with him; not a man showed anything but determination on either occasion.

As for the Captain himself, he had been aboard some of those 38-gun British frigates armed with 18-pounders, which were their standard heavy cruisers, and he believed that the powerful battery and fine speed of his own ship would make her more than a match for any one of them. His insubordination was thus rooted in the most relentless New England logic. He did not care what precedent or appearances prescribed; he decided on the basis of what the situation itself contained, without reference to any other authority.

One hundred and thirty-one years later, on the red afternoon of Philippine Sea, Admiral Raymond Spruance said: "If the destroyers run out of fuel, send them back and we will proceed without them. I am going to strike that fleet and I will not be distracted by details."

v

Hull took his ship up to the region of Cape Race, in the main traffic lane for transatlantic crossings, where he captured a couple of small British craft and retook a pair of captured Americans before falling in on August 18 with a Newburyport privateer, who said a British frigate was cruising to the southward; had lately held the privateer in chase. *Constitution* turned in that direction with doubled lookouts posted; at two in the next afternoon a strange sail was sighted, close-hauled on the starboard tack. A heavy frigate, and there could be no doubt that she was British. *Constitution* came down toward her, running free; the stranger backed his main topsail to kill way and show a readiness to fight.

And ready to fight he was, for this was H.M.S. *Guerrière,* 38, that had practically held the American coast under blockade during the last months of uneasy peace, and only a few days before had sent in a note to New York daring *President* "or any other American frigate of equal force" to come out and "have a tête-à-tête." On her quarterdeck there was no doubt of a happy issue. Her captain, James Dacres, a tall, knightly-looking man, stood beside the skipper of a captured merchant and remarked that *Constitution* moved in rather too boldly for an

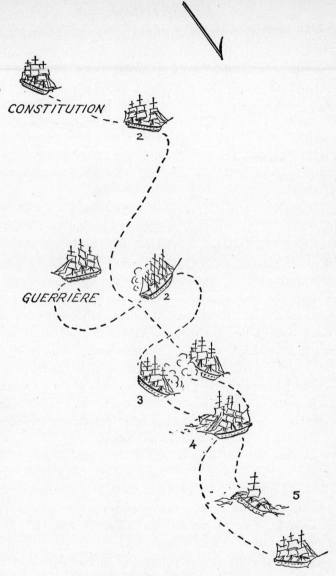

Constitution—Guerrière

(1) *Guerrière* waits. (2) *Guerrière* tries to rake; *Constitution* maneuvers to prevent it. (3) Broadside action. (4) *Guerrière* loses her mizzen-mast; *Constitution* taken aback. (5) *Guerrière's* foremast goes; the surrender.

American—"however, the better he behaves, the more honor we shall gain by taking him." At five the colors were set; as the American frigate approached, *Guerrière* fired and ran off, fired and ran off repeatedly, trying to rake her enemy, but was always foiled by the speed of Hull's countermaneuver. After nearly an hour of this Dacres ran free under short canvas, indicating willingness to accept level broadside battle.

Aboard *Constitution* everyone was at concert pitch. The guns were double-shotted; the men were shouting, "Her sides are made of iron!" as *Guerrière's* long-range shot bounced from the heavy scantling. Once, twice, three times, Lieutenant Morris asked anxiously, "Shall I open fire, sir?" And each time Hull replied, "Not yet, sir, not yet," trotting back and forth like an agitated and pudgy honey-bear. Balls began to sing through the rigging and holes appeared in the sails; two or three men were hit; and *Constitution* slid up one side of a long swell, down the other into position beside her antagonist.

"Now, boys, pour it into them!" screamed Hull, leaping into the air with such energy that his tight breeches split from waist to knee. Every gun in the frigate's broadside let go at once; on *Guerrière* a man below "heard a terrible crash, the *Guerrière* reeled and trembled as though she had received the shock of an earthquake. The next minute the cockpit was full of wounded." Aloft, the British frigate's mainyard was shot away in the slings and the balls that crashed into her hull sent a cloud of splinters high as the mizzentop.

"By heaven, that ship is ours!" cried Hull, leaping up and down, careless of his bare behind. "Hull her, boys!" the men along the gun-deck were shouting, as they strained at the tackles. For fifteen minutes the two ships ran side by side, *Constitution* shooting both faster and lower from her leeward position—and then the Britisher's mizzenmast toppled over her counter with a crash.

Tackle still holding the dragging gear twisted her head round against the pressure of the wheel, and *Constitution* luffed up to cross her bows for a rake. In the excitement she was driven too far into the wind and hung, with her topsails aback, while the enemy's bowsprit jutted over her quarterdeck. The bugles called boarders on both ships; there was a fierce blaze of musketry, but the sea was running too heavily for anyone to leap the gap, and Hull ordered his vessel's sails filled for a run ahead and another try at raking the crippled *Guerrière*. Just as *Constitution* swung clear, the British frigate's foremast, wounded at its base, stumbled over the side, and, with nearly all the system of bracing that is a sailing ship's rigging gone, the mainmast followed.

Constitution ran off to a little distance to replace damaged ropes, then swung round toward the hulk that lay heaving under the red twilight of high latitudes, and for the first time in nine years of uninterrupted war Saint George's blood-red cross came down at the end of a cruiser battle. The two captains had known each other well; the oft-repeated and probably veracious tale is that they had even bet a hat on the outcome of a contest; and that when Dacres, shamefaced and shot through the shoulder, mounted to his captor's deck, Hull offered his hand and refused to accept his adversary's sword: "But I will trouble you for that hat."

VI

The effect of the victory was explosive, and out of all proportion to its physical importance. Nor was this effect lessened when the British Admiralty, forced to make explanations in a field where these had never before been necessary, called *Constitution* "a disguised ship of the line" and pointed out that her weight of metal in a broadside was as 3 to *Guerrière's* 2. The unanswerable answer was that the relative personnel casualties were as 6 to 1 (*Constitution* had only 14) and that the British frigate was so smashed that they had to burn her in the evening because she was in danger of sinking before they could take her crew out. Hull had not merely won a battle, which is something that can usually be accounted for by the defeated side if it searches long enough for a soothing reason; he had destroyed his opponent.

And he had done so at a time and place calculated to give the achievement its maximum value. The war was going badly. Fort Dearborn had fallen to the Indians, who killed everyone in it, and the news of Hull's victory reached most places only a few hours after the less pleasant tidings that his own uncle, General William Hull, had surrendered Detroit to the enemy in the most pusillanimous manner. A people who had borne many wrongs and were starved for a victory heard with almost incredulous delight that they had received one from the most unexpected quarter possible, and that the verdict of the Revolution about American seamen's being no match for British was a reversible error.

Even the hard-boiled Federalists of Boston capitulated to enthusiasm, for the navy was their institution, *Constitution* was their ship, and most of her crew their men. They brought Hull ashore amid music and saluting artillery; New York raised a subscription to buy swords for the Captain and his officers; Philadelphia sent them services of plate; at Baltimore bells were rung and cannon fired, all day long. Most important of all, Congress, which at the beginning of the war had voted only $300,000 to repair naval vessels, now heartily rushed through a bill to construct four line-of-battleships and six more frigates like *Constitution*.

In the midst of the shouting and illuminations, Hull retained his Yankee reserve. He avoided as many of the public dinners as he decently could, and when he learned that his brother had just died, asked to have Bainbridge relieve him in command of the frigate—which saved everybody a good deal of embarrassment in view of the order that had been sent him before he sailed. The new assignment was to the harbor defense of New York. On his way to Washington to make a personal report he paused long enough in Philadelphia to call on a reigning beauty named Ann Hart. Eleven years before, when he was a lieutenant superintending some repairs to *Constitution*, the girl had visited the ship, expressing a desire for a piece of the curiously hard tarred rope of her cordage. After she left Hull sent her a piece of it, made into a necklace. Now when he returned a hero, she was wearing the necklace, and they were married in February.

It was a singularly happy match, and probably one of the reasons why the Captain saw little sea-service thereafter. After a short tour of duty at New York, he was sent up to Portsmouth to superintend the construction of the new 74-gun ship of the line *Washington*, which would normally have made him her commander on completion, but he stepped aside for Bainbridge. After the war, when a law setting up the new board of Navy Commissioners was passed, he was named one of three, but resigned after a brief period, apparently because he found the expenses and social duties of the capital a strain. Two of his recommendations while in office were for the establishment of the rank of admiral and for a regular building program. There followed commands at various navy yards, a three-year cruise to the Pacific as ranking officer on station, and another to the Mediterranean in the new battleship *Ohio*, which ended in a mild controversy with the department and some unhappiness for Hull—the quiet life of a peace-time officer until his death in 1843.

During this time his influence was not outstanding in the service or out of it, and nobody regarded him as a leader of thought, like the stormy Porter or the intellectual Rodgers. At first glance, indeed, Hull's contribution to the body of thought and tradition that ulti-mately gave the American navy a character of its own seems entirely concentrated around the events of August, 1812. This is true to a de-gree, though the whole picture might have turned out very differently if he had been a less modest man or a more demanding one.

But the background of that sea-fight, the circumstances under which it took place, and the fact that it was Hull who won it, made it of paramount importance in determining both the ideals of the naval service and the spirit in which those ideals were approached. In the Revolution, John Paul Jones had won an even more splendid victory at a moment as unexpected, and he left a legacy of unconquerable per-sistence and dauntless courage that was an inspiration to all future na-val officers. Yet precisely because the odds that faced Jones were so great, there was about him something of the superman. He founded no school, trained no successors. Simple, plain Isaac Hull, the Con-necticut nutmeg, did nothing but what any ordinary man could do, provided that man assembled his conduct in the proper pattern. The lesson was not lost on others.

His extraordinary skill in handling a ship was something individ-ual, to be sure, but this could be seen, and in fact was seen, as the re-sult of application. The fact that he was always so ready for trouble—the fact that he had the ship cleared for action before trouble arrived (as in the exit from Portsmouth)—the fact that when he reached a situation not covered by orders, he made his own orders: these were things that any ordinary man could file for imitation. No doubt Hull had absorbed much of this from Preble. But he also added something of his own, just as, in a sense, Preble's campaign against Tripoli constituted a small victory, while Hull's over *Guerrière* was a great one. That something can be best described as moral courage; the thing that took Hull to sea without orders and into an engagement which everyone else was sure would end in defeat. Not that Preble lacked the quality; he never had the opportunity to employ it in a manner that would fix public attention. The important point about Hull's moral courage was that it was not the sort of bravery that must be called upon when all resources but courage are exhausted. Hull showed this sort, too, in the moment when he proposed to fight his ship till she sank if the British fleet caught up with him. What counted, in his case, was reasoned courage, confidence in the validity of his own intellectual process.

In the hot business of war, there are always risks and they are not always from the enemy. It was Hull's merit to investigate those risks; and when he found unreal the danger which his contemporaries thought most deadly, he acted on his own judgment, and thus overcame the greater risk that the navy might be withheld from its business of making war unprofitable to the enemy.

In so doing he not only established a pattern for his service, but also struck the first blow in the long fight against the idea that Americans live on a separate planet. "Shall the great mammoth of the American forests leave his native element and engage in a mad contest with the shark?" demanded John Randolph of Roanoke. "I see no disgrace in saying to the mistress of the seas, 'We are unable to contend with you.' " Words were spoken in reply at the time, but they have been forgotten; the real answer was given by *Constitution's* long 24s.

Chapter 3

A Delaware Squire:
Jacob Jones

Now drink to *Decatur* and *Rodgers* and *Hull*
   And to every brave heart, to his country that's true;
And never forget while the glass circles round
   The fame of the *Wasp,* her *Commander* and *crew.*

                        —Old Song

O F ALL PREBLE'S BOYS NONE REMAINS MORE ESSENTIALLY MYS-
terious than Captain Jacob Jones, the least boyish of that remarkable group. There was something about him that inspired other
people to clichés; his contemporaries speak of him as brave, upright,
temperate, benevolent, plain—a compendium of Sunday-school virtues,
in fact. The man himself has not left us much help. He was one of
the most word-sparing individuals in the history of the U.S. navy; private letters in his hand practically do not exist, he committed public
documents only under press of urgent necessity, and those he did
produce are perfectly correct (the cliché again) but about as colorful
as a worn-out sail.

This would hardly matter if he had lived an ordinary life, even the
normal life of an extroverted naval officer, which could be described
in terms of voyage, technique, and battle. He did nothing of the kind;
and merely citing the record in the case of Jacob Jones leaves a great
deal unexplained. Why did he spend so much time at sea, especially
after reaching an age when most officers were quite willing to accept
shore duty? What was there about him that made successive secretaries of the navy find sea commands for him when there were so few

ships in commission that it was hard to find ships for anybody? Above all, what was he doing in the navy in the first place?

On the last question there is some background of information, but its real meaning cannot be the apparent one. The navy was certainly not the career for which Jacob Jones was destined, by either his family or himself. He was born near Smyrna, Delaware, in 1768, on what is described as a small farm, but the family must have been reasonably well off, for there was money enough to give him a good classical education. In the meanwhile, his mother died while he was a tot, his father remarried and himself died when Jacob was only four, leaving the boy to be brought up by his stepmother, Penelope Hope Jones.

She appears to have made a good job of it. Jones always spoke of her later in terms of the most intense admiration and affection, and she surrounded the boy with a host of friends. One of these was a Dr. James Sykes of Dover; having opted for the medical profession, Jones did four years of practical internship with this doctor, took a course at the University of Pennsylvania, married Dr. Sykes's sister, and returned to his native Kent County to set up in practice. As of those days he is reported as a big man with a long nose and a hammerhead chin, much seen in the Delaware society whose elegance was so like that of country-gentleman England, with riding to hounds and hunt breakfasts on partridges and wild boar hams brought from the forests of Pennsylvania; apples, cheese, and two or three bottles of port per man in the evening. There was not a better seat in Kent County than Dr. Jones, nor a better companion; but he made himself remarkable in that hard-drinking group by his abstemiousness.

He seemed settled for life; but the trouble about this easy-going country-gentleman existence was that Jones could not make enough money to live on. Whether the "benevolence" ascribed to him means that he did too much work without pay, or whether his poverty was comparative and related to the social necessities of maintaining a stable and a kennel, is uncertain. The fixed point is that some time in the presidency of George Washington, Jones decided to improve his prospects by abandoning medicine for the study of law. He had not gone very deeply into it when Governor Joshua Clayton, a personal friend, appointed him clerk of the Superior Court, the highest in the state.

Jacob Jones

Jones moved to Kent City and lived there until the death of his wife in 1799. Shortly after this he threw up everything and entered the navy as a midshipman.

On the face of it, this looks like a case of the world lost for love, for it was about the most impossible step that could be taken by a man who had any thought of a career, or even of personal happiness. Jones was 31 at the time, and had never been to sea in his life. In the cockpit of a warship he would be thrown with lads in the early teens; on deck he would be performing such drudgery tasks as mending signal flags and carrying messages. Completely ignorant of the profession, he could hardly expect to be advanced faster than these boys, so that when they reached the age of command he would be eligible only for retirement. But the romantic explanation of Jones's enlistment is rather damaged by the fact that when he returned from his second cruise, he promptly married another girl, who bore him a son and lived with him until her own death, nearly twenty years later.

No, a broken heart will hardly answer. Jones himself gave as a reason for signing on, that he wanted a more active life; but there are other possibilities. He had certainly been a failure as a doctor, and in spite of political friends, there is no evidence that he was considered a rising star of the legal profession. One could make out a case for the idea that he regarded himself as a failure and was willing to enter a business that offered him some economic security even at a sacrifice in dignity.

The weight of the evidence is that his thinking was not done on so materialistic a level. Thomas Truxtun, the famous and brilliantly successful privateer captain of the Revolution, was living in Philadelphia; had become a close friend of Jones and a frequent caller at his house. Himself on intimate terms with most of the government heads at the capital, Truxtun was an obvious choice for one of the six captaincies when the navy was re-established, and President Adams gave him the fifth place on the list, with command of the *Constellation* frigate. There would be a good deal of talk about French aggression and the prospect of war around Kent City; talk in the high tone, somewhat stiff and formal, that characterized the end of the 18th century—the duty of a citizen to his country, sirs.

Preble's Boys

Now, one of the few facts that shine through all the records concerning Jacob Jones is that his whole mind was irradiated with an emotion currently somewhat out of fashion, but which was a real force in the generation that saw the escape from English rule. It was an ardent personal identification with the United States of America, not as a state in the modern sense, but as an association of free men, born equal. Jones had the faces of three ancestral silver tankards melted down to erase from them the family coat of arms, and when his second wife asked what it had been, refused to tell her, with the remark, "I am a Welshman and my coat of arms is the leek."

Thus it can be taken that Jacob Jones did not join the navy as a career. He waited till the guns were shooting, till American ships were at sea in search of enemies of the nation. Upon a mind oriented like his the fact of actual war would be decisive. He joined the navy; and as he felt his lack of experience did not justify him in asking for any higher station than that of midshipman, he persuaded his friend Captain Truxtun to obtain for him a warrant to that post. The same high-mindedness kept him from applying for a billet aboard *Constellation*. Instead he entered the general list, (in April 1799) and went out for a short cruise in *United States*, 44, which voyage was chiefly important in introducing Jones to the head of the midshipmen's mess, with whom he formed an acquaintance of mutual liking—Stephen Decatur.

As soon as *United States* reached port, Jones was transferred to the new corvette *Delaware*, 24. This cruise was a hard one. *Delaware* captured one French privateer and recaptured a couple of American merchants, which meant prize-money for all hands: but after some six months in the West Indies was ordered to the area of Curaçao, and there ran into trouble. *Delaware* was a purchased merchant craft, her length less than four times her beam, which made a sidewise drift her best point of sailing. She never came up with the French known to be operating in the region, but easily caught tropical fevers, which struck down the captain, Baker, and so many of the crew that the ship had to lie over in Curaçao harbor for nearly three months. There were barely enough men left to work the ropes when she sailed for home without orders.

When the ship reached port after more than a year at sea, Jones paused only for his second marriage, received his step to lieutenant, and put to sea again. This time it was *Ganges,* 24, a rebuilt merchantman that had been the first vessel of the new navy to leave harbor. She was destined for a cruise to Java on Preble's track, but never made it, because she behaved so badly that a board of commissioners which was called found her totally unseaworthy. Not long later the French treaty was ratified and the peace establishment came into force. Jacob Jones ranked at the very bottom of the list of 36 lieutenants who were not dismissed.

II

Here is another mild mystery, and no tools but conjecture to solve it with, for any documentation that existed has disappeared. It is easy enough to see why Mr. Lieutenant Jones was retained when two-thirds of the lieutenants on the list were let out. His conduct had been correct, if not particularly distinguished, and Truxtun, who had become a national hero by virtue of his two victories during the war, would be sure to put in a good word for him. But it is a little harder to understand why the lieutenant should have accepted a post in a service that now had few attractions when he had a new bride at home, and the impulse to patriotism was somewhat dimmed by the peace.

Possibly economics had something to do with it this time. Jones's friend Clayton was no longer governor, which meant no more political preferment. Without some such backing the prospect of making a fresh start in a stable and ordered community where small gains were the rule cannot have been an exciting one. But in view of Jones's later life, it seems quite as probable that the sea itself had already exercised upon him that pull which led so many younger Americans of his time to leave home for the life of a sailor. The attraction is somewhat difficult to analyze precisely—compounded in varying amounts of the spirit of adventure rampant in all men and nations when they are young, the quest of foreign lands in an age when travel was extremely difficult under ordinary circumstances, and the offering of the sea itself. Jones felt that pull; not six months after he reached home, he asked for sea service and got it—as Fifth of *Constellation,* 38, for the Mediterranean under Captain Alexander Murray.

That officer had seen a good deal of service in the rowdy navy of the Revolution, and was determined that there should be no similar lack of discipline aboard any ship he commanded in the revived marine. He was oldish for the service, arbitrary by habit of mind, and rather deaf, and he suffered a good deal from old wounds when rainy weather was toward. The result was a series of clashes of temperament with his juniors which made *Constellation* a peculiarly unhappy ship.

Jones was involved twice, once being placed under arrest for acting as second in a duel and shortly after in a more dangerous business. The ship had picked up a pilot and was coming into port with the Fifth Lieutenant in charge of the deck, when Captain Murray ducked out of the cabin and gave the order to shorten sail. Jones, who had not heard him, but saw the sails being clewed up contrary to any ideas of his, asked the pilot to have them shaken out; whereupon Murray flew at his lieutenant, using such language that Jones requested relief from the deck.

This sort of thing happens aboard warships frequently enough to make it no special cause for excitement. In the navy of that day the usual end would have been a personal interview, followed by a note of apology on one side and a note of explanation on the other. But when Jones appeared before the Captain, Murray began shouting again, answered his junior's protest about the words he had used by ordering the lieutenant from the cabin, and sent him below, under orders of arrest for the voyage.

One of the other lieutenants had already been arrested for murder on the heels of the duel in which Jones was a second; another was sick; so the shape in which *Constellation* arrived in port can be imagined. The rather odd part of the story is that when word of the occurrence reached Washington, the department backed the lieutenants against their captain, ordering the ship home and sending Murray ashore, where he remained for the rest of his life except one brief cruise against smugglers off the St. Mary's. The fact that the lieutenant's first arrest was for dueling was a factor in this decision, there being no law that authorized an arrest for murder on such grounds. But Jones's own reputation for punctilious behavior certainly played its part, since he received a vote of official confidence in the form of an order to return to the Mediterranean at once, as one of the very junior officers assigned to Commodore Preble's squadron.

His appointment was that of Second Lieutenant of *Philadelphia*, 38, under William Bainbridge as captain. The latter, who took the unusual step of turning in written reports on his lieutenants, could find no terms for Jones but the familiar ones of cliché—"a brave, good officer and a correct man," which would indicate that the Captain was satisfied but did not see anything remarkable in his lieutenant. Preble did; had Jones aboard the flag a couple of times for dinner, and talked things out with him extensively. There is no record of what the two reticent men said to each other, but a good portion of it must have been professional shop, since neither of them was given to the abstract. The contact was a brief one, for Preble was bound to Morocco and the overawing of the sullen Emperor there, while Jones had an appointment with an unhappy destiny on the rocks outside Tripoli harbor, where—as has been told—*Philadelphia* grounded and was taken by the Turks at the end of October 1803.

Officers and crew spent over 19 miserable months in captivity, the men being forced to work on the fortifications, the officers on short commons whenever anything aroused the peevish temper of Peter Lisle, a renegade Scotsman who had made himself the Bashaw's war minister under the style of Murad Reis. Jones functioned as prison doctor, and the mortality rate was less than might have been expected. There is very little else to say about this experience, except that it was followed by the longest period Jones had spent ashore since entering the navy. But then, everyone was ashore those days; it was the period when the ships were laid up and the government built gunboats to defend its harbors.

In the course of the period Jones was chosen to make personal presentation of the gold medal which Congress had voted to Preble, with whom he spent some time, finding him very ill; then sat as junior member of the court-martial which condemned James Barron for his conduct in the *Leopard-Chesapeake* affair. There followed a short period of shore duty at the New Orleans station under David Porter, who had been in Tripoli with him.

In 1810 seniority brought Jones to a master-commandant's rank, and the following year he was ordered north to place the sloop-of-war *Wasp*, 18, in commission. She was a remarkable little ship, originally intended to be one of the brigs for inshore work against the Barbaries, but not completed in time because the work of design fell into the. hands of one Josiah Fox. This Fox was an Englishman and a Quaker, trained in the shipbuilding art, who came to this country originally to buy ship-timber. In Philadelphia he met a fellow-Quaker and ship-designer, Joshua Humphreys, who had just received a commission to design six frigates for the re-established U.S. navy. Humphreys needed an assistant; the two Quakers hit it off at once, and Fox remained in America for the rest of his life.

It is probable that he contributed to the combination a good deal in the way of sound methods and constructional details, but he certainly gained more than he gave, for Humphreys was one of the master-figures of the history of naval architecture, a profound and original thinker. "As our navy for a considerable time will be inferior in numbers," he wrote in answer to President Washington's request for information about what ships to build, "we have to consider what size ships will be most formidable and be an overmatch for those of an enemy. Frigates will be the first object, and none ought to be built less than one hundred fifty foot keel, to carry thirty twenty-four pounders on the gun-deck. Ships of this construction have everything in their favor; their great length gives them an advantage in sailing,* which is an object of the first magnitude. They are superior to any European frigate, and if others be in company, our frigates can always lead ahead and never be obliged to go into action but on their own terms."

Now, as the normal heavy cruiser had a keel length of between 125 feet and 130, and mounted a main battery of twenty-eight 18-pounders, this was revolutionary. But Fox considered it heretical. So big a frigate

---

* It takes less power to drive a long, narrow ship through the water than a shorter one of the same beam; and on a long ship it would be possible to use taller masts, hence larger sails.

would be as clumsy and hard to handle as a battleship, slow on every bearing except when the wind was dead astern. Humphreys had an answer for that: he would give his ships a hull-form modified from that developed through long years into the clipper schooners of Chesapeake Bay—great length in proportion to beam, the hull hollowed out aft to fish-tail shape, and with so much keel-drag that the draft under their counters was nearly a quarter again that at the bow.

Fox remained unconvinced. The two men were as near disagreement as Quakers can ever come, and being appointed to handle one of the new frigates, *Chesapeake*, the man from England brought her out as a normal and very fine 38-gun, 18-pounder ship, instead of the American freak he was supposed to build. After the Humphreys-designed ships showed their wonderful sailing and fighting qualities in the West Indies and before Tripoli, Fox suffered a change of heart. Now that he had the chance, he decided to apply similar theories of construction to a sloop-of-war. The norm of the class was a brig of not over 90 feet length; he went to 115 feet for *Wasp* and her sister, *Hornet*, with the fine entry, clean running lines, cut-away deadwood, and deep keel aft of the Baltimore clipper. They were flush-deckers, without the poop and forecastle found in the sloops of other nations.

They steered hard, but in every other respect were sensationally successful ships, fast as dolphins, handling sharply, steady gun platforms, and prodigiously weatherly. Master-Commandant Jones must have been pleased with his new ship. She was armed with eighteen 32-pound carronades and two long 12s; he worked his men hard.

III

By the date *Wasp* put to sea, American naval policy had become that of sending the ships along the coast in training cruises, with instructions to do what they could in holding down British impressments, and the air was heavy with angers. Jones sailed along the coast of the middle states for some months without event; then, putting in for stores, was given the mission of carrying dispatches to our ministers in Europe. It was now 1812; before *Wasp* left France on her homeward journey there was a rumor that President Madison would go to war with England, and as a matter of fact the declaration had already been issued, though no one in Europe knew it as yet.

The ship made a good passage; when she reached America, the orders were to put out again at once, for the incredible news of *Constitution's* victory over *Guerrière* had come and there was no longer any disposition to use the American navy for anything but fighting. Jones cruised up to the region broad off Boston, but made only one prize, a British merchant that had already been captured by a Yankee privateer and retaken by a British frigate.

Rough weather brought a necessity for small repairs; Jones ran into the Delaware, his normal home port at New York being under blockade. When he came out again, on October 13, he headed generally toward the Bermudas, reasoning that the English West India trade would keep wide of the American coast, though not so wide as to run east of this group of islands and so lose the help of the Gulf Stream in the voyage to Europe. His mission was primarily a raiding one.

Three days out the ship found winds of hurricane force and lost her jib-boom during the night. The weather did not moderate till morning, when it left behind so heavy a swell that no spare spar could be rigged. That night at about 11 several sail were made out through night glasses on a sea still running high, but as two of them appeared to be large ships Jones did not close them in the dark. He cleared for action and set his ship on the same course as the strangers, but under a little less canvas, so that he gradually dropped astern but remained to windward. *Wasp's* speed and weatherliness would allow him to work clear of heavy enemies, even though the missing jib-boom deprived her of two-thirds of her headsail, and made fast tacks impossible.

Morning exhibited the chase as six ships, of which at least four were clearly big Indiamen and another a heavy brig-sloop. *Wasp* made sail to close; the brig shortened in willingness to accept battle, and as the two drew together it could be seen that she too had had a bout with the winds, for her mainyard was on deck.

She was H.M.S. *Frolic,* 18, more powerful than *Wasp* by about 10 per cent (274 pounds weight of broadside to 250), with the incomparable tradition of the British navy behind her. Her captain was

Thomas Whinyates; he had drilled his men at the great guns until they could fire them as fast as any ship in the Royal Navy and maybe faster, for he was an ambitious man and wished much to make a good prize in battle. This was why he had signaled the Indiamen to stand on, though one of them carried as many guns as the American now coming down under his queer flag of fifteen stripes and wreath of stars.

The remains of the storm were still in the swell; upon it now worked a breeze both sharp and freshening, so that as the two ships slid down a broad reach on the starboard tack they rolled violently. The dipping prows flung spray across the decks and the men worked barefoot, finding it hard to stand. Aboard *Wasp* the gun-breechings were doubled; the sponge-and-rammer men rubbed their hands in sand from the deck, and made obscene remarks about His Majesty's jollies. Jones kept his ship a little more off the wind than his adversary, the tracks slanting together. He wanted broadside action, being in no shape to jockey for position without his jib. At half-past 11 they were side by side; *Frolic* opened fire at 60 yards, repeating so rapidly that she was shooting three times to *Wasp's* two, which surprised the American officers, who had trained their own gunners long and well.

Nor was the British fire resultless; five minutes from the first gun, the American sloop's main-topmast was shot away and went crashing into the fore braces, making it impossible to work the yards on that mast. Three minutes later the gaff and mizzen-topgallantmast followed. *Wasp*, cut to pieces aloft, was so nearly unmanageable that she could only hold her course, but few men had been hit and it was evident that the Britisher was firing from the trough of the sea, just as his starboard side began to rise on the swell, so that most of his rapidly delivered shot were going high. Not so with *Wasp*; as Captain Preble had taught in the old days before Tripoli, her guns were being fired from the wave-top as they began the descent that would presently carry their muzzles under—and they were making splinters fly aboard the enemy.

Now the two were so close together that the American rammers struck *Frolic's* side, but before the guns could be fired from that posi-

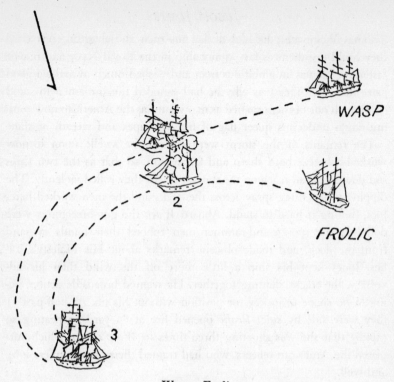

Wasp—Frolic
(1) The approach. (2) *Wasp* cut up aloft. (3) *Wasp*
nearly unmanageable; but *Frolic* has lost too many men
to handle her sails.

tion the brig's gaff-head braces went and her spanker came down on
the run. With more sail still drawing, *Wasp* pulled slightly ahead. The
slant of her motion brought *Frolic's* bowsprit jabbing into the rigging just above Jones's head, where it caught, dragging *Wasp* into a
raking position under her enemy's bows.

The broadside let go with a crash; Jones shouted to hold her there
and give *Frolic* another, but there was a seaman named Jack Lang,
who had once been impressed in the British navy. With a snarl, Lang
swung himself onto the overhanging bowsprit, cutlass in hand, to
take his personal revenge. Lieutenant Biddle followed, crying on the
rest to come on, and, seeing it was useless to restrain them, Captain
Jones ordered his bugler to blow "Boarders away!"

Jacob Jones

The smoke whipped down the wind; as the shouting Americans reached the foot of their opponent's bowsprit, they paused in astonishment, for the only living persons on a deck slippery with blood were an old oak-hearted quartermaster gripping the wheel and three wounded officers, who threw their swords at the victors' feet. The last raking broadside had completed the deadly work of Jones's artillery; of *Frolic's* 107 men, 90 were dead or wounded and the survivors had fled below to escape that terrible rain of iron. *Wasp* herself had 5 killed, 5 wounded.

IV

In a sense the victory was Pyrrhic. Biddle and a prize crew were placed aboard *Frolic*, but she lost both her badly wounded masts soon after the ships separated, and when *Wasp* shook her own sails out it was discovered that they had been cut to ribbons by the high fire of the Englishman. This was unfortunate, since two hours later, before repairs could be much more than begun, there hove over the horizon H.M.S. *Poictiers*, a 74-gun battleship, which of course captured both without any trouble.

They were carried into Bermuda, where *Frolic* was found so smashed that she had to be condemned. The British naval men were much angered; they took away from Jones and his officers their watches and everything but the clothes they stood in. But the civilian Bermudans, with that sportsmanlike admiration for men who can beat them at their own game that Britons not infrequently show, entertained the prisoners with a series of balls and dinners.

Exchange was only a matter of a couple of weeks; all the *Wasps* were in New York before the end of November, being greeted with an enthusiasm which compared only with that for Hull's triumph over *Guerrière*. New York voted Jones a sword and a banquet, and Philadelphia put on a public entertainment for officers and crew. Congress sent a gold medal to Jones, and silver impressions of the same to his officers, and voted that $35,000 should be distributed among all hands as prize money for *Frolic*. We may take it that Jones, always a great hand for minor social pleasures, enjoyed all this hugely; he made a kind of progress through Philadelphia and his old home in Delaware to Washington, where he was informed that as another reward he had been promoted captain and placed in command of *Macedonian*, 38.

In February 1813, he joined his ship, which had recruited a full crew and was lying at New London, Conn. By this date the government had adopted a policy of sending out, or trying to send out, every available ship in small squadrons, strong enough to destroy any but the most heavily escorted convoys and to deal with their escorts as well. These groups were to sweep out generally in the direction of the gap between Africa and Brazil, along which line they would cut across the lines of British trade with both the East and the West Indies. *Macedonian* was one of a group headed by Stephen Decatur, who had *United States,* 44, as his flag and *Hornet,* 18, with him; but the difficulty was that by early 1813 the British had posted heavy blockading forces off all the American ports, and there was a big one at Nantucket to watch the exit of Long Island Sound.

Decatur took his ships down to New York (where there was another banquet) and tried the Sandy Hook outlet, but found it closed by watchful ships; took them back through Hell Gate to New London and tried the Sound again, but to no purpose. There were always at least four British frigates on guard, usually backed by a two-decker. A whole year went by in this frustration, the ships spending most of their time at wharves in the Thames under the guns of forts built to cover them against landing expeditions, with now and then a short jog out for drill.

The only relief for Jones was a call to New York. As one of the best-educated men in the service, he was placed on a board to report on the plans and model of a stream-propelled frigate designed by Mr. Fulton, the ingenious inventor. The ship was to be called *Demologos*; she was to be arranged as a catamaran, having a paddle-wheel between two enormous hulls so thick as to be impervious to any ordinary shot. The battery was to consist of 30 32-pounders, battleship guns, on a single deck, and as long as she had fire aboard anyway, there was a furnace for heating the balls red-hot, and a pump to squirt potential boarders with boiling water. No masts except a couple of light poles for signaling.

Jacob Jones

Jones did not think her a seagoing craft, but was otherwise wholly favorable. Her sides would be impregnable (he wrote), and "in a light breeze she can take her choice of position or distance from an enemy." The only stipulation concerned her engines: if they were worth as much as four knots, the ship "can be rendered more formidable to an enemy than any kind of engine yet invented for the defence of ports, harbors, bays and sounds." Build her, by all means, was the Captain's advice, and the government took it, though they did not complete her till the war was over, so that she became a marine curiosity instead of a new weapon of destructive effect and far-reaching influence.

At the break of spring in 1814 the government changed naval policy again. The heavy ships in harbors having sheltered approach waters that permitted the British to maintain blockade in all weathers were to be laid up, and their crews sent overland to lakes Champlain and Ontario, where campaigns of doubtful issue were in progress. *Macedonian* was one of the ships laid up; Jones and his crew went up to Sackett's Harbor, N. Y. (on Lake Ontario), where they were detailed to *Mohawk*, 48, a heavy frigate on two decks, then still uncompleted.

It was a distinctly odd campaign among the woods that came down on all sides to the shores of the lake. The two commanders, Isaac Chauncey on the American side and Sir James Lucas Yeo on the other, were men much alike—good organizers, but cautious as fighting leaders. Moreover, each was filled with a vivid sense of the disaster that could come to the cause if his fleet were destroyed, like the British on Lake Erie during the previous year. There had been a couple of mild partial battles, a few cases of small craft cut off and destroyed, but the main contest was in the building yards.

The procedure was this: the commodore on each side remained in port until he had completed a new ship that gave him superiority, then blockaded his adversary in turn and carried out whatever ulterior projects he had in mind, such as descents on the shore, the transport of supplies, the covering of military movements. The contest had begun with 16-gun brigs and little schooners; by the date of Jones's arrival it had grown into one of quite respectable fleets.

At this time it was Yeo's turn to hold the lake; he was off Sackett's with a two-decked 58, a 42-gun frigate, two strong corvettes, and three brigs. Chauncey himself had a two-decker, slightly bigger than the British flagship, two corvettes, two heavy brigs, and two light ones, but he liked the look of the British frigate so little that he would not sail until *Mohawk* was ready. This was on July 25; the squadron put out, caught one of the British brigs without a keeper and destroyed her, then turned back to maintain a blockade of the enemy base at Kingston until mid-October. Now Yeo appeared with a 110-gun ship of the line which could have taken on Chauncey's whole squadron; the Americans returned to Sackett's and stayed there till the freeze.

By the spring of 1815 news of the peace had come, and Jones was ordered back to *Macedonian* with his men; objective, the Mediterranean, where some business had developed with Algiers, largest of the Barbary powers. The story of that expedition is Decatur's, who was in command; Jones and his ship were merely among those present.

When he returned he was given three months' leave, the first he had had since entering the navy, except for a few weeks at a time while waiting for a ship to be ready. It is possible that the period represents the illness and death of Jones's second wife, a personage even more mysterious than the Captain himself, in that surviving records do not even give her name. In 1821 Jones married for a third time and took his new bride on a three years' honeymoon tour of the Mediterranean, aboard *Constitution*, 44, of which he had been made captain; it was a skipper's privilege in those days to take his family aboard. They had a son who became an officer in the Marine Corps and went with Matthew Perry to Japan.

There followed various sea commands and a temporary seat on the board of Navy Commissioners, then a final cruise to the Pacific, with a commodore's broad pennant, in *Brandywine*, 44, the famous "roaring *Brandywine*" so celebrated for her speed, the toughness of her crews, and the hilarity of her officers. They caught rather a tartar in Jacob Jones, who reports from Callao that he has hanged one sailor from the yardarm for fatally stabbing another while drunk. One of the accounts of his life contains a queer little item from this period: "He is a

great promoter of temperance among his crew; and has been successful in reclaiming many a valuable seaman from the pernicious habits
of intoxication."

Return from the Pacific found him aged 62, which was considered
too old for sea work in sailing-ship days, but he never was retired
from the service, holding various shore posts which ended with command of the Naval Asylum at Philadelphia, where he died in 1850, 82
years old. He had asked to be buried in his native Delaware, and his
coffin was followed by "the largest and most interesting collection of
military ever seen in the state," not to mention such organizations as the
Masons, the Odd Fellows, the Society of Cordwainers, and the Sons of
Temperance.

The item about the funeral supplies a clue. Jones seems to have been
a member of every one of this extraordinary array of fraternal bodies,
which was a great deal more peculiar in his day than it would be now.
That is, he was an early American joiner; he was a friendly man; he
liked people, and was liked by them so thoroughly that when they
came to praise him, they could do so only by seeing in him an intensification of the group virtues. Nobody ever claimed he was an intellectual giant, and his failure in the professions rather suggests that his ca-
pacities were not too high—though there is no reason to set him down
as an incompetent doctor, or to reject his own explanation of sheer
boredom with any task that did not keep him active and in the open.

To the last, there was that strain of intense drive in the man. On
his final cruise, for instance, he could easily have had one of the new
ships of the line and a comfortable trip to Europe, but he took *Brandywine* and the lonely Pacific. He is also described as hardly knowing
the meaning of the word fatigue; riding horseback while late in his
seventies. But his contribution to the accumulating body of naval tradition lay not so much in this as in his influence on a view of duty that
was in danger of becoming cheerless. He added a touch of geniality,
worked on the principle that duty is for the hours of duty and may
be performed without damage to normal human relations.

The great age he reached and his 52 years of service, nearly half
of them at sea, added not a little to the influence he had among the
younger officers. They could and often did look at this plain, kindly,

sociable old man and reflect that he wore a gold medal for the most murderously effective single-ship action of the War of 1812. That action was not without importance in confirming the verdict of *Constitution-Guerrière* and bolstering the confidence of the nation in the navy and of the navy in itself; but it was probably more important that the man who won it was an educated gentleman, who remained for so long as a living exhibition of qualities that can make a successful naval officer.

Chapter 4

Hero of Romance: Stephen Decatur

Decatur and his hardy tars were cruising on the deep,
When off the Western Islands they to and fro did sweep,
　The *Macedonian* they espied,
　"Huzza! bravo!" Decatur cried,
　"We'll humble Britain's pride,
　　My brave Yankee boys."

Now chain-shot, grape and langrage pierce through their oaken sides,
And many a gallant sailor's blood runs purpling in the tides
　While death flew nimbly o'er their decks,
　Some lost their legs, and some their necks,　.
　And Glory's wreath our ship bedecks
　　For brave Yankee boys.

Then homeward steered the captive ship, now safe in port she lies,
The old and young with rapture viewed our sailors' novel prize,
　Through seas of wine, their health we'll drink,
　And wish them sweet-hearts, friends, and chink,
　Who, 'fore they'd strike, will nobly sink,
　　Our brave Yankee boys.

　　—Broadsheet ballad: "The *United States* and *Macedonian*"

ON THE NIGHT OF DECEMBER 28, 1812, THERE WAS A NAVAL BALL
in Washington. The guests of honor were Captain Stewart of
the frigate *Constellation* and Isaac Hull, who had done so much to
change the official mind with regard to the place of the navy in national
defense. Behind the dais where the musicians played hung the captured

battle-flag of H.M.S. *Guerrière*, and opposite the colors of the British corvette *Alert,* lately taken by the frigate *Essex.* Dolly Madison was present, looking queenly. At midnight, under a thousand candles, an exciting rumor began to pass from lip to lip and then, as the orchestra struck up "Hail, Columbia," a young midshipman entered the door, and marching down an alley of delirious applause, laid at the feet of the President's wife still a third British battle-flag.

It had belonged to a heavy frigate, and the delight of those who heard the news of the capture was in no way dimmed by the fact that it had been taken by Captain Stephen Decatur, Jr. For Decatur was the darling of the nation, the man every youth wished to be; already famous for more than one exploit before he had reached 25; proud, courteous, and gallant; who simply could not avoid giving an atmosphere of high romance to the most prosaic transaction.

It is an extremely good man who can do this without stepping over the shadow-line that separates the superb from the absurd, but Decatur stayed firmly on the sunny side of that line. Perhaps his French blood had something to do with it. He was really the third Stephen Decatur in direct descent—though the first of the three had spelled it Étienne. Perhaps it was because he was the product of a childhood spent in surroundings touched with romance; for he was born while his mother was in flight from the British occupation of Philadelphia and his father on the quarterdeck of a privateer cruiser; he reached the years of full consciousness in a colonial capital where French officers, Indians, grave Quakers, and the government of the new United States passed through the streets in continual pageant, and where many tales were told.

As for the romance of the sea, Stephen Decatur, Jr., drank of it early, being a sickly boy. At the age of eight he had so severe a bout with whooping-cough that it left him in one of those "declines" which the people of his age found popular as ailments. His father pre-scribed a long sea voyage. It was to France, with the senior Stephen Decatur as captain, therefore in the most pleasant circumstances pos-sible; and as a cure it was so successful that there is no record of young Decatur's ever being sick again.

Stephen Decatur

This just may indicate that there was something psychosomatic about the malady; his mother had always kept the boy close to home and expressed her hope that he would grow up to be a bishop. The ambition became clean impossible after the boy once tasted salt water, but the mother persisted, sending him to the academy of one Dr. Abercrombie, where the discipline was strict, the educational standards low, and the code of conduct derived from that current at the court of Louis XVI. At the school young Decatur became great cronies with three other boys who were to turn up later—Richard Rush, Richard Somers, and Charles Stewart. They lived much out of doors, boating, swimming, fishing. Somers was the strongest of the four, but Decatur the best skater, very quick at repartee and a clever mimic.

All were high-spirited as eagles and they were involved in not a few fisticuff "duels," settled in the old Quaker burying-ground. When the French King went down and the partisans of the new doctrines began to demand that everyone in the streets sport a tricolor cockade to show French and revolutionary sympathies, some of these combats were transferred to public places. At fourteen Decatur was involved in a famous one with a whole gang of roughs and was brought home in rather battered condition, but still hanging onto his cockade of American blue. Two years later the academy had done all it could for him; he was taken from Dr. Abercrombie and sent to the University of Pennsylvania.

This was his mother's last try to win him for the church. The Stephen Decatur of those days is described as an almost preternaturally sensitive boy and he loved Ann Decatur deeply. There is no doubt that he tried hard to please her, but the malaise that would be the beginning of another decline came on him at being shut indoors. He was downcast in spirit, his academic grades suffered. At the end of a year, his mother was glad to compromise the silent struggle by letting him quit the university for a clerk's post in the counting house of Gurney & Smith, the shipping agents for whom his father sailed.

The young Decatur was now launched toward the sea; it was noted of him that although mathematics had been one of his weakest subjects at school, he now studied it in private and at night for the help it would give him in navigation. When Gurney & Smith, as navy agents, launched the new frigate *United States*, 44, he rode down the ways with her, and when she went into commission he went with her as a midshipman. So did his old friend Richard Somers; Charles Stewart was the Fourth Lieutenant. At this date Decatur was not quite 20 years old.

II

The captain of the ship was honest John Barry, whose reputation has suffered from the overenthusiastic efforts of Catholic writers to make him a kind of superman. He was really a kindly, generous old soul of wide experience, who treated his lieutenants to a glass of sherry in the cabin and depended for obedience less on discipline than on his own dignity and reputation. He was the head of the new service, the only surviving officer of the Revolution who had really done well in that war. A genuine 18th-century period piece.

Aboard the frigate he was surrounded by young men whom he liked personally, but whose ardors were unfamiliar and perhaps even a little embarrassing to him. If he knew of the rows in the midshipmen's mess, it was policy to ignore them; the young bloods must work out the world for themselves. Decatur had no trouble; his quick wit and keen sympathy carried him easily through all the pranks played on newcomers. But the more stolid Somers found the going difficult, and the climax was reached when in a single day three of the other mids told him he was "too fond of the lee of the mizzen-mast."

There was only one thing to be done about such an imputation of cowardice. Somers challenged all three to battle, named Decatur as his second, and said he would take them all on in a single day. Edward Wyer, the senior midshipman, said that fighting was forbidden, but gave in when Decatur declared that this was no brawl, but a genuine affair of honor, which had better be settled this way than in blood. Somers knocked the wind out of his first adversary and piled the second into a bulkhead with a pair of black eyes, not without damage to himself. Decatur offered to take on the third, but Somers refused

Stephen Decatur

to let him, terminated the bout successfully, and earned the name of "Old Reliable."

The Third Lieutenant was a dour, powerfully built Virginian named James Barron, who saved the ship when she ran into the Gulf Stream in October during her second cruise, there meeting a warm nine-day gale which slacked off all the rigging set up on a clear, cold day at Newcastle. Heaving seas tore away the ship's figurehead; the old captain could do nothing but gaze at the quavering masts and speak words of worry to his subordinates. Barron stepped out of rank to suggest that the rigging be set up as she ran—aye, and made good the almost impossible task, with gangs standing to the waist in the boiling water, heaving at the word of command and confirming each tiny gain by means of lanyards. It was a consummate feat of seamanship, of group timing at the word of command, and of points skilfully chosen for the application of force.

Barry recommended Barron for promotion when the ship reached port, and Secretary Stoddert, anxious to bring leadership to the fore in a service that was still experimental, promptly jumped the lieutenant to a captaincy. It was a good precedent for Stoddert's purpose, but there was a by-product of trouble, since the new captain was not transferred out of the ship. As commodore of one of the two squadrons in the West Indies, Barry now had a full captain to handle his flagship, and every other group-commander desired the same honor in an outburst of "avarice of rank" which much bedeviled the Secretary.

Among the islands *United States* ran down two French privateers, and when a third tried a quick tack in an effort to run out to windward of the less-handy frigate, she was given just one shot from a main-deck 24-pounder. It went right through the privateer at the waterline (Barry was a great hand at drilling his men with the guns), and her crew jumped overboard as she began to sink. Mr. Midshipman Decatur was in charge of the first boat away. He picked up the privateer's captain, who looked at the flag flying from the frigate's gaff and (perhaps for the record) said:

"I am very much astonished, sir. I did not know that the United States was at war with the French Republic."

"No, sir," replied Decatur sharply, "but you knew that the French

Republic was at war with the United States; that you were taking our merchant vessels every day and crowding our countrymen into prison at Basseterre to die like sheep."

This was one sign of the man to come; another appeared the day a man fell overboard. Decatur dived after him like an arrow and kept the seaman afloat on his own back till rescue arrived, after which no officer aboard received more ready obedience from the crew.

When the ship returned to Chester, Barry recommended lieutenancies for both Somers and Decatur, which being recorded, the latter was sent to Philadelphia on recruiting duty. The new lieutenant soon found some of his detachment missing; his petty officer said they had run to join a big Indiaman lying at the quay, which promised them higher wages. It was not merely a matter of letting the rascals go, for they had already taken advances on pay. Decatur went aboard the merchant and found the mate not only undisposed to co-operation, but downright abusive, both of himself and the whole curs't U.S. navy. He kept cool and took back his men, but when he reached home that night asked his father what he should do. There was only one course open to a gentleman (said the elder Decatur, who had just reached port with his own ship, the corvette *Delaware*) : the mate must be called out.

Somers was Decatur's second. Our lieutenant, who had practiced pistol-play till he was something of an expert, remarked that his skill made the duel somewhat unfair; he would merely cripple the fellow with a ball in the hip. So he did at the first fire, then turned his back and strode stiffly from the dueling-ground with lips pressed tight to keep from showing emotion.

The new cruise was to Lisbon, carrying commissioners for peace. The ship met storms and had to go into dock on her return; Lieutenant Decatur was transferred to the brig *Norfolk,* 18, for one more brief trip to the Caribbean before peace became definite and the navy was altogether changed. So solid a Federalist as the elder Decatur had to take one of the dismissals, of course, but young Stephen and his brother James, now also a midshipman, had John Barry's backing, and both were kept. There was clearly something more than favor behind the retention, however; Stephen Decatur was immediately appointed First Lieutenant of *Essex*, 32, an almost unheard-of rank for a young man of 22.

William Bainbridge was her captain, and she was for the coasts of Barbary in the 1801 cruise of Commodore Dale. From Gibraltar, *Essex* was assigned to convoy an important merchant vessel to Tunis, then to pick up American ships from Marseille all down the Spanish coast to Alicante and guard them through the Gates of Hercules. All went smoothly till Barcelona was reached. There the Spaniards had a big xebec as guardship in the harbor, with a captain who was determined to increase the honor of his own nation over foreigners, after the manner of those days. One night he fired several shots over Captain Bainbridge's gig as it pulled out from shore, and tried to make the American come aboard for recognition. Bainbridge came alongside but refused to go aboard, not mincing his words over the insult. On the following night the xebec fired over Decatur's boat, and the morning after saw the coldly handsome lieutenant on the Spaniard's deck, demanding to see her captain. He was ashore. "Very well," said Decatur; "tell him that Lieutenant Decatur of the frigate *Essex* pronounces him a cowardly scoundrel and that when they meet on shore he will cut his ears off."

The Spaniard did not send seconds, but there were diplomatic repercussions of the most violent sort, heard all the way back to Madrid. The Captain-general of Barcelona tried to persuade Bainbridge to keep his officers aboard; Bainbridge refused to do anything of the kind, as he was taking in provisions. The end of it was that the Spanish top brass recognized that the xebec's captain had placed himself in an unlovely position and sent down an order that the officers of the United States were to be treated with courtesy and respect, "more especially those attached to the frigate *Essex*."

It is a little difficult for moderns to realize that such passages had a major importance. The atmosphere was that of the great European war, which had been going on for eleven years; long enough to make it a normal part of life. The air was filled with testy arrogances, and dueling was the most natural sport in the world, something like a dangerous form of athletics. Nearly a year later Decatur was involved again—at Malta, after *Essex* had gone home and he had been transferred into *New York*, 36, still as First Lieutenant. The young British officers at the base considered that Americans did not observe a proper humility and should be taught their places. One night in the opera lobby a resplendent personage jostled Midshipman Joseph Bainbridge. The American moved; was jostled again; moved once more and once more was given the shoulder, together with a high-pitched remark that these Americans would never stand the smell of powder. Young Bainbridge knocked the man down.

Next morning a challenge came aboard from Mr. Cochran, secretary to Governor Sir Alexander Ball. The junior Bainbridge was totally unskilled in this form of exercise, but just as he was about to ask another midshipman, as inexperienced as himself, to second him, there came a summons to the cabin of First Lieutenant Decatur. Did Mr. Bainbridge realize that he had been called out by a professional duelist, who would certainly try to kill him? Standing very erect, he did. Would he accept the services of Lieutenant Decatur? He would, with the lines in his face softening a little.

Decatur met the secretary's man and coolly proposed pistols at four paces. "This looks like murder, sir," said the Englishman, somewhat aghast at such close work.

"No, sir, it looks like death. Your friend is a duelist and mine is totally inexperienced. If you insist upon the usual ten paces, I will fight your man."

Four paces it was; at the first fire, Cochran missed, but Bainbridge's ball took his hat off. The normal procedure at this point would have been an apology and honor satisfied, but Mr. Cochran furiously demanded another round. "Hold lower if you wish to live," Decatur told his man; young Bainbridge did hold lower, and shot the Englishman dead, right below the eyes. There was a terrible row, with Governor Ball demanding that both Bainbridge and Decatur be turned over to him for civil punishment. Commodore Morris, who then held the Mediterranean command, refused this, but relieved both officers from duty and sent them home with a report. Ball was a fairminded man, and after he got over his annoyance he and Decatur became good friends.

Stephen Decatur

III

Now a curtain rolled back and onto the stage stepped the spare figure of Edward Preble. The Navy Department's only reaction to the report of the Malta duel was to make Joseph Bainbridge a lieutenant and to send both young officers back to the Mediterranean, Decatur in command of *Argus,* 16, the beautiful new black-masted brig which the Commodore himself had sent down the ways at Boston. The lieutenant was quite evidently considered something more than a ruffler, for he had been promoted fast and had given satisfaction as an exec both to Bainbridge and to James Barron, who commanded *New York.* Yet it is quite within the bounds of possibility that one of the subsidiary reasons for placing him and some of the other young officers under Preble was to give that old martinet the opportunity of bringing them to heel. There is no proof of this in the surviving documents— there would not be, since they rarely deal in personal factors—but the whole navy was still in a formative and not a very satisfactory state; and some of the Commodore's procedures seem explicable only by the idea that he had been given an oral mission.

An intimacy between him and Decatur sprang up as soon as the latter arrived at Gibraltar. They ate together regularly and talked on many things all through the campaign, and Preble, who had pushed Jacob Jones, restrained and counseled with Decatur. He could not let him keep *Argus* of course, since Isaac Hull was the senior officer and the more experienced, but in return for the brig Decatur received the fine schooner *Enterprise,* 12, which could work closer to the reefs than any other ship in the squadron and therefore offered the greatest prospect of action. She was detached to escort a supply ship to Syracuse, where Preble joined her with *Constitution* at the close of November 1803, bringing the news of the loss of *Philadelphia.*

The Commodore took both ships to Tripoli at once, reconnoitered the harbor, and then returned to make plans. Even before seeing the place, Preble had written that the captured frigate must be destroyed, though "it will undoubtedly cost many lives." Now, with the project at the level of practical discussion, Decatur was desirous of taking *Enterprise* right in under the batteries to do the job.

This was clearly impracticable. *Argus* had to remain west for the time being to guard the Gibraltar gate, where the conduct of the Emperor of Morocco was still equivocal; there were only three other small ships—*Nautilus, Siren, Vixen*—all now absent on such duties as convoy or carrying dispatches. If *Enterprise* were lost on the desperate venture, the blockade would be virtually ended, for Preble could not trust his one heavy frigate close to the reefs without the support of a light ship in case of accident. Violation of that precaution had cost him *Philadelphia*.

But during the reconnaissance of Tripoli, the schooner had captured a blockade-running ketch some sixty feet long, a craft well known to those ashore. A plan was gradually beaten out—the fact that he was placed in charge of the execution makes it seem that Decatur had a part in the scheming—to load this ketch with 70 men from *Enterprise,* "If that number can be induced to volunteer," take her in at night, lay the captured frigate aboard, and burn her. Five midshipmen from *Constitution* were to go; so was a brave Sicilian pilot named Salvatore Catalano, who deserves a place in American history. As might be expected of a crew of Decatur's, every man jack in his ship volunteered. He took 63 of them, which with his own officers and those from *Constitution* made up a total of 74, one leader to every five men, a noteworthy proportion of supervisors. The ketch was named *Intrepid*.

The details of what was to be done were most elaborately allocated. The spar- and gun-decks of the frigate were to be cleared first. While Decatur himself, with two mids and 15 men, kept control of the topsides, parties told off for the job were to descend to various points on the lower decks and set her afire. Every man was rehearsed aboard *Constitution* in exactly what moves he was to make, whom he was to follow, and what he was to do if his officer were killed. The brig *Siren,* 16, under Decatur's old friend Charles Stewart, had joined; she would convoy *Intrepid* to the reef line after dark, then move in to cover the raider in case she were attacked by Tripolitan gunboats as she beat out. It is probable that few aboard believed she could beat out, though nobody said so.

Stephen Decatur

On February 7, 1804, the two ships brought the minarets of Tripoli over the horizon, but that night it came on to blow hard and held a northward gale for five days, during which all the provisions aboard *Intrepid* went foul—no food at all for the better part of a week but salt beef that was three-quarters rancid fat and attacked by maggots: an example in support of the observation that adventure is somebody a thousand miles away having a hard time. February 16 at last dawned clear; *Intrepid* bore down toward Tripoli, but with drags astern to hold her back till after dark, and only one or two men on deck, bare-legged and wearing Turkish jackets, the rest penned close in the stinking hold. The breeze fell light with sundown; the ketch barely ghosted through the pass of the rocks and closed in toward *Philadelphia* with all hands but Catalano well hidden below. The pilot hailed; in the *lingua franca* of the Mediterranean he said he had run the blockade with stores, but had lost both anchors in the gale and wished to tie to the frigate for the night. Permission granted; *Intrepid's* side bumped that of the frigate, a rope was taken aboard——

"*Americanos!*"

The watch had seen them. "Board!" yelled Decatur, and did board, one step behind Midshipman Charles Morris. There was a brief flash of pistol, cutlass, and shouting across *Philadelphia's* deck, the Americans too strong and too organized for the opposition. Those not cut down dived into the harbor, and Decatur's men began to pass combustibles up. The forts were silent, the Tripolitan fleet silent as the flames gained so rapidly that it was hard for all to get away. Sheets of fire were already blowing overhead as *Intrepid* began to work out under her sweeps, but now she was clean visible, the batteries woke, the Tripolitan ships woke, firing from where they lay and trying to unmoor for a pursuit. *Philadelphia's* own guns went off in succession as they were heated by the blaze, but the ketch worked out to where *Siren's* boats took her in tow with never a man hurt. When Lord Nelson heard of it, he called it "the most bold and daring act of the age," and he was a man who did not lightly scatter praise.

The question once was and occasionally still is debated as to why Decatur did not attempt to bring the frigate out instead of destroying her after he had gained possession. Those who argue that it could have been done seem to have forgotten one thing: Bainbridge had cut away her foremast before surrendering, and it had not been replaced. She therefore had no headsail and, as the breeze was onshore, could not have been worked out under canvas. It does not seem likely that 74 men could have towed her out by hand with everybody shooting at them and the Tripolitan gunboats certain to intervene.

The burning of the frigate completely changed the strategic situation. It was now no longer necessary to hold *Constitution* in reserve; there was no longer an enemy heavy ship that could drive off our light cruisers. The big frigate could therefore be used in the direct attacks on the city which Preble had intended; but it was late summer before the elimination of a threatened difficulty with Tunis and the end of the onshore gales gave opportunity.

August 3 was the first real fighting day. *Constitution* would bombard the water-batteries, with the brigs and schooners in support. Six gunboats, borrowed from the King of the Two Sicilies, were to work along the edge of the reefs and deal with the Tripolitan craft of similar class; theirs were much larger. Somers was a division commander; he led three gunboats against nine of the enemy at the leeward or western gap of the reefs. Decatur had the other three Americans opposing five of the enemy at the eastern pass.

As the shooting against the castle began, the Barbaries came straight on toward contact, with their guns banging through the powder-smoke, for they prided themselves greatly at hand-to-hand fighting and their equals in the game had not been found in the Mediterranean during 300 years. They got their bellyful from Decatur, who slammed his bow against one of their boats, boarded against odds of two to one, and in ten minutes had the Turks all down or overboard except five who hid in the hold.

Lieutenant Trippe carried another after a desperate battle in which he drove a boarding-pike through the Tripolitan captain after taking 11 scimitar wounds. Joseph Bainbridge's boat of Decatur's division had her lateen-yard shot away and could not close; neither could two of Somers's craft, which were unable to beat against a contrary wind fast enough to reach hand-to-hand action. But Lieutenant James Decatur of his division came down to join his brother's battle, and delivered into one of the Tripolitans a fire so fierce that she hauled down her flag. He swept alongside to take possession; just as he mounted the rail, the Tripolitan captain produced a pistol and shot him through the head.

The news came to Stephen Decatur as he was towing out his prize. He shouted to the eleven men who remained unhurt in his own boat and turned back toward the treacherous Moor in a rage that was a close approach to madness, slamming into her side and leaping aboard almost in unison. The Tripolitan captain was a giant of a man; Decatur's cutlass snapped off against his boarding pike, and the American took a thrust that tore his arm and chest, but grappled with the big man, and the two went to the deck, Decatur on top. Another Moor swung a deadly blow at his head, an incredibly courageous seaman named Daniel Frazier, already wounded in both arms, pushed in to take the blow on his own skull. The struggling pair rolled over, the Moor working one arm free to yank out a dagger; but Decatur managed to hold his wrist with one hand while with the other he fired a pistol through his pocket, bringing down his huge enemy like the carcass of a bear.

That finished it; the rest of the Tripolitans on this gunboat gave up, the others had fled. After the stormy interview with Preble on *Constitution's* deck and the reconciliation that followed, the Captain's barge was sent for James Decatur, who would die before sunset, and there was a sad, proud evening in the squadron as it prepared for another bout. Another there was and more than one, but the Tripolitans would try handgrips no more, and Lieutenant-Commandant Decatur saw nothing but bombardment work until the arrival of the relieving squadron. It brought out a captain's commission for him, dated as of the hour when he burned *Philadelphia,* and shortly after there came an order to "repair to Malta and there take command of U.S.S. *Constitution.*"

IV

It was not a fighting command, of course. There were no more fighting commands, the squadron was going home, where Decatur found he was a hero, and also found the girl he married after a brief courtship, Susan Wheeler. The era of the gunboat blight had come upon the navy; the young captain was caught in it and was kept busy superintending the construction of those useless craft in Rhode Island until the *Chesapeake-Leopard* affair arose.

The department sent Decatur to the frigate at Norfolk to investigate. What he heard from officers and crew convinced him that James Barron, though a man of personal courage, had been grossly negligent in the face of probable trouble, and it was so reported. As the result of the investigation a court-martial was called and Decatur was appointed to the court, along with four other captains, three masters-commandant, and four lieutenants. It was within Barron's rights to protest his presence on the bench, but the proud, dark-faced man would not; took his condemnation and laid up in the back of his mind a grudge against Stephen Decatur as the true author of his misfortunes.

When the skies changed with the coming of Madison, Captain Decatur received one of the first seagoing commands—that of *United States,* his first ship, now somewhat altered since he had sailed in her as a midshipman. She sailed first with fourteen long 12-pounders on quarterdeck and forecastle; in the interval all the 44s had exchanged these light long guns for twenty-two 42-pounder carronades, to give close-range smashing power. But it was found that only *United States,* which was built under Joshua Humphreys' own hand, could carry so prodigious a battery without racking. Heavier-built than the others, she was so slow that they called her "Old Waggoner"* during her first commission, but since then her spars had been altered and her masts shifted; still no racer, she could now move along respectably well. She was very weatherly and a good sea-boat; rolling deep but easy; a steady platform for guns. Decatur was to cruise her on the South Atlantic station, which meant the southern coast of the United States, with Norfolk as a base.

* Theodore Roosevelt remarks that "the weak point of all the 44s was their lack of speed." There is no evidence of this except in the case of *United States. President* was an exceptionally fast ship, and so was the later *Guerrière;* in action *Constitution* proved faster than any of her opponents except *Java,* which was built at the Toulon yard—at least partly on the lines the French constructors had taken from *President!*

Stephen Decatur

The captain was much interested in the hydrography and zoology of the region; did a lot of sounding and collected specimens, using a marine drag of his own invention. More especially was he interested in the gunnery of his ship, which he considered should be both attack and defense, as it had been with *Constitution* under the walls of Tripoli and against three times her own weight of metal. The French had never lost at Trafalgar, Decatur used to say, if their gunnery had been what it should.

He did not believe in boarding—which seemed so wild a doctrine to the British officers who visited the base that they twitted him about it, saying that a theory of winning a naval battle by guns alone would never be much use to Americans. Captain John Carden of H.M.S. *Macedonian* explained the matter to Decatur one evening over the candles and port, after a dinner of fresh beef and wild turkeys, a great treat for a man so long at sea.

The 24-pounder was too heavy (he said) to be handled as rapidly and efficiently as a British 18. "Besides, Decatur, though your ships may be good enough, and you are a clever set of fellows, what practice have you had in war? There's the rub."

Decatur had his own ideas on this point; exercised his men daily, firing at floating targets, with prizes from his own pocket for hits. He was so easy and considerate with the men that they touched their hats when they met him ashore, and the word they passed was "Good luck to him—he has a soul to save."

The seas rolled and the hours rolled; there was war. *United States* sailed with John Rodgers's squadron, which futilely chased the British *Belvidera,* 36, then made its way to Boston. The orders there were for all the ships to put out in small groups for raids toward the eastern Atlantic. Decatur sailed on October 8, with *Argus,* 16, in company, but halfway across the ocean he detached the lighter ship, as she added little to his own force and could damage the enemy more on independent cruise. One capture of no great importance was made; then *United States* slid through empty seas until October 25, 1812, a Sunday, when she was 500 miles west of the Canaries, and a ship was sighted, the stranger being 12 miles distant and to windward. She swung to show the yellow-and-black checkers of a heavy British frigate—"Nelson's checkers"—hung out three battle-flags, fired a gun in challenge, and came down through smooth seas with a long swell.

As she approached there was a small eddy on the American frigate's deck; an old quartermaster came aft, marching ship's boy Jack Creamer in his huge paw. Decatur, dressed in the plain homespun and battered straw hat he always affected at sea, paused and lowered his glass: "Well, Jack, what's wanting now?"

"Commodore, will you please put my name on the muster-roll?"

He was only ten and below the legal age for enlistment. "What for, my lad?"

"So that I can share in the prize-money when we take that Britisher, sir."

No doubt there; nor aboard the enemy, neither, for that matter. She was H.M.S. *Macedonian,* 38, a new, strongly built ship, still under the command of that Captain Carden who had pointed out to Decatur that an American 24-pounder frigate could never equal the British type of heavy cruiser. He was a gentleman with gentlemen, but famous even in his own service for the severity of his discipline; once gave a man 300 lashes for stealing a handkerchief. Yet under that rod of iron he had made *Macedonian* esteemed as a crack ship. He had not heard of the loss of *Guerrière,* and to many others besides Decatur had mentioned his confidence that he could take an American 44, though the odds in weight of metal were as 5 to 7 against him. Actually, he thought this would be a much easier game, having taken his opponent for *Essex,* which was only a 32 and was armed exclusively with the short-range carronades. Therefore he decided to hold the weather-gauge and fight at long range; the preliminary jockeying showed he could do this, as he had the speed of his enemy.

He kept the wind easily; at a mile apart fire was opened on both sides. *United States* wore twice to bring her adversary broad abeam, both ships now steering rap-full as it is called—not hauled close to the wind, but with mizzen topsails aback to give them steadiness and a little way. The Old Waggoner was suffering little from her opponent's fire and that mostly aloft; as *Macedonian* edged in, Decatur eased his ship off and then came to again to hold the range as steady as might be. His guns were firing by divisions, as they had been schooled through three years; wholly together and not at the mere loom of the enemy frigate but at specific targets aboard, which was a thing almost without precedent. They were shooting twice to the Britisher's once; everything was in order.

On *Macedonian's* deck, where Captain Carden had by this time realized his mistake in identification, the scene was different. One of her sailors has left a picture that is the very best eye-witness account of a sea-fight from the side that is taking punishment:

"I heard the shot strike the side of our ship; the whole scene grew indescribably confused and horrible. The cries of the wounded ran through all parts of the ship. The boys belonging to the guns next to mine were wounded in the early part of the action, and I had to spring with all my might to keep three or four guns supplied with cartridges. A man named Aldrich had one of his hands cut off by a shot, and almost at the same time he received another, which tore open his bowels in a terrible manner. As he fell two or three men caught him in their arms and threw him overboard. The schoolmaster received his death wound. A fellow named John was carried past me, wounded. I distinctly heard the large blood-drops fall pat, pat, pat, on the deck; his wounds were mortal. Not only had we men killed and wounded, but several of our guns were now disabled. The one I belonged to had a piece of the muzzle knocked out. The large shot passed through the ship's timbers, scattering terrific splinters which did a more appalling work than their own blows. So terrible had become the work of destruction around us that that part of the ship was afterward termed 'the slaughter-house.'"

There was something over thirty minutes of this; then *Macedonian's* mizzen-mast came crashing down over her lee quarter. "Huzza, Jack!" cried a quarter-gunner on the American frigate. "We've made a brig of her; give her another and make her a sloop."

"No, no," said Decatur, coolly. "Her spars are going fast enough. Aim for the yellow streak; she must have more hulling."

Brave Carden saw he was being beaten at long bowls; let his ship's head fall off and rushed in to close, but in that charge ran into the full force of *United States'* tremendous battery of 42-pounders, firing in such sheets of flame that the British tars, stripped to the waist and fighting on bravely, thought they had set their enemy afire and began to cheer. But the cheers died and *Macedonian's* rush died, as her fore-topmast came cracking down, the main-topmast followed it, and she drifted off to leeward, out of control, with all her upper-deck guns knocked out. As *United States* swept round in a graceful tack and stood under the Britisher's stern, down came her flag.

"How do you do, Doctor?" said the American lieutenant who came aboard to take possession, recognizing a man he had known in Norfolk.

"I have enough to do. You have made wretched work for us with your guns."

"Would you like some of our surgeons to help you?"

The Englishman's eyebrows lifted. "I should think they would have work enough tending to your own wounded."

"Oh, no. There were only seven, and their injuries were dressed long ago."

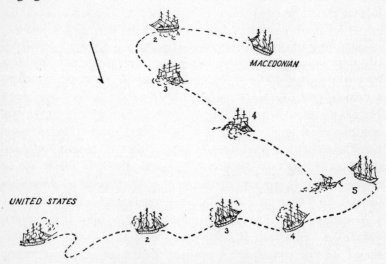

United States—Macedonian
(1) The approach. (2) Firing begins at long range.
(3) *Macedonian* badly hurt; Captain Carden decides to
close; *United States* holds off and on. (4) *Macedonian*
loses her mizzen-mast and makes her last rush. (5)
Macedonian adrift and helpless; the surrender.

United States had five killed besides those wounded; *Macedonian's* casualties numbered 105 in a crew of just over 300, and Decatur had proved his theory of gunnery. He greeted Carden in the high style: "Sir, I cannot receive the sword of a man who has so bravely defended his ship. But I will receive your hand."

The British captain was a picture of misery, announcing that he was an undone man, "the first British naval officer that has struck his flag to an American. What will they do to me?" Decatur offered him the somewhat chilly comfort of the news that *Guerrière* had already been captured, and did everything he could to make Carden comfortable, remarking to one of his lieutenants that half the pleasure of victory was spoiled by seeing his late opponent's unhappiness. A prize-crew put *Macedonian* to rights as well as it could be done outside a dock, for she was in bad shape, with over 100 shot in her hull, and Decatur broke off his cruise to convoy her to New London.

v

There was a perfect passion of receptions at New York when the two ships came up the Sound during January of 1813, with free grog for navy sailors at all the shops, and the musical honors performed by a French band which *Macedonian* had originally taken from one of Napoleon's ships. After the turn of the year the captured frigate was refitted and Decatur's old shipmate, Jacob Jones, came up to command her. The assignment was for her to go on cruise with *United States* and the sloop *Hornet,* but the British blockade off Sandy Hook was so massive and so closely kept up that in May, Decatur led all three ships through Hell Gate for a try at the exit via Long Island Sound.

As they were moving eastward on the night of May 24 a thunder-squall blew up; a flash of lightning struck *United States'* mainmast, ripped off the commodore's pennant, and, after a zigzag course through the ship, plunged into the sea. There was no damage except a sheet of copper torn loose from the bottom, but the sailors took the incident very ill, saying that Decatur's luck had been torn away with his flag.

And so it seemed, for certain. Not only were the British off the

Montauk outlet in great force, but they had a vigilant leader, Sir Thomas Hardy, Lord Nelson's old flag captain. There was also more than a suspicion that they were getting help from disloyal New Englanders ashore. Twice during night and the gales of early winter Decatur tried to run free; each time blue lights were burned on the New London headlands and the enemy gathered before he could drop land out of sight.

The only relief from the monotony was the consideration of a steam vessel of war proposed by Mr. Fulton (which Decatur enthusiastically approved, after having Jones look into it), and an effort to entice some of the British into single-ship duels for the honor of the flag. Decatur's first proposal was that *Macedonian* should meet *Statira,* 38, which was her sister-ship, while *United States* paired off with *Endymion,* 40, the latter a British 24-pounder frigate, a good deal stronger than the usual English heavy cruiser. Commodore Hardy found the idea magnificent but not war; refused to let *Endymion* meet *United States* under any conditions and attached so many provisos to the other duel that the whole idea was dropped. The blockade went on; after a year of waiting, the two ships were placed out of commission and Decatur came down to New York to take over *President.*

She had slipped into harbor in February 1814, after her fourth wartime cruise, all of them successful as raids, though no fighting enemies were met—was considered the finest of the 44-gun frigates, and was certainly the fastest, since a certain lightness of construction had been more than made good for strength by a novel and ingenious system of jointure in her planking. *Hornet* and the new sloop *Peacock,* 20, were placed under Decatur's orders. He was to run out on the first westerly gale that drove the blockaders offshore and take his squadron on a raid against the British in the East Indies.

The opportunity was long in coming. But on January 14, 1815, a strong wind, low-hung clouds, and a driving sea offered a favorable conjunction. *President* had been anchored under Staten Island; she put out on a following sea to find the tide running more strongly than usual across the harbor bar against the wind. Her pilot made an error in direction; the ship struck on the bar and pounded heavily for an hour and a half before wind and good seamanship carried her across. Now it was clear that the ill-luck of the lightning stroke was still with Decatur; in the dark beyond the bar he found his frigate damaged all along her false keel, her rudder-braces broke and the masts sprung, changed by this accident from a fast ship to one dead slow and hard to handle. The sensible thing to do was turn back, and Decatur tried that; but *President* was now on an ebb-tide, with the wind so strong against her that she could not work in. He held eastward, close under the shore of Long Island.

The hour and a half lost on the bar was fatal. At five next morning the British fleet were sighted, turning back toward New York from the offing into which they had been driven. They came about in chase at once, the big 50-gun razee *Majestic* leading. Now the airs fell light and baffling; *President* began to pull away from the dull-sailing razee, but another of the pursuers pulled up fast—*Endymion,* the ship Decatur had challenged. The American captain did everything he could: cut away his boats and anchors, started out the water, threw overboard provisions and spare spars; but *Endymion* kept hauling up, hand over fist. By five in the evening, under a sky like lead, she had a position on *President's* quarter and began to shoot, hitting frequently enough to cause a good many casualties aboard the American frigate, which could not reply without turning, and so losing ground to the others in the chase.

Two of Decatur's lieutenants fell, and the first firing showed that some of *President's* powder was bad. After an hour of pounding, almost without return, Decatur mustered his crew aft and addressed them:

"My lads, that ship is coming up with us. As our ship won't sail, we'll go on board of theirs, every man and boy of us, and carry her back into New York. All I ask of you is to follow me."

The American frigate swung round with her crew cheering valorously. But the British captain, Henry Hope, was an experienced man and a clever one, who perceived at once the purpose of the maneuver; he kept off, and the two ships ran southward, side by side, through the gathering dark, firing into each other. Decatur saw that his ship's poor sailing and sluggish response to her helm would not let him close unless the enemy wished it, and changed his plan midstream to one of dismantling *Endymion.*

The range was somewhat long, but *President's* marksmen had been trained by an expert in gunnery, and in two hours of firing they had done their work. *Endymion* dropped away astern with her sails in ribbons, braces shot away, and masts wounded; moreover so badly mauled along the strakes as hardly to be able to fire a gun. Her last shot killed Lieutenant Hamilton, who as a midshipman had carried *Macedonian's* flag into the ballroom. Decatur himself was twice wounded, by a splinter in the chest and a numbing blow on the head.

It had become nine o'clock; as *President* resumed her course, now slower than ever with some of her ropes missing, the clouds blew clear and bright starshine picked her out for the British, who came crowding along on a favorable slant of wind. By eleven *Pomone,* 38, was in position to shoot without reply, as *Endymion* had been before; *Tenedos,* 38, came legging forward on the other quarter, and even *Majestic* was gaining. A fifth of Decatur's crew were down, and the rest, though not demoralized, were disorganized, with three of the five lieutenants gone. At 11:30 he hove to and hauled down his flag.

The ship that had been his lost all her masts as she was being taken into Bermuda and *Endymion* lost two of hers. Neither was ever good for anything thereafter, which shows that the defense had been carried about as far as the equipment permitted, without counting the loss of key personnel, which made it hard to get anything significant out of what equipment there was. But neither this nor a reception more as a guest than a captive could salve Decatur's inner hurt; he had lost his ship and was miserable. Yet if he thought any blame was imputed to him, he was speedily undeceived when he reached home at the end of February with the war over.

New London received him like a conqueror with music and an illumination; the ship carpenters of New York pledged 1600 hours of labor on a new frigate for Decatur to replace the one he had lost. The Navy Department was both complimentary and practical: it offered him his choice of a shore billet, the command of the new frigate *Guer-*

rière, 44, with the first squadron for the Mediterranean, or the command of the new line-of-battleship *Washington,* 74, and the flag of the second Mediterranean squadron.

VI

These squadrons were going forth to trouble, because Decatur's old friends, the Barbaries, had been up to new tricks while we were busy with the War of 1812. Algiers, the most powerful of the regencies, was at the head of it; she had declared war against America, enslaved the crews of a pair of American ships, and ordered out her fleet of five frigates, three corvettes, two brigs, a xebec, and a schooner against our shipping. With the victories over England behind him, President Madison was not inclined to stand for such nonsense; nor had he any intention of placating Algiers by resuming payment of the tribute that had gone thither from President Washington's time down to 1812. Decatur chose *Guerrière* and the first squadron; in addition there were speedily equipped for him *Macedonian,* 38, *Constellation,* 38, the new ship-sloop *Ontario,* 20, the brigs *Épervier,* 18, *Flambeau,* 14, *Spark,* 14, and the schooners *Spitfire* and *Torch,* each of 12.

The squadron reached Gilbraltar on the 15th of June and caused a prodigious buzz, the British coming aboard the flag in droves to see one of these American 44s of which they had heard so much. Moors at the Rock sent dispatch vessels to warn the Algerines, but others told Decatur that their ships were cruising in loose squadron, probably off Cape de Gat, under their admiral, Rais Hammida. As soon as he had taken on water the American Commodore went out in search. Sure enough off Cape de Gat on the 17th a large ship was sighted eastward, and the whole formation bore in chase. *Constellation* was the most forwardly and gained on the enemy; the stranger saw he would be caught on that bearing and wore round to head for the security of Spanish waters, which brought *Guerrière* into favorable position, and as she was a very swift ship she pulled up rapidly.

The Algerine opened with musketry from his tops; Decatur allowed no reply to be made until he was right alongside, with yard-arms barely clearing; then let go with the heavy broadsides by divisions which his men were always so well schooled to deliver. They caused havoc aboard the pirate, and the second fire drove his people from their great guns. The musketry kept on, but Decatur was now sure he had her and, wishing to spare life, he clapped on sail to pull ahead, while the speedy *Épervier* maneuvered adroitly under the frigate's stern, raking her again and again until flag and sails came down. She proved to be the Algerine flagship *Meshouda,* 46, now having over 30 dead, including Rais Hammida, who had been cut in two by a cannon-ball just before his crew panicked.

Two days later, off Cape Palos, another Algerine was sighted, a heavy brig, which ran into shoal water where the frigates could not follow. The brigs and schooners went in after her, caught up to her after a running fight that cost the corsair about a fifth of his crew, and presently returned with *Estedio,* 22, in tow. The prizes were sent on to Cartagena for safekeeping; Decatur bore for Algiers, sailed boldly into the bay and hung out signals indicating that he wished to negotiate through the Swedish consul. The captain of the port came off, inclined to be lofty; said any negotiation must take place in the Dey's palace and that his fleet was safe in harbors where the Americans dared not touch it.

This gave Decatur an opening. "Not all of it," said he, and had the lieutenant of *Meshouda* led forward, trembling with fear lest he have his head cut off, to confirm Rais Hammida's death and the capture of the frigate. This brusque action set the keynote of the parley, which was conducted by the Americans in such a tone as Preble might have used—on *Guerrière's* deck, at the foot of a mast whose peak bore a sword and a branch of olive. Tribute in any form was refused; indeed, the instant release of the enslaved seamen was demanded, with an indemnity. The Algerines shifted and squalled like camels, said that such an instrument would be contrary to the whole policy of the Barbary regencies, asked for an amnesty of ten days, gradually cutting it to three hours.

"Not a minute," quoth Decatur, at last. "If your squadron appears in sight before the treaty is actually signed by the Dey and the prisoners sent off, ours will capture them."

Stephen Decatur

That was precisely what worried the Algerines, since the port captain had of course lied about their ships' being safe. Something over two hours had passed after the Commodore's last word had gone ashore, when one of the pirate corvettes was sighted, inward bound. Decatur hung out the signal for a general chase and was just having *Guerrière* hove short when a barge with a white flag put out from the shore in frantic haste. It contained all the enslaved Americans and a treaty such as no Barbary power had ever signed before.

The mission was thus completed, but even before leaving Gibraltar Decatur had learned that he had another. During the war, the Boston privateer *Abaellino* had operated in the Mediterranean with great success, sending three prizes each into Tunis and Tripoli, which was good international custom in those days, as the two states were neutrals in the Anglo-American struggle. The Barbaries confiscated all the prizes and turned them over to the British. News of this had not yet reached the United States, so Decatur had no instructions in the matter, but he wrote his own, sailing into Tunis harbor with a demand for a $46,000 indemnity.

The Bey tried indifference, but was told the news from Algiers, with the addition that the American commander was "the Frank who burned the frigate at Trablis in Sidi Yusuf's time." At this point he called for a comb, combed his beard for a few minutes, asked why the Americans sent wild young men to conduct their negotiations, and grumblingly yielded. The British consul was called in and given a wigging for having promised protection against these people from beyond the Atlantic.

At Tripoli it was much the same story: angry refusal at first, but, after the tidings from the other states came, sour acquiescence. On the way down the Mediterranean with *Guerrière* alone, Decatur encountered the whole Algerine fleet, seven ships cruising in company. He cleared for action, rather hoping their superiority of force would induce them to attack him. They only asked where he was bound, to which the Commodore replied in words that would be spoken again by Admiral Halsey 132 years later: "American ships sail where they please."

Back in the United States, Decatur was appointed to the board of Navy Commissioners with John Rodgers and David Porter. He moved to Washington and into a whirl of activity, setting up regulations for the government of a service which had grown up more or less haphazard. A scheme of inspection for defective vessels, standard orders for harbor defense, for gunnery drills, for ships on cruise and medical attention, all were drawn up at this time. It is hard to determine who made the specific contributions to these laws of the navy, but in at least one case Decatur's imprint is clear because the two other commissioners dissented. He was the man who chose the Norfolk-Hampton Roads area as the major base fronting the Atlantic, and a good choice it was.

The Commodore should have been very comfortable. His wife was both beautiful and popular and he adored her. President Madison had become his close friend; they saw each other almost daily. There were frequent social exchanges with the Monroes and John Quincy Adams, who could be as engaging as any man alive when he chose, and who usually chose with Decatur. The couple were living in circumstances somewhat more than easy; the Naval Commissioner's salary was a good one, the prize-money from *Macedonian* provided a backlog, and to it was added a considerable sum appropriated by Congress in recompense for the capture of *Meshouda,* which had been returned to the Algerines after the peace was signed. There were dinners and balls; Baltimore presented a service of silver and Philadelphia a set of plate.

Yet through it all ran a rivulet of discontents. Decatur hated dealing with contractors, hated detail-chasing, and in 1818 is found writing to a friend; "What shall I do? We have no war, nor sign of a war, and I shall feel ashamed to die in my bed." The fact is that he was a son of Mars, born in wartime and nurtured on war; a mind good in many other aspects had become set in the mold of regarding conflict as the normal way of life.

Perhaps the final act grew in some way hard to explain out of this accumulated *cafard.* Perhaps; for the story has not only obvious intricacies, but a suggestion of darker tides still, lying below the surface. It begins with Oliver Hazard Perry, the victor of Lake Erie. After that famous triumph—the only one to lighten the gloom of the black year 1813—there was a good deal of question about the manner in which Captain Jesse D. Elliott had hung back with one of the two most powerful ships in the American squadron until Perry's flagship was nearly beaten to pieces. The two men never liked each other afterward, and when Perry fell on an altercation with Captain Heath of the Marines, Elliott offered to be the latter's second in a duel.

Elliott knew very well that Perry had criticized his conduct in the lake fight, and, the Heath matter having given him an opening, he wrote Perry a series of increasingly angry letters, ending with a challenge, three times repeated. Perry had struck Heath in public, and felt that he owed that officer personal satisfaction; he asked Decatur to be his second. To Elliott's challenges he replied coldly that the criticisms were official acts, for which he would not be held personally accountable. Since Elliott felt aggrieved, however, charges would be presented and the matter would be settled by a court-martial. The Heath affair passed off in a puff of gallantry when Perry bore his opponent's fire unflinchingly, then had the charge drawn from his own pistol. But the quarrel with Elliott was still unresolved when Perry died of yellow fever in the West Indies.

Jesse Elliott was a man who spent a great deal of time in brooding over his wrongs and in writing about them. To him, the sequence of events was now clear: Perry's friend Decatur had prevented the meeting on the field of honor, and so had left him, Elliott, under a shadow of disgrace that could now never be lifted, since the dead Perry was the only person who could legally have preferred the charges leading to court-martial. Elliott himself had no excuse to pick a quarrel with Decatur, but he could and did reach into the background for the gloomy figure of Captain James Barron.

They were old friends; malcontents often hang together. Elliott had been a witness for Barron at the latter's court-martial, and remained in correspondence with him when the condemned man went abroad during the five years of his suspension. Now it happened that just at the time of the Perry-Heath duel the new ship-of-the-line *Columbus,*

74, was approaching completion. Barron applied to command her and the application went before the board of Navy Commissioners.

Decatur opposed the appointment with all of his considerable verbal force, pointing out that the *Leopard-Chesapeake* affair was the worst disgrace that had ever befallen the American navy, and that although Barron's suspension had expired during the early months of the War of 1812, the man had remained abroad till the fighting was over. Barron's excuse was that he lacked the money for a passage home, and perhaps it was a true reason, though not a very good one, since it bore the mark of the same lack of capacity for resolute swift action that was seen on *Chesapeake's* deck when the British cruiser followed her to sea.

Never mind the details; Decatur opposed Barron's application and it was rejected. The next step was a letter from Barron to Decatur, June 19, 1818: "I have been informed in Norfolk that you said that you could insult me with impunity, or words to that effect. If you have said so, you will, no doubt, avow it."

Who was the informant? Barron never told, but neither then nor later was there much question in anyone's mind that it was Captain Jesse D. Elliott who, after the exchanges of letters usual in such a business, turned up as Barron's second. It is clear throughout the correspondence that Decatur is trying to avoid bringing the matter to pistols, and equally clear that Barron is pushing things in that direction. He accepts Decatur's disclaimer of the "insult" remark as an apology, and replies to another letter from the Commodore with the accusation that the latter has attempted to ruin his reputation, and had brought on him the "unmerited sentence" of the court-martial of 1807. The two men met at Bladensburg on the morning of March 22, 1820; Barron was wounded, but Stephen Decatur was shot through the intestines and died in agony before another dawn.

So passed the brightest spirit of the early navy, the man who had more to do with its making than any other man except Preble himself. In that process which made Decatur the exemplar of the service, even the manner of his death helped. Barron was to a degree the head of the party in the navy which held that nothing was so important as seamanship and all the rest must come after. "The fact is that Decatur was no seaman," a junior officer heard one of his elders remark years later, when the loss of *President* was being discussed.

During peace, there is in every navy a quite natural and not wholly unreasonable tendency to concentrate effort toward making ships efficient instruments for traveling the ocean, as opposed to fighting machines. It was such a concentration that overtook the British navy and prepared the way for the American victories in the War of 1812. They had a war on, but their enemies had become so inefficient that battle was less important than sea-keeping.

That the American navy was saved from a similar fate during the long years down to the Civil War was largely Decatur's doing. Not only did he help freeze the doctrine of battle efficiency into the structure of the navy through his work on the board of commissioners. There was also the fact that his party, the party of Preble's boys, triumphed even in his death. Nearly everyone who heard of the fatal duel hastened to take the side of the man who had been killed in that murderous act of rancor.

No doubt the duel and its results furnished the lesser part of the influence. Decatur had proved his case long before on the ocean, when *Macedonian* was cut to pieces and *Meshouda* crushed. But the fact that there was a contest was emphasized when the principals of the two sides met in person. In choosing a precursor to imitate—and all young officers must imitate someone—the junior could hardly fail to select the victorious and beloved Decatur over the morose and unsuccessful Barron.

When they came to specific items for imitation, the younger officers found two that were easy and obvious above all others. "Good luck to him—he has a soul to save," said the sailors of Decatur; and Decatur insisted that naval battles are won by the accurate fire of big guns, which is attained by constant practice. He was not alone in making both these elements a part of the American naval tradition, but he surrounded both with so dazzling an aura of glory and success that none thereafter could overlook them.

Chapter 5
Child of Misfortune: William Bainbridge

At length through the wave as she plow'd in her pride,
The *Java* our seamen exultingly spied,
And as usual, all strangers to cowardly fear,
To the brazen-fac'd huzzy, we quickly drew near.

Cho.—So our cans with good liquor were flowing quite full,
To Bainbridge, and Jones, and Decatur, and Hull.

And now did our bull-dogs most merrily bark,
Sure Miss *Java* ne'er met such a deuced rough spark
For we tore her fine rigging and cut up her dress,
Till she'd not a spar standing her carcase to bless.

Cho.—So our cans with good liquor were flowing quite full,
To Bainbridge, and Jones, and Decatur, and Hull.

—Broadsheet ballad: "Bainbridge's Victory, or
Huzza for the Constitution, Once More!"

ROME CHOSE ITS MILITARY COMMANDERS LESS FOR ABILITY THAN ON evidence that they were lucky men. As Rome conquered the world, it was probably right; but there is some evidence that good fortune is not an indispensable requisite for success in the profession of arms.

The story of William Bainbridge is part of that evidence. Throughout his life he was attended by so unbroken a series of misfortunes that no one could have been blamed for talking about an evil fairy

William Bainbridge

at the cradle. It was not that he did things wrong, either, or was one of those humanly defective characters who can do the right thing in a way that makes everyone hate the name of it, like John Paul Jones. On the contrary: he was a friendly man, whom people liked on first sight and were glad to oblige. He maintained a voluminous correspondence with acquaintances all over the world; he persuaded Congressmen to agree with him, and—what is more—to stick to their agreements. An able man, who pushed rapidly to the front in whatever he undertook, and who undertook a wide variety of different things. What makes his case so strange is that out of the ill-luck which simply dropped on him from the skies he never failed to produce something to his own and the national advantage.

His father was a doctor and William Bainbridge was born at Princeton, N. J., in May of 1774, which means that he must have had a rather lively childhood, since a good part of the War of the Revolution revolved around his birthplace as though it were an axis. The boy's maternal grandfather was named Taylor; since Dr. Bainbridge already had three sons when William was born, the older man asked permission to bring up this one. The permission was given and as soon as the boy could read, he was trained toward college and one of the professions. Vain effort; before he was fifteen young William Bainbridge decided that the only profession he wished to follow was that of the sea. He was observable then, on his fifteenth birthday, going aboard the ship *Ariel,* Captain Waldron, for a voyage to Europe.

Given the background this is commonplace enough. Young Bainbridge rescues the narrative from the ordinary by going aboard with an outfit which consists mainly of books and spending every off-duty hour at sea in reading and studying—not mathematics and the professional subjects alone, but history, philosophy, poetry, the whole range of available literature. He later became known as the most cultured of Preble's boys—never quite the writer Charles Stewart was, who had something of a special talent for marshaling his thoughts on paper, but possessed of an infinitely wider range of interests and the ability fully to hold his own in any group of the great turn-of-the-century conversationalists.

That is, he had intellectual capacity, and he made such good use of it that by the age of eighteen he was first mate of the ship *Cantor,* in the Holland trade under a captain named Stebbins. At this time Bainbridge looked a good deal older than he was; stood five feet eleven, had enormously broad shoulders, and was muscled like a gorilla. It was just as well he had this physical equipment, for the crew of *Cantor* were a hard lot, strongly addicted to the bottle, while Captain Stebbins himself was alternately drunk and in the grip of savage hangovers. Matters came to a head in Rotterdam one night, when Bainbridge leaped from his cabin toward the sound of a struggle on deck to find the captain already prostrate, and five men struggling with the old second mate, shouting that they were going to throw both officers overboard. Two of the assailants Bainbridge stretched on the deck with blows from the barrel of his pistol; a third wrestled him down and narrowly missed with a knife-blow. But a faithful sailor came to the rescue for long enough to let Bainbridge join him in laying out the other mutineers. The merchant marine under sail was no place for rubber-spines.

Captain Stebbins would appear to have had a certain amount of gutta percha in his backbone, for he quitted his command when *Cantor* returned to the United States. The owners rewarded William Bainbridge by placing him in command of the ship at the age of 19—a considerable responsibility in those blue-water days, since contrary winds or some contact with the great war might force a vessel into a port quite other than her destination, whereupon the captain had to sell his cargo to the best advantage, arrange for provisions, stores, and a new charter, and conduct the intricate banking details of a period without commercial clearing houses.

Presumably Bainbridge handled the commercial details to satisfaction. He altered *Cantor's* rig in an unspecified manner, which improved her sailing, made three successful voyages, then was placed in charge of a new and larger ship belonging to the same firm: *Hope.* His studies continued, but the surviving records are all concerned with the man of action, and when they next speak of the young captain he is getting people out of trouble again. This was in 1796, when *Hope* was lying in the Garonne off Bordeaux. A hail from a South

William Bainbridge

Carolinan ship anchored in the stream announced they had mutiny aboard.

Bainbridge caught up his pistols and climbed to the other vessel's deck, followed by the crew of his gig, and the mutiny dissolved in growls and black looks. But as the young captain was putting away his weapons in his own cabin, some movement of tide or current caused the ship to lurch slightly. The lid of the heavy arms chest fell forward, striking the hammer of one of the pistols. It went off right into a bag of powder; there was a violent explosion and Captain Bainbridge found himself lying against the opposite bulkhead, badly burned about the body and injured in the legs.

It was the first sample of the misfortunes that were to dog him all his life, and it is therefore worth examining. Carelessness with firearms will not do as an explanation. Sea-captains in those days did not draw the charge of a pistol except to see that it was in working order; if wanted at all it would be in a hurry, and a pistol took long to load. It was pure accident; but the sequel also laid down a pattern. The mates and crew put their captain to bed and nursed him so carefully that he was up and around again in five weeks, even before *Hope* weighed anchor for St. Thomas in the West Indies.

By this date the Royal Navy of Britain was already feeling the strain of one war, and the practice that was to bring on another had begun —that of impressing seamen out of American ships. A vessel which had lost men in this way put into Bordeaux with the news that impressments were being stepped up. Bainbridge mustered his crew and told them he did not propose to see them dragged off to fight for England, and that they should not be if they would stand by him. The crew of eight were told off into divisions and set to practicing with the four brass 9-pounders *Hope* carried.

The precaution was taken just in time; off the Grand Banks on the run down to the Indies, a schooner showing four ports on a side hailed *Hope* and ordered her to heave to. She was British; Bainbridge sailed on, but called his men to quarters and double-shotted the guns. A shot crossed his bow, and as he still made no move toward halting, the stranger captain's voice was clearly heard shouting, "Fire into her!"

Hope's two guns let go simultaneously with the schooner's, and the American's were the better laid, for one double shot carried away the Britisher's gaff and main-topmast, while the other took out his flying-jibboom and fore-topmast stay. Bainbridge had to make a quick tack to avoid being run aboard as the schooner fell off, and as he did so he let her have the other broadside. It was as sharp a fire as the first, dismounting one of the schooner's guns and knocking a hole in her water-line. Down came her flag; Bainbridge refused his crew's importunities to take possession, since we were not officially at war with Britain, but hailed the schooner to say she should report to her masters that if they wanted his ship they would have to send a greater force or a more skilled commander.

Tales of this type spread with astounding rapidity and thoroughness in sailing-ship days. The fact that he had established himself as a pi-jawing Yankee had some influence on Bainbridge's next encounter with H.M. navy, which came on the following voyage, homeward from Bordeaux with wines and silk. About 300 miles off the American coast a large razee, H.M.S. *Indefatigable*, 44, drew alongside *Hope*. Her skipper was Sir Edward Pellew, an able officer and a great adventurer, whose career bears a rather striking resemblance to that of the fictional Captain Horatio Hornblower, but a man very lofty in dealing with races outside the law. He sent a boat and a lieutenant, who demanded *Hope's* papers, then declared he was going to have the second mate, Allan McKinsey, whose name made it obvious that he was a Scot. Bainbridge told McKinsey to go to the captain's cabin and "look over the pair of loaded pistols and the cutlass" that lay on his bunk. The lieutenant was not quite ready for blows; he took one of the seamen instead, and retired, doubtless satisfied that he had taught Bainbridge a lesson.

Actually, the lesson was to be on the other side. Three days later Bainbridge came across a British merchant brig; hove to under her bows, with his guns run out, and sent a boat which took a British seaman out of her, leaving in exchange a letter to Sir Edward Pellew telling precisely why he had taken the man.

Now came more voyaging—New Orleans, England, and back to the West Indies, where Bainbridge put in at the island of St. Bartholomew and was becalmed in its harbor. As he walked ashore with a friendly merchant, the sound of a girl's voice, singing to a harp, drifted from a window behind a tall hedge. Who was she? The granddaughter of a Dutch commercial man, her name Susan Heyliger (said the merchant); would the Captain care to meet her? He would, and was presently being introduced to a tall, beautiful girl with gray eyes and masses of brown hair. The calm lasted for three weeks, which could be considered bad luck for a ship engaged in moving. But it was not so to Bainbridge, for he saw Susan Heyliger every day, and on the next trip carried her away as his bride.

II

It was 1798. Captain Bainbridge was 24, considered handsome, and a marked man in the merchant service. He was offered the fourth ranking lieutenant's commission in the new navy and, soon after he accepted it, received a ship of his own. She was a fine schooner of 14 guns, which had been the French privateer *Incroyable* till she was taken by *Delaware,* 20, off the New Jersey capes; now renamed *Retaliation.* In September Bainbridge took her down to cruise off Guadeloupe and St. Martins in company with the small corvette *Montezuma,* 20, and the brig *Norfolk,* 14.

During the first month the little squadron did nothing but speak several British frigates and recapture an American brig the French had taken, but on the morning of November 20 two ships were discovered to leeward. Captain Alexander Murray, who had a broad pennant in *Montezuma,* ordered chase. At the same time two more ships appeared to windward and began to come down fast. Bainbridge with *Retaliation* was the nearest to them of the Americans. He set the private signal for British ships, which remained unanswered, then that for Americans. In reply one of the strangers hoisted a flag at the mizzen-mast which could not be made out, but it was probably all right, since the two, now clear as large frigates, maneuvered in the British manner. Error; two hours later the big ships were close aboard with French colors flying, one of them firing into the schooner and ordering her to strike.

There was no chance for Bainbridge whatever. There never had been, since the frigates could easily run down his tiny ship off the wind, and in the dawn position *Retaliation* was so boxed in against the island by the pair that an attempt to beat to windward would have left the schooner making tacks, which is the slowest point of sailing, while the big ships were on a reach, which is the fastest. Bainbridge gave up his sword aboard *Volontaire*, 44, Commodore St. Laurent, the French flagship of the station—and in accordance with the guiding custom of his life, immediately turned misfortune to advantage. The other frigate had pushed on after *Montezuma* and *Norfolk* while *Volontaire* paused to take possession of Bainbridge's ship. She was *Insurgente*, 38, and could easily have eaten them both alive; moreover she was the fastest ship in those waters, as our people discovered after Captain Truxtun took her in battle; now she was rapidly pulling up on the chase. As St. Laurent stood watching on the forecastle of his own ship, he turned to Bainbridge:

"What is the force of your two consorts?"

"The ship mounts twenty-eight long twelves and the brig twenty long nines," said the American without the slightest hesitation, a little more than doubling the strength of Murray's two ships, and throwing a very dirty face on the matter for the French, for if they were really of that strength, they could cripple *Insurgente* a couple of hours before the arrival of her consort.

What made the lie effective was that St. Laurent was already familiar with the Americans' custom of arming their cruisers heavily. He hoisted a signal of recall; the captain of *Insurgente* came back in a fine rage, for he had been near enough to learn the real weakness of the two ships he was pursuing and had seen his prize-money vanish beyond recall.

Nevertheless, Bainbridge was well treated on arriving at Guadeloupe and for a special reason. The governor there was an Étienne Desfourneaux, one of those midnight characters thrown up by the French Revolution, who saw an opportunity for enormous riches if he could only carry through a scheme he had hatched. It was to keep Guadeloupe neutral in the war, so that the goods of the French islands would pass through it for transit to the United States, paying for the privilege.

The bait he offered was the release of all American prisoners; Bainbridge, as an officer of the U.S. government, should sign the agreement and be the emissary to obtain its confirmation. When he was brought ashore to talk on the matter, he found his men and the prisoners from American merchant ships in horrible shape, nearly naked, beaten daily, and subsisting on a diet of raw salt pork. Desfourneaux made his proposition: he would gladly see that his friends the Americans were better treated. Bainbridge refused to sign anything, but a month later the ingenious Frenchman was back with a new version: this time the American lieutenant and his men would be placed aboard *Retaliation* and sent back to the United States as evidence of the good faith of their embassy. There was only one condition—Bainbridge must promise not to attack any French ships he met.

It was a somewhat embarrassing position for the young lieutenant, particularly since Desfourneaux' treatment of the prisoners had so little improved that some falling in with the Frenchman's scheme was evidently a tacit conditon of their betterment. But he refused. Desfourneaux threatened to throw him in a dungeon; he refused again. Desfourneaux began to talk wildly about putting all the prisoners to the sword; Bainbridge remained unmoved, whereupon the Frenchman threw up his hands and sent all his prisoners home in a cartel on parole.

Bainbridge reached Philadelphia early in 1799. The Department not only approved his procedures with regard to the release of the ship but also made him a master-commandant and sent him back to the islands in charge of *Norfolk,* 18. This cruise was mainly on convoy duty, varied by a bit of blockade work off Havana, where a heavy French privateer was in port. There was only one noteworthy incident—when a French frigate bore down on the convoy under *Norfolk's* charge near St. Thomas. The merchant ships were ordered to scatter, while Bainbridge took his ship so close to the frigate that she came on in chase, whereupon Bainbridge led her into an offing, lost her in the night, returned and brought every one of his convoy safe to port.

Now this was no mean feat of seamanship, for those French frigates were all fast and *Norfolk* was a mere purchased vessel that had never shown any particular turn of speed. Bainbridge thought he had done well, and was so much chagrined to find five other lieutenants promoted over his head to captaincies that he talked of resigning from the service. In the case of James Barron, who had saved *United States*, 44, in a storm, there was some reason for the jump, but the others had done nothing remarkable, and the thing looked like pure favoritism. Secretary Stoddert felt he could hardly rescind the promotions, but he did make Bainbridge a captain at this point and gave him the corvette *George Washington*, 24, with a mission carrying the annual tribute to Algiers. To this was added, as soon as the new administration came in, the welcome news that William Bainbridge was chosen as one of the nine captains retained on the list of the peace establishment.

III

In the course of a varied maritime career, young Captain Bainbridge had been in some odd corners, but he was never to encounter anything stranger than this first contact with the semi-Oriental world of the Barbary states; and it left him with a detestation for their system which lasted the rest of his life. "I hope I may never again be sent to Algiers with a *tribute* except it be from the mouth of a cannon," he wrote in a report when the journey was over.

There was excellent reason for this vehemence. At the pirate stronghold he was taken to see the Dey—"a huge, shaggy beast, sitting on his rump upon a low bench, with his hind legs gathered up like a tailor or a bear, who extended his fore paw as if to receive something to eat. 'Kiss the Dey's hand!' our guide exclaimed. The animal seemed at that moment to be in a harmless mode; he grinned several times, but made very little noise."

Nevertheless he informed the Captain through an interpreter that *George Washington* was ordered to carry presents and an embassy from Algiers to Constantinople. Bainbridge protested that this was none of his business, and was answered: "You pay me tribute, by which you become my slaves. I have a right to order my slaves as I please." To a man of the American's temperament there could hardly have been anything more galling, but there was very little he could do about it. His ship lay under some 200 guns of the Algerine fortifications, which insured he must take the embassy aboard; if he failed to execute the mission, the corsairs would be loosed against American merchants. So *George Washington* set sail with the ambassador and his suite, 100 Negro women, two lions, three tigers, five antelopes, two ostriches, and 20 parrots in cages. Where they all slept is a mystery; *George Washington* was only a merchant ship purchased into the service, 108 feet long, and already had 220 men of her own.

It was an extremely unpleasant trip, against headwinds most of the way and in poor company. The Americans derived what amusement they could from tacking the ship rapidly while the Mussulmans were at prayer, so they had to flop back and forth on the deck like dying fish to keep their faces properly turned toward Mecca. At the entrance to the Dardanelles a pilot was picked up; he said it was regulation that the ship should lie under the forts until a firman came down from the Sultan, giving permission to enter. Already disgusted and bored, Bainbridge found an answer to this new indignity in a device of seamanship. He had the pilot steer in; as the level of the forts was reached, the people began to clew up the light sails and let go the jib in preparation for anchoring, while the guns of both broadsides fired salutes with double charges, making a prodigious smoke. The forts replied into more smoke-puffs; under that cover, Bainbridge set everything and was well out of range before the Turks discovered what he was doing.

At the Golden Horn, the officer who came off to visit the ship had never heard of the United States and would not believe in such a country until informed that it was part of the new world discovered by Columbus. On his second visit he brought word that his master regarded it as a good omen that the flag of the unknown nation, like that of the Turks, bore a representation of heavenly bodies. The menagerie was landed; the Capudan Pasha, high admiral of Turkey, stamped and spat on the Dey's letter and in order to emphasize his point showed all the courtesy he could to the Dey's unwilling messenger. There was a series of dinners, very friendly, at one of which Bainbridge met the noted English traveler, Edward D. Clarke, with whom he maintained a correspondence as long as they both lived. The American captain's culture and natural charm stood him in good stead with such Turks as the Capudan Pasha, who was an educated gentleman and who obtained a firman placing Bainbridge under the special protection of the Sultan. There was also some talk of a trade treaty with the nation discovered by Columbus; Bainbridge may be said to have laid the ground for the document later negotiated upon such peculiar terms.

Another seed of diplomacy was planted at Algiers on the return voyage. The Dey had just cut down the French consul's flagstaff and ordered all his nationals out of the regency under pain of enslavement, but would give no ships to carry them away. Bainbridge produced his firman, which made the Dey surprisingly agreeable, and took the Frenchmen aboard, to the number of 40 men and women, for passage to Alicante. From this point *George Washington* sailed for home.

Bainbridge had not been there a month before he was ordered to take over *Essex*, 32, and return to the Mediterranean in a squadron sailing under Richard Dale, since the Tripolitan regency had been growing very bold and exacting and President Jefferson thought the presence of American warships on the coast might be a restraining influence. It was an emergency appointment for Bainbridge; the frigate was really Edward Preble's command, but he had fallen too ill to take her out. The two men met for the first time and grew to like each other much during the weeks while the exchange was being effected; Preble was at once added to Bainbridge's growing list of correspondents.

Essex' cruise was an unremarkable tour of convoying except for the incident at Barcelona, when the captain of the Spanish guardship fired over Bainbridge's boat, then over that of Lieutenant Stephen Decatur, and was loftily brought to terms by the latter. She reached the United States in 1802, and for a little over a year Bainbridge was on a tour of shore duty at Philadelphia, supervising the construction of two new light-draft vessels for Mediterranean service, a brig named *Siren* and the schooner *Vixen*.

The Captain had seen very little of his wife since their marriage, and would have liked to stay ashore longer, but by the middle of 1803 the situation with regard to the Tripolitan war had become so unsatisfactory that Secretary Smith had decided on a complete change of system. Preble was sent out as Commodore, partly because he was almost unknown to the rest of the service and hence was immune to the intricacies of personal relationships that had affected earlier squadrons, partly because he made no secret of an intention to come down on the Tripolitans with something more vigorous than the only occasionally maintained blockades set up by Commodores Dale and Morris. He was to have five small ships with two frigates instead of the exclusively frigate commands that had gone out earlier. An officer of captain rank was needed for one of the frigates, and Preble himself was so very junior that only three captains ranked below him. Two of these had just come in from long cruises, which left Bainbridge as the only choice.

His new command was *Philadelphia*, 38, the gift of the city for which she was named—a beautiful ship, designed by Josiah Fox, Humphreys' assistant, as a somewhat lighter and less expensive version of one of the famous 44s. She was armed, like the ordinary French or British heavy frigate, with 18-pounders along the gundeck, but carried heavier carronades topside than they (being large and stoutly built); underwater she had the famous Humphreys lines, and aloft a quite unusual spread of sail, which made her exceptionally fast. David Porter was her First Lieutenant and Jacob Jones her Second; Bainbridge thought the former was one of the best officers he had known, and also begged to direct the Secretary's attention to one of the midshipmen, named James Biddle, whom he thought worthy of a lieutenant's commission.

Philadelphia was the first vessel of the new Mediterranean squadron to reach Gibraltar, arriving to find rumors that since war with the United States had proved so little damaging to Tripoli, the other Barbary powers were likely to try it, especially the Empire of Morocco. Bainbridge paused only to take in water, then went cruising along the trade routes into the inland sea to find if the corsairs were loose. On the evening of August 26, off Cape de Gat, he sighted a large ship under a foresail only, without flag and having a brig in company. It was blowing fresh and too dark to make out with certainty the character of either vessel, but the cut of the brig looked American, and that of the ship suspicious. *Philadelphia* was kept near them during the night and in the morning cleared for action and closed with the ship, which was ordered to send a boat aboard.

Sure enough, it contained an officer from one of the Emperor of Morocco's cruisers, *Mirboka,* 22; he said the brig was American, but not a prize, merely keeping close to him for security. The idea of anyone seeking security under the wing of a pirate seemed so fantastic to Bainbridge that he sent Lieutenant Porter over with a boatload of armed men, who found the brig's captain and seven of his crew in the Moroccan's hold. The Moorish captain was named Ibrahim Lubarez; he said that no authority had been issued to take Americans, but he had captured this one in anticipation of war. Bainbridge said that in this case Lubarez was a common pirate and should instantly be hanged from a yardarm, whereupon the Moor reluctantly produced a commission against Americans, signed by the Governor of Tangier.

Taking his capture and recapture into Gibraltar, Bainbridge found the Commodore with *Constitution,* 44, as well as two ships of last year's squadron, outward bound. The Moorish matter required immediate resolution, but in the meanwhile Preble was most unwilling to leave Tripoli uncovered. He therefore took his own frigate and the last year's ships over to Tangier, while Bainbridge, with his own ship and the schooner *Vixen,* 12, was sent up to blockade Tripoli until the rest should arrive.

Philadelphia raised the minarets of the city on October 7, 1803. On the 31st, the wind having blown her somewhat to the eastward, she was returning to station when a sail was made out, inshore. The frigate bore up in chase, with the leadline going constantly and getting 7 to 10 fathoms. At 11:30 it suddenly shoaled to half 6; Bainbridge had the helm put hard down and the yards braced sharp up, but the ship had so much way on that before she could lose it, misfortune once more struck at her captain. She was hard and fast on an uncharted reef. Bainbridge did everything a seaman's ingenuity could suggest, but to no purpose. Canted over, unable to fire a gun at the numerous Tripolitan gunboats which presently came out, the frigate had to be surrendered, and for the second time in his career one of the best ship-handlers and best captains in the American navy found himself a prisoner.

In Tripoli, the Danish consul, N. C. Nissen, was wonderfully helpful in arranging comforts for the captured officers and crew, even smuggling out communications to Commodore Preble, which Bainbridge wrote in sympathetic ink. These letters helped the Commodore greatly, giving an accurate picture of both the psychology and the physical dispositions in the city, and included the suggestion that the frigate might be destroyed by sending in a chartered merchant vessel with American seamen secreted below.

Bainbridge and his officers were tolerably well treated (since to the Tripolitan mind they represented an asset which could be exchanged for cash) until the February night when *Philadelphia* was burned. They saw the glare through their windows and gave three cheers for the sight, offering bets as to whether Decatur or Richard Somers had led the storming party; but in the morning they were all placed in close confinement in a cell. It might have been a good deal worse but for Napoleon, First Consul of France; he heard what had happened and repaid a debt of gratitude to Captain Bainbridge for the earlier transaction at Algiers by letting the Bashaw know he was personally interested in the case.

Nevertheless it was a very thin time for the prisoners until the day in 1805 when Bainbridge stood before a court of inquiry at Syracuse and was honorably acquitted of all blame for the loss of the ship. At home, he and his crew were received with public dinners, respect, and the to-be-expected demands to narrate their experiences. Bainbridge received command of the Navy Yard at New York, with the duty of building gunboats. It was as good a command as there was in the service during those melancholy years following the Tripolitan war, but it was only a half-pay job, and, as Susan Bainbridge does not seem to have been the best of managers, the family finances fell into some disorder. There was no war nor likelihood of one while the current administration policy remained; the Captain applied for a furlough to seek service in the merchant marine.

He got it, and it nearly cost him his life. In the Gulf Stream during a southward voyage, his ship encountered one commanded by an old friend, and as the day was fine Bainbridge had his gig out to go aboard for a visit. Just as he was about to spring for the ship's side a swell capsized his boat, throwing him between it and the ship. It furnishes an odd commentary on how things were ordered in those days to learn that he could not swim. Down he went, broke water, then a second time down and up; just as he was sinking for the third time, some distance from the ship, he barely managed to grip the leadline which his mulatto bodyservant threw out, and was dragged to safety.

The commercial venture lasted until the end of 1808; with the coming of the Madison administration and its decision to send the big ships to sea again, Bainbridge was recalled to the service, being placed in charge of *President,* 44. There was a good deal of repair work to be done on her, so she did not go to sea until July 1809, but then the Captain made a real deep-sea cruise of it, well off the Atlantic coast, not returning to port until the following May. This is noteworthy in showing how the man's mind worked, for it was not then the custom in any navy to stay so long at sea unless blockade duty made it necessary. Bainbridge further emphasized his point by using the cruise for a training program so thorough that when he brought the ship in, other captains reported they had never seen a better drilled or disciplined body of men—a vague remark perhaps, but one passed sufficiently rarely to make it worth recording. But *President* reached port to find there was a fair prospect that peace with Britain would be kept by negotiation. Bainbridge had to give up the ship, there was no other immediately available, and rather than take more shore duty, he applied for another furlough to the commercial service.

His voyage was to St. Petersburg. Passing through the Danish Sound, his ship was halted by a Danish privateer and sent in to Copenhagen for adjudication. This looked bad, since Denmark was an ally of France and followed Napoleon's rule that ships that touched at British ports were tainted, subject to condemnation. But fortune quickly reversed herself by arranging that at the very moment Bainbridge's ship was brought in, his old friend Consul Nissen should be unpacking a fine silver bowl which the Captain had sent him. He rowed out at once to renew the acquaintanceship and, being a man of considerable influence, arranged everything. The voyage turned out a great success commercially, 'in no small measure because Bainbridge was a man of sufficient consequence to be presented at court, and of sufficient culture to make a fine impression when presented. He was asked to return to St. Petersburg, and in the following year he did so.

IV

That was the year 1811, the year when H.M.S. *Little Belt,* 22, slid alongside *President* during the night, fired a shot into her to make her stop, followed it with a broadside, and was instantly crushed by the return fire of one of the heaviest frigates afloat. The news reached St. Petersburg in October. "This means war!" cried Bainbridge, who knew full well that the arrogant Britons had made war on other small nations for far less.

He waited on Minister John Quincy Adams to say he must leave his ship in charge of the mate and make his way home as quickly as possible. Adams gave him some sort of dispatches and a courier's passport, while the Tsar provided an officer as escort and interpreter. The Baltic was already iced in for the winter; the pair set out to cross the Scandinavian peninsula. There were no inns along the Gulf of Bothnia; Bainbridge and his companion had to carry their own food and sleep in their carriage. The only possible route was by way of the Åland Islands; the carriage was taken to pieces and sent from one island to another in a convoy of small boats, which were hauled by hand over recurring patches of floe ice. On the way from Stockholm to Göteborg, Bainbridge had a piece of his usual luck: his coachman made an error that sent the vehicle tumbling down a thirty-foot precipice, killing the driver and three of the horses and painfully injuring the Captain.

He pressed on, nevertheless. The ship he took was English, part of a small convoy. No sooner were they at sea than they were assailed by a terrible gale that foundered three vessels and would have taken

Bainbridge's as well had not the injured Captain assumed command by sheer force of personality, shouting orders which box-hauled the ship off a lee shore.*

It was February of 1812 when the Captain came to Boston after as bad a journey as could well be imagined, but he pushed on at once to Washington to ask for a ship. But the first news he met was that there would be no ships. The long roll of English aggression was indeed to be countersigned with war; Congress was even then debating it. But Chief Clerk Goldsborough of the navy office had prepared an order at the President's direction that American warships should play their part in the struggle by being moored at harbor entrances as floating batteries, with half their guns ashore.

Captain Charles Stewart had been staying at the Indian Queen in Washington, having arrived on an errand like Bainbridge's own. The two men went around to see Navy Secretary Hamilton. He was deeply sympathetic with their attitude of protest, but said that the matter had already been decided in a full meeting of the Cabinet, and the order must stand. The ships' spars were to be struck; New York would be the station for most of them. The gentlemen would understand that this would entail no loss of advancement for naval officers, as they would continue in command of their ships.

Stewart had a fine flow of eloquence and Bainbridge was no incompetent debater himself. They pressed the Secretary so severely, with arguments so cogent, that he finally agreed to take them round to President Madison. We know what those arguments were, for they have been recorded:

---

* Box-hauling is an extremely neat trick, almost never done. It is tried when a ship is close-hauled—that is, with her prow as close to the direction of the wind as possible—and it becomes necessary to tack: i.e., to bring the wind on the other side of her bow. Because of the lee shore, there is no room to wear (swing her through the circle with the wind temporarily astern); because of her own clumsiness, or damage to the rigging, or the force of the wind she refuses to tack; that is, swing through the circle with the wind momentarily right ahead. In box-hauling, the headsail is thrown aback, and the ship is made to back around; but it takes a genius at seamanship to do it, because the commands to haul or let go braces must be given at precisely the right second in the process, and there are a great many such commands. Anyone who wishes to find out how chancy a matter it is can do so in Cooper's *The Pilot*.

"Eight times out of ten, sir, with equal force we can hardly fail; our men are better men, better disciplined. Our guns are sighted, which is an improvement of our own the English know nothing of. While we fire cannon, with as sure an aim as musketry or almost rifles, striking twice out of every three shot, they must fire at random, without sight of their object or regard for the undulations of the sea, shooting over our heads, seldom hitting us. We may be captured and probably shall be, even after taking prizes from them, because their numbers are much greater than ours. But the American flag will never be dishonored, seldom, if ever, struck to equal force."

They pointed out that the sheet-lead cartridges used in American ships gave an advantage of almost one gun in three in rate of fire; that the U.S. Marines were made up of riflemen from the backwoods, the best marksmen in the world; and that the system under which they were used made the most of this, six men in each top loading, while the best aim of all fired the pieces.

People were wont to call President Madison "poor Jemmy," the epithet's undertone being that he was pretty much the plaything of forces too big for him to handle; but the brain that produced a good part of the Constitution and of *The Federalist* could absorb a telling point when it encountered one. After a time the President sighed and said:

"You'll give us victories, then, you think?"

"We do," said Stewart, "and not upon irrational premises."

"Which victories," Madison mused aloud, "will give us ships; for with victories Congress will supply them faster than they can be lost."

Next day a Cabinet meeting was called to reconsider the order laying up the ships. Bainbridge and Stewart sat it out in Secretary Hamilton's office, but he returned in the afternoon to say the news was bad. A. A. Gallatin, the sharp-nosed Swiss financial genius of the Treasury, was the opponent, a man so accurate in most of his judgments that Jefferson had always deferred to him and Madison accepted as gospel almost everything he said on almost any subject with which he concerned himself. Gallatin thought of warships in terms of investment; they would be lost uselessly on the sea, for it was not only in numbers that the Royal Navy excelled ours, but also in the quality of those British seamen who, for nearly twenty years, had met the four quarters of the world in arms. Our men had no experience of war, and the New York merchants were really haunted by the thought of a British fleet sailing up their harbor and treating their town as Copenhagen had been treated, with a burning bombardment. Decision as before: ships to be laid up.

The two captains would not quit. That evening they retired to the Indian Queen and drew up a letter of protest, Stewart furnishing most of the structure, while Bainbridge set everything in order.* Secretary Hamilton, when he saw it, wanted them to rewrite it, as containing expressions too strong for the Presidential eye, but the captains would not yield an inch. When Madison read the missive, he decided on the (for him) unprecedented step of overruling his Cabinet. The ships should go out for at least one cruise apiece as an experiment.

That one cruise led *Constitution* to her tête-à-tête with *Guerrière,* and Bainbridge had no personal part in the victory. Yet as the long tide of glory rolled in from the Atlantic up to the moment when *Macedonian's* flag was laid at the feet of Dolly Madison, Secretary Hamilton cried over the heads of the rapturous audience: "Never forget that it is to Captains Bainbridge and Stewart that you really owe these victories!"

Unknown to the Secretary, unknown to any present in that hall, Captain Bainbridge at that very hour was far below the Equator, winning a reward he would infinitely have preferred.

v

After the one-cruise decision had been taken, the Department gave Bainbridge *Constellation,* 38, then lying at Washington, but she had been lying in ordinary beside *New York,* 36, with her guns and all spars except the lower masts out, for nearly seven years. Even some of her main beams were rotten and the Captain found he could drive his thumb into many places in her planking. Repair would obviously be too long a business for the immediate recruitment of a crew; Bain-

---

* That letter disappeared, presumably in the burning of Washington in 1814, but there is no doubt of its existence or its general terms. Too many people saw it.

bridge could only indicate what was necessary after a close inspection and set the work in train.

While it was still going on, the Captain traveled up to Boston to see his family, and was present when Isaac Hull brought *Constitution* triumphantly home, then applied for a furlough because of his brother's death. Bainbridge requested a transfer to the 44 and immediately received it, with orders to cruise to the coast of the Brazils as head of a small squadron which should include *Essex,* 32, and *Hornet,* 18.

Essex was in the Delaware under David Porter; Bainbridge made arrangements to leave instructions for him at Porto Praya in the Cape Verdes and again at Fernando Noronha, which he expected to reach in mid-December, after which he would slant across toward Africa in an effort to pick up some of the Honourable East India Company's ships.

Constitution and *Hornet* sailed together on October 22, 1812; the long cruise down to Fernando Noronha was almost eventless. The place was then a Portuguese penal colony and Portugal was an ally of England. Bainbridge dressed his ships with British colors and made such minor changes as were necessary to convert American officers' uniforms to British, described his own frigate as H.M.S. *Acasta,* 44, and left a letter addressed to Sir James Yeo of H.M.S. *Southampton,* which was the style Porter was to assume, with an interlineation in the same sympathetic ink both men had used while imprisoned in Tripoli. The frigate and the sloop now cruised southward, intending to see what might be found on this coast before striking across to the Cape Verdes. At Bahia a British 20 was discovered in the harbor and challenged to combat by *Hornet,* but refused to come out and fight, since she was carrying a great treasure. Bainbridge left the American sloop on blockade and himself pushed on toward Rio.

At nine in the morning of December 29, two sail were made out against the dark, low-lying tropic coast. One stood on; the other made toward *Constitution* along light airs from the east-northeast, and by eleven stood out clearly as a heavy frigate. Bainbridge had long since cleared for action; now he tacked to the south and east, setting his royals, to draw well away from neutral waters where a beaten ship might take shelter. The stranger came sliding through a smooth, bright sea in pursuit, eager for battle, and doubtless with some comment on her quarterdeck that the American was seeking to avoid it; for if the British then had some inkling of the size and power of the American 44s, their own ship was a good deal beyond the strength of the average British 38, and her captain was James Lambert, a fearless man and a skilled one.

She was H.M.S. *Java,* which had been the French *Renommée* until taken in battle the year before; one of the cruisers that Napoleon's naval architects built slightly stronger than their British counterparts, with guns firing a heavier shot, so that her 18s were almost equal in individual weight of metal to *Constitution's* 24s, which fired the short-weight American ball. Moreover, she was bound for the East Indies, with parts of the crews of three other ships, so that there were 446 seamen on her decks, which meant that her ropes and sails could be handled with lightning speed.

By noon, when colors were set on both sides, it was already clear that *Java* had the speed of the American; but it was twenty past one before Bainbridge dropped land below the horizon and took in his maincourses and royals, indicating willingness to engage. At 2 P.M., distant half a mile and both ships on a reach, *Constitution* fired a gun, *Java* returned it with a broadside, and a rapid cannonade began. The sea was smooth and the sun brilliant; men tore off piece after piece of clothing, and runnels of sweat through the black, thick powder-cinders striped their bare backs like zebras as they hove on the tackles. Both ships were hit at once; *Java* drew gradually ahead and began to keep off for a rake, but *Constitution* wore sharp round and they were running in the opposite direction, again wing to wing, but with the other broadsides bearing.

Once more *Java* reached ahead and wore for a bow-rake; but *Constitution* came round as fast and they were back on the original course. Now, 30 minutes after the first gun, damage began to show on both sides; *Java's* jib-boom was splintered, while a round shot carried away *Constitution's* wheel and drove a copper bolt deep into her captain's hip. The loss of the wheel might have been deadly, particularly with the Captain hurt, but Bainbridge pressed his hand to the wound while

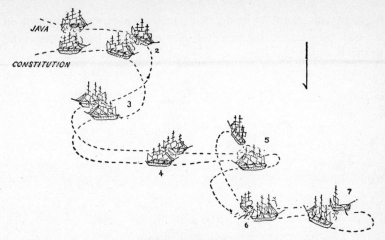

Constitution—Java

(1) Both ships open fire. (2) *Java* forereaches; wears to rake; misses, and loses her jib-boom. (3) The second turn; *Java* forereaches once more. (4) *Java* still gaining on the third run. (5) *Java* misses her tack, hangs in stays, and is raked. (6) Lambert tries to board; *Java's* foremast goes. (7) The last run; *Constitution* gains, wears, and rakes again; *Java* loses her mizzen-mast.

he directed the rigging of tackles to the rudder-post below-decks, with a line of midshipmen to pass down the word for alterations of course. Not satisfied with what his guns were doing, the American Captain determined to take partial rakes in order to close. He ordered the top-gallants flown and the rudder simultaneously ported for a luff; and his calculation was just, for exactly as the sails were sheeted home with a shout, the order reached the rudder-tackle men, and she swung prettily. As the frigates approached each other, *Java* fore-reached for a third time; but the ships were now so near each other that Captain Lambert feared he would lose his windwardly position if he wore again, so ordered a quick tack in the smoke.

Now the effect of the American gunnery became apparent; for *Java* had lost so many control-ropes that she missed her tack, hung in stays as *Constitution* wore sharp round, and was raked dreadfully from astern by those long 24s. The fight was clearly going against the Britisher; her lieutenants were screaming and beating men with their speaking trumpets, but there was nothing they could do about that dreadful sleet of iron, and her gunfire became slower and disorderly. Lambert got his ship's head round by wearing and came charging in with desperate valor to restore the battle by a hand-to-hand fight on the enemy's deck. Bainbridge coolly luffed up and raked *Java* once— twice—three times from ahead. The English frigate's bowsprit came stabbing across *Constitution's* quarter, the bugles bawled "Boarders away!" and Lambert came running forward to lead them, cutlass in hand. An American marine's bullet went right through him, the boarders broke under small-arms fire, and as the ships jerked apart, down came *Java's* foremast, partly masking the guns as the two ships ran off free, resuming their cannonade at pistol-shot.

Java's deck was in dreadful shape by this time, the British cheers had turned to screams and sobs, the gunnery was all disorganized, the hamper of the broken foremast was burning at every discharge; and *Constitution* now fore-reached with her greater spread of sail. Bainbridge luffed up and fired a semiraking broadside, wore round and raked the Britisher again from astern. More than half *Java's* guns had been dismounted or silenced for lack of people. As *Constitution* wore round once more to come abeam, the British frigate's mizzen-mast came down and so did her mainyard. She was a wrecked ship; a beaten ship; not another gun was fired as the American shot proudly ahead to repair a few cut ropes, then came back to force the downfall of a flag which had been kept flying only for show.

Java had made the best defense of any of the British ships, and had inflicted 34 casualties on her opponent (while herself taking 60 killed, 101 wounded); but this did not much help the feelings of the British, who found it difficult to understand how such events could come about at all. They had begun the war with the London *Times* speculating delicately on how long it would take to bring into British ports the "handful of fir-built frigates under a bit of striped bunting, manned by bastards and outlaws." When *Guerrière* went, there was an explanation; she was an old ship and early in the action had the "accident" of losing her mizzen-mast. *Macedonian* was obviously no match for the "disguised ship-of-the-line" *United States*. Bad enough; but now had come something hardest of all to take, for *Constitution* had the misfortune of a lost wheel and a wounded captain early in the action, and the forces were not far from equal.

"Good God! Can such things be?" inquired the now-mournful London *Times*, while the *Pilot*, organ of the shipping trade, sang a threnody that has ever since been remembered:

"The Public will learn, with sentiments which we shall not presume to anticipate, that a third British frigate has struck her flag to an American. This is an occurrence that calls for serious reflection—this and the fact that Lloyd's list contains notices of upwards of 500 British vessels captured in seven months by the Americans. Five hundred merchantmen and three frigates! Anyone who had predicted such a result of an American war this time last year would have been treated as a madman or a traitor."

And the great Viscount Wellington, swinging forward on the high tide of his success in Spain, wrote homeward: "I have been very uneasy about the American naval successes. I think we should have peace with America before the season for opening the campaign in Canada, if we could take one or two of those damned frigates."

VI

Bainbridge had received a second wound, from a musket-ball in the leg, and had to be supported on deck when he accepted surrender from the British First Lieutenant, for Captain Lambert was a dying man. Both the injuries became inflamed; the victorious Captain had to remain in his cot for three weeks during the homeward voyage, which was undertaken at once, since he now had a ship filled with prisoners. *Java's* hull was not in too bad shape, but she could hardly have been taken home without a thorough refit in port, which would have meant taking chances with the highly pro-British government of Portuguese Brazil; therefore the captured frigate was burned. The new Governor of Bombay, who had been aboard, was sent in to Rio under parole. His name was Hislop; he and Bainbridge became good friends and carried on a long correspondence halfway round the world, full of assurances of mutual esteem, descriptions of natural objects, and (on Hislop's part) a running account of the Mahratta wars.

Constitution reached Boston early in February 1813, where her second victorious return completed Isaac Hull's work in cutting the ground from under the New England disloyalty campaign. The legislature passed a resolution: "It becomes the Representatives of the People of Massachusetts (whatever may be their opinions in relation to the existing war) to testify their high appreciation of the gallant and able conduct of those officers and crews of the Navy, to whom the fortunate opportunities have occurred, of giving reputation to the American arms, and of signalizing their own valour, enterprize and skill." There were the usual dinners and celebrations; then Bainbridge went on to Washington to make a personal report (as the custom was) and to assist Decatur and Hull in drawing up a new set of naval signals.

There was also a good deal of consultation on a technical level with regard to the construction of the new line-of-battleship *Independence*, 74, to which Captain Bainbridge had been named as supervisor and prospective commander. It is not quite certain who designed her; probably William Doughty, altering a plan Joshua Humphreys had drawn for a 74 in the '90s to take a battery heavy enough for our battleships to overmatch the British. In the sequel this did not turn out too well, as *Independence* and her sisters, though fast, proved to be insufficiently beamy to carry so much metal topside with comfort. Bainbridge proposed one main alteration in the design—that of giving her frigate bows, with a bowsprit running down two decks, instead of terminating that spar at a heavy bulkhead as was usual in heavy ships. The Captain believed the change would strengthen the ship forward and make her a better sea-boat in rough weather; he was right.

Independence was built at Boston, the busiest naval port of the country during the war years, and Bainbridge was commandant of the yard as well as of the battleship, so he had charge of seeing into the water the new sloops-of-war *Wasp* and *Frolic*. During this construction he introduced another improvement which seems so obvious that it is hard to believe contemporaries were startled—that of building his big ships on housed-in ways, so that the mechanics could work all through the winter. The success of the plan was so instantaneous that Bainbridge's housed-in ways were copied at all the navy yards of the United States, and American ships were built under cover right down to the Civil War. This had one very curious result: as it was possible to keep a large ship, nearly completed, housed in and safe from the forces of decay until needed, it became the custom to do so, and the U.S. navy became famous for the number of its ships on the stocks. Thus *St. Lawrence,* 44, was over 20 years "building"; *Santee,* 44, and *Sabine,* 44, were even longer in the process; and at the outbreak of the Civil War the line-of-battleships *Alabama, Virginia,* and *New York,* which had been laid down in the 1820s, still rested snugly under their houses on the stocks. The idea was recommended to the British Admiralty in 1816 by their best constructor, Seppings, but they refused to have anything to do with it, on the ground that it made mechanics lazy.

Toward the end of 1814 *Independence* was ready except for guns and a crew. Bainbridge bombarded Washington with requests for both, and the suggestion that, as soon as ready, the battleship be sent with a heavy frigate and a tender to cruise off the coasts of India. The plan had more strategic thinking in it than appears on the surface. The British were in the habit of covering the frequent and highly valuable India convoys with nothing heavier than a 50-gun ship, and even if they had stepped up to 74s, it would have taken at least two of them for every convoy to give real protection against such a striking force as Bainbridge proposed—say half-a-dozen to half-a-score battleships, all told. This was as many as it took to blockade one of the French fleet harbors, and would have been a severe strain on a war-weary England which was laying up battleships to provide light vessels for covering convoys against the depredations of Yankee privateers.

But *Independence* was not to get to sea during the war; the British blockade prevented her receiving her guns by water, those that reached her by land came only in a trickle, and she was still an uncompleted ship when, in the fall of 1814, the scared Governor Caleb Strong requested Bainbridge to anchor her outside the harbor since a British expedition might come to Boston, "the public ships were the exclusive objects of attack, and if the *Independence* remained at her present anchorage, the fire of the enemy would be drawn on the towns of Boston and Charlestown, and thus involve them in the ruin of the national property." The Captain's reply has not been preserved, perhaps because nobody had any paper on which it could be written; but it was spring before his guns were all on hand, and the news of peace came first.

With it came new orders. Bainbridge was to go to the Mediterranean with his own new ship, *United States,* 44, *Congress,* 38, *Erie,* 20, and four brigs taking general command of operations against the Algerines, who had opened a war on American shipping while we were busy with England. Stephen Decatur was to sail from New York at the same time with three frigates and six smaller vessels, falling under Bainbridge's command at Gibraltar—how different from the days when Preble had a single frigate against Tripoli!

The installation of the flagship's guns took so long that Bainbridge could not leave Boston until July 3. This was Bainbridge's usual luck; when he reached Gibraltar it was to discover that Decatur had done all the fighting and had all the fun, and was already homeward bound, not only with an Algerine treaty that renounced tribute forever, but also with indemnities from two of the other Barbary powers which had behaved badly. Bainbridge went on up the Mediterranean in any case, as there was a good chance that any given Barbary power would become less peaceful when it lost sight of the American flag waving over tiers of guns. It was as well he did so; the rulers of Tunis and Tripoli were indeed beginning to wonder whether Decatur's appearance had been a flash in the pan, and the British had told them England had forbidden the Americans to build battleships. The appearance of *Independence* was a *pièce de conviction*; everything went smoothly, and the Commodore of the largest fleet yet assembled under the American flag sailed for home in the fall.

After this Bainbridge settled down to the routine duties of a peacetime officer: in command of *Independence* as station ship at Boston, another trip as Commodore Mediterranean in *Columbus,* 74, duty at the Navy Yard in Philadelphia, a trip to Canada to visit the Earl of Dalhousie, with whom he had formed a friendship. There were the usual small incidents, such as adjusting a difference with the Governor of Gibraltar, who had issued an order that American officers were not to come ashore because of numerous quarrels with the British. (Bainbridge refused to touch any point of the current disputes until the order was withdrawn.)

None of these items are very important, except for the Commodore's vigorous and long-continued effort in favor of a naval school. The peculiar concept of democracy during the period defeated him here, but he at least laid some foundation by setting up a school for his own young officers while in the Boston command, and in 1817 he fitted out the brig *Prometheus,* 14, and sent her on a long training cruise with all the midshipmen he could lay his hands on. Nothing came of it immediately, but the results were good enough to be cited later when the Academy was founded.

In 1831 Bainbridge fell foul of the Secretary of the Navy, John Branch, the "miserable old woman," who had been appointed principally because he could make North Carolina safe for Jacksonian Democracy. The Commodore had been serving on various special boards and surveys over a period of years, and, as the custom then was, applied for extra compensation for his overtime work, the salary of shore-bound officers being niggardly to the last degree. Jacksonian Democracy had many lovely aspects, but its handling of veteran public servants was not one; Branch said things were going to be ordered differently under his administration, and refused to pay a cent. Bainbridge wrote him an indignant letter; Branch promptly removed the Commodore from his command of the Philadelphia yard and sent him home "to await orders." This action against the third ranking officer of the service and one of its most distinguished members so exercised the citizens of the town that they gave Bainbridge an enormous public dinner and deluged Washington with petitions, but it was a year later when a new Secretary consoled him with command of the Boston yard.

By this time it was too late; the cup of misfortune had been filled by family trouble. The Commodore's brother began it; he had started well in the navy and was a mid under Preble during the 40 days of Tripoli, but there seems to have been some element of stability missing from his character. In the war of 1812 he had mounted far enough up the list to be a master-commandant and was given the new sloop-of-war *Frolic*, 20, one of the famous Doughty racers, perhaps the finest ships the navy had, weight for weight.

On his very first cruise he fell in with a British 32 and was taken without resistance after throwing overboard all his guns in an effort to escape. There was nothing disgraceful about the last procedure, which was common in cases where no real fight could be made, and the court of inquiry found him without blame. But there was no escaping general service opinion that with a ship like that something better could have been done; all *Frolic's* sisters got out of tight corners with ease. Under the shadow of that mute disapproval Joseph Bainbridge took to drink, and in 1824 he died of the resulting complications. This left the William Bainbridge line the only naval one of the family, and in 1831, just when Secretary Branch was delivering his blow, William's only son died also. The Commodore never quire recovered. Shortly after taking up the Boston command he had to quit it for Philadelphia, suffering from an ailment described as a combination of neuralgia, pneumonia, and inflamed bowels, which means that the doctors did not know what it was. Early in 1833 he died, calling on all hands to board the enemy.

He was the most cultured of Preble's boys, and probably the one who owed least to that iron commodore, his mental equipment being already nearly complete when he went out to the Mediterranean in 1803. But one catches more than hints of what might be called Preble-ism—for instance, in the bold plan to take the offensive against the British in the waters of India, which no one else had attempted since the days of French Suffren. Another thing Bainbridge certainly owed to the older man: before the Tripoli cruise he was known as one of the strictest commanders in the service or in the merchant marine either, but after that comparatively brief contact Bainbridge became one of the easiest, almost as much beloved by the sailors for his kindness as Decatur himself.

There is also the fact that he became one of the party of Preble's boys, thinking like them and acting with them whenever there was a moment of decision. This was not unimportant in the period when a somewhat accidental play of circumstances seemed to set apart a group that trained for seamanship in opposition to one that trained for battle.

William Bainbridge

Bainbridge belonged to the "battle" party, but there could not be alleged against him as against Decatur a lack of seamanship, for he was unquestionably one of the best ship-handlers in the War of 1812. Hardly anyone else could have handled the slower *Constitution,* with her wheel shot away, so that she not only avoided being raked by *Java,* but three times inflicted that crushing enfilade on her opponent. To be sure, Bainbridge inherited a crew carefully trained for both seamanship and battle by Isaac Hull, but he knew all about training, too; the deep-sea cruise of *President* shows it.

But it was not emphasis on training and education alone that Bainbridge had to give the navy. He was also the completest of officers; one who did his own thinking all along the line. In command of *Cantor,* he immediately altered her rig to improve her sailing; he built roofs over his ships, and dared challenge the master-shipbuilder, Joshua Humphreys, on the constructional details of a battleship. His wide general culture made it possible for him to get along with all sorts and conditions of men; he was almost the founder of the tradition of naval officers in diplomacy, which played so large a part in the development of American seaborne trade in the years between the War of 1812 and the Civil War. Above all stood Bainbridge's confidence in his own intellectual process; he rejected both superstitition and the semisuperstition of received ideas.

It is impossible to separate the parts that he and Stewart had in the vital decision to send the frigates out over Gallatin's opposition, and to claim the major share for either is pointless. But without that decision it is clear that the history of the navy, and indeed of the nation, would have been very different, for the second War of Independence had been lost but for those ships.

THE BRITISH REPLY

Chapter 6

Honor: James Lawrence

And art thou gone in time of need?
Brave Lawrence, hast thou fled indeed?
And will that noble heart again
Ne'er feel the throb of joy or pain?
That heart that beat with patriot fire,
And will it ne'er again aspire
To meet our foemen on the main
And teach Britannia's sons again
That valor, armed in Freedom's cause,
Can never shrink, or never pause;
Lawrence was merciful as brave,
He loved to conquer—and to *save;*
A fallen foe should be forgiven,
Mercy is the attribute of Heaven.

—A Young Lady of New York

O N OCTOBER I, 1781, JAMES LAWRENCE WAS BORN AT BURLINGTON, N. J. It is a river town, and at the date of his birth the family house was still pockmarked by shot from the British warships that had been in the stream in '77. It is not clear whether Lawrence *père* was in prison at the date of his son's birth, but he certainly had been during a good part of the Revolution, for he was a most contumacious Loyalist to the cause of England and King George.

In the atmosphere of burning patriotism that followed the release from British bonds, the knowledge of such a parentage must have been bitter to a growing boy. Moreover, James Lawrence was the somewhat unwanted son of his father's late second marriage, and his mother died while he was quite a baby. Psychologists can work out the details of how this affected his choice of a career. For the present it is sufficient to note that there were torts in his childhood, and of a character that has been used by a softer age to explain more than one juvenile delinquency.

There was nothing delinquent about the youth of this child. After his mother's death, he fell into the hands of a half sister named Elizabeth, fifteen years his senior, who had married an Irishman named Michael Kearney and established herself as the leading blue-stocking of Perth Amboy, N.J. She signed herself "Mme. Scribberus" or "Pindarina" after the fashion of the period, and appears to have thought rather highly of her own poetry, one specimen of which has survived —because Lawrence was its subject:

> "My brave, brave Jim's a sailor Jack—
> Upon the treacherous sea—
> A sailor who loves poetry
> All taught to him by me."

The Romantic revival had evidently not reached northern New Jersey at the time of this composition, which is clearly later than 1796, the date when the elder Lawrence died and brave, brave Jim began his career as a sailor Jack. We are told that he had expressed a preference for this profession as early as the age of 12, but at this point it would only be a boyhood search for romance. Persistence in the resolve was probably due to the opposition of his father, who wished James Lawrence to follow the law.

There was enough money in the family so that instead of beginning as a 'prentice hand on a merchant vessel, like most young seaman, Lawrence was sent back to Burlington, where he was tutored in astronomy and theoretical navigation by a Mr. Griscomb. In fact, he never entered the merchant service at all; when his education had progressed far enough for him to go to sea, he received a midshipman's warrant and sailed in U.S.S. *Ganges,* 24, Captain Thomas Tingey.

Perhaps Tingey got him the appointment; he was a New Jersey neighbor, and in the normal course of events would be allowed to select some of his own mids. The Captain was a rather peculiar customer to bring a young man up in the ways of a new service; an active, loquacious man, who commanded so much esteem in high places that, although without naval experience, he was made Commodore of the small squadron operating in the Windward Passage, between Cuba and Santo Domingo. Later he was for many years superintendent of the Washington Navy Yard, the only nonseagoing captain in the service. His ideas on construction and equipment were heard with the utmost respect. The reason for this is not easy to understand, since most of the ideas were bad; and though he did lay three French privateers by the heels during his cruise to the Indies, his ship fired upward of 40 cannon at one without once touching her or her crew. Such a performance from a vessel commanded by Truxtun or Barry would have produced a tempest on the quarterdeck and some hard practice for the gunners.

Lawrence seems to have done well enough aboard, and when *Ganges* returned from her cruise he was immediately transferred to the new frigate *New York*, 36, as one of the senior mids, under a captain named Thomas Robinson. Robinson is a shadowy figure, of whom little is recorded beyond the fact that he was one of the captains dismissed under the peace establishment of 1801, and that when he transferred to another new ship, *Adams*, 28, he took his senior midshipman with him, and made him an acting lieutenant, although Lawrence was not yet 20.

It was the first instance of something that was to be a repeating pattern in the young man's life—his singular capacity for friendship, for making people like him. Long after, when the midshipmen of the Mediterranean squadron held a meeting to settle details of a dinner they were giving for Commodore John Rodgers, it was decided that inviting the lieutenants would put too heavy a strain on short purses. "What! Not even Mr. Lawrence?" one of them burst out, whereupon all the others began clapping their hands and Lawrence became the only lieutenant at the table.

The cruise of *Adams* was without events that were thought worthy of record. When she reached New York for laying up at the end of the French War, there was waiting for Lawrence one of those letters by means of which Mr. Secretary Smith disembarrassed himself of so many of the officers crowding his navy list. He had a place for Lawrence in the service, but the list of allowed lieutenants was full; the young man could not be confirmed in that rank, and would have to remain a midshipman.

It must be remembered that the service offered anything but attractive prospects at the time. The blanket dismissals, many of them without regard to service reputation, hinted that any officer's career stood at the mercy of a caprice. On the other hand the demand for qualified navigators in the merchant marine was so prodigious that many a youth no older than Lawrence had his own ship and a share in a venture whose success could almost be guaranteed. But he accepted the midshipman's billet in a letter expressing the hope that "I shall not be forgot." In the meanwhile, he was ashore on half pay, which amounted to the magnificent sum of $9.50 a month. A patriotism which took no account of material considerations, commonly mingled with an almost medieval sense of honor, formed much of the stuff of the early navy, but at this date it was yet as formless as an urge, and without a directing force.

Well, Lawrence was not forgot. When Lieutenant John Rush of the schooner *Enterprise,* 12, resigned the service just as the ship was ordered to the Mediterranean in the second squadron, that of 1802, Lawrence received the vacancy and his lieutenant's commission together. It was a young ship, which had been commanded by the youthful Lieutenant Andrew Sterrett, and now by the equally junior Isaac Hull; also the only light vessel in the squadron. Therefore when summer came, and the ships moved up toward Tripoli, most of the work devolved on *Enterprise*—as inshore chases, actions with the Moors alongshore, and an occasional brush with the batteries. In June, after the languid Commodore Morris left things in the hands of John Rodgers, there were a couple of passages of fairly warm work, the first coming when a whole covey of provision-coasters was flushed along the beach, and the boats of the squadron went in to burn them. Lawrence had the *Enterprise's* cutter, with a boat carronade in the bows and as many bags of grapeshot as it could carry. There was a good deal of shooting against a two-gun battery and about a thousand of the Tripolitans who came out from the city. Two weeks later a Tripolitan cruiser of 22 was sighted east of the town. Hull handled his lighter ship beautifully to cut her off and, when the corsair ran into a deep bay, went in after her with the support of *John Adams,* 28, and blew her up.

II

Officers and crew were thus already cocky veterans when the schooner ran down to Gibraltar in October of 1803. There they met the frigate *Constitution* and the new Commodore, Edward Preble. He was no m&ore than a name to those aboard *Enterprise,* but they were happy when the fire-eating Decatur, already famous for the duel at Malta, was exchanged into command of their ship; and even happier over the orders that came with him: "Continue to cruize before Tripoly until the season makes it dangerous, but you must even in the worst season go out, and show yourself off Tripoly, if only for a day or two at a time, as it will have a good effect in convincing those *Barbarians* that their Vessels is not safe, in leaving port at any season of the year." This was a different tone from that taken by previous commodores; it looked as though the old man really meant it when he spoke of substituting active operations against the enemy for passive and partial blockades.

He certainly did mean it, as they learned when they reached Syracuse. Plans for cutting out the lost frigate *Philadelphia* at once fell under discussion. Lawrence took part in those discussions as second-ranking officer of *Enterprise,* for it was determined from the beginning that she and her crew would have the adventure. In the meanwhile the young lieutenant had a run-in with one of the mids, a burly fellow named Boyd, somewhat older than the rest and not too bright. Boyd got drunk in Syracuse, beat up one of the natives, and—when Lawrence tried to get him into a boat—grabbed the lieutenant by the throat and whipped out his dirk. Lawrence took the weapon away from him and handed him into the boat like a child, which was no mean physical feat; but the interesting point is how Preble treated the affair. Instead of ordering a court-martial, as most commanders would have done, he made Boyd apologize both to Lawrence and to Decatur, hat in hand, then write a letter of apology to the Commodore himself;

and finally, the guilty mid was refused a place in the ketch *Intrepid* when she went in to burn the frigate. Boyd was later given one of the gunboats in the fighting off the harbor, and did well.

Lawrence was with the burners, of course, second in command. Congress voted him two months' pay for his part in the exploit, and it throws a little extra light on his character to hear that he refused the money as " 'this sordid and paltry reward,' with an indignation scarcely repressed by respect for the hand that offered it." There is no further special mention of him until the attacks on Tripoli in August 1804. In the first, the battle when the gunboats were captured, he remained aboard *Enterprise* as her skipper while Decatur went into the light craft, having the duty of going in under the fire of the batteries to tow out prizes—a task which he performed so smartly as to earn the special thanks of the Commodore. In the attack of August 28, Lawrence commanded one of the gunboats himself. When the big squadron arrived with Commodore Barron, he was sent home as First Lieutenant of *John Adams,* 28, carrying time-expired men and Commodore Preble as a passenger. The young man and the older were much together during the voyage.

On reaching New York, Lawrence asked for a month's leave, "as some material alterations have taken place in my family"; there is not the slightest clue to the nature of these alterations. The request was apparently denied, as he was ordered to fit out Gunboat *No. 6* at once and take her to the Mediterranean. She was one of the earliest of a new type of naval vessel, the result of an inspiration on the part of a President profoundly interested in inventions and himself an inventor. Jefferson followed his news sources closely; he knew that the small craft borrowed from Sicily by Preble had done very well off Tripoli, and that the gunboats with which Napoleon was intending to cover the invasion of England were proving very formidable in close waters, several times capturing small inshore blockaders and making attacks on harbors most difficult. In similar craft he saw a means of obtaining the essentials of naval defense without building large, expensive warships and maintaining a military establishment that might become a danger to liberty. They would defend our bays and harbors against the insults of a rapacious power; a republic should attempt to do no more.

James Lawrence

The President accordingly abandoned the construction of the six battleships authorized by Congress, and began to put the timber assembled for them into gunboats.

No. 6 was one of the first lot of 9, built to a design by Josiah Fox which was pretty much an experiment in finding a type suited to American conditions. She was 71 feet long and 18 in beam; double-ended, so the rudder could be shifted; carried two lateen sails and a long 32-pounder at either end, which should make her dangerous even to a frigate. Her deadrise was almost nil, so that she rowed much better than she sailed, and her depth of hold was only 5 feet 6—into which space was crowded the incredible crew of two officers, 16 men, and 5 marines.* The fighting at Tripoli was over, but it was determined to send several of the new craft across the Atlantic to determine how seaworthy they were.

When Lawrence saw his new command, he placed it on record that he did not think she could sail to the Mediterranean "or anywhere else," and Gunboat *No. 1* had already fetched up in a Georgia cornfield on her maiden voyage. Nevertheless, she represented an independent command, the young lieutenant's first, and he set to work with a right good will, stowing one of the big guns below and sending another on shore, fitting a false keel and altering her rig to that of a yawl or "dandy" for the long traverse.

When these preparations had been made, the gunboat showed only a single foot of freeboard. Out in the Atlantic a British frigate came tearing down on the little craft, under the impression that she was a raft carrying sailors whose ship had foundered. With a captain's devotion to his own ship, Lawrence nevertheless reported that *No. 6* was "a good sea-boat and sails very fast."

He had his troubles, however, not with the boat, but as the result of an incident off Cadiz, where his route carried him into the midst of Admiral Collingwood's blockading fleet. A British boat came aboard for the customary visit; three of the gunboat's crew, who had been "very unruly" all the way over, announced that they were British subjects and claimed the protection of the flag. The boat officer said

* Yachting magazines today not infrequently carry advertisements for vessels of this size. They usually specify "sleeps six."

that of course they should receive it; he would send an armed boat over immediately to pick them up.

Lawrence went aboard H.M.S. *Dreadnaught,* 74, to protest that these men had taken the pay of the United States and an oath of allegiance to it. The Admiral gave him little comfort; would not even consent that the matter should be adjudicated at Gibraltar; the seamen said they were British, so must be delivered up. Returning to his own ship, the young lieutenant found things were even worse than this attitude indicated. He had left word with his mid, Mr. James Roach, that the departure of the men was to be prevented—by force if necessary; he found the armed boat had come and taken the three men, Mr. Roach not having made the smallest move to detain them.

This was so little like the spirit his old Commodore had taught that Lawrence sent Roach home by the next ship, never again to be employed by the navy. But his real grudge was against the arrogance of the British in taking men out of a warship belonging to another nation. He expected the home government to do something about it. It did not; and the fact that it did not could be seen as one of the reasons why H.M.S. *Leopard* two years later fired into the frigate *Chesapeake* and took out four men who said they were by no means British, and in fact were not.

Lawrence was on the court which condemned Captain James Barron of *Chesapeake* for his disgraceful unreadiness on that occasion, coming down from Portland, Maine, where he had been named inspector of gunboats in succession to Preble. The old man was confined to his bed when the younger arrived, and died before he left.

Soon after the Barron court, Lawrence married a lady named Julia Mountaindevert, about whom not much is known. This was at the close of 1808; when the new administration decided to lay up the gunboats and place the big ships in commission again, he was appointed First Lieutenant of *Constitution.* Lawrence served one commission in her, commanded two of the navy's light brigs for brief periods, then received his promotion to master-commandant, with command of the fine ship-sloop *Hornet,* 18, and orders to proceed to Europe with dispatches.

The ship was lying at New York. Certain merchants of that city, having a large shipment of specie to make to England, besought Lawrence to carry the money for them, which he said he would do, notifying Washington in accordance with protocol. To his surprise he received a letter forbidding him to do any such thing. The government's position was not entirely unreasonable, since the date was November 1811, and war with England had become so imminent a prospect that Treasury Secretary Gallatin did not wish to see cash reserves depart from the country in that direction. But Lawrence was deeply hurt, pointing out in his reply that the honor of his pledged word was involved, that Captain Evans of *Chesapeake* had been allowed to carry money abroad, and that it was an imputation on an officer not to allow him to do what was permitted to others.

His protest was without result, but the voyage was an interesting one, including a visit to St-Cloud, where the Imperial court was in residence and gave the American naval officer a warm welcome. There was so much talk of hostilities that Lawrence cleared his ship for action every time he saw a British ship during the return voyage, and soon after he reached New York the hostilities came.

III

President, 44, *United States,* 44, *Congress,* 38, and *Argus,* 16, were in port, in addition to *Hornet,* all under the general command of John Rodgers. He put out with his squadron as soon as permission was received from Washington and cruised deep into the Atlantic, hoping to catch the British plate fleet homeward bound from Jamaica. In this he failed, as he did in the pursuit of a British frigate, and took his ships nearly empty-handed to Boston at the end of August. *Constitution* had only lately preceded him, garlanded with her tremendous victory over *Guerrière,* and the navy men found themselves unexpectedly popular; but the occasion provided another blow for the high-strung Lawrence.

At that time it was the custom in the British navy to promote the first lieutenant of a victorious ship, since as executive he did most of the hard work of preparing vessel and crew for battle and must have been more than a little responsible for the triumph. Secretary Hamilton thought this custom would be a valuable one for our own service;

but, instead of merely promoting First Lieutenant Charles Morris of *Constitution,* jumped him clear up to the rank of captain, passing over the whole grade of master-commandant. This now made Morris superior in rank to Lawrence (as the latter pointed out in his letter to the Secretary); and it bore particularly hard on Lawrence, for he had been executive officer and second in command when *Philadelphia* was burned, and had been offered nothing but the sordid and paltry two months' pay. The lack of promotion for that exploit implied that the burning of the frigate had been unimportant or ill-performed.

Commodore Rodgers cordially supported Lawrence; Morris himself had been consulted and was in agreement. But Secretary of the Navy Paul Hamilton was one of those obtuse persons who cannot bear admitting a mistake. He replied coldly that "if you leave the service of our country, there still remain heroes and patriots to support the honor of its flag."

Lawrence actually did speak about resigning the service, but he was already under orders for a cruise to the South Atlantic in company with *Constitution,* and decided to talk it over with her captain, William Bainbridge. The latter, who had a good deal of political sense, persuaded Lawrence that the proper thing to do was to memorialize the Senate, at the same time expressing regret if his previous letter had been indecorous. It was done; the Senators agreed with his point of view and held up the Morris promotion until one came through for Lawrence as well, and the two could be confirmed on the same day. The navy was still finding its customs.

But this was still in the future when "Captain Jim," as his men called him, put to sea toward the end of October 1812. The trip down the latitudes was eventless until Bahia in Brazil was reached. A British 20-gun sloop was lying in the harbor there, with a shipment of a half-million in specie aboard, *Bonne Citoyenne;* a little heavier than *Hornet,* but only by so much that the result of a battle between the two would depend upon the better seamen and gunners. Lawrence had commanded his ship for over a year now, training the men daily in firing with the great guns as Preble had taught him; he almost trembled in delight at the prospect of a combat, and sent in a challenge to be delivered through the British consul. Bainbridge promised to sail away in his frigate and not to interfere.

It has been remarked that the Britisher's refusal to come out and fight was "proper," on the ground that it was his business to deliver the money; but this was not the reason he gave. A stiff return note said that Bainbridge obviously "could not reserve so much from the paramount duty he owes to his country, as to become an inactive spectator, and see a ship belonging to the squadron under his orders fall into the hands of an enemy." The imputation on their own honor by a man who they felt was not behaving very honorably made both the American captains very angry. Bainbridge turned his prow southward to be in fact out of the way. *Hornet* remained on blockade, with the hope that her mission would force *Bonne Citoyenne* out of port.

The expectation proved vain. *Constitution* returned with the prisoners from captured *Java* and sailed away home; the British sloop remained obstinately at anchor for nearly a month, or until January 24, 1813, when a British 74 appeared, having been summoned by smack from the Rio station to drive *Hornet* off. Lawrence ran into the harbor on the battleship's arrival, but, not trusting Portuguese ability to make their neutrality respected, slipped out again during the night. His course was northward, such being Bainbridge's order, since hunting for British ships off the Brazils had been so poor that only one was taken. Off Pernambuco *Hornet* captured another, a valuable one with $20,000 in her hold; then pushed on toward Cayenne, Surinam, and Demerara, where there was considerable British trade and something might be accomplished.

On 24 February, the mouth of the Demerara River was reached, where the British had a fort on the spit at the entrance. Dawn showed a merchant brig to leeward, which evidently spotted the sloop as a raider. She threw up all sail in flight and made good her escape, since *Hornet* soon reached shoaling waters and was without a pilot. The chase brought Lawrence's ship close enough in to make out another brig, evidently a heavy British brig-of-war, lying at anchor outside the river bar but inside the long shoal known as Carobano Bank. *Hornet* began beating round the shoal to get at her, when still another sail was sighted, coming down from sea on our sloop's weather quarter and soon revealing herself as a warship and British.

She was H.M.S. *Peacock,* 18, Captain William Peake, a vessel known in her own service as a crack ship, called "the yacht," since no other in the Royal Navy had whiter canvas breechings lining her carronades, more carefully polished brasswork, or better drilled boats' crews. By time she was near, the chase of the first brig and the maneuver round Carobano Bank had killed most of the day. It was 4:20 in the afternoon when *Peacock* set her colors, whereupon Lawrence beat to quarters and cleared for action. He held his ship close-hauled to the wind, with the intention of gaining the weather-gauge if he could, since he had a battle plan already in mind for using it. *Hornet* was one of the clipper-model sloops and a notably weatherly vessel; she footed so high that Lawrence soon saw he would easily weather his opponent. Accordingly, he tacked sharply and stood for the enemy along a broad reach, the ships on opposite courses, the American on the starboard tack, the British on the port.

In those light airs there was plenty of time before the combat would begin, and its terms were obvious; Lawrence walked slowly down the deck, telling each gun captain to fire as soon as his piece bore, aiming low and reloading for a second shot before the enemy passed. Aye, aye, Captain Jim. At 5:25, from pistol-shot distance, the first cannon went off, then the rest, one line of explosions running evenly down the deck, the last guns of the first broadside mingling with the earliest discharges of the second. The British fire was not quite so rapid or well-timed and mostly flew high, only one of *Hornet's* men being killed, and he in the mizzentop. As soon as they were clear, *Peacock* wore round, apparently with some idea of getting in a rake, but Lawrence was looking for just this. He wore even more rapidly and in a narrower circle, so that *Hornet* came down on her opponent close aboard and somewhat on her starboard quarter, a diagonal raking position, firing quick broadsides "like successive claps of thunder." The shot could be heard tearing right through the Englishman's side; he made hardly any reply, and at 5:39, fourteen minutes from the first gun, his ensign came down. It was almost immediately hoisted again in the fore-rigging, union reversed in signal of distress. At the same moment his mainmast went by the board.

Lieutenant Shubrick, who went over to take possession, found *Peacock* in dreadful shape, her captain killed, 37 other casualties, or more

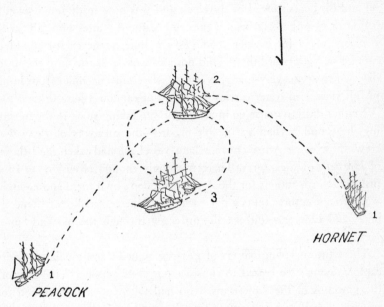

Hornet—Peacock

(1) The approach; *Hornet* weathers *Peacock*. (2) The broadsides, passing. (3) Both ships wear; *Peacock* is raked, surrenders, and sinks.

than a third of her crew, six feet of water in her hold, and more coming in in torrents. The last was the dividend of Lawrence's clever maneuver in engaging from windward; as his enemy heeled to the gust, *Hornet's* low-aimed shot had cut her to pieces right along the waterline. Another lieutenant and a working party were sent over to try to save the prize; they toiled like mad, throwing guns overboard, working pumps, and trying to plug shot-holes, while the boats were saving the wounded. It was all no use; *Peacock* went down suddenly into the first black tropic dark, taking 15 of her own people and three of the Americans: a ship destroyed by an opponent only a little stronger than she—the proportion in metal, 13 to 11—after a defense which cost our side but three casualties.

Hornet's sails were a good deal rent. Lawrence had a new suit bent on and his boats stowed by 9 o'clock and was now ready for a second action in case the brig behind the bank came out after him. She was *Espiègle,* 18, a bit heavier than *Hornet,* but she never stirred. Her captain said afterward that he did not know of the battle until the next day, which seems very queer, as it took place only six miles from him, in full view, and water carries the sound of cannon a long distance.

Neither did Lawrence go in after him. On taking stock in the morning, he found he had 277 people aboard—the survivors of *Peacock's* crew, those of an American merchant vessel she had taken, and those of *Hornet's* own captures. There were only enough provisions to furnish two-thirds rations for the American sloop's own men, and enough water to allow three pints a day each. It was best to make for home at once, and Lawrence did so, sliding easily through the blockade into New York.

There the surviving officers of *Peacock* signed a testimonial to their captor, saying "we ceased to consider ourselves prisoners" in view of the kindness of the Americans, who had taken up a subscription to provide each British sailor with two shirts, a blue jacket, and a pair of trousers, since they had lost everything they owned in the sinking ship. One of the Britishers needed an amputation, but would not permit it unless Lawrence stayed with him through the ordeal and promised, in case it proved fatal, to be a father to his little son.

IV

On *Hornet's* return, Lawrence found that Secretary Hamilton had been replaced by a somewhat more efficient but rather disoriented gentleman named William Jones, and Captain Jim promptly had another run-in with authority. He received his captain's commission and, in line with the general plan of promoting victorious officers to better ships, he was offered command of *Constitution.* But the offer was to be made good only if neither Captain Porter nor Captain Evans (who were senior to Lawrence) wanted that frigate. This flicked Lawrence on his touchy sense of honor; he refused the conditional command as a piece of haggling; was told that he could have *Constitution* without conditions, and then (by the next mail) that he could not have her at all, but must go up to Boston and take over *Chesapeake,* 38.

He did not want her. *Chesapeake* was a fine ship with a nice turn of speed, but she had established a thorough reputation for being at cross-purposes with her masters ever since Josiah Fox built her as a British-type 38 instead of the 44 he was supposed to turn out. At the launch she had stuck twice coming down the ways, a presage of bad luck. In the French War, she cruised for two years and made only one miserable prize at the very end of the struggle; in the Tripolitan fighting, an unprecedented series of foul gales kept her from even getting in sight of Tripoli on the one occasion when she was turned in that direction. She had been the victim of the most disgraceful episode in the history of the young navy, and in the current war she had made only one cruise.

To be sure, she took six prizes on that outing, some of them very valuable, but the shadow that hung over her turned even success into bad luck. She put in at Boston; the navy agent there was so dilatory and inefficient that two months after the frigate arrived, and three months after most of the prizes, her crew had not touched a cent of their money and were in a state of almost open mutiny. One of the lieutenants was ill ashore. Lawrence wrote no fewer than four letters, trying to get his *Hornet* back instead of this madhouse ship, but Secretary Jones never bothered to answer any of them, so he had to carry on with fitting his new command for sea, a process nearly completed when he arrived.

Off the port at this time lay a single blockader, H.M.S. *Shannon,* 38, Captain Philip Bowes Vere Broke, quite a different kettle of fish from the average British naval officer thus far encountered in the war—one of those characters thrown up from time to time by the British race, who ride a hobby-horse to the edge of aberration. Broke's aberration was gunnery. "From the day when he joined her on the 14th of September, 1806, the *Shannon* began to feel the effects of her captain's proficiency as a gunner." He personally taught his men how to lay the pieces and had the guns all carefully sighted—a freakish thing for a Britisher to do, as Bainbridge and Stewart had noted. He transgressed regulations by wasting ammunition on mere practice. "Every day, for about an hour and a half in the forenoon, the men were exercised in training the guns, and for the same time in the afternoon in the exercise of the broadsword, pike, musket, &c." He gave a pound of tobacco to the man who put a shot through the bull's eye and often had a cask thrown overboard, ordering some gun to sink it impromptu. When inspection of Boston harbor showed that *Chesapeake* was lying in the stream with her yards crossed, Broke sent in a challenge to come out and fight, as Lawrence himself had once challenged *Bonne Citoyenne* at Bahia.

At midnight of June 1, 1813, then, *Chesapeake* weighed anchor and stood down the roadstead. It was the following afternoon when she found *Shannon* waiting about six leagues off Boston Light, hove to without way, her head to the southeast and her main-topsail backed to the mast. The wind was light from southwesterly; the American frigate came on from the west at a good rate of speed. Lawrence might have kept away and tried for a stern rake on the stationary ship, but this seemed to him too obvious against an enemy who knew any part of his business. He chose instead to luff sharp up and run down *Shannon's* weather broadside at close range, with the idea that in the light airs then blowing he would blanket her sails, fore-reach on her, then turn short under her bows and grip her by the throat.

He luffed, then, at a distance of 50 yards. At 5:50, the captain of *Shannon's* aftermost gun, who had been told not to fire until his piece bore into the American's second port, pulled his lanyard. Both ships began shooting as rapidly as they could. Both were hitting and being hit, very hard; *Shannon* taking the worse at this stage, from the more rapid service of *Chesapeake's* guns. But now Lawrence found there were disadvantages as well as advantages to keeping the weather position, for if the British cannon had to fire into smoke, the same smoke was swept clear from the American's deck, and the fire of the British Marines from their tops was beyond all expectation accurate and deadly. *Chesapeake's* First Lieutenant was mortally wounded, the Fourth Lieutenant killed, with the sailing-master, the Marine officer, and the boatswain; two helmsmen were shot down in less than six minutes.

Now also came a disaster that was true mischance. At almost the same moment, *Chesapeake's* jib-sheet and fore-topsail tie were shot away and the brails of her spanker. The last sail bellied to the wind, the jib and fore-topsail lost their air—that is, the frigate lost all her headsail and the draw of her aftersail was enormously increased—just as a third helmsman was shot at the wheel. She flew unmanageably into the wind, took two or three diagonally raking broadsides, and began to drift down on *Shannon,* gathering sternway, her port quarter toward her enemy.

Lawrence ordered the foresail filled to draw round, but saw the ships must make contact before his own could fill away, and gave the word for all hands to be summoned from the gundeck to board or repel boarders. The Negro bugler was too frightened to toot a note, and as the Captain opened his mouth to give the order by shout, one of those bullets from the cursed British marines went through his body. He fell to the deck, and was carried below, saying feebly: "Don't give up the ship."

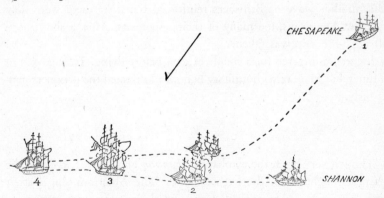

Shannon—Chesapeake
(1) *Shannon* waits; *Chesapeake* comes down. (2) *Chesapeake* pulls up on *Shannon*; the gunnery action begins.
(3) *Chesapeake* loses her headsail while her spanker is cut free; she drifts down. (4) Captain Broke boards; end of the battle.

Third Lieutenant William Cox accompanied him and was later court-martialed for it, since he should have been commanding the ship, the only other surviving major officer being Second Lieutenant George Budd, who was where he belonged, in charge of the forward division of the gundeck. There were thus no American leaders at all topside as Broke shouted, "Come on, *Shannons!*" and swarmed aboard, wearing a plug hat, waving a cutlass that had been made for him in Spain, and followed by 20 men.

Only *Chesapeake's* chaplain met him on the quarterdeck, firing a pistol; Broke nearly took his arm off with a stroke of the Toledo blade. *Chesapeake's* marines put up a fierce struggle, but there were only a third of them left, and these were quickly put down. The men in the American frigate's mizzen-top fired down into the boarders, killing one of the British lieutenants and a couple of men, but were knocked out by the fire of *Shannon's* maintop and a 9-pounder pointed aloft. It was not until this moment that Lieutenant Budd learned what was going on overhead; he came charging up at the head of what gundeck men he could gather, so violently that for a space the boarders were driven back and Broke himself was cut down, desperately wounded. But another wave of Britishers reinforced the first; there were now too few Americans, too many of their opponents. After a short, hard struggle the ship was taken.

Lawrence lingered for a couple of days before dying. They gave him a funeral at Halifax with military honors and treated the prisoners generously.

v

Though very brief, the combat of *Shannon* and *Chesapeake* was the hardest fought of all the frigate battles. The American ship lost 61 killed, 85 wounded in a crew of 379—nearly half the total, more than any beaten frigate in the war. She inflicted on her enemy a far heavier loss than that suffered by any victorious ship—33 killed, 50 wounded, or a proportion such as caused the surrender of more than one ship in the war. In addition *Shannon* took a heavy battering about the hull. No discredit to anyone.

Yet the battle produced the same effect as *Constitution-Guerrière* with the rôles reversed—extravagant delight on the one side, a passion of dismay on the other. At last a British frigate had taken an American! A song was written about Broke:

> "Brave Broke waved his sword,
> And cried, 'Now, lads, aboard!
> 'And we'll soon stop their singing Yankee-
> doodle-dandy-o!'"

which was still sung by schoolboys fifty years later. The King made him a baronet, which was only one point less than Nelson's reward for taking a whole French battle-fleet at the Nile.

On the American side, the newspapers began to pile up excuses as soon as the tidings came in, and in a manner reminiscent of the way the British had tried to talk themselves out of their own defeats. *Shannon* was called a 50-gun ship, while *Chesapeake* was a 38. The latter's crew contained a large number of untrained landsmen, including a big group of Portuguese, who ran below under fire, headed by a boatswain's mate. The whole thing was sheer bad luck. Lawrence was altogether too rash in taking out a ship he had commanded only a few days, and over-chivalrous in seeking broadside combat instead of coming down to rake *Shannon* from astern, as he might easily have done.

Almost none of this is true. The complaint about relative armament is an instructive piece of special pleading, the actual case being that both frigates were rated 38s, *Chesapeake* actually mounting 50 and *Shannon* 52 guns, the latter being heavier in weight of broadside metal by about the proportion by which *Frolic* exceeded *Wasp,* which latter simply slaughtered her British opponent.* *Chesapeake's* muster-

---

* The difference between rated and actual armament has made difficulties for many readers. It came about in this way: in the old days a 38-gun frigate would actually have had 38 guns—28 of them, usually 18-pounders, in her main battery along the gundeck, with 10 smaller guns, 9- or 12-pounders, on quarterdeck and forecastle. At the time of the American Revolution the carronade was invented, a gun with a lighter and shorter barrel. It could shoot only to short ranges, but weighed so much less than the normal long guns that greatly increased calibers, and a larger number of guns, could be used without straining the decks; and when carronades were used, they gave a tremendous smashing effect at close

roll has been preserved; it shows not a single landsman beyond the 15 boys who were powder-monkeys. If there were any Portuguese aboard, they must have changed their names before signing on, since the muster-roll fails to reveal them. (As a matter of fact, Lawrence had quite a number of men who had been old *Constitution* hands under Hull and Bainbridge; it was their handling of the maindeck artillery that smashed *Shannon* up so badly in the early part of the action.)

Lawrence may have cherished a fairly low opinion of British commanders after his contacts with *Bonne Citoyenne, Peacock,* and *Espiègle,* but his actions do nothing to show it, for his battle-plan of coming down *Shannon's* weather side with good way on, taking and giving equal damage till he could blanket the wind from her sails and round under her bows, was considerably more acute than the hindsight plan of trying to rake the Britisher from astern. The latter assumes that Broke would have waited passively to be raked.

Hard luck there certainly was, for the damage during the precession down *Shannon's* flank was not equal; and not equal chiefly because of the shots which cut loose *Chesapeake's* headsail and spanker brails. These shots were wild—overs, which missed their target in the American's hull. But this was not the essential, not the fatal damage. In view of what happened when Broke and his first party of boarders met only a handful of leaderless Americans on *Chesapeake's* deck, it is fair to say that if Lawrence's whole crew had come piling up through the hatches to the sound of the bugle, they could have beaten off the hand-to-hand attack, and perhaps counterboarded, as Yankee seamen were to do in a battle later in the war. The fact that the bugle did not sound was another misfortune, but one that would have been overcome if *Chesapeake* had had any officers left. The British captain put his finger on it exactly—"The American resistance was desperate, but disorganized," he said. That is, there was no leadership, the same defect that cost us *President.*

Partly, this was due to the British Marines, who shot down all the

---

quarters. Thus *Shannon* had the standard 28 long 18s on her gundeck; but up above, she carried 16 32-pound carronades instead of the 10 long 9s that were her theoretical armament as a 38-gun frigate. Indeed, she never had the long 9s; but she was rated a 38 as though she did.

James Lawrence

American officers except one incompetent and one man who did not know what was going on. But this is not the whole story. Later in the war a ship was to win her battle while her captain lay mortally wounded on her quarterdeck; earlier, Decatur's *United States* had fired by divisions without orders, under direction of midshipmen, and the only thing her captain had to do was maneuver his ship to give the gunners the maximum advantage. "The American resistance was desperate but disorganized"; they fought as brave and skilful individuals, but not as a team. Lawrence had been in command only a few days, knew neither the lieutenants nor the men, and had not had time to weld them together. It is hard to believe that Captain Jim, who on other ships knew his people so well, would not have detected the cowardly bugler and eliminated him, given time. Given time, he could have integrated in other ways. No excuses, then; *Chesapeake* was beaten by the better ship.

There remains the imputation of rashness; why did Lawrence put to sea with a ship unprepared for battle? Among the other recriminations following the defeat, there was a story that Bainbridge, then in command at Boston, had advised against going out. Bainbridge promptly denied it, but even if the tale were true it is unlikely that his or any other protest would have had the slightest effect on James Lawrence. For Lawrence had positive orders from Washington to go to sea as soon as his ship was physically ready. He had also been challenged to battle by a British captain in almost the same terms he himself had used to challenge one. Honor forbade him to take any other course.

VI

It was also to some extent fortuitous that *Chesapeake* should meet the very best enemy cruiser off the American coast. Yet as 1813 deepened, it became increasingly apparent that after a first shock—due to not taking an American war seriously—the Royal Navy was getting things in hand. The frigate *President* managed to get away for one cruise to the coasts of Norway, and took 13 prizes; but on her return was closely blockaded in New York by a squadron that counted four frigates and a line-of-battleship. *Congress*, 38, was tightly confined in

Portsmouth and needed docking for the repair of her rotten timbers; and Portsmouth had no dock. The ship was laid up and her guns taken out. *Constitution* was long under repair at Boston. *United States,* 44, and *Macedonian,* 38, were in New London; at the end of Long Island Sound five British frigates and a battleship were waiting for them. *Constellation,* 38, lay at Norfolk, watched by a British force so large and so close in that they even attempted to take her by a boat expedition. The new *Guerrière,* 44, was completing at Philadelphia and the new *Java,* 44, at Baltimore, but the Delaware was tightly blockaded and Chesapeake Bay was held by a British battle-fleet, which made periodic and rather despicable descents on the coast to burn farmers' houses and run off their livestock. Attacks on Baltimore and Washington were in preparation.

In addition to the collective process of blockade for dealing with American heavy cruisers, H.M. Admiralty took up the problem on an individual basis. A new class of ships, even more superior to the 44s (it was hoped) than the 44s were to the British 38s, was laid down and placed under orders for rapid completion. In the meanwhile the 38-gun, 18-pounder frigates were ordered to cruise in pairs, and not to engage American 44s except in company. Two of them, sighted successively and alone by *President* during her cruise, simply ran away. No doubt this was not quite the fashion in which England was accustomed to winning her naval wars, but it was a fashion which could bring results.

Even the American commerce-raiders seemed likely to be snuffed out by the end of 1813. Privateering showed a decline; many vessels were taken, and others held in port by the ever more stringent blockade. The light cruisers of the regular navy did very little during the year. To be sure, old Commodore Preble's beautiful black-masted brig, *Argus,* 16, did get away from the blockade in May, and made a frightfully destructive raid into the English Channel, during which she caught 21 British merchant vessels worth over two and a half millions, and burned them all. But she, too, came to a bad end. One night she captured a ship laden with Spanish wine, her crew got drunk on the captured cargo, and with the dawn they had to fight the British *Pelican,* a brig of considerably greater force. *Argus* was taken after the only battle of the war in which it could be said that an American crew behaved badly.

No; the loss of *Chesapeake* and of the brilliant, the impetuous, the beloved Lawrence, seemed clearly to mark the beginning of the end for the U.S. navy on the ocean. It was as Bainbridge and Stewart had told President Madison in that White House interview before the ships were set free: "We may be captured and probably shall be, even after taking prizes." The only thing to survive the disaster was the tradition of irreducible courage represented by "Don't give up the ship."

Oliver Hazard Perry set those words on his battle standard when he went forth to break the British line on Lake Erie, and they have ever since remained the memorial of Lawrence in American naval tradition, as "I have not yet begun to fight" is the memorial of John Paul Jones. Every fighting service needs some such tradition that the struggle is not hopeless while anyone remains alive, and its source is perhaps not germane to the question; it is fortunate that in the American navy that tradition should be associated with the name of Lawrence, who to his courage united both talent and a heart. Decatur was asked once whether Lawrence's intrinsic merit as an officer justified the veneration in which the nation held his memory.

"Yes, sir, it did," replied Decatur; "and the fellow died as well as he lived, but it is part of a soldier's life to die well. He had no talk, but he inspired all about him with ardor; he always saw the best thing to be done; he knew the best way to do it; and he had no more dodge in him than the mainmast."

Chapter 7

An Anomaly:
Isaac Chauncey

I T IS EASY TO EXAGGERATE THE DIFFERENCES AMONG THE TYPES OF
thought and conduct-pattern that were built into the structure of
the U.S. navy by the men at the head of the service during the
primary-school days of the French War. The ideas which were considered of doctrinal importance by John Barry, Samuel Barron,
Richard Dale, and even Thomas Truxtun covered relatively limited
and not always coterminous areas, so that a young officer trained by
one of these leaders never found it too difficult to give satisfaction to
another. Many of the doctrines themselves were profoundly modified
when brought into relation with each other by the events between
1803 and 1815. In any case, the men affected, the juniors of the French
War, put into action ideas of their own as soon as they reached the position of absolute authority that was conferred by command of a sailing ship at sea.

Or ideas they thought were their own. For no man can wholly escape his past, and an officer who thinks of himself as obstinately original is, more often than not, only slightly modifying something he
learned long ago. That is why it was so important to the navy to have
a Truxtun in the days of the French war; and why it was important
that Truxtun made himself the premier officer of the service by winning the only two first-class sea-fights of the conflict, one through brilliant maneuver and sharp gunnery, the other through sheer hard te-
nacity. He was a close disciplinarian, but he made the brash young lieutenants discover the fighting man's reason for discipline. "I do assure

you," one of those lieutenants wrote home, "that we would put a man to death merely for looking pale aboard *this* ship."

Truxtun was also a good deal more than a disciplinarian. When the big, rubicund man took U.S.S. *Constellation*, 38, to sea in June 1798, all the navy regulations there were could have been written on a couple of sheets of foolscap. Such matters as the duties of a master gunner, the proper post for the Third Lieutenant during action, the responsibility for maintaining the standing rigging in good condition, were delegated according to the whim of the individual captain. They were usually delegated on a day-to-day basis, which meant that the captain had to see to everything himself, with his lieutenants as messenger-boys. It was Truxtun's peculiar merit that he decided in the beginning this was no way to run a navy. He set out to remedy the condition in the most practical manner. When regulations for the government of the service were drawn during the 1820s, the officers in charge of the task found they could not do much better than go back to the long series of letters Truxtun had addressed to each of the officers and petty officers of *Constellation*, telling them precisely what was expected of them on all occasions, military and social.

In short, he ran his ship like a business enterprise, and on lines that would warm the cockles of a modern efficiency expert's heart. It was an admirable method; and it had so much to do with getting the nascent service off on the right foot that Truxtun has frequently been called "The Father of the Navy." But at least one of his pupils absorbed so much efficiency that he became immune to other and perhaps more desirable influences.

For Isaac Chauncey already had a strong bent toward the business side of the service when he entered it at the age of 27 in 1799. He had already so great a reputation as a seagoing businessman that Secretary Stoddert predated his commission by nine months to "make him an old lieutenant and First Lieutenant of the frigate which he is desired to supervise." There is very little about how Chauncey obtained this reputation. In fact, there is very little of anything about him before he gets into the navy; he never attained the apotheosis which sets people searching out childhood memories of the hero. The sole surviving detail about his background is that his father was from Connecticut, a

farmer who presumably belonged to the local squirearchy, being de-
scended from the second president of Harvard College. The surviving details about Isaac Chauncey himself are that he was the fifth of
seven children, tall and corpulent from an early age, and that (in the
words which beat a metronome through contemporary notices of
nearly all Preble's boys) he "had little taste for the quiet, though enno-
bling, pursuits of agriculture, but at an early age longed for the more
adventurous and exciting pursuits of the sea."

The family let him go; indeed, they helped him by placing him as a
'prentice with a shipmaster of New York. Young Chauncey did so
well that he earned his own command at the age of 19, which is more
than usually creditable since it came before the great European war
set up a furious demand for American bottoms in the carrying trade.
After this date there is an eight-year hiatus in the story. It contains
Chauncey's marriage and the acquisition of the good reputation mentioned earlier. At the end of the period he steps forth as superintendent of construction and prospective First Lieutenant of U.S.S. *President*, 44, then building at New York.

Truxtun, who had been moved up to this heavier frigate as a reward
for his victories in *Constellation*, does not seem to have been pleased at
the Chauncey appointment. He was an obstinate and strong-minded
man; what he really wanted was to take to his new command the officers he had carefully welded into a unit aboard the old. Secretary Stoddert had to write him a sharp letter to the effect that if he had trained
one set of juniors, he could train another, and that *President* already
possessed a "very well qualified lieutenant."

This was a background that hardly promised a happy relationship
between captain and executive, but they were both men of business,
portly fellows, good-natured in social intercourse; men who thought
rather well of their victuals. They hit things off at once. *President* was
a happy ship during the one brief cruise she made before the French
War ended, and in April 1801 we find Truxtun requesting the Commandant of the Marine Corps to order two lieutenants of that service
out of the ship, as "I fear they will never, after what has passed, live in
cordiality with Mr. Chauncey."

What had passed is obscure, but it was nothing that told against the record of the lieutenant from Connecticut, who was one of those retained on the Peace Establishment, sixth of his rank on the list. Truxtun's approval probably had something to do with his retention, but there is no record on the point. The efficiency reports of those days were normally a matter of personal interview between the Secretary and the captain of a ship just in from cruise, neither making any notes.

Chauncey remained First Lieutenant of *President* when Richard Dale took her out for the first Mediterranean cruise, and gave satisfaction there also. As soon as he returned to the United States, in 1802, he was appointed to command the light frigate *General Greene*, 28, for the Mediterranean with 100 gun-carriages as tribute to the Emperor of Morocco, and $18,000 in cash for the same purpose to the Dey of Algiers. Before the ship was ready, word arrived that the Moroccans were disposed to be nasty. President Jefferson so hated the whole business of tribute that he seized every occasion not to pay it. *General Greene's* sailing was canceled and Chauncey with his crew was transferred to *New York*, 36.

Commodore Richard V. Morris had this ship his flag when she reached the Mediterranean, and as he had the general business of the squadron to handle as well as diplomatic affairs, Chauncey was practically in full command of the ship. This turned out to be a good thing. On April 10, 1803, while *New York* was making the passage from Gibraltar to Malta in company with *John Adams*, 28, there was a violent explosion and smoke came rolling up the hatchways from the region of the magazine. Chauncey instantly told the drummer to beat to quarters, but as the long roll thrummed through the disciplined confusion of men hurrying to their places at the guns, Morris completely lost his head and ordered the boats swung out.

Nothing communicates itself through a group of men so quickly as panic at the source of command; in an instant the sailors broke, running forward to crowd bowsprit, jibboom, and knightheads, every space that was farthest from the magazine. Some even jumped overboard. The quartermaster, as unnerved as the worst, ran up the signal for "Mutiny on board" instead of "Fire on board"; *John Adams* opened her ports and came down with guns run out to quell a rising.

Chauncey saved the day and the ship. Crying that he might as well be blown up through one deck as through three, he rallied a few men with the help of Lieutenant David Porter, and led them down into passages rolling in smoke, where they attacked the fire with wetted blankets and a bucket-chain. They got the blaze in hand just as it was eating through the bulkhead into the magazine; then discovered that there were 14 dead, including the master-gunner, whose carelessness had left a quantity of loose powder near the magazine door.

The ship was a good deal shattered and had to have major repairs, therefore took little further part in the campaign, which was not much of a campaign in any case. The squadron had already destroyed one of the two major Tripolitan cruisers and captured the other, so that Commodore Morris believed a close blockade of the city was unnecessary. When the Navy Department disagreed and ordered him home as a passenger, Chauncey was left in technical as well as actual command of *New York*. In that capacity he waited on the new commodore, Edward Preble, when the latter arrived at Gibraltar in September of 1803. The two New Englanders made favorable impressions on each other, Preble through his energy of expression and forthright manner of command, Chauncey by his orderliness and capacity for system. The Commodore appointed him head of a board to fix values on the Tripolitan prize *Meshouda,* and on *Mirboka,* the captured Moroccan ship, since the prize-money would be due their captors.

This done, Chauncey sailed for home. He had hardly arrived and made his report before he received his step to master-commandant and was ordered out again, this time as skipper of *John Adams*. She was armed *en flûte*—that is, with most of her cannon in the hold, the deck space being taken up with supplies for the squadron. An indication of what the Department thought of Chauncey is furnished by the fact that while his ship was fitting they sent him up to New York on a budget of business errands—to buy 24 gun-carriages for mounting the new carronades of *United States*; to hire ship-carpenters for Washington Navy Yard; to locate a number of sailing-masters, master-gunners, boatswains, and sailmakers, whose characters and talents made them suitable to receive warrants in the naval service.

Isaac Chauncey

II

John Adams dropped the Chesapeake capes astern on June 26, 1804, barely touched at Gibraltar, and joined the squadron before Tripoli at dawn on August 7. The atmosphere was charged with lightning; four days earlier Stephen Decatur had led the fierce battle of the gunboats and the fleet was going in again that morning. All the young lieutenants were swaggering, in love with fighting and the hope of renown, eager as hunting hawks at the hand of the grim old dyspeptic on *Constitution's* quarterdeck. Preble had many officers out in the gunboats, and the affairs of the squadron to deal with; when Chauncey and several of his people volunteered for the fighting, they were accepted with pleasure. In the day's battle and from that point on till the close of the campaign, the new Master-Commandant maneuvered *Constitution,* and did it in a manner that evoked a letter of commendation from Preble as well as the admiration of the other ship-captains, some of them by no means poor seamen.

When the fighting ended with the arrival of Preble's relief, *John Adams* had her guns mounted again and was for home with a batch of time-expired seamen, a mid sent back to answer charges, a marine who had gone insane, and Commodore Preble. The ship made the circuit of the southern Mediterranean to pick up dispatches, and at Naples nearly came on tragedy during a big blow. The sheet-anchor parted, so did one of the bowers, and *John Adams* drifted in to where her prow was among the breakers. H.M.S. *Renown,* which was in the harbor, dropped an anchor and passed the cable to the American frigate, whereupon Chauncey windlassed it in and clawed his vessel clear.

It was characteristic of him to be so concerned about the failure of his anchors to hold that he delayed his departure till he had spent some time in fishing them up. He found "both broke off in the shank. They are of American Manufactory and the worst I ever saw; what prevented the Ship's going on shore, God only knows." At the turn of the century American ironwork had a well-deserved reputation for inferiority; even the 24-pounders mounted aboard the big frigates came from England and bore the royal crown. This changed gradually as the deepening of the great war made it difficult to obtain military supplies from abroad, and by 1813 American-made cannon were as good as any, but the powder was always of uncertain quality, and the shot was 7 to 10 per cent light in weight.

Chauncey's return to the States found the navy sliding into its lowest ebb, ships being laid up in favor of the miserable gunboats, and captains on half pay. The prospect revolted his methodical soul. "I see no prospect of Congress doing anything for the Navy or officers," he wrote to Preble, "therefore the sooner we can get good employ in private Ships, the better at least for those who have no fortune to depend on." He was one of the first officers to apply for a furlough to make a commercial voyage, and since he had been almost continuously at sea for five years Mr. Secretary Smith felt constrained to grant the request.

One thing first, however. Two new sloops-of-war, *Hornet* and *Wasp,* 18 each, of very original design, were just completing. They were identical as to lines, but the former was rigged as a brig and the latter as a ship. The Secretary was anxious to have them put through their paces for comparison by officers in whose seamanship he had confidence, and Mr. Chauncey was asked to do the trial cruise in *Hornet.*

She was launched out at Baltimore in July of 1805, ran down the coast to Charleston and then back up to New York, on one of the few deep-water cruises made by the navy during the second Jefferson administration. On the way, her mainmast sprung so badly it had to be replaced, being evidently too tall a stick to stand without the support of the system of cross-stays connecting to a third mast. Chauncey also reported that with her great deadrise and ballast placed low for the sake of speed, the tall masts made her something less than desirably stable; she should be made into a ship-rigged vessel. It was done, but not until 1811; quite aside from the languid pace of ship construction at the period, there was a shortage of money.

Early in 1806 Chauncey received his captaincy and his furlough, and sailed for China as master of the ship *Beaver* for the account of that notable financier and scoundrel, John Jacob Astor. The captain had a run-in with the Royal Navy at the mouth of the Whampoa, when he was dropping down with a cargo of teas, nankeens, and China ware. H.M.S. *Lion*, 64, was lying inside the bar as *Beaver* appeared. She sent a boat with an officer who required that Chauncey muster his crew for examination as to whether there were British deserters among them. The Captain refused and drove the boarding party from his quarter-deck. The Britisher shouted across to *Lion* for help; all the boats of the battleship came over with 50 armed men, who struck *Beaver's* American flag, placed guards at the hatchways, and demanded that Chauncey produce his ship's papers, with certificates proving each of his men to be an American citizen. Chauncey said he'd be damned if he did, whereupon one of the boats took him aboard *Lion*, whose captain treated the American to a flood of billingsgate and said that if proofs of their Americanism were not furnished he would impress every man of *Beaver's* crew.

Chauncey replied coldly that this was now a matter of perfect indifference to him; by the Briton's action, he had made a prize of the ship and all she contained; what happened thenceforth would be a matter for international adjudication. At this point the British captain, who had clearly gone beyond what was authorized, began to have qualms about what they would say at Whitehall. He ramped around a bit more, ground out a few oaths, and then sent Chauncey back to his ship, one of the few American captains who had found a way to keep the British from taking two or three men.

The voyage seems to have been a commercial success, but Chauncey did not repeat it, for on his return to the United States in 1807 he found waiting an appointment to the New York yard, then the most considerable in the country, a place well suited to his taste and talent for conducting administrative business. President Madison kept him at the same post until August 31, 1812, then suddenly ordered him up to Sackett's Harbor on Lake Ontario, as commander of all forces for that body of water and Erie as well.

III

It was the most important appointment in the navy at the time, covering the one area where the war could turn into really decisive triumph or defeat. Troops could be moved through the forests that swung a great arc from north of Albany to beyond Lake Superior, but only slowly and with the utmost difficulty; supplies in significant amounts could not be carried at all except by water. The fortified posts of both sides thus occupied somewhat the position of islands. There were nine such posts that had military importance. American Detroit faced British Malden at the western end of Lake Erie. At its eastern end a complex of four covered the entrance and the exit of the Niagara River—Fort Erie and Fort George on the Canadian side, Buffalo and Fort Niagara on the American. York was the British base at the western end of Lake Ontario; at the lake's eastern exit Canadian Kingston stood across from American Sackett's Harbor.

When the war began, the British had on Lake Erie a squadron consisting of a small ship, two brigs, and three 2-gun schooners. The Americans had no force on the water, and on land a set of commanders whose record of combined cowardice and incompetence has seldom been equaled and never surpassed. One of them was General William Hull, the sea-captain's uncle, a stout fellow before age rotted out his faculties. The British warships cut his supply routes across Lake Erie and forced him to retreat from before Malden to his base at Detroit; and he surrendered his whole army to about half its number of enemies. With Detroit went the whole Northwest; the American frontier was set back to a defensive line along the Wabash and Maumee rivers.

The bulk of the British forces now hurried down the Lake to make good the defense of the Niagara frontier against another fumbling attack. It was clear to Chauncey that nothing could be accomplished in that direction without some ships on Erie. He sent a draft of ocean seamen to Buffalo under a fat, vigorous lieutenant, Jesse D. Elliott, then followed him with a still better officer, Captain Oliver Hazard Perry, who had instructions to set up a base at Presqu'Ile and build there two brigs, powerful enough to win command of the lake. No more could be done before snow flew in 1812.

The Ontario situation was prevented from being as desperate as Erie's only by the fact that the British leadership was less crisp than on the upper lake. Our forces opened the war in possession of a single bluff-bowed brig, *Oneida*, 16, stoutly built, but as sluggish a sailer as ever refused to work to windward. The enemy had a ship-rigged corvette, *Royal George*, 22, a small ship-sloop, *Earl of Moira*, 14, two brigs, *Prince Regent*, 16, and *Duke of Gloucester*, 10, and a pair of schooners, *Seneca* and *Simcoe*, 8 each.

On July 19, a month after the war opened, they all came over to Sackett's to do business under a Canadian commodore named Earle. Lieutenant Melancthon Woolsey, who had *Oneida*, tried to beat out past the enemy squadron to the open lake, found his ship too dull to make it, and, returning to the harbor, moored her under a bank covering the entrance, with the guns on one side taken out and mounted ashore. The British force was sufficient to have eaten the brig alive, with Sackett's Harbor for dessert, for the place was defended only by a "battery" mounting a single gun and a handful of militia, whose training consisted of a keg-party once every three months. But the enemy force was only a kind of Canadian naval militia, as wanting in training or discipline as the troops on the American side. They paraded their ships past *Oneida* at long range, firing irregularly and wild. At the end of two hours they had hit nothing, but had lost a few spars and suffered a few casualties from the return fire, so Commodore Earle decided it was a poor day for conquests and went home to Kingston.

Chauncey learned of this ridiculous passage from the dispatches before he went north. There was a promise of feeble opposition in it, but he was realist enough to know that the British would never let things rest on such a basis, and businessman enough to be aware that the problem of both sides was essentially the same—that of creating a navy from the ground up. In this contest all the advantages lay with the enemy. They had a fleet in being; his was to build. They had direct water transportation for such heavy items as cannon and cables up the St. Lawrence, while his own stores must come by the Hudson and Mohawk rivers to Lake Oneida, and thence down to Oswego. The route contained toilsome portages, could not be used at all during the winter, and w?s generally so bad that the elapsed time from London to Kingston was actually less than that from New York to Sackett's. If the British had command of the lake, they could gobble up supply convoys during the journey from Oswego to the American base.

The only possible solution must be sought in better organization and in details more accurately and energetically carried through. Chauncey accordingly remained in New York for the time, building up his background: arranging for the purchase and transit of the necessary stores and for the recruiting of seamen, ship carpenters, mechanics. Cordage he foresaw as one of the big difficulties; he hired workmen and sent them at once to Sackett's to establish a ropewalk on the ground. The necessary people for setting up a hospital went at the same time; and also those for establishing a naval school, since in a moment of prescience Chauncey perceived he would have to take many untrained men. A hundred officers and sailors were on their way by September 18, taking with them supplies of guns, shot, and dry provisions; almost as many ship carpenters had already left New York by that date.

In the meanwhile, Lieutenant Woolsey was ordered to examine some of the commercial lake schooners and purchase as many as he thought worth the trouble of converting into warships. These schooners were a poor proposition—shallow-draft vessels of 50 to 90 tons, quite without bulwarks or quarters, and having a great deal of sail area in proportion to their size. They would be distinctly unsteady in a breeze with the heavy topweight of guns on their decks, but they would have to do until better warships could be provided. The need was for hurry; for getting some gun power afloat that would cover the passage of convoys from Oswego to Sackett's during the crucial weeks before winter closed navigation.

As superintendent of construction, Chauncey chose and sent on at once a Brooklyn shipbuilder, Mr. Henry Eckford. After an apprenticeship in Quebec, this gentleman had set up his business on the shores of New York Harbor to take advantage of the abundant American timber, which made it possible to build ships in this country at little over half the price per ton required for construction in England.

Isaac Chauncey

This Eckford had no such radical theories of hull design as the great Humphreys of Philadelphia, but had become quite well known as a constructor through his refinements of details. His ships were noted for strength and speed; when a new vessel of his construction returned from her first voyage, he questioned the captain closely about her performance under all circumstances, and not infrequently took her into dock for alteration at his own charges. This repeated process had led him to cut down considerably on stern framing and deadwood aft in ships. A sound man, who could be trusted to allow in his designs for green timber, rapid building, and the peculiarities of lake navigation—which made it unnecessary to carry water, for example, but required ships of shallow draft which could move well in light airs. By the time Chauncey reached the base in person, Eckford had laid down a ship-rigged corvette to mount 24 guns and a fast dispatch-schooner, besides sending on designs for Perry's two brigs on Lake Erie.

Chauncey came on October 6, to find that Woolsey had taken six schooners into service, and Eckford had armed each with a long 24 or 32 on a circle in the center of the deck, the larger of the schooners having up to six 6-pounders along their sides in addition. The two of the latter class were named *Hamilton* and *Governor Tompkins*; the remainder were *Julia, Growler, Conquest,* and *Pert,* most of which carried a 12-pounder in addition to the big gun.

Some vagueness about the armament of these vessels is unavoidable, since it is next to impossible to say how any one of them was armed at a given time. All were subject to a continuing process of change in the quite futile effort to give them better sea-keeping qualities. No accurate record of the changes was kept. The one big gun per ship remained a general rule.

With his pennant flying in *Oneida,* Chauncey put out at the head of these vessels on November 8 and steered for the north shore, where the British squadron had been covering various movements of transport. *Royal George* was sighted by *Oneida,* then alone, off the False Duck Islands. In spite of being more than double the American brig's force, the Canadian fled. Chauncey missed her in the night, but caught sight of her again early in the morning, beating up toward Kingston, and considered that since she was handled with so little stomach for combat, it would be worth while going in to board her whenever she anchored.

On the next day, then, he took the squadron into Kingston Bay, *Conquest* leading, followed by *Julia, Pert,* and *Growler,* with the flagship last, since she was armed only with short-range carronades and needed the cover of the schooners' long guns through the gauntlet of the batteries at the entrance. *Pert's* big gun blew up and put her out of action, but the other schooners smothered the fire from ashore; *Oneida* slid past and opened on *Royal George* so effectively that after 20 minutes of it the latter cut her cables, ran upstream, and tied herself to a dock. Most of her people scrambled ashore in a panic, but so large a body of troops gathered that any attempt to carry her by boarding was clearly out of the question.

Chauncey hauled off for the night, with the intention of adding *Hamilton* and *Governor Tompkins* to his line and going in for a gunnery attack the next day. But dawn brought a gale of wind, followed by another and another, in such rapid succession that nothing could be done but blockade the port until the end of the month, when gathering ice would bring navigation of the lake to a close. Just before movement became impossible, Eckford got his 24-gun corvette into the water and christened her *Madison.* Four more schooners had been made into warships by this time—*Fair American, Asp, Ontario,* and *Scourge,* the last a Canadian provincial vessel which *Oneida* ran down and captured on the lake under the name of *Lord Nelson*, a fairly considerable craft able to carry a long 32 and eight 12-pounder carronades.

It was a hard winter at Sackett's Harbor; the inadequately sheltered people were racked by typhoid and pneumonia and many of them died. Heavy snows cut off communication with Albany; builders' supplies did not come through, food was short, and there was word that the British were preparing a powerful effort to win command of the lake.

Isaac Chauncey

IV

The word was true enough. H.M. Government had sent out a soldier of some experience, Sir George Prevost, to take command in Canada, with a contingent of regular troops. On the naval side, four captains, eight lieutenants, 24 midshipmen, and 450 hand-picked regular seamen came to take over from the undisciplined Canadians. At their head was Captain Sir James Lucas Yeo, an officer who had made a good record in amphibious warfare under outré conditions. He had led the Portuguese expedition from the Brazils which captured Cayenne. During the winter he fortified the entrance to Kingston harbor and laid down a couple of schooners, a brig, and a 24-gun corvette; another corvette of the same force was begun at York.

Detailed news of this reached Chauncey and Eckford after the turn of the year. They brought up a new gang of shipwrights by sleigh through the snows of February. As soon as it became possible to cut timber in early April, Eckford laid the keel of a powerful small frigate, *General Pike,* to mount 28 guns, all of them long 24s, the same as those in the main batteries of the ocean-going 44-gun frigates. Two of these were mounted on circles, quarterdeck and forecastle, a design feature dreamed up by Eckford which was to bear abundant fruit.

As spring approached there was a good deal of strategic discussion among army and navy heads. *Madison* was so forwardly in her construction that the American fleet would have command of the lake at the break of spring, and would hold that command until the British completed their new corvettes. A waterborne offensive to kill one of these dragons before it hatched was indicated, and Washington suggested it should go to Kingston. But General Dearborn, who commanded the small army gathering at Sackett's, thought the defenses there too heavy for him, opting instead for a descent on York, to be followed by the clearing of the Niagara frontier.

The plan was approved; in the last days of April, the squadron sailed, with 1700 troops and some ship carpenters to complete the British 24 after she should be taken. On April 27 the fleet reached York. Here the schooners proved very useful, since they could work inshore, where *Madison* and *Oneida* could not, replying to the British shore batteries with their heavy guns, while their light artillery deluged the flank of the British-Canadian line ashore with showers of grape; Chauncey pulled among the ships in his gig, directing the debarkation in person.

The attack had come as a strategic surprise; the defenders were three times outnumbered and much shaken by artillery fire from the ships. As General Zebulon Pike went storming in on them with the bayonet, they broke. York town surrendered together with *Duke of Gloucester,* 10, which was lying at a dock, but during the fighting the British had gained enough time to put their unfinished corvette to the torch. In the last moments of the battle a big magazine blew up, killing General Pike with 52 other American soldiers and wounding 180.

The general situation was now this: one of the British corvettes had been disposed of, but the other (named *Wolfe*) had her lower masts in. With *Royal George* and the smaller vessels, she would give the British incontestable superiority until the completion of *General Pike* some time during the summer, so that whatever was done must be done quickly. After a week during which the American squadron was held at York by contrary winds, Dearborn's army was carried to an encampment at Fort Niagara. Supplies and reinforcements were brought forward from Sackett's and on May 27 an attack was launched against Fort George. *Growler, Julia,* and *Ontario* fired on a battery near the mouth of the river; *Governor Tompkins* and *Conquest* attacked a fort that covered the best available landing beach, drove the British from their guns, and covered the assault wave, which was led by Colonel Winfield Scott and Captain Oliver Hazard Perry, who had come on from Lake Erie.

The loss of the beachhead took all the fight out of the British, who had faced General Dearborn's 4,500 men with only 1,000 and had lost a quarter of these, chiefly to the fire of the well-handled schooners. With the rest of the Niagara frontier Fort Erie fell—a key event in the chain that decided the fate of the Northwest, for the guns of Fort Erie held penned in Buffalo five schooners Perry had equipped for war. Now they were free; they sailed for Presqu'Ile and furnished the gunnery cover under which Perry was able to lift his two brigs across the bar to the lake, a task that had to be performed with the ships' guns out.

In the meanwhile, Commodore Yeo had completed his *Wolfe* earlier than the Americans expected. On the very May 27 that saw Scott winning the Niagara frontier, he embarked Sir George Prevost and 800 British regulars for Sackett's Harbor, where the British commander counted on destroying the base and *General Pike,* which was not yet launched. The landing was made on the 29th, on a long spit west of the town; 400 militia who attempted to dispute it were dispersed into the woods by the first fire, and the British came washing up against the stockade which defended the place. There were but 400 Americans inside, many of them convalescent sick. British ships were firing into their flank, and the case looked so evil that the officer in charge of the American storehouses ordered them fired.

Here it was touch and go with the whole campaign, the American fleet likely to be cut from its base in the face of a far superior British squadron. But Sir George Prevost was in the presence of a master spirit. Just as the British were closing on the stockade, there emerged from the woods on their flank one of the greatest soldiers of American history—Jacob Brown, the sanguinary Quaker, leading the runaway militia, whom he had rallied to such a fever of fighting as no man had seen in militia before. They flung themselves upon the enemy with the bayonet; Prevost was driven to his boats, with a third of his men casualties.

Chauncey was lying at the mouth of the Niagara when he learned that Yeo was on the lake with *Wolfe*; he had no choice but to slip back in to Sackett's and await the completion of his frigate. Yeo followed him up, seized some small vessels along the southern shore, and hurried to the St. Lawrence, where there was being prepared the tragically burlesque invasion of Canada by General James Wilkinson. It is not likely that any movement led by that scoundrel, poltroon, and traitor would have been a success, but the British fleet helped greatly in producing the ultimate failure by capturing many of Wilkinson's supplies on the water and operating a gunboat flotilla in the stream.

June went by in that way; July saw little cruising by either side, but on the 21st of that month Chauncey had *General Pike* ready and put out, again turning toward the Niagara. There Colonel Scott was embarked with some troops to complete the work of destroying York as a base, the army still considering Kingston beyond its resources. The defense was no better than before; Scott captured some stores and ammunition, burned the barracks and building facilities, and was taken back to Fort Niagara. Anchored there, the American fleet for the first time sighted their opponents in open lake, coming down from the westsouthwest on August 7.

The composition of the two squadrons now stood so: Chauncey had *General Pike*, 28, *Madison*, 24, *Oneida*, 16, with the schooners *Hamilton*, 10, *Scourge*, 9, *Governor Tompkins*, 8, *Julia, Growler, Ontario,* and *Fair American*, 2 each, *Pert* and *Asp*, 1 each. Under Yeo's flag were *Wolfe*, 24, *Royal George*, 22, *Melville*, brig, 14, *Earl of Moira*, brig, 14, *Sidney Smith*, schooner, 12, and *Beresford*, schooner, 8.* Ninety-two British guns to 112 American; 1,374 pounds weight of metal in the British broadsides, 1,390 in Chauncey's.

This is not far from an even match on the face of it; but there were several factors that made the two fleets so little like each other as to be in fact incomparable. To begin with, *Pike's* long 24s made her a match for the two biggest ships together at long range; but at close quarters they could bring 68-pound carronades into play, and things would be changed. The heavy guns of the American schooners were also formidable at a distance, but their smaller pieces were only 6-pounders and no sort of use in a fleet action. More: the American schooners had no bulwarks and therefore very little resistance to shot, and they were so unsteady they could not fire their guns in a wind. In anything but the lightest airs they were intolerably slow; and *Oneida* was such a slug that she did much of her cruising at the end of a tow-line from *Madison*. The British ships were all built as men o' war; could cruise and fight as a unit in any weather.

That is, Chauncey wanted to engage at long range in a light breeze, or, failing that, to take formation and make the British run down

---

* What happened to *Prince Regent*, 16, of the previous year's squadron is not clear. She may be the same as *Melville*; the British records, like the American, were badly kept.

to close him through a belt of fire. Yeo wanted to fight in blowing weather; or so to maneuver as to reach close quarters before the Americans could use their long guns effectively. Neither was the sort of man who would sacrifice an advantage for the mere sake of having a nice little battle. Therefore all the day of the 7th was spent in maneuvers, each commander seeking an opportunity to pounce, and not a gun was fired. During the night a heavy squall struck both squadrons; the two largest American schooners, *Hamilton* and *Scourge,* capsized, carrying down all but 16 of their combined crews, a great encouragement to the men in the other vessels of the same type.

The accident brought the American fleet down to as much of an inferiority as it had previously enjoyed superiority in weight of metal, but it did nothing whatever to spoil the taste of either commander for interesting but resultless maneuver. All through the 8th, 9th, and 10th the squadrons jigged slowly past each other out of range, through variable winds. Each commodore closed the day by writing a report which demonstrated how the other had run away from him.

Toward sunset of the fourth day of paradings, when they were fairly near each other, a shift of wind gave the weather-gauge to the British. Yeo's fleet was in a single line at the time, with his two biggest ships leading. Chauncey had formed two lines, the weatherly one consisting of *Julia, Growler, Pert, Asp, Ontario,* and *Fair American;* the leeward containing *Pike, Oneida, Madison, Governor Tompkins,* and *Conquest.* The courses were slightly converging. Chauncey's thought was that his outer line of schooners would draw the enemy down; his orders were that they were to engage until the enemy reached carronade range, then bear away through the line of heavier ships.

The British held on their course, and at 11 in the evening, under a big round moon, began exchanging fires with the weather line of American schooners. A few spars came down; at half past the hour, things had become so warm that it was time for the schooners to bear away, but Sailing Master James Trant of *Julia* and Lieutenant David Deacon of *Growler* thought they knew a trick worth two of that. Instead of running free, they tacked sharp up, with some idea of getting round the head of the British line and doubling on it. They reached the desired position all right, but at the same moment Chauncey, in a burst of inspiration, decided to get more out of his long guns by bearing away two points to open the range.

Sir James, to whom two birds in the hand seemed worth more than any number in the bush, promptly tacked with all ships in the opposite direction, cutting off *Julia* and *Growler*. The main American squadron was left far down-wind; the two schooners clawed desperately to windward, but soon found themselves with the northern shore of the lake, the enemy's coast, close aboard. Now they turned and tried to run back through the line of pursuers; were fired into, crippled, and forced to strike. Yeo furnished a commentary on their quality as warships by refusing to have them in his squadron, sending them to the St. Lawrence to act as armed transports; and Chauncey, having lost four of his ships and being almost out of provision, retreated to the Niagara and then to Sackett's.

There he picked up a reinforcement in the new schooner *Sylph,* built by Eckford for the special purpose of whittling the group speed of the British squadron down to a point where they would be forced to accept action on American terms. She was very fast and weatherly, armed with six 6-pounders along her bulwarks, but—more important —with four long 32s on circles between her masts, with which heavy pieces it was hoped that she could knock a mast out of one of the British vessels, forcing Yeo either to fight or to leave an important ship behind. Now the squadron put out again; Yeo and his ships were not discovered until September 11, off the mouth of the Genesee River, in winds so light as to be only a little beyond a flat calm. This was so clearly Chauncey weather that the British stretched away out of action across the lake, and there was only a little shooting at long range. No damage on the American side; the British took a few casualties and had one of their brigs badly holed on the waterline before escaping into Kingston Harbor.

Chauncey left them there while he escorted the troops from the Niagara down to Sackett's for the Wilkinson invasion. This took two weeks, during which first the rumor and then the definite news of Perry's dazzling victory on Lake Erie drifted in—an entire British fleet wiped out, for the first time in history. Could it be done again?

Perhaps; the news was that Yeo had sailed up the lake to York, where there was no defense for the anchorage, and Chauncey raised all sail in pursuit.

On September 28 the enemy were in sight, inshore and to the west, while the wind was easterly, giving Chauncey the weather-gauge. The breeze was strong enough to favor Britain, but the American Commodore had now hit on the device of having his schooners towed by the larger ships in such airs. *General Pike* led his line, with *Asp* in tow; well behind was *Madison,* towing *Conquest*; then *Sylph* with another schooner, and *Oneida,* towing herself as best she could. *Governor Tompkins,* the fastest of the schooners and the best handled, occupied the place between *Pike* and *Madison.*

The British were formed on the port tack, heavy ships ahead. Chauncey did not try to parallel them, but bore straight for the center of their line, closing so rapidly that Yeo began to fear his lighter vessels would be cut off, and tacked round in succession to cover them. This brought his flagship *Wolfe* into gunnery range of *General Pike, Asp,* and *Tompkins*; and now, though the squadrons were passing on opposite courses, at last, at long last, the broadsides of fighting ships flashed and rumbled across the clean surface of the lake.

Not many had been fired when Yeo discovered that the competition against the accurately served long 24s of *Pike* and *Tompkins* was more than his corvette could bear. Death strode along *Wolfe's* decks; down came her main-topmast, her mizzen-topmast and mainyard, and the British commander was forced to crowd on every sail his forward spars would bear and fly madly down through the rest of the fleet. *Royal George,* under Captain William Mulcaster, the best seaman the enemy had, luffed up valorously to cover his Commodore's retreat, but his ship was no match for the American frigate and was driven away with her fore-topmast down and a fifth of her crew casualties. *Madison* came into action and gave *Melville* more than she could stand; they all fled.

Now was Chauncey's great chance, a pursuing action against an enemy already badly hurt and retreating in disorder. But he obstinately refused to part company with his schooners, keeping them in tow of the bigger ships which slowed all down and let the British escape

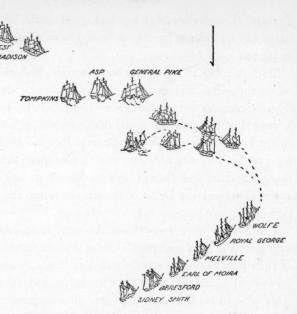

"The Burlington Races"
The British approach (below); *Wolfe* beaten out of line;
Royal George tries to cover her; the British fleet in
confusion.

into Burlington Bay—from which the engagement is known not as a battle but as "the Burlington Races."

There was still opportunity to wreck the British, for Burlington Bay is an open roadstead, and Chauncey had before him a crippled enemy, whose gunnery had proved inferior to that of his own, in both weight and accuracy. He chose rather to haul up for the Niagara, on the grounds that *General Pike's* spars were wounded and one of her bow-chasers had blown up; that the wind was rising and might throw both fleets on shore; that *Oneida's* guns were so crowded together that she was no use as a chasing ship—with various other reasons of a similar order. By next day the chance had vanished, for a gale began, and when it had blown itself out Yeo slipped past Chauncey's long-range blockade. The American pursued toward Kingston; missed the enemy's fighting fleet, but off the False Ducks came upon seven of his schooner-gunboats, carrying a regiment of troops. One of these was burned and five taken, two of them being *Julia* and *Growler*. Yeo remained in harbor till navigation closed.

v

Thus the Lake Ontario campaign of 1813 ended on a note of mutual melancholy. During the winter Wilkinson's invasion failed. All the regular troops had been pulled out of the Niagara frontier to maintain it, leaving in charge a silly officer of militia named McClure, who evacuated Forts George and Niagara at the Ontario end of the lake. For his pains he was driven into the woods by some British bands and Buffalo was burned behind him. Thus all the gains of the year were lost, save those won by Perry on Lake Erie; and now both sides settled down to gain a clear mastery of Lake Ontario in 1814.

On the American side all the purchased schooners were retired to transport duty. Two famous shipbuilders of New York, Adam and Noah Brown, came on from Lake Erie, where they had built the ships for Perry's victory. They were not Eckford's equals as designers, but the efficiency of their methods, their ability to handle work-gangs, contributed much. A two-decked frigate of 50 was laid down and named *Superior,* as well as two heavy brigs, *Jefferson* and *Jones,* 22s.

Early in March some British deserters came in, bearing word that the new enemy ship, of which there had been some rumor earlier, would be a 56, mounting long 24-pounders on the main deck, and that she would have a 40-gun companion, while a vessel much larger than either was being laid down. This was frightening, for not a gun or a cable of all those ordered from New York had yet reached Albany—nor would, until April. Seamen were desperately hard to come by for the thankless service of the lakes, where there was so little chance of prize-money and so much of being struck down by fevers. The conditions in the Sackett's Harbor camp were almost incredible: no shelter but huts built of branches, no heat but fires of green wood, no sanitation at all, and the food so monotonous a procession of salt beef, salt pork, and dried peas that scurvy was added to the other diseases.

Moreover, the news from Kingston was even short of the truth. Napoleon was tottering to his fall in Europe, and Britain was pouring a flood of troops, sailors, shipbuilders, and supplies into Canada for the grand strategic plan of cutting off northern New York and isolating New England during 1814, the British Cabinet having some expectation of erecting the latter territory into an independent republic, supported by their bayonets. Their Ontario fleet was completely reorganized, supplied with more men; most of the ships were rearmed and, as a measure of deception, all of them were renamed. Thus *Wolfe* became *Montreal,* receiving a battery of twenty-five long 18s and 24s instead of her carronades; *Royal George,* 22, was called *Niagara; Melville, Earl of Moira,* and *Beresford* all became 16-gun brigs, under the names *Cherwell, Star,* and *Netley. Sidney Smith* received 14 guns and the name *Magnet.* The new big ships were *Princess Charlotte,* 42, and *Prince Regent,* 56; they led the fleet out of Kingston on May 3.

Superior had been launched only the day before, after the indefatigable Eckford put down a strike of mechanics and lengthened and strengthened her to be a 58, with long 32s on the main deck. He instantly laid down a 42 on her blocks, the ship that was to be the frigate *Mohawk,* Captain Jacob Jones commanding. In the incredible time of 34 days she was sliding into the water.

Meanwhile Yeo was trying to use his control of the lake. He took Oswego in an amphibious operation on May 5, the poor old *Julia* and *Growler* being scuttled in the harbor. The operation did not pay very well; the British lost 95 men, had *Montreal* a good deal cut up by shore batteries, and captured only insignificant quantities of stores. But now they came back to place Sackett's Harbor under strict blockade, and this was serious; light guns could be carried to the American base through the woods, but not the heavy pieces for *Superior* and *Mohawk,* nor their great anchor cables, 22 inches in diameter. Chauncey entrusted the task of getting the stores in to Melancthon Woolsey, now a captain. He organized a system of carrying the goods along the shore by night in convoys of bateaux as far as Stony Creek, then up that stream to a point three miles from the harbor, from which point on land transportation was practicable.

This led to a brush on May 29, when a convoy of 19 barges was surprised by daylight off Big Sandy Creek. Woolsey ran into the stream, but one of his bateaux got lost, was taken by the British, and gave news of where the convoy was. Yeo placed 180 of his people in the ships' longboats, armed them with light carronades, and sent them into the creek to gobble up the convoy under a couple of captains named Popham and Spilsbury. Popham had been the hero of a gallant cutting-out expedition on the French coast, with far fewer men, and refused reinforcement, thinking this affair would be a lark. He deceived himself; Woolsey had scouted his approach, and as the British seamen pulled up the creek, with Marines marching along both banks, they were suddenly hit with deadly rifle fire from cover, and found themselves surrounded; 14 were killed, 28 wounded, and all the rest captured.

By June 6 *Superior* had her yards crossed and her sails bent on. Yeo raised his blockade, though the last guns for the big ship did not arrive until two days later, and *Mohawk* still lacked her rigging and most of her crew. The latter arrived before the end of the month; so did the first of a series of letters from General Jacob Brown, who had been placed in command of the Niagara frontier. He was having hard work holding on against the British, who had been strongly reinforced in that quarter while Yeo held the lake. Brown crossed from Buffalo through Fort Erie and won a brilliant victory at Chippewa on July 4.

Now he wanted supplies and reinforcements from Sackett's, but above all the presence of the fleet to keep the enemy from bringing in men by the water route from York to Forts George and Niagara. On July 13 he wrote:

"I do not doubt my ability to meet the enemy in the field and to march in any direction over his country, your fleet carrying for me the necessary supplies. We can threaten Forts George and Niagara, and carry Burlington Heights and York, and proceed to Kingston and carry that place. All accounts represent the force of the enemy at Kingston as very little. Sir James will not fight. For God's sake, let me see you. I have looked for your fleet with the greatest anxiety since the 10th."

And where was Chauncey when this appeal came through? Chauncey was in bed. He had come down with an attack of a fever of unspecified nature, was doubtless ridden by the thought that he had missed greatness at the Burlington Races, and was now determined to have every nail in place when he met the enemy again—now that he had a fleet which could match the enemy for speed and in gunpower excelled it. Brown's urgings, presently reinforced by others from Washington, added to the irritability of a sick man and that over the lost opportunity of the previous September. To General Brown he replied with peevishness, to the government with excuses; after a long silence, he is writing to the Secretary of the Navy: "The squadron has been prevented being earlier fitted for sea in consequence of the delay in obtaining blocks and ironwork."

Not until July 31 did he hoist sail, and then made only one short circuit of the upper lake, in the course of which he caught and destroyed *Cherwell,* 16; then he sailed back to blockade Kingston. He was too late and in the wrong place; on the very day of his flimsy letter of excuse to Washington, Brown had fought and won the terrific battle of Lundy's Lane, the hardest in American history; then had been forced by reinforcement from York, which Chauncey could have prevented, to retreat to Fort Erie. Now he was under siege there.

President Madison had always thought highly of Chauncey; he recommended to Congress that the supreme commander of the lakes receive part of the honors for the victory on Erie. But now his patience gave way; he ordered Decatur to take the command, and it may be considered a pity that the order was canceled on the news that Chauncey had sailed.

The Commodore remained unimpressed and cantankerous. From before Kingston, where Yeo was looking through his spyglass and commenting on the portly figure of the officer at *Superior's* gangway, he wrote his doctrine of sea power to Brown:

"That you might find the fleet somewhat of a convenience in the transportation of provisions and stores for the use of the army and an agreeable appendage to attend its marching and countermarching, I am ready to believe; but Sir, the Secretary of the Navy has honored me with a high destiny; we intend to seek and fight the enemy's fleet. This is the great purpose of the government in creating this fleet and I shall not be diverted in my efforts to effectuate it by any sinister attempt to render it subordinate to the army."

So this campaign also ended in black disappointment, though later in August *Jefferson, Sylph,* and *Oneida* were sent to the Niagara, where they put down a blockade which caused the British siege of Fort Erie to abort—with the help of some more hard fighting by the inextinguishable Brown.

Yeo is reported as being much annoyed at not being allowed to go out and demonstrate that he was a fighting leader, and the retreat at the Burlington Races had been an unavoidable accident. Perhaps; but he never showed any disagreement with the orders that came after the British disaster on Lake Erie forbidding him to engage superior forces. (The proportion in August was 5 to 6 in weight of metal.) Moreover it was exactly his game to accept blockade in order to keep Chauncey idly busy for a couple of months, since Yeo held the key of the situation in his new three-decker line-of-battleship, *St. Lawrence,* 100, now approaching completion. When she was ready in October, the British put out and it was Chauncey's turn to be shut in harbor—another step in a process that might have gone a long way, for by this time Eckford was nearly ready with *New Orleans,* 110, and frames were rising on *Plattsburg,* 58, and a still greater monster, *Chippewa,* 130.

VI

After the war Henry Eckford returned to his business with a greatly enhanced reputation, and later he was appointed to design the *Ohio* class of 80-gun battleships, the most successful the United States ever had. The Humphreys model ships of the *Independence* type might have been all right with their original armament of 32-pounders throughout —long guns on the orlop and main decks, carronades aloft—but captains were then permitted to change the armament of their ships, and the American captains, heavy-gun men ever, put 42-pounder longs on the orlop decks of their liners. This brought the port-sills down to within three feet of the waterline, too far; and the ships rolled badly from not having enough displacement to carry such a weight. Eckford allowed for the habit, and produced a vessel which carried her guns high, sailed well, and was so solidly built that she lasted for forty years.

He died in Turkey in 1832, a result of one of the most extraordinary treaties in history. The Ottoman Porte, in return for a general trade agreement with the United States, demanded that a first-class naval constructor be sent over to build the Sultan a fleet, and Eckford was chosen.

Chauncey was sent to command the Portsmouth Navy Yard after the war, and in 1816 he was Commodore Mediterranean. Things rather got out of hand with him there, and it was his last sea command. All the rest of his life, until 1840, was spent either as head of the New York yard or on the board of Naval Commissioners. He did the administrative jobs superbly, as always; was much seen in society, pompous, greatly respected, and supposed to be the original of Old Grimes in the well-known poem by Greene.

The respect was due, for his services on Ontario were considerable. With much inferior resources he and Eckford and the Browns built up the great triumph on Erie, and on their own lake achieved something better than a draw, since they held command of the water for the greater period, inflicted the greater loss, and accomplished whatever was undertaken in a strategic sense. It was all done by orderliness, hard work, close attention to human relations, and precision in handling detail.

But this was not the method by which the rest of Preble's boys attained their results, nor were the results of the kind attained by the rest of Preble's boys. The question is what was the matter with Chauncey? Why did he not drive in at Burlington? In 1759, in an exactly similar situation, Sir Edward Hawke took his fleet by storm and night in among the shoals of Quiberon Bay and crushed the French. Why did not Chauncey adopt Brown's strategy of using the fleet in support of the army?

The point is probably that he was too good a businessman to be a good fighting man. Not that he shrank from wounds and death; his personal conduct was always gallant, most especially in the landing at York. But he was a builder, to whom a ship was a beautiful object, which he hated to see destroyed or even damaged, as *General Pike* was at the Burlington Races. That this damage was relative, that he had hurt the enemy more than himself, that if he pressed on he might destroy them all—these were considerations foreign to his mind.

That is, he wished to produce the defeat of the enemy without material loss to his own side. He was not with Preble when the old commodore said "I expect we may suffer much" but signified his intention of going in against the forts of Tripoli anyway. In fact, when Chauncey reached the Mediterranean, it was already clear that *Constitution* was not going to suffer much from the type of gunnery the Moors put out. Chauncey was a builder; but this still does not answer the question why he, who had the opportunity to be the most thoroughly Preble of all Preble's boys, who indeed invented the phrase, should have adopted so extraordinary a view of strategy as that set forth in the letter to Brown.

The part of the question about the letter is the easiest to answer. Chauncey certainly enunciated sound naval doctrine when he said that the objective of the forces afloat was to seek out and destroy those of the enemy. What he failed to consider was the purpose of this destruction. Absolute sea power is not an end in itself, but a means to the end of transmitting goods, troops, every form of military force, to a point where it can be brought to bear on areas vital to the enemy.

In the case of the Lake Ontario campaign, this is peculiarly sharpened by Jacob Brown's clearer view. Napoleon tried to eliminate the Royal Navy from his vast combination by closing the ports of the continent to England's commercial shipping; he left to the arrogant islanders nothing but the ports of a world. But Lake Ontario was a little world in itself. Had Brown been able to carry through the project of a waterborne descent on Kingston, there would have been quite literally no place for Yeo's ships to go. They must come out and fight, at whatever cost. In fact, they must come out and fight to beat off the landing, as the Japanese navy, 132 years later, was forced to fight disastrous naval battles in the effort to prevent the landings on Saipan and Leyte.

That is, Chauncey's principle was correct, but limited. He failed to look beyond objective toward purpose; he had too narrow a mind. This is a defect that not infrequently goes with the very qualities he displayed—the capacity for businesslike administration, for effective handling of detail, for getting things done. The man who can describe every tree rarely has a good eye for the wood. The only surprising thing is that the contact with Preble did not give to Chauncey, as it did to others, a different and wider set of views. There is perhaps no wholly satisfactory answer to this Why, save in some unresolved mystery of human personality.

Yet one can suggest that the ideas, the doctrines, that Hull, Bainbridge, Decatur, required for the completion of their mental equipment as naval officers were relatively simple. In Chauncey's case, the need was for a high concept of strategy that no one had yet formulated. No one would really think the thing through and spell it out until the days of Mahan. Preble acted as though he knew all about the doctrine of sea power, but there is no record of his having spoken on the subject, and for his pupils it was a matter of deduction.

Well, Isaac Chauncey did not make the deduction and so missed his chance. It is not too much to say that if he had been as truly one of Preble's boys as the rest, the Burlington Races would have been the Battle of Lake Ontario, and the war could have been ended in 1813 by a series of victories on the northern frontier that would have placed the British cause there beyond redemption. As it was, Perry's battle for a time remained an isolated and far-away accident, and the year as a whole was one of American disasters, which convinced the British they could beat the young republic into a humbling peace. They had taken one of "those damned frigates" and the rest were sealed in port by a blockade more tightly maintained than that against the Empire of Europe. The privateers were on the wane, and with Russia and Austria hammering at the gates of Paris, British armies could follow British sea power to conquer any part of America they chose.

Chapter 8

The Turbulent Yankee:
David Porter

> The saucy Essex, she sail'd out,
>   To see what she could do;
> Her captain is from Yankey land,
>   And so are all his crew.
>
> Away she sail'd, so gay and trim
>   Down to the Gallipagos
> And toted all the terrapins,
>   And nabb'd the slipp'ry whalers.
>
> Then sail'd about the ocean wide,
>   Sinking, burning, taking,
> Filling pocket, spilling oil,
>   While John Bull's heart was aching.
>
>   —A Pleasant New Song from the Analectic

H E WAS REALLY ONLY TECHNICALLY A YANKEE, THOUGH BORN IN Boston of New England stock in 1780. His father, also David, was then sailing out of the port in command of a Massachusetts State ship; but from the age of three the boy was brought up in Baltimore or at sea.

The reason for this was that a grateful government recognized the services of the elder Porter by placing him in charge of a signal station on the Chesapeake, and he moved his family down in the expectation that the employment would be permanent. When it turned out to be both too inactive and insufficiently rewarding for a seafaring man with a family of six children, there was an appointment to the revenue cutter service, still with Baltimore as the home port. Young David Porter thus grew up in an atmosphere where pulses beat rather more quickly than in his native city; the background that produced Decatur rather than that of Hull and Chauncey. The only recorded remark from his boyhood illustrates the point: "If a man tread on my toes, I will retaliate upon him ninety-nine fold!"

There might have been some difficulty about this on occasion, for David Porter was a pale youth, undersized and sickly, whose mother wished to keep him at home. She was up against the sea-tales of her husband, famous even in Baltimore as a spinner of yarns, and the fact—well known to everyone in the period—that a long·sea voyage was sovereign against every malady from constipation to consumption. At sixteen young David was allowed to ship on the merchant schooner *Eliza* for a voyage to the sugar ports of the West Indies, his father having left the revenue service to be her skipper.

The adventures that were to accompany everything David Porter did throughout his life began at Jérémie in Santo Domingo. There was a British warship in port which, after the manner of British warships in 1796, needed men and sent a press-gang to pick up a couple from the American. Captain David Porter, Sr., met them at the gangway with weapons and there was a stiff, bloody fight, in which a sailor was shot at Porter's side before the attackers were beaten off.

Why the British did not come back with more men, and how *Eliza* escaped the harbor, are matters of mystery; not even the son of David Porter, Jr., who wrote his father's biography, has anything to say on the subject. Nor is the detail on Porter's next adventure much better. He was out of his father's ship by this time, first officer (though so very young) of a small brig, which put in at one of the ports of Santo Domingo, where she was boarded by a boat from an English frigate, on the usual errand.

Instead of taking one or two men, however, this British captain carried the brig's whole crew aboard his ship, including Porter, and ordered them into irons until they should accept enlistment in the Royal Navy. They refused to a man; the Captain ordered them to the gangway to be flogged for "the bad example set the crew of His Majesty's ship."

David Porter

This procedure apparently aroused the British sense of fair play among some of the man-o'-war's crew. A word was whispered to Porter, he wrenched out of his captors' hands and hid somewhere below, where a "search" failed to find him. The British captain may have suspected what was up, but remarked that the rat would come out of his hole when he got hungry enough. However, he was not quite ready to hoist anchor; during the night young Porter slipped through a port-hole and swam under water to a Danish brig, whose deck he reached by climbing a cable. The Dane took care of him and at her home port of Copenhagen transferred him to a vessel bound for America. But now Porter had neither money nor clothes of his own, and had to work his way as a common seaman through one of the bitterest winters the Atlantic had seen, with spray freezing on the ropes.

He made at least one more West Indian voyage after this, and the son's memoir says that Porter was actually impressed into a British ship for a time, but without giving any details either of the impressment or of the escape that must have been made, for Porter certainly spent no great period in a British ship. The next really fixed date is December of 1798, when the elder Porter announces that he has placed his son as a midshipman aboard U.S.S. *Constellation,* 38, then just in from a cruise on convoy duty, and about to go out to the West Indies. The captain of that ship was Thomas Truxtun, the disciplinarian and schoolmaster of the early navy, and one of the few men in it who did not adopt British practice as the all-sufficient rule, but set up his own system. It seems to have been rather a rough one at times; one day when young Porter was at the Captain's table in response to an order that "the midshipmen will dine with me in rotation at 1/4 past 2," the lad complained of his hard treatment and avowed his intention of quitting the service. Truxtun's face went red.

"Why, you young dog!" he cried. "If I can help it you shall never leave the navy! Swear at you? Damn it, sir—every time I do that up you go a round on the ladder of promotion! As for the first lieutenant's blowing you up every day, why, sir, 'tis because he loves you and would not have you grow up a conceited young coxcomb. Go forward and let us have no more whining."

That was Tom Truxtun, delivering a lesson Porter never forgot. It was presently reinforced by another of a different kind, when Midshipman Porter fell foul of Lieutenant Simon Gross—not the First Lieutenant of Truxtun's speech, who was John Rodgers and a proper man, but one of those sullen alcoholics who managed to creep into the service through a reputation for hard driving gained in the merchant marine, though all they really did was hard drinking. Gross came down hard on Porter for some small offense one day and reinforced a storm of verbal abuse by giving the undersized young man a series of slaps. Porter knocked him down.

Now this was striking a superior officer, which in any naval service—and particularly in sailing-ship days—constitutes mutiny, punishable by death. In a solidly established navy the next step would have been a court-martial; but the U.S. navy was by no means solidly established in 1799 and Truxtun did not want a court-martial, especially on a case that would be sure to see someone disgraced in a manner reflecting little credit on the young service. He summoned both officers to his cabin and, after questioning them closely, gave Porter a certificate that he had "full provocation as an officer and a gentleman" for his act.

Gross was sent out of the ship and was never heard from again.

II

The precise date of the row, like so many dates in the early history of the navy, cannot be established. But Gross was certainly not aboard the frigate at noon of February 9, 1799, when five leagues off the northeast point of Nevis Island *Constellation* sighted a large ship to the southward, and bore down on her through heavy blowing weather. She was a frigate clearly enough; there was apparently something wrong with her top hamper. Truxtun thought her British at first, but as she did not answer signals she must be French. He pressed toward her with the drums rolling quarters and excitement running like a wave along the decks, for this would be the young navy's first battle.

The stranger was in fact *Insurgente,* 38, the extremely fast ship which had helped capture William Bainbridge and the little *Retaliation* in November. A heavy squall that morning had cracked her main-topmast, so that the American frigate now had the legs of her. She fired a gun to windward, a challenge; Truxtun took *Constellation* toward her lee beam, since his own ship was somewhat crank and working guns to leeward in a seaway would be troublesome. As the two ships came abreast, the order to fire was given: shoot into the hull.

The first broadside nearly cleared the Frenchman's quarterdeck, where his heavy carronades were mounted, but like most Gallic ships he carried a huge crew, therefore called away boarders and came rushing down to try things hand-to-hand. Truxtun caught the indications of this move before it was fairly begun; though the ships were only fifty yards apart, he clapped on sail quickly enough to draw ahead, giving *Insurgente* a diagonal rake as he did so; then swung across her bows and administered another diagonal rake from the opposite beam.

Things were now going all to pieces aboard the French frigate, but just at this juncture a ball from one of the long 18s on her forecastle struck *Constellation's* foremast just below the cap, damaging it so badly that the topmast threatened to go overside at the next severe strain. With the pitching sea, press of sail, and quick maneuvering, this would not be long in coming. David Porter was mid of the foretop. He hailed the deck to report the injury, could get no answer through the din of cannon and shouting, so without orders went up himself to cut the slings and lower the foreyard, relieving the pressure. The American frigate's fire had meanwhile been dismantling *Insurgente*; her mizzentopmast came down, all her forward braces were shot away, she could no longer maneuver. *Constellation* danced back and forth across her bows, pouring in broadsides until she surrendered.

Truxtun commanded a ship certainly more heavily armed than his opponent's, having long 24s on her gundeck as against the long 12s of the French ship, though the short weight of the American shot, the overweight of the French, and the heavy carronades on *Insurgente's* upper deck made the proportion in weight of broadside metal 369 pounds to 338, no impossible odds. What chiefly impressed was the brilliance of Truxtun's tactic and the accuracy of the gunners he had trained, who inflicted 70 casualties while taking only 4 themselves, and completely wrecked the French ship.

John Rodgers, as First Lieutenant, was sent to take possession with 13 seamen and a mid. He chose "that youngster Porter, who seems to be able to get out of his own way," and boats began bringing the prisoners over. There was not much daylight left when the process started, and as night began to fall the wind rose, making transit between the two ships flatly impossible. French sailors to the number of 170 were still aboard *Insurgente*; now without officers and in the nasty mood of defeat. As Rodgers soon discovered, they had thrown overboard all the handcuffs and shackles in the ship, as well as the hatch gratings by which they could have been kept below-decks.

Moreover many of the ship's control-ropes were gone, her decks were cluttered with dead men, and a storm was rising. The two American officers placed a man with a blunderbuss and a pile of loaded muskets at each hatch and tipped a loaded carronade to point down the main one; then with their tiny work force rushed back and forth madly throughout the night, splicing ropes and handling sails on a ship that normally required a crew of 300. Dawn found them on a sea roughened by the storm and *Constellation* nowhere to be seen.

Now began a prodigious struggle with wind, sea, and the malevolence of men. It lasted for three days and two nights more, during which the French could doubtless have retaken the ship had there been among them a couple of suicidal heroes willing to accept the first bullets in their chests so that the rest could rush up before a reload. But there were none such; Rodgers and Porter brought their frigate safely to St. Kitts Bay, where the former was made a captain and Porter received his first round up the ladder of promotion—to be a lieutenant at the age of 19.

Like everything else in his career, this led to another adventure—after *Insurgente* had been taken to Baltimore and Porter was sent ashore to look for deserters. The search led him to a waterfront dive which was suspected of being a crimping-den. He ordered a beer and asked the proprietor whether any navy sailors had been in. The innkeeper, a rare old specimen of his species named M'Glossin, replied by ordering the young lieutenant off the premises. "Not until I have finished my drink," said Porter, and coolly did so. M'Glossin rushed around the bar, knocked him down, missed with a furious kick, and was advancing to repeat the dose when Porter rolled under a table and came up on the other side with his dirk out. Beside himself with fury and alcohol, the tavern-keeper charged right in; took the point through the chest and fell down dead.

The navy was not too popular along the Baltimore waterfront in those days. Angry yells from bystanders brought a crowd, red-hot for lynching the lieutenant, who had to back all the way to the quay with his blade up. Stones were thrown before he reached his boat, one of them laying open his face. Nor was this the end, for the local authorities filed a civil charge of murder against him. He was rather unexpectedly saved when at the trial the widow of the late M'Glossin testified that her husband had received exactly what was coming to him. Very likely she had been looking for a chance like this for some time; in any case the event left no scar on the record of Lieut. Porter, who was immediately ordered to sea again.

Not in *Constellation,* however. She had come and gone during his trial, so Porter was made lieutenant of the new schooner *Experiment.* She was Baltimore-built, one of a pair designed to provide ships for work among the reefs and light airs of the West Indies, since there had been some dissatisfaction with the earlier light ships, which were short, heavy, and usually slow corvettes of from 20 to 24 guns, built on models inherited from the Revolutionary War. These new ships were 60-footers, each mounting twelve 6-pounders, with very fine lines, the deadwood cut away aft, narrow cheeks forward, and a sharp deadrise, like the commercial craft which sailed so very rapidly in Chesapeake Bay. The name of Porter's ship indicates correctly that there was a good deal of question as to how this type of vessel would do as a warship, with her slenderness and the heavy topweight of cannon; but there need have been no worry. *Experiment* turned out to be an ideal ship for Caribbean waters: fast as a streak, able to work to windward far better than a square-rigger, and capable of ghosting right along through the semi-calms of the islands.

Her skipper was a newly appointed lieutenant-commandant named William Maley, a somewhat singular character for an officer of the navy, as was demonstrated on his ship's first cruise. She was given four merchantmen to convoy; on New Year's Day of 1800, a calm found the five in the Bight of Léogane, north of Gonaïve Island of Haiti, a place where calms are frequent. At this time all southern Haiti was in the hands of a ruffian named General Hyacinthe Rigaud, the pattern of future Caribbean dictators—loud and willful, with no more morals than a tiger-shark. He claimed the authority of France, but actually lived by piracy, his people being called "picaroons." As *Experiment* and her four sheep lay becalmed, these picaroons came rowing out from Gonaïve to the number of four or five hundred, in ten barges, big enough so that each carried at least a 4-pounder in its bow.

The sight so unnerved Lieutenant-Commandant Maley that he proposed making signals of surrender to save bloodshed. Porter pushed him aside and began to give orders: Marines to the quarterdeck and forecastle, hidden behind the bulwarks; guns double-shotted with grape, but ports closed. By this time the picaroons were within musket-shot, making for all the ships at once, evidently taking *Experiment* for one of the merchantmen. Her ports flew open, the Marines stood up, and a storm of fire beat against the attackers, so hot and quick that they pulled out of range with many oars missing.

Men who live by robbery cannot afford to be easily discouraged, and these were not. They lay on their oars for a while, talking things over, then pulled back toward the shore of Gonaïve, where other barges took out their casualties and furnished a reinforcement. When they came back they were split into three squadrons of four barges each, steering so as to take *Experiment* on both beams and the bow simultaneously, firing their boat-guns and screaming as they came. This was a hard round; the combat lasted nearly three hours. Porter was hit in the arm by a bullet as he stood on the rail directing the defense, and two of the barges were sunk before the rest had had enough.

Toward the end of this fight two other barges attacked one of the merchant vessels from the off side, where they thought themselves out of reach of the war-schooner's guns. The crew of one barge misestimated the angle and ended up in the bellies of sharks; Porter had a gun loaded with round and laid it himself, so accurately that he sank the barge with a single shot. The other attacker got in on a ship and murdered her captain, the only man who remained aboard; but when *Experiment* threw a few rounds of grape into the vessel, the picaroons climbed over her side without having done anything further save plunder the cabin.

David Porter

In the evening the picaroons tried again and this time succeeded in towing away two of the convoy that had drifted out of gunshot from the schooner, but *Experiment* was considered to have behaved herself with enormous credit, most of which belonged to her young lieutenant. A consular officer who was aboard at the time thought it wise to write a report making Maley the hero of the occasion; but of course tongues wagged and, as there were not a few other complaints against the gentleman, he was deprived of his ship and allowed quietly to resign from the service. Porter thought he might have been given the command, in spite of his youth, and was disappointed when it went to another. But the disappointment lasted only until he made the acquaintance of that other, who was Lieutenant Charles Stewart, Bainbridge's old schoolfellow, a young man of such wit and address that he could have charmed snakes out of their holes merely by talking to them.

He and young Porter hit it off famously, and had many adventures together, the most notable following the capture, after a little shooting, of the French schooner privateer, *Deux Amis,* 8. Porter with four men went to take possession, but before a single man of *Deux Amis'* 40 could be transferred to her captor, another sail came over the horizon. *Experiment* ran off in chase and was soon hull down. Now Porter was in as bad a situation as he had been aboard *Insurgente,* for the Frenchmen began to murmur and shuffle, and this time he had no John Rodgers to lead. But he had his own high spirit and the precedent of that previous occasion. A pot of paint was produced; Porter drew a line across the deck, just forward of the mainmast, cocked a pistol, and announced he would blow the head off the first man who crossed. In the meanwhile his four had dragged round one of the after guns and loaded it with langridge (which is any sort of hard metal junk that comes to hand) as a reinforcement to the pistol. There was no rising, but no sleep either for Porter and his prize-crew until they brought the ship into St. Christopher three days later.

The exploit made the slight young lieutenant something of a marked man, and Silas Talbot, commanding *Constitution,* 44, asked for his services. The news occasioned Porter some dismay. Not only had he acquired a taste for the excitements and freedoms of small ship work, but there was a personal difficulty. A year or so before, there had been a dispute between Talbot and Truxtun over their relative rank, and Porter had exhibited rather violent partisanship for his old commander. He need not have been troubled; old Talbot was an honest man. When the new Lieutenant reported for duty, he was informed to his passionate delight that, although borne on the frigate's muster-roll, he was actually to command a navy ship of his own.

She was only a diminutive schooner, bearing the odd name of *Amphitheatre*,* with a crew of 15; recently captured and now being fitted as a seagoing errand boy to *Constitution,* with five little brass swivel guns from the latter's tops. The date was March 1800; Porter and his fifteen men enjoyed two months of active service in the craft, doing all sorts of chasing before they found some real action.

This came about while *Constitution* was cruising the waters at the eastern end of Santo Domingo. Near Cape Samana there is a rather deep bay with a line of reefs at the entrance, then a frequent haunt of picaroons. Talbot dispatched *Amphitheatre* for a look. Sure enough there were ships inside the reef—a brig, which by her shape and rigging must be American, and alongside her a three-masted schooner and a lugger-rigged barge, one of the type that normally carried 30 to 40 men. This seemed to Porter about the kind of odds that would provide good sport. He begged Talbot to let him go in, and the Captain consented, after putting half a dozen marines aboard *Amphitheatre* and ordering a couple of the frigate's longboats to follow her. As Porter's schooner bore through the reef, both picaroon ships came at him, opening up not only with swivels but also with a long 12-pounder and a pair of 6s. He held right on in to close action.

In the only contemporary account of the action, the details are obscured by a period phrase about "the heroism Porter inspired into his crew." This is a pity; it would be interesting to know how he maneuvered his ship to keep the enemy within the range of those little brass popguns, without being hurt by their bigger pieces or letting them come close enough to board. But there is nothing indefinite about the result. The schooner struck, with 7 killed and 15 wounded, proving to be named *Ester* and to have a French privateer's commission; the brig

* She is called *Amphitrite* in most books, but this is a case of recent authors prettying things up; the contemporary documents all give the right name.

was repossessed and Porter was in hot pursuit of the barge, when *Amphitheatre* touched a wing of the reef and thumped her rudder off before she could be pried loose.

III

At the end of June *Constitution's* time on station ran out. She went home, taking *Amphitheatre* with her, and before she could be put into commission again the war was over and the navy had entered its peace establishment. Porter had seen as much active service as any officer on the list, and always with credit, so there was never any question about his being one of the officers retained on the list. In fact he received what amounted to a promotion, being named Second Lieutenant of *Enterprise*, 12, *Experiment's* sister, a ship which moved perpetually through an atmosphere of valor and wonderful good luck. During the French War she saw more fighting and captured more enemies than any other vessel of the navy. Porter's new skipper was Lieutenant-Commandant Andrew Sterrett, one of those who "blew up" the young man when he was a mid aboard *Constellation*; they were good friends now.

Enterprise was a member of Commodore Dale's squadron, for the Mediterranean on a mission whose orders said it was exploratory rather than punitive: to show the flag to the Barbary states and warn them against aggressions on the young republic of the West. Dale arrived at Gibraltar in July 1801, to find the aggressions already taking place, the American Consul's flagstaff at Tripoli chopped down, and the Tripolitan corsairs out on cruise with orders to take American ships.

Two of them were at Gibraltar when he reached the place, a 26-gun ship and a brig of 16, taking in stores, apparently for a venture into the Atlantic. Dale dropped *Philadelphia*, 38, to watch them, sent *Essex*, 32, to gather up American shipping in the Mediterranean and convoy it through the Straits. Himself, in *President*, 44, with *Enterprise* in company, moved along the Barbary Coast. There were matters to be settled at Tunis and Algiers, and he wanted a big ship to impress these people.

Enterprise was employed much as *Amphitheatre* had been, as a dispatch-boat. Nevertheless, the little schooner achieved the first contact with the enemy. On August 1, while en route to Malta, she came upon the polacre-rigged ship *Tripoli,* 14, and at once commenced a hot and close action. A polacre handles very well in the light Mediterranean airs of summer; the Tripolitans kept trying to close and board, since their decks were crowded with men. But Sterrett was as good a seaman as the navy had; he maneuvered sharply, kept it a gunnery fight, in which he achieved several rakes, and at the end of three hours had the satisfaction of seeing the enemy strike.

As soon as *Enterprise* hove to to take possession, however, *Tripoli* hung out her flags again and came rushing in, with the evident intention of boarding her stationary opponent. *Enterprise* just barely escaped; but escaping, was forewarned when the corsair struck a second time, and a second time changed his mind and tried to continue the action by catching *Enterprise* at a disadvantage. Now the sailors on the American's deck were thoroughly roused; when the Tripolitan hauled down his flag for the third time they were all for keeping right on shooting till they sank him, but the corsair's mainmast broke across her bulwarks and her captain came to the waist of his ship, bowing low and casting the colors into the sea.

He was a bearded person of deceptively benign aspect, named Mohammed Sous, who begged the Americans to take him prisoner, because (he said) he feared what the Bashaw of Tripoli would do to him when that gentleman discovered the fate of the ship. Sterrett told him the perfect truth: that without a declaration of war by Congress there was no authority from the American government to take prisoners or prizes. Instead of taking possession, he cut away all *Tripoli's* sticks except the stump of the foremast, threw overboard all her guns and equipment save one patched sail, and left her to crawl homeward in that shape, doubtless hoping that a gale would rise and deprive the world of a scoundrel.

If so, he was disappointed. *Tripoli* made her home port, but Mohammed Sous got exactly what he expected, being ridden through the streets backward on a jackass while people pelted him with filth, and was afterward bastinadoed. At this date it was considered disgraceful for any ship to yield to an American, the nation which had lost its entire navy in the War of Independence. As for Sterrett, Porter, and the ship that had come to be known as the "lucky little *Enterprise*," they sailed for home, since Commodore Dale did not believe it safe to cruise the Mediterranean in winter.

In those days there were few lieutenants who had the reputation for doing things, and they were worked hard. Porter had barely reached the United States, and certainly was without opportunity for any but the most casual shore leave, when he was ordered to the Mediterranean again as First Lieutenant of *New York,* 36. She was originally intended to be under command of John Rodgers, Porter's old superior in *Constellation,* but there were some command changes when the Mediterranean was reached, and Porter found himself Second Lieutenant to Isaac Chauncey's first, in a ship nominally commanded by Richard V. Morris, who was actually commodore of the squadron. The service was rather disagreeable to the young lieutenant, who grumbled that it was "too close to the flag" though this may merely have meant that he found himself too close to Morris, whom he did not like very well; especially after the incident on the way to Malta, when there was an explosion in a passage near the ship's magazine. The only orders Morris gave on that occasion produced a confusion bordering on panic. It was Chauncey and the diminutive Porter who led a few hands into the choking berth-deck, put out the fire, and saved the ship.

Yet even under the rather soft command of Morris, Porter found an opportunity for action. On the single occasion when *New York* approached Tripoli, on May 20, 1803, she was lucky enough to sight eleven felucca-rigged grain vessels crawling along the coast toward the port. The frigate made for them; they all ran ashore near a large stone building, and a great assembly of Moors, including some cavalry and a couple of pieces of artillery, poured out of town and began to build breast-works with sacks of grain taken from the feluccas. Porter wanted to lead the squadron's boats in for a night attack, but Morris said no, it was too dangerous. The effort was held over till morning; James Lawrence of *Enterprise* was Porter's second in command of the boats. By this time the Moors were well established ashore and the attackers had to pull in through a heavy fire of musketry which killed or wounded fifteen, including Porter, shot through both thighs. He nevertheless led the landing party right up the beach, so close that the defenders were throwing stones. Some of the party fired the feluccas; on the way out Porter had the boats pull to one side so that the ships in the rear could break up any effort at salvage by gunfire. Morris did fire, but from such a distance that the Moors were able to save all their boats, so the attack was in vain, except as it established the more firmly Lieutenant Porter's reputation for gallantry.

IV

In September, *New York* went down to Gibraltar, under orders of recall. *Philadelphia,* 38, was in harbor, having just come from the United States with a First Lieutenant named Cox, who was desirous of retiring from the service. Commodore Preble, who took an instant liking to young Porter on meeting him, suggested that he exchange places with Cox, and Captain William Bainbridge of *Philadelphia* agreed. Neither the captain nor his new executive had any cause to regret the arrangement. Bainbridge's culture and wide experience fascinated the younger man, who had been at sea so steadily since childhood as to have missed educational opportunities; and as for the Captain, he was writing to Washington even before the frigate sailed up the Mediterranean that "Lieutenant Porter is fit for any command."

The combination could have produced a sensationally effective warship, but destiny decided otherwise. At the close of October *Philadelphia* ran on that uncharted reef off Tripoli, heeled over on one side, and was taken with all her crew. The most interesting thing about the 18-month period of captivity that followed is that while Captain Bainbridge was busy trying to smuggle information to Preble by means of sympathetic inks, and Lieutenant Jones was occupying himself with the health of the prisoners, Porter was intent on employing his time educationally.

Contact with Preble and Bainbridge had shown the Lieutenant what he lacked—book knowledge and the regimen that goes with it, the ability to apply the touchstone of general theory to the specific case. Mr. N. C. Nissen, the Danish consul, supplied a few books; Porter grasped them avidly and announced the foundation of the University of the Prison in Tripoli. *Philadelphia's* officers were by turns students, instructors, and independent researchers. Porter taught himself French and spoke it well ever after; he practiced drawing, on paper when he had it, on the wall when paper there was none. A course in history was given, one in the theory of seamanship and another in practical navigation. With blocks of wood as model ships, the floor of the prison became a maneuvering board on which doctrines of tactics were worked out.

Yet even this was not enough to keep Porter from getting into trouble; probably nothing would have been. The enlisted prisoners were led daily to and from their forced labor on the fortifications down a passage past the room where the officers were confined. Porter found it out and easily bored a hole through the soft masonry of the party wall to the passage, through which notes were passed. A good idea until someone became indiscreet enough to use the aperture for word-of-mouth communication. Of course, the guard caught them at it and rushed into the officers' quarters, breathing fire and threatening a bastinado all round.

"I alone am responsible," said Porter and, being led before the Bashaw for judgment, delivered a harangue to the effect that any man worthy of the name would try to make a prisoner's lot easier; "and meanwhile, if the Bashaw thinks that none but his corsairs possess courage, then he has something to learn from the Christians." It is not recorded that his Bashawship was impressed; but the Vizier, Mohammed D'Ghies, was a man of some culture in the erratic Moslem style, and Porter had hit upon the line of appeal most perfectly in concord with that philosophy. D'Ghies sent him back to join the others without penalty.

After the release Porter saw no particular reason for going home. His old chief, John Rodgers, was now Commodore Mediterranean and wanted the young Lieutenant as nominal First and acting captain of his flagship, but Porter's health was too run down for him to handle so complex an administrative task, so Rodgers placed him in *Enterprise* as lieutenant-commandant. The shooting war was over and *Enterprise* was already under orders for home, but this did not prevent Porter from finding trouble. His ship was anchored in Malta harbor when a British sailor, presumably drunk, came out in a shore boat and rowed round and round her, cursing the American flag and damning the eyes of everyone aboard. After a certain amount of it, Porter told him to keep off; the sailor only cursed the more heartily, daring the Americans to do something about it. Porter needed no second challenge of this sort. He lowered a boat with an armed guard, hauled the impertinent Briton aboard, triced him up to a mast, and amid the hearty applause of *Enterprise's* crew had him given a round dozen with the cat-o'-nine tails.

The next morning there was an emissary from the Governor of Malta on hand with a solemn pronouncement: the flogging of a seaman of H.M. navy aboard an American warship was an event of international importance. *Enterprise* was not to leave Malta until the matter was settled, and the forts at the entrance had instructions to stop her if she tried to go out. Porter replied that he had fixed his hour of sailing, and if the forts attempted to stop him the subsequent events would have even greater international importance; then hove short, beat to quarters, and went down the harbor with guns run out and battle-flags flying.

It would be an error to view the recurrence of such incidents as merely acts of individual truculence, though Porter was, even beyond the norm of Preble's boys, quick to take offense. What he and the others did has to be viewed against the background of the time. A great war had been going on for many years and violence was in the very air; moreover British arrogance and the repeated, burning wrong of the impressments formed an essential part of that atmosphere. Decatur, in the incident of the Malta duel, Porter flogging the British seaman, doubtless felt some resentment over the individual incident, but neither really acted on impulse. They did what they did coolly and taking time to think things over. They were perfectly aware that the world was in flux, international law was being rewritten, and the men who piled words on sheets of foolscap in the chanceries were mainly occupied with rationalizing acts already performed; yet acts which, being established as precedent, would control the movements of generations unborn. If *Enterprise* submitted to being detained for this reason, there would be some other reason for holding the next American ship that came in; and presently the right of British port officers to grant or withhold exit passes would be established. A British frigate fired into a Dane once because she did not lower her fore-topsail when they met, in "customary" acknowledgment of Britain's rule of the seas.

But it would be a long time before David Porter had another chance to speak for the honor of his flag, for he reached home to find the big ships laid up, and everybody building the fatuous Jefferson gunboats, while the Embargo that was to halt American sea-adventuring lay just over the horizon. In the meanwhile Porter went down to Washington, where Captain Thomas Tingey had the Navy Yard.

As the custom then was with anyone who had visited the more bar-barous foreign parts, the Lieutenant was exhibited as a social curiosity and asked to give accounts of his captivity in Tripoli. On one of these occasions, at the house of Tingey's brother William, Porter saw a beauti-ful girl of fifteen playing with a doll, and instantly decided he wanted to marry her. Her name was Evalina Anderson; he pushed his suit so vigorously that she sent him to her father, a Congressman who lived in Chester, Pa. At Chester, Porter was received by Evalina's brother in-stead of her parent. This gentleman protested that the girl was too young for marriage; Porter remarked that she had already been pre-sented in society, an act which carried with it at least a guarantee of willingness to consider marriage offers. The brother said the family ob-jected to naval men; Porter offered to throw him out the window, whereupon Congressman Anderson, who had apparently been listen-ing, judged it time to intervene with the statement that if Evalina felt the same way about it after a year, he would interpose no further ob-jections.

She did feel the same; they were married, and the Congressman made them a wedding present of a fine house called Greenbank, over-looking the Delaware. The Lieutenant's wedding present from the de-partment was a master-commandant's commission and appointment to the New Orleans naval station, with general charge of 15 gunboats and the duty of enforcing the Embargo. Three of the gunboats were supposed to be ready at Pittsburgh, to which place the honeymoon couple proceeded over the mountains. Porter found the craft nowhere near ready, so chartered a river-boat to take him to his station; the gov-ernment refused to make good the money he spent.

At New Orleans he found things just as bad as they could be. One of his gunboats was already so rotten after only 18 months of service that she had to be beached. The rigging of all had been furnished by a contractor who scandalously cheated the government; the theoretical force of 400 seamen was far below standard, the terms of the men in service were fast running out and no recruits to be had. The Governor of the territory was William C. C. Claiborne, "a man of many private virtues and few public ones" vain, high-handed, and weak. The French and Spanish creoles addressed him to his face as "*ce bête*," for he did not know a word of either language. He told Porter that he could supply neither money nor men nor stores, and when the commandant of the naval station at New Orleans drew on Washington to pay his official bills, the drafts were dishonored, to the accompaniment of furious letters from Secretary of the Navy Robert Smith.

That was how things stood in the service during those days; and, to crown all, Porter had hardly reached his post before he came down with an attack of yellow fever, so severe that his life was despaired of. By the time he recovered, he had found the one really good officer in his command, a purser named Hambleton, and they managed to get the worst of the administrative problems in hand before looking around for exterior troubles. They did not have to look far; piracy was rampant all along the Gulf coast. Armed ships of every description were making whatever captures they chose under privateers' commissions only too readily granted by the colonial authorities of England, France, and Spain. There were a good many who did not even bother with commissions.

One of the worst of these rogues was a three-masted schooner of 14 guns named *Montebello*. She had originally cleared from Baltimore as a merchant craft bound for St. Bartholomew, but instead put into Savannah where she took aboard her guns and a new crew. She had preyed so heavily on Spanish shipping that the Governor of Havana posted a reward of $60,000 for her capture. Porter learned that this *Montebello* had arrived at the Pilot Town suburb of New Orleans, flying the French flag with an obviously faked signal of distress to give her an excuse for coming in. She was accompanied by two more vessels of the same kidney, a Spanish-built schooner named *Intrepido* with a commission originally granted to a pirogue (which is a dugout) and a brig-rigged job named *Petit Chance,* which had no papers at all.

Porter went to Pilot Town with all the gunboats that were service-able, forced the surrender of the three craft, and placed libels against them in the Federal district court. Now his troubles really began. The Federal attorney, a personage named D. A. Grymes, who had been doing good business with these and other "gentlemen of the coast," gave an opinion that the navy had no authority to capture ships in distress. To do Claiborne justice, he was really trying to put down pi-racy, but he said he could not go behind the attorney's ruling. Porter pre-pared the attachment papers himself, and announced that if the hearing were not held at once he would take all three ships to Philadelphia. A menacing-looking crowd armed with pistols surrounded the court and forced the judge to adjourn the case. The next day they reappeared; so did Porter, with the Marines of the station in full war kit and loaded muskets. Himself acting as attorney amid the lowering glances and mut-tered threats of the mob, the Master-Commandant called up the case and secured the condemnation of the three ships. The incident did not end piracy in the Gulf, but it cramped the style of the freebooters and left the commandant of the naval station free to take part in another event which had far-reaching consequences.

Old David Porter Sr., now far gone in years, had returned to the reve-nue service after his son entered the navy, and was still in it, since no one retired in those days. At his own request, he was sent down to New Orleans to serve under his son, and became well known around the place as a cheery ancient with a strong sense of humor, who spent most of his time writing a book called *The Origin of Man* in which he demonstrated that humans had developed from jellyfish through a variety of forms to mermen and so up to their present estate. One day he went fishing on Lake Pontchartrain and, while in the boat, suffered a stroke that left him lying helpless. He was found by a man named Farragut, who carried the old revenue officer to his own home, put him to bed, and cared for him tenderly until he died, since he was too sick to be moved.

After his father was gone, Porter wished to do something for Farra-gut, who was far from prosperous. He had enough delicacy not to offer money; instead he arranged to adopt the son, young Davey Farragut, then nine years old. Just at this point Porter had become so disgusted with the business in which he was engaged that he was trying to resign the service. "The navy is a glass of weak whiskey and water," he wrote, "the weak addition of the naval element having only diluted the draft without improving the taste. Burn the wretched gunboats and build some useful vessels!" The resignation went to Paul Hamilton, the new naval Secretary who came in with President Madison; on looking over the records he considered that Porter had done extremely well, and refused the resignation in a singularly flattering letter. As a kind of reward for staying in the service, Porter was allowed to give the Farragut boy a midshipman's warrant, place him on inactive duty at half pay and send him to school. At the same time there was the promise of a sea command—a sloop of war or one of the light frigates, since as a master-commandant, Porter was still too junior to have a heavy ship.

v

The family came north up the Mississippi in 1811, when the skies were deepening toward war with England. They established themselves at Greenbank; Porter learned that his ship was to be *Essex,* 32. When he looked her over, he was so dissatisfied that he asked for *Hornet,* 18, or *Adams,* 28, instead.

There was reason for this. *Essex* was a beautifully and honestly built ship, the gift to the government of Salem town, designed by old William Hackett, who had turned out the wonderful *Hancock* and *Alliance* during the Revolution, the finest and fastest frigates of their time. Commodore Preble took *Essex* to the East Indies during the French War, and on the voyage she showed that Hackett's hand had never lost its skill, for she was a refinement on his Continental frigates, with better lines under water and better proportions above, perhaps the fastest ship in the new navy.

But it was a long way from 1777 to 1809; when Captain John Smith was placed in command of *Essex* during the latter year, he decided that the appearance on the seas of so many 38-gun, 18-pounder frigates had outmoded his ship's armament of twenty-six long 12s on the main deck, sixteen 24-pounder carronades above. She had speed enough to choose her station in action; he therefore gave her more fire power by exchanging the gundeck battery for twenty-four 32-pound carronades and hoisted four of the long 12s to the spar-deck.

Not only did this spoil the ship's sailing by throwing out the delicate balances Hackett had given her. It also left *Essex* a completely short-range ship, which could be pounded to pieces from a distance by a vessel mounting nothing beyond long 9s, if the slightest accident of battle produced damage among the spars. Porter pointed this out and wanted to rearm her as before; but the prospect of war was too pressing as the year turned to 1812, and he had to do the best he could with what he had.

He did a good best. Given that he could not hope to maintain a maneuver-and-gunnery action with a ship of anything like *Essex'* force, he argued that the way to win was to get close to an opponent (under disguise, if possible), fire one thundering broadside from his heavy carronades, then board through the smoke. Well, then: he enlisted a heavier crew than normal, heavier than he was supposed to have, 319 men. Having enlisted them, he proceeded to give them such a training for hand-to-hand work as few crews ever had. Daily there were hours of practice at pistol work and singlestick, man against man. "I never saw an old *Essex* sailor in the navy later but he was the best swordsman in the ship," related Farragut later, he having been ordered out of school to active duty by his adoptive father, a full-fledged naval officer not quite eleven years old.

Every day a bugle blared and a drum beat to quarters; all hands seized cutlasses sharpened to a razor's edge and rushed to their posts. Sometimes the drum was beat at dead of night, or an alarm of fire given; the men turned to, with blanket in one hand and cutlass in the other—always the cutlass—and if all were at their stations within ten minutes, an extra issue of rum went round. There is a spirit in such preparations; the men caught it, and swaggered proudly ashore under sailor hats lettered Essex, exhibiting their sharpened dirks, cocky as young bulls. They were delighted when on the third of July the ship catheaded her anchors and stood down New York bay with war orders under Captain Porter, he having been promoted to that rank the day before.

This was part of the first experimental cruise the ships were being allowed to make, before they were laid up for harbor defense, and as Porter knew this was their only chance, probably his crew did also, for he was always careful to keep them informed of what was toward. There would be a sense that the fate of the navy rested on them, an excitement that did not check when, a week out of port, *Essex* found herself by night overhauling a little fleet bound northward. Porter ran down on the sternmost, hailed her, and held her in converse without arousing suspicion. It was a convoy of troops, bound from the West Indies to Quebec, under escort of a bomb ketch and H.M.S. *Minerva,* 32, the warship being now well toward the head of the column.

Porter knew about *Minerva*; she was a ship of *Essex'* own type and nominal force, but armed as the American cruiser once had been, with long 12s on the gundeck. He summoned all hands, announced his intention in a little speech, sent everyone to quarters in the dark, and with only running lights showing, cracked on sail and bore through the fleet, with the intention of closing the British frigate and boarding her by surprise in the dark. But the next ship he passed grew suspicious, hailed, and threatened to fire a signal-gun unless *Essex* clearly identified herself. There was now nothing to do but haul alongside the other ship and announce that this was an American frigate, which would blow the stranger out of the water unless she backed a topsail and gave up. She proved to be a transport with 200 soldiers and some specie aboard, a good capture, but it took so much time to move all those soldiers from ship to ship by rowboat that dawn found the convoy beyond pursuit.

Essex pushed on up to the region of Newfoundland, and there made good hunting, retaking five sail of American merchantmen captured by the British, with eight of the enemy's ships—$300,000 worth together. On August 13 a man-o'-war was identified, far out to windward and bearing down. Porter struck his topgallant masts, trimmed his sails in a slovenly manner, and put a drag astern to give the appearance of a slow-sailing merchant ship trying to escape. The stranger, revealing herself as a ship-sloop, came galloping down, rounded under *Essex'* quarter, gave three cheers and fired a broadside, which did no harm whatever.

Porter put *Essex'* helm hard up; her ports flew open, and from fifty yards' distance she let the Britisher have a broadside so destructive that the order to board was unnecessary; she fired a single musket and struck. The prize was *Alert,* 20, which had been sent out in search of *Hornet*; the first British fighting ship taken in the war.

This was good, but it might have ended badly, for as *Essex* turned homeward, so packed with prisoners that they lay one against another on deck like sardines, little Davey Farragut woke in his hammock one night to see a man standing over him, whom he recognized as one of the British. The fellow had a pistol; it took no great feat of deduction to determine that a prisoners' rising was in the wind. The boy lay without moving a muscle till the Britisher turned away, satisfied he was asleep; then slipped to the deck and crept barefooted down the passages to the Captain's cabin with his tale. Porter leaped from his bunk shouting "Fire! Fire!" All the American sailors came rushing on deck with blanket and cutlass, and the rising never really began; but Porter judged it was time to get rid of these prisoners, therefore paroled them and made a cartel of *Alert* to take them to Halifax. The sloop was in any case so shot to pieces that she had only ornamental value; it would be cheaper to build a new ship than repair her.

The news from New York being that it was closed by blockade, Porter now made into the Delaware, where he and his crew were no little surprised to see people come out of their houses along the banks and cheer *Essex* all the way up the river. It was the news of *Constitution's* victory over *Guerrière* they were saluting; and the next news was that Porter was to put out again in company with the triumphant cruiser, now under his old captain, William Bainbridge. It would be a long cruise, down to the Cape Verde Islands, then back across the Atlantic to the Brazils. *Constitution* was in Boston; by correspondence Bainbridge made arrangements to leave instructions for Porter at Porto Praya in the Cape Verdes, and again at Fernando Noronha. *Hornet* would accompany *Constitution.*

Preble's Boys

Sailing day was October 27, 1812. Porter himself has described the departure in what is perhaps the best surviving account of the house-keeping arrangements of a frigate bound out on cruise:

"Previous to leaving the river, the crew had been put on allowance of half a gallon of water each man per day;* and being desirous of making our provisions hold out as long as possible, having views, at the same time, with regard to the health of the crew, I caused the allowance of bread to be reduced one half, and issued in lieu of the remainder, half a pound of potatoes, or the same quantity of apples, every other article of provisions was reduced one third, excepting rum, of which the full allowance was served out raw to the cook of each mess (the crew being divided into messes of eight, and a cook allowed to each), who was accountable for its faithful distribution. For the undrawn provisions, the purser steward was directed to issue due-bills, with assurances on my part that they would be paid the amount on our arrival in port. Orders were given to lose no opportunity of catching rain-water for the stock, of which we had a large quantity on board, every mess in the ship being supplied with pigs and poultry. The allowance of candles was reduced one half, and economy established respecting the consumption of wood and the expenditure of the ship's stores. Habits of cleanliness and care with respect to clothing were strongly recommended to the officers and crew. I now gave a general pardon for all offenses committed on board; recommended the strictest attention to the discipline of the ship; held out prospects of reward to those who should be vigilant in the performance of their duty; and gave assurances that the first man I was under the necessity of punishing should receive three dozen lashes; expressing a hope, however, that punishment during the cruise would be altogether unnecessary. I directed, as a standing regular, that the ship should be fumigated in every part every morning, by pouring vinegar on a red

---

* This includes not only drinking water, but water for whatever washing a man did not care to do in salt water. For a voyage as long as this was anticipated to be, it was an uncommonly generous allowance.

hot shot, and confided in Lieutenant Finch the superintendance of the birthdeck,* in order to preserve it in a cleanly and wholesome state. Lime being provided in tight casks, for the purpose of white-washing and sand for dry-rubbing it, and orders given not to wet it if there should be a possibility of avoiding it, a comfortable place was fitted up for the accommodation of the sick on the birthdeck; cleats were put up for slinging as many hammocks as possible on the gundeck; and orders given that no wet clothes or wet provisions should be permitted to remain on the birthdeck, nor the crew be permitted to eat any where but on the gun-deck, except in bad weather. Having established the above and other regulations, as regarded the health and comfort of the crew, I exhorted the officers to keep them occupied constantly during working hours, in some useful employment, and directed that two hours between four and six in the afternoon, should be allowed to them for amusement, when the duties of the ship would admit."

The voyage down to Porto Praya was without event, save for the visit of Neptune and his consort Amphitrite (they came aboard at the Tropic in those days, not the Equator) who were so convivial during the ceremonies as to lose the ability to stand. When the boat went in, the governor of the Cape Verdes was taking his siesta, but his deputy sent out to say the gentleman would be glad to receive the officers of an American frigate. There had been no others of their nation in the islands, save a privateer from Boston, and they would be glad if *Essex* could spare them a little flour, as they were destitute of bread.

Porter went ashore to have dinner with the Governor and found that the garrison at Praya consisted of 400 Negro soldiers, none with any clothing above the waist. Most of their muskets were without locks and had the stocks broken off; it was not uncommon to see one mounting guard with nothing but a musket barrel over his shoulder. The cavalry troop had only jackasses to ride; their swords were all broken and none of the garrison had received pay, clothes, or arms in ten years' time. There was little variety in the meats, but a great

---

* The "birthdeck" (*sic*) was below the main gundeck; it had no portholes and therefore no light of its own, but the ventilation, by means of windsails, was fairly good. In most frigates, a good part of the crew habitually slept there.

quantity of tropical fruits, of which the oranges were especially fine. Over 100,000 of these were taken aboard, with pigs, fowls, and turkeys in great abundance. "My principal care was the health of my people," Porter reported, and a few days out, when he discovered that the consumption of water was somewhat excessive, because of the amount of livestock aboard, he ordered that all the pigs be butchered.

On December 12, just as they had crossed the Equator, a brig was sighted to windward; she bore every appearance of a warship. Porter hoisted English colors and, by using the signals he had found aboard *Alert,* brought her into a range from which she could not escape. She was the armed mail packet *Nocton,* 10, with $55,000 in specie aboard, which proved useful later in paying *Essex'* crew.

At Fernando Noronha, the second rendezvous, the ship approached under British colors and Lieutenant Downes went ashore in plain clothes. He came back to report that H.M.S. *Acasta,* 40, had visited the place with a sloop of war a week before and had left a letter for Sir James Lucas Yeo of *Southampton,* 32. This was so exactly in Bainbridge's style that Porter sent in for the letter, saying he was Yeo. The salutation was "My Mediterranean friend" and it contained the line "I should be happy to meet and converse on old affairs of captivity; recollect our secret of those times," which seemed so clear a reference to sympathetic ink that Porter tested the document for it. So it was—the hidden message was from Bainbridge, bidding Porter meet him off the coast near Rio.

Thither he accordingly set his course, but on the way met a small vessel lately from the Brazilian capital with news: namely, that an American frigate had sunk a British cruiser of the same class after a terrific battle in which the latter lost her masts; that the British 74 normally stationed at Rio had gone in pursuit of the American, but a 60-gun ship was on her way from the Cape station to the Brazils, besides several ships from England. Porter now considered that with so many enemy ships of such great force in the region, he would have no place to get provisions without running the risk of being blockaded. His consorts had evidently gone north; therefore he decided to pass into the Pacific and wage war on the British whale fishery while protecting the American.

David Porter

As very heavy weather was to be expected off the Horn in this season, the ship was prepared by sending down the royal masts and every heavy article from the tops; the shot were placed below except six for each gun; the cannon at bow and stern were removed amidships and the cables overhauled, being cut and spliced where they showed weakness. The strictest orders were given to the cook that the seamen were not to be allowed to fry their bread (a habit to which they were greatly addicted), as scurvy had frequently been traced to this practice.

The ship made south; albatrosses began to assemble; it grew colder, and on February 13, in thick and heavy weather, breakers were sighted ahead, with the ship plunging forecastle under and no room to wear. By the utmost exertion the mainsail was set and *Essex* hove round in stays, though the jib was blown to pieces in the process. All night the ship clawed perilously off a lee shore; but at seven in the morning, to the unspeakable joy of all, the sea became smooth and a sight of land confirmed that they were now in the Strait of Le Maire. No other part of the world presents a more horrible and dreary appearance than the shore of Staten Land, now visible.

Porter steered south in the hope of gaining enough offing to weather Tierra del Fuego, but encountered a succession of heavy gales from the northwest working around to west, with occasional dreadful squalls accompanied by hail. Calculation, with a due allowance for currents, showed that the ship must have reached 79 west longitude and, the wind favoring, she hauled around toward north on the 22nd; but that night a lunar could be taken for the first time, and to the Captain's mortification it showed they were only at 75 west, the Cape still to be rounded. The casks of peas and beans, when opened, proved to contain nothing but a mass of chaff and worms, but the weevils had not much attacked the bread and could be extracted with a knife. It was the last of February before the prow could be set north; and now came another succession of gales that left all hands fatigued and some men bruised, while the sails were so worn as to be little reliable. On March 6 calm seas and a fair air were at last their lot; they reached the island of Mocha, where parties went ashore to shoot some of the wild hogs and horses in which the place abounds. The meat of the latter was the better.

There was much doubt in the Captain's mind as to how he would be received at Valparaiso, since Spain was an ally of England; but to his infinite joy he found that the Chileans had thrown off their allegiance to King Ferdinand and adopted a republican form of government. The Americans were hospitably received and *Essex'* wants in provisions, wood, and water were met in every respect. The Governor held a ball for the frigate's officers; the ladies, except for their teeth, were very handsome, but the dance of the country in which they engaged was indelicate and lascivious. Captain Porter was informed that the Viceroy of Peru had equipped ships against American whalers; there was also obtained a specification of the British whalers then in the Pacific, most of which carried letters of marque and all of which were armed. *Essex'* gunner was detected smuggling rum on board and placed in irons; and the carpenter, a worthless fellow who overstayed his shore leave, was not permitted to come on board again. One wonders about this drunken American carpenter and worthless fellow, marooned in a strange, Spanish-speaking land; but there is nothing more of him, in Porter's or any other journal.

The frigate now stood north along the coast; on the 25th March she met the American whaler *Charles,* which said that a Peruvian cruiser had taken two of our ships. Off Coquimbo a vessel was sighted that must be the cruiser in question; Porter set English colors, had *Charles* hoist an English jack over the American flag, and ran down. The stranger was *Nereyda,* 15; she sent a lieutenant aboard, who proudly explained that the Peruvians were friends and allies of the British, that his ship had taken two American whalers and had their crews aboard at the moment. By this time the Peruvian was close under the frigate's lee. Porter undeceived his visitor as to the true nationality of *Essex* and fired a couple of shot over *Nereyda,* which induced her to strike. This ship the Captain served in the same fashion as *Tripoli* in the old war—i.e., by throwing overboard all her spars, guns, and shot (which were observed to be of copper, since iron was scarce on that coast), and sending her home with a letter advising the Viceroy of Peru on how to maintain friendly relations with the Americans.

Essex sailed on northward; in mid-April she was lucky enough to come up with *Barclay,* one of the captured whalers, and to retake her,

most of her crew entering aboard the frigate, while her master decided
to employ his ship as a tender for Porter's. The ocean, which looks so
blank on charts, is really limited to a certain number of avenues by
winds, currents, the prevalence of whales, and the necessity of ships
to find places of resort for food and water. In this region one of the
greatest points of assembly was in the Galápagos Islands, toward
which Porter now directed his course. On Charles Island there was a
famous letter-box, where ships left intelligence for each other, but it
contained nothing of recent date. Even the genius of the place had departed: an Irishman who called himself "the fatherless Oberlus" and
who formerly lived on the place wild and hairy, exchanging the few
potatoes he raised to visiting ships for rum.

The other islands yielded nothing but quantities of the monstrous
tortoises which stay alive so well in the hold of a ship, and whose flesh
is superior to beef. The cruise was thus a disappintment until the 29th
April. That morning Porter was roused from the cot where he had
spent a sleepless and anxious night by a hail from masthead. He went
on deck to see a large ship bearing westward, which he made no
doubt was a whaler and British. She was overhauled about nine and
found to be *Montezuma* of two guns, with her tanks nearly full of oil.
During the chase two other ships were sighted ahead; when it fell calm,
as usual with the approach of noon, *Essex'* boats were hoisted out and
made for the pair, who fired some signal guns to each other, but surrendered without resistance as the boats came into range. They proved
to be *Georgiana* of six 18-pounders and *Policy* of ten 6-pounders, the
former built as an Indiaman and pierced with 18 ports. Porter had
the guns of both prizes put into her and commissioned her to cruise
independently under First Lieutenant Downes, giving him a rendezvous for Tumbez. All three whalers were filled with stores, such as
paints, cordage, and sails, of which the frigate stood in great need.

No more sails were sighted until May 28, when two together appeared about evening. One, the letter-of-marque whaler *Atlantic,* of 10
guns, proved a remarkably fast sailer and was taken only after a good
deal of maneuvering by *Essex, Policy, Barclay,* and *Montezuma* together. The other was the letter-of-marque *Greenwich,* also of 10; her
captain was drunk and so abusive that Porter had to order him into

irons. The number of prizes and prisoners was now a great embarrassment, as was the fact that so many officers were now out in the captured ships that the Lieutenant of Marines was in command of one, and only the chaplain and the Captain's clerk remained aboard the frigate. The mids had watches, each aided by a bo'sun's mate, who (as is well known) can never be received in Hell and therefore may do what he pleases. Porter accordingly shaped his course for Tumbez, arriving on the 19th June. The inhabitants offered a warm reception and fresh provisions, but Second Lieutenant Wilson, who had several times been disgracefully drunk, being found in that condition in his cabin, produced a pistol against the Captain. Porter threw him across the room and placed him in arrest.

On the 24th, three large vessels stood in, proving to be *Georgiana* with two prizes, one of which, *Hector,* 11, she had taken after a sharp action. Lieutenant Downes said there had been a third capture, *Rose,* which he had given up to the prisoners, as their total more than seven times outnumbered his own crew. The whole squadron was now reorganized. *Georgiana* was loaded with whale-oil and sent round to America under Lieutenant Wilmer. *Atlantic,* as the best sailer, was armed with 20 guns and commissioned under Lieutenant Downes as *Essex Jr;* *Greenwich* was made into an armed store-ship under Marine Lieutenant Gamble. Four of the prizes were sent to Valparaiso for disposal under escort of *Essex Jr.,* even little Davey Farragut being put in command of one.

On the last day of June the frigate sailed for the Galápagos once more, with *Georgiana* and *Greenwich* in company. En route three more whalers were discovered. Gamble of *Greenwich* borrowed some men from *Georgiana,* closed with the heaviest of these, *Seringapatam,* 14, and captured her after a fight; the other two surrendered without trouble.

Now there was a period of fruitless cruising until mid-September, when the last British whaler in the Pacific was taken. At the end of the month Downes returned from Valparaiso with his ship to report that the government there was seeking to return to the rule of Spain, had become very pro-British and unco-operative. Several ships of war had been dispatched in pursuit of *Essex.* The frigate was greatly in need of heaving down for repairs to her bottom and had defects in her masts. Porter accordingly decided to go to the barbarous Marquesas, first giving up another of the prizes to take some of the prisoners home, and commissioning *Seringapatam,* which was cruiser-built with 22 guns.

The fleet reached the bay of Nukuhiva on October 25. Almost immediately a canoe came out with three white men, tattooed all over like natives. To the astonishment of everyone aboard, one of them proved to be a midshipman of the American navy; his name was John Maury and he had been left on the island to gather sandalwood while on a commercial voyage and had been abandoned in consequence of the war. The natives were friendly and, to the delight of the sailors, their women were decidedly amoral; they served feasts of baked bread-fruit and pork, which everyone pronounced delicious. The valley at whose foot the frigate lay, with her carpenters and metalsmiths working busily, belonged to a tribe called the Taeehs. They were at war with the neighboring tribe of Happahs, who raided the Taeeh bread-fruit grove. Porter said he would protect his friends against these enemies if they would carry a six-pounder to the top of the mountain, which they accomplished in a single night. When the Happahs attacked the fort around this gun, Lieutenant Downes killed five of their people, including one of the chiefs, and compelled them to peace.

But this did not in the least discourage the Typees, a warlike tribe on the other side of the island, who sent messengers to declare they would drive the white lizards into the sea. Porter had to undertake an expedition against them, accompanied by the Taeehs, who showed no great stomach for combat. The night it sailed had been chosen by some of the prisoners for an attempt to seize *Essex Jr.,* which they proposed to do by getting the guard drunk on rum mixed with laudanum.

Porter had in fact been aware of this plot from the beginning and was only letting it run until he was ready. Now he assembled the Englishmen under guard, reproached them for their ingratitude in thus repaying his kindness in allowing them at liberty ashore, and put them all in irons. The Typee war was much harder than that with the Happahs, these people using their slings and thrown spears with great effect from ambush. There was even one retreat, and Lieutenant Downes was wounded by a stone; but in the end Porter's men marched through the Typee valley, burned all their villages, and persuaded them to be friends.

It was now December of 1813; 1500 rats had been smoked out of *Essex,* the copper of her bottom repaired as well as a rotten maintopmast. She sailed for Valparaiso with *Essex Jr.,* on the 17th, and reached it on February 3, going in for supply. On the 8th, *Essex Jr.,* which was cruising in the offing, came into the bay firing signal guns, followed at no great distance by a pair of British cruisers, H.M.SS. *Phoebe,* 36, and *Cherub,* 20. Porter instantly recalled his people and beat to quarters. This was a wise precaution, for as *Phoebe* came into the harbor, she luffed up within ten or fifteen feet of *Essex,* her captain calling out: "Captain Hillyar's compliments to Captain Porter and hopes he is well."

"Very well, I thank you," said Porter, and warned the Britisher that if he ran *Essex* aboard there would be bloodshed.

"Oh, sir, I have no such intention," replied Hillyar, but his ship came right on, and allowed herself to be taken aback with her bowsprit jutting over *Essex'* forecastle.

"You have no business where you are," shouted Porter, "and I warn you that if you touch a rope yarn of this ship I shall board instantly."

Now Hillyar could see how every man was in place at the American frigate's guns, with boarders along the gangways, pistol and cutlass in hand, while his own ship was bows on, in position to be raked. He backed her away, expostulating frantically, and anchored at the other side of the harbor. A couple of days later the two captains met ashore, established friendly personal relations, and agreed to respect Chilean neutrality within the three-mile limit.

On the 24th Hillyar put out and began to cruise back and forth off the port. Several times Porter took his ship into the offing, trying to bring on an engagement against *Phoebe* without having to fight *Cherub* as well, but Hillyar soon found out that his much heavier ship could not maneuver against *Essex,* and he liked the look of the American cruiser's preparations for close action so little that he kept close to his consort. *Essex Jr.* was no good in company with regular warships; her biggest guns were 18-pounder carronades and her sides were weak.

Thus matters stood at a deadlock until March 28, when a strong gale from the southward swept across open Valparaiso Bay. One of *Essex'* cables parted and the other anchor began to drag. Porter hastily got sail on his ship and, sighting the British off the westward point, made a snap decision to break away to sea from them, out to windward. *Phoebe* could never catch him; he could handle *Cherub*.

Now destiny took a hand, as with *Philadelphia* at Tripoli. A flaw in the gust struck *Essex,* and as she heeled to it the weak main-topmast that had been repaired in the Marquesas went cracking over the side. The British were too close for the crippled frigate to make it past them to her anchorage inside, but she was run off the wind and brought to in a little bay about a quarter of a mile from shore. *Phoebe* and *Cherub* followed her right in; Captain Hillyar forgot about his agreement, took station where not one of the American frigate's carronades would bear, and began to shoot.

Porter made one of the most desperate defenses in naval history. The only guns he could use were the long 12s on his upper deck, but with these he made such good practice that once he drove both opponents out of action with damaged spars, and once succeeded in maneuvering his limping ship close enough to exchange three broadsides at a terrific pace. But it was all no use against the odds; after two hours of firing, with three-fifths of her crew killed or wounded and not a whole rope left in the ship, the long saga of *Essex* came to a melancholy end in surrender. She had destroyed an industry and raised one up; for after her cruise the whale fishery remained almost exclusively American until the coming of coal-oil and the Civil War put an end to it.

She had cruised for over a year in an unfriendly ocean, supplying herself from her enemies; had damaged them to the extent of some eight or nine times her own value; and was brought to book at last only because her commander was a more honorable man than his opponent.

VII

It was agreed that *Essex Jr.* should be disarmed and carry the prisoners to some American port under parole. The home voyage was without incident until the coast of Long Island was reached in July

1814, when the ship was brought to for an examination of papers by *Saturn,* 74, one of the squadron blockading New York. Porter went aboard; Captain Nash of the battleship gave him some oranges and newspapers, and told him to proceed, but two hours later signaled a halt and sent over a lieutenant, who said *Essex Jr.* was not to go in to New York after all. Porter demanded to know why; was told that Captain Nash "had his reasons" and flashed into a rage.

"I am your prisoner, then," he said. "I do not consider myself any longer bound by my contract with Captain Hillyar, which has been violated, and I shall act accordingly."

He made good on it. At seven the next morning a whaleboat was dropped over *Essex Jr.'s* side, Porter and an armed crew slipped into it and began to pull like mad for shore. They were not spied for several minutes, and when *Saturn* did come around in pursuit a friendly fog rolled in, so that Captain Porter reached Babylon, Long Island, in safety—or relative safety, since a local vigilance committee was all for stringing him up as a spy until he produced his captain's commission and found someone who recognized him. From this point on to Washington it was a triumphal progress. The windows of New York were illuminated for him, at Philadelphia sailors pulled his carriage through the street by hand and carried him on their shoulders to his tavern. In Washington, he was taken at once to a lunch with President Madison and Navy Secretary Jones, who offered him the command of the new 44 building at the capital.

He would take the frigate if ordered, said Porter, but thought he had a better plan. The way really to damage Britain in this war was through opening the arteries of her commerce, and the best means would be to use some of those light clipper-built raiders which were proving so sensationally successful in the hands of the privateers. Let a squadron of these get into a trade area, as *Essex* had operated in the Pacific, not making prizes to be sent in, but under orders to sink, burn, destroy; they would make John Bull howl.

The Secretary was much taken with the idea and Mr. Madison was easily persuaded. They not only told Porter to go ahead, but ordered Oliver Perry to assemble a second raider squadron. Porter purchased two brigs, *Spark* and *Firefly,* and three schooners, *Torch, Spitfire,* and

David Porter

Eagle, which had all been laid down as privateers. They were armed with eight to ten 18-pound carronades and four long guns of the same caliber, being intended to cruise in the West Indies. But all needed some alterations to fit them as warships, and the unit never put to sea, as news of peace prevented. *Spark* remained in the navy many years and was a notably fast-sailing vessel.

As soon as peace became definite Porter was appointed to the new board of Navy Commissioners with Isaac Hull and his old superior and friend, John Rodgers. As he liked Washington, he bought a farm of 157 acres a mile north of the White House, and built upon it a fine house which he called Meridian Hill. The prize-money from his Pacific cruise and the income from the excellent journal he wrote about it made him at the close of hostilities a fairly wealthy man. This was fortunate, for he farmed on the lordliest scale, keeping the building filled with guests, who were always sent away loaded with presents from the vegetable garden, so that the family had to buy for their own winter consumption. It had become a fairly large family, with six stout sons, every one of whom turned out to be a head taller than his father. The work at the Commissioner's office went well, the navy's new regulations showed progress, and the board obtained from Congress a series of acts which established the navy on a permanent basis of 12 line-of-battleships, 14 heavy frigates, and three 38s.

In short, after so much voyaging and adventuring, Captain Porter seemed about to settle down into a sage. But he had not yet exhausted his singular capacity for trouble. The new movement began in that fruitful source of difficulties, the Caribbean, where picarooning had once more become a popular pastime, under the impulse of the endemic lack of peace—one cannot call it war—between Spain and her revolted American colonies. The trade of the sugar centers was rich, and the authority of Spain, itself in confusion, was so feeble as to offer little restraint on piracy. In 1820 the British felt it necessary to send a pair of sloops-of-war to the north coast of Cuba. They captured one or two piratical craft, but this did not notably discourage the rest, and by 1822 the situation had become so bad that the United States decided to set up a regular West Indian squadron, consisting of four frigates, two sloops-of-war, and six of the light vessels originally intended to raid those very waters under Porter and Perry.

Some fairly good work was done that year, but even the light raiders turned out to be rather clumsy for the close inshore work needed. Moreover, international law required that unless the pirates were caught in the act they had to be turned over to the Spanish local authorities, who only said they could not prevent such things happening and let the rascals go. At the beginning of 1823, accordingly, Porter was appointed to reorganize the whole business of pirate-hunting, with a free hand as to his ships. The official instructions were stiff and correct; unofficially, he seems to have been told that he need not be too nice about such matters as pursuing the pirates ashore into Spanish territory as long as he could made a plausible case and get results.

Of the frigates, Porter retained only *John Adams,* 28, as a flag and administrative headquarters. He added eight of the small, fast Chesapeake schooners called "bay-boats," arming them with three guns each, a steam-powered "galliot" named *Sea Gull,** and a half-dozen big 20-oared barges.

The disposition of the Spaniards was made abundantly clear on March 6, 1823, soon after Porter arrived on station. The Commodore sent one of his bay-boats in to San Juan, Puerto Rico, with a request that the Governor furnish a list of the ships legally commissioned as privateers by his office. The bay-boat did not return; after two days Porter sent another of his schooners in to seek the reason. The forts at San Juan entrance opened up and killed the lieutenant commanding. Of course, the matter was smoothed over with a great many fine words, but the event left its mark, and the mark was not erased when Porter began sending in landing parties to smoke out piratical nests ashore.

He was getting things fairly well in hand when an epidemic of yellow fever hit the squadron in August, so severely that he had to send practically all the ships north to save the lives of their crews. This produced another outbreak of piracy, which lasted until Porter came back

* This inconsiderable pot seems to have been the first seagoing steam warship in the world. Fulton's *Demologos* never left New York harbor.

in the winter and began hammering them again. By this date the British patrols had also been considerably increased, and Porter made an area-of-operations agreement with them—a very convenient arrangement, since it was always possible to discover that a given group of captured pirates had been working in the British-patrolled area. In such a case the prisoners had to be turned over, not to the Spaniards but the Royal Navy; the Royal Navy took them to Jamaica and hanged them.

In 1824 the yellowjack struck early, and Porter had to send most of his ships north in July, going north himself. He returned to the base anchorage at St. Thomas in the Virgins aboard *John Adams* on November 12, and there he heard a tale from Lieutenant Charles T. Platt, commanding the bay-schooner *Beagle,* 3.

About a month before, someone had broken into the warehouse of Cabot, Bailey & Co., American merchants of St. Thomas, and had stolen a considerable quantity of goods. The firm discovered that the merchandise had been taken to Fajardo, at the eastern end of Puerto Rico, and asked Platt to recover it for them if he could. The Lieutenant reached Fajardo in his ship on October 26, and went to call on the captain of the port, wearing civilian clothes, since his mission was nonmilitary. He was well received and taken to the Alcalde, who promised his good offices. Platt left him to have breakfast in a public-house; as he was thus engaged, a couple of soldiers interrupted his meal to take him back before an Alcalde suddenly become very stern, who demanded the register of his ship. Platt replied that *Beagle* was a warship and did not have a register, but he sent a boat out for his commission and his uniform, which he proceeded to don. The Alcalde pronounced the uniform a fake, the commission a forgery, and Platt a damned pirate; had him thrown into jail and did not release him until the other people of the schooner came ashore with a copy of her official orders.

The motives and business connections of the Alcalde were obvious; what struck Porter, what would strike any naval officer, was the insult to the American uniform and flag, the sort of thing he had been fighting all his life. He sailed at once for Fajardo; two days later, one of the schooners towed *John Adams'* boats with 200 armed men into the little harbor. The Alcalde was summoned to give a formal apology, which done, salutes were exchanged and the Commodore departed, satisfied that he had done his duty.

It is possible that he did not realize he was past the hot days of the great European war, when honor was at such a premium. It is probable that he did not know how delicate the diplomatic position was in Washington, where the Monroe Doctrine had just been promulgated, to the anger and derision of the Continental powers; and where it was regarded as not unlikely that Spain would seek some excuse to show her resentment. But even had Porter taken all this into account, he could hardly have been prepared for the letter that presently arrived from Navy Secretary S. L. Southard. It disapproved everything the Commodore had done, removed him from command, and ordered him home to face a court of inquiry.

To Porter (and to many people since his time) this seemed the most appalling mistreatment for an act which merited reward instead of punishment. He made no bones about saying so, both privately and through the press, and as he had plenty of information and a neat turn of phrase the remarks he made left welts. It was unfortunate that the man on whom the welts were left was Samuel Southard, a professional politician and one of the most tactlessly irritable characters who ever sat in the Cabinet.

Southard translated Porter from the court of inquiry to a special court-martial, of which James Barron was named president and Jesse D. Elliott the next senior member, all the other judges being junior to Porter himself.

To understand the import of this, one must remember that David Porter had sat on the court which thirteen years before had condemned Barron for the disgraceful unreadiness of the frigate *Chesapeake* when H.M.S. *Leopard* shot her up and impressed four of her men. Then, five years before, had come the duel in which Barron killed Stephen Decatur in the sorry aftermath of the *Chesapeake* business; Porter was Decatur's second then, Elliott had seconded Barron—and fled from the field when he saw both men fall, persuaded that he would be arrested as an accessory to a double murder. It was Porter who helped the surgeon care for the wounded Barron on that occasion, then pursued Elliott and shouted at him: "Go back to your friend, you coward, and do what you can."

These were the two men who led the court in the trial of David Porter. The charge was "disobedience of orders," on the ground that nothing in the Commodore's instructions authorized him to go ashore for such a purpose as obtaining an apology. The result was what might be expected. Porter was found guilty and sentenced to six months' suspension from the service.

VIII

His resignation went in at once. The ink on it was hardly dry before he was visited by a polite and persuasive emissary from the new Republic of Mexico. Spain still refused to recognize the independence of that nation, and maintained a garrison in the fortress of San Juan de Ulua outside Vera Cruz, from which the town was occasionally bombarded. This was a case of substantive warfare, and the only means open to the Mexican government for damaging the Spaniards was on the sea. A loan had been floated in England, and with the proceeds the new nation had purchased several warships to be the foundation of a national navy. Would Commodore Porter consent to head the service, with a free hand to do as he pleased, the title of "General of Marine," a salary of $12,000 a year, and the usual arrangements regarding prize-money and perquisites?

Commodore Porter hesitated a little while and decided that he would, leaving for Mexico in April 1826, with a nephew, David H. Porter, and two of his own sons, David Dixon and Thomas. The four went up to Mexico City at once, where President Victoria handed the new admiral a deed to an enormous estate in Texas and another in southern Mexico. Porter swiftly discovered that "for political intrigue, Mexico compares to Washington as Mt. Orizaba compares to a level plain," but there was no difficulty about his commission, and he hurried down to Vera Cruz to look over his fleet. It consisted of a 32, *Libertad,* with four good new brig-sloops and a couple of small gunboats of antique vintage. The officers were younger sons of wealthy families, who spent most of their time dressing in gorgeous uniforms and exercising their fascination on various ladies; the seamen were almost nonexistent. But some men came in from New Orleans, attracted by Porter's name—international adventurers assembled from various parts of the Caribbean; the ships were gradually whipped into shape, and by early spring of 1827 the General of Marine of the Republic of Mexico was able to take his fleet to sea.

He made for the coast of Cuba, and put into effect the plan of raiding warfare he had intended to use against the British in those same waters. The Spanish Caribbean squadron consisted of two 50-gun ships, two frigates, and three brigs, but they were not very efficient and the commanders knew nothing about the proper methods of handling convoy. Porter had learned the shoals and reefs of the region throughly during his command against the pirates. He established a base at the Dry Tortugas and was able to slip in and out at will, capturing ships by the dozen, and—as he had in the Pacific—making war support war by sending their cargoes in to New Orleans for sale.

There was only one difficulty. David Porter was an honest man, who paid the expenses of his cruisers out of their captures, then remitted the rest of his take to Mexico, expecting that after the usual clerical procedure sums of prize-money would be placed to his credit. Of course, nothing of the kind happened; the money was pocketed, and the government soon found itself in debt to its admiral not only for considerable sums of prize-money, but also for nearly two years' salary. That bird of singularly ill omen, Antonio Lopez de Santa Anna, had by this date become the controlling force at the capital. He recalled Porter for a series of conferences about nothing, gave him profuse promises of payment as soon as this detail or that had been settled, then sent him down to Vera Cruz on a "tour of inspection." On the road, two men tried to assassinate the General of Marine; as soon as he was asleep in his bed in Vera Cruz, two others tried it.

Their lack of success was conspicuous. Porter shot one of the road agents and cut an arm off the other with his razor-edged cutlass; in Vera Cruz he split the skulls of both assailants. But it was clear that the Mexican jig was up, and it was probably a great relief to Porter to get a letter from an old friend named Mahlon Dickerson. General Andrew

David Porter

Jackson had just been elected President of the United States (the letter said), a man who had received from the government much the same injustice as Porter himself, when he followed his duty rather than his orders in pursuing some Indians over the Florida border. He was determined to redress the injustice done by the court-martial. If the Commodore would return to his native country, something substantial would be done for him.

Porter accepted with alacrity, but felt he had been too much hurt by the naval service to resume his place in it, so Jackson sent him out as consul to Algiers. Even here there was no rest for the troublous spirit; when he arrived at his station Porter discovered that France had just conquered the old pirate hold, and there was no need of an American consul. He remained in the Mediterranean, however, and Jackson presently cleared matters up by making him the first U.S. resident minister at Constantinople.

There he spent the rest of his life, a good many years of it, not dying till 1843, much respected by the local diplomatic corps. Toward the end it was a rather lonely life, far from home and family. The Commodore read a good deal and became a noted authority on travel in the East, being much consulted by passing Europeans. Every 4th of July there would be a ceremony before the residency, with the raising of the Stars and Stripes and the firing of a salute, at the end of which Porter would remark in a loud voice, "*Mashallah!* That was well done!"

A lonely end; but it had been a full life and a useful one. No other of Preble's boys carried so much so directly to the future; for of the first two active admirals of the American navy, one was his son and the other his foster-son, and the influence of both was prodigious. For that matter, so was David Porter's own. His whole life was a series of anecdotes, and he seemed to exist in a state of hair-trigger temper; but temper was not without survival value for the nation in the days of British aggression. There is also a good deal more to him than that.

Specifically, there is the thing Porter caught from his old teacher Preble, the thing so completely transmitted through the service later— the spirit of make-do, of finding a way to use the means in hand to produce the desired result, although the means may be less than one is entitled to expect and the result may seem unattainably distant. *Essex* cannot fight a broadside action? Very well, we will prepare her to fight by surprise and boarding. Her consorts in the South Atlantic have disappeared? Very well, we will take her to the Pacific. There is no friendly dock? We will make one in the South Seas. The frigates are kept in port by the British blockade? Run the blockade with fast schooner-raiders.

That spirit has never entirely left the American navy from Porter's day down and, through all errors, all fumblings and temporary defeats, has had much to do with its triumphs.

Chapter 9

The Eccentric:
William Burrows

I remember the sea-fight far away,
How it thundered o'er the tide!
And the dead captains, as they lay
In their graves, o'erlooking the tranquil bay
Where they in battle died.
—LONGFELLOW: "My Lost Youth"

WHEN THE NAVY WAS RE-ESTABLISHED TO THE STRAINS OF THE new "President's March," fifteen years after the Continental Congress sold into the India trade the last of the ships that had fought in the Revolution, President Adams felt the propriety of enlisting a regiment of marine soldiers. They were to operate according to British precedent, a seagoing police force to keep unruly sailors in order, to lead shore expeditions and boarding parties, and in battle to act as small-arms men. As it was anticipated that they would identify themselves with the service in general rather than with a particular ship (which sailors follow), their term of enlistment was fixed at one year, or until ten days after reaching port if the year had expired while they were at sea. No Negroes, mulattoes, or Indians were to be entered, and the foreign-born, even if naturalized, only in the proportion of one in three. The pay was to be six dollars per month, with one ration.

To head this marine regiment, Mr. Stoddert, the new Secretary of the Navy, besought the services of one William W. Burrows, providing him with a commission as major-commandant. He was a respectable gentleman of South Carolinan origin and some wealth, a true

Federalist (politics played a not unimportant part in military appointments in those days), who had served his state during the Revolution and subsequently established himself at Kinderton near Philadelphia, then the seat of government. This Burrows had a son of thirteen, also named William, who was being educated under his parent's eye with the greatest care, though without any view toward preparing him for a particular profession. Even at so tender an age, the boy showed a lively intelligence, an inclination to the pursuits of literature, and so particular a skill in living languages that German was already as familiar to him as his mother tongue. For French, on the other hand, although his parents insisted rigidly that he should study it, he experienced a profound and almost inexplicable aversion.

Among the subjects he was taught, art had a place. His drawing-master was surprised to observe that young Burrows not infrequently neglected his allotted tasks in the other departments of a polite education to produce the likeness of a gallant ship of war. When this news was carried to his father, it became evident to the latter where the secret bent of his son's inclination lay. He accordingly arranged for the boy's tutelage in the various aspects of naval science and, after the instruction had proceeded in a satisfactory manner for something over a year, procured for his son a warrant as midshipman of the navy.

Young Burrows was assigned to the corvette *Portsmouth,* 24, built for the government by the city of the same name in New Hampshire. This ship was commanded by Captain Daniel McNeill, often referred to as "the gallant but eccentric McNeill." There was certainly something in his conduct strikingly divergent from the norm. In 1802 he was eased out of the service after a cruise to the Mediterranean in command of *Boston,* 28, during which he sailed about wherever he pleased, without paying any attention to the orders of Commodore Dale, and at Toulon left three of his own lieutenants on the beach and put to sea with as many French officers "for a change of company." At the time of Burrows' first cruise, this eccentricity had not burst into full bloom, though there was a hint of it in the perfectly towering row in which McNeill involved himself with the British governor of Paramaribo.

The details are now impossible to recover fully; it had something to do with the bad conduct of one of *Portsmouth's* midshipmen ashore. The Governor told McNeill not to go to sea until the matter was settled, and McNeill replied with a letter couched in terms that produced a formal diplomatic complaint from London. At the time the Captain was held to have behaved in a manner that sustained the dignity of the flag, and the Commandant of the Marine Corps doubtless considered his son fortunate in going to sea under so energetic an officer. But, without making too much of a point of it, one may inquire whether association with McNeill was not an encouragement toward straying from the beaten track for a mind which already showed tendencies of its own in that direction. The first leader under whom a young officer serves, especially if he be admired, can often fix a character beyond recall.

At all events, Midshipman Burrows was something of an odd fish in the steerage mess. When the fork was set in the table at four bells of the evening watch, as a sign that the warrants and senior mids wished to converse on subjects proper only for those who had passed their examinations in vice, he tumbled off to his hammock without even trying to listen. He saved up his rum, and would be found sharing it with the old seaman who acted as body-servant-of-all-work, discussing some such point as how a flying moor was made.

It was only with difficulty that the Captain could persuade him to wear his uniform. He said he wanted to do something to deserve it first, and when one of the lieutenants inquired why Burrows was so tonguetied about giving orders to the sailors, the midshipman replied that the men knew what to do better than he did.

The ship voyaged to France under a flag of truce, with envoys to negotiate a definite treaty. On her return the 15-year-old Burrows asked for a furlough of several months to complete his studies. Those he undertook were the mathematics of navigation, in which he had found himself weak, and the French language, of whose utility he had received a convincing demonstration during the trip.

All this would seem to make him out a rather solemncholy youth, intensely ambitious within the confines of his profession, caring for very little else—and so he appeared to others at the time. During his next cruise, which was to the Mediterranean in *Philadelphia,* 38, Captain

Samuel Barron, he was noted chiefly for his reserve and his close application to the technical details of seamanship. In that recondite art, he could hardly have found a better teacher than the Virginia Captain, probably the best ship-handler in the services and one of the few men who ever succeeded in box-hauling a frigate off a lee shore during a gale. But the service itself was uneventful, the ship spending most of her time at Malta. When the ship returned to the United States, Burrows was allowed to remain on shore for nearly nine months before being appointed to *Constitution,* 44, then fitting for the Mediterranean as flagship of the new commodore, Edward Preble.

Behind this official neglect there seems to have lain a difficulty at which the reticent written record only hints. The elder Burrows was certainly not in sympathy with the politics of the Jefferson administration, and still less so with its attitude toward the navy. In February 1804, he resigned his commission, not even remaining in Philadelphia, but going back to the old home in Charleston. Secretary Smith accepted the resignation in a cold note, with the addendum: "As there is a large debit to your account on the books of the department, it is expected that you will without delay repair to this place, for the purpose of settling the balance." There is nothing to indicate how the commandant of the Marine Corps, a man of independent means, could have run up "a large debit," nor is there anything to indicate the ultimate outcome of the transaction. But the whole business can hardly have been pleasant for the midshipman of eighteen, so determined to make the navy his profession. His taciturnity developed to the edge of moroseness during the voyage out.

Burrows's assigned working station was at the main and main-topsail braces, a post for a seaman and probably the most important a midshipman could have. The manner in which he performed his duty attracted the attention of the old Commodore, who marked him down as one of the best seaman aboard, and often had him to dinner. In those days, ships carried an officer called the sailing master, a kind of warrant machinist or gang-boss, the technical head of the department dealing with propulsion. When the man who held this place aboard the schooner *Vixen* fell ill during the winter, Preble gave Burrows the appointment on a temporary basis.

William Burrows

He acquitted himself so well during a stormy voyage to Tunis that when *Vixen's* sailing master recovered, Burrows was transferred in the same capacity to *Siren,* 16, the new brig commanded by red-headed Charles Stewart. Wherever that officer went there was action, and Burrows saw every bit of it the navy could offer during the summer, with long weeks of rocking on blockade off a lee shore, an occasional pursuit or capture; finally the growing sense of perilous excitement as Preble prepared for the direct attack on Tripoli's castles, in which "I expect we may suffer much." Then August and its series of battles, with a promotion; for between casualties and the necessity of manning the gunboats that did the close-in work, there was a shortage of officers, and Burrows found himself an acting lieutenant at 19, one of Preble's boys. In the company of that league of youth, under the approval of the frosty old demon on *Constitution's* quarterdeck, he began to live the life he wanted, and his character opened out and developed.

The signs were apparent to others who saw him after the Preble campaign was over, when Burrows remained in the Mediterranean as Fifth Lieutenant of *Essex,* 32, and therefore a full member of the wardroom mess. At this time he is described as still somewhat aloof in his manner and, when addressed quickly, rather blunt. No one ever sees him laugh; but from the earlier moroseness there has been a significant change. "During the hours of hilarity, without moving a muscle of his face, he would set the table in a roar. Everything he said or did was odd and whimsical." His fund of anecdotes was bottomless, for he was in the habit of going ashore, dressed as and acting like a common sailor, to explore all the dives of the seaport towns in search of matters of interest.

These Haroun-al-Raschid activities gave Burrows a personal contact with the enlisted men which was thoroughly unusual among young officers. He spoke the language of the seamen, understood their agitations and, when they had any, their ambitions; was always ready to get them out of trouble, and did so on numerous occasions. No officer but Decatur had so good a reputation with the lower deck.

Nevertheless, as time went on and the ships were called home to be laid up in favor of Mr. Jefferson's gunboats, the old melancholy was observed to be repossessing him. There was good reason for this; he had devoted his life to the U.S. navy so completely as to have almost no other interest, and the U.S. navy had become singularly reluctant to recognize either his devotion or the ability with which he did his work. Midshipmen who had been under him in Preble's squadron were moved up to First Lieutenancies and even small commands, while Burrows came back from the Mediterranean over two years after the close of the Tripolitan War, still an acting Fifth.

It is a little difficult to account for this. Certainly, even Mr. Robert Smith, one of the less effective Secretaries of the Navy, knew what sort of man he had in Preble, listened to his recommendations, and pushed forward the graduates of the school before Tripoli as rapidly as they could be pushed under the circumstances. Certainly Preble considered Burrows one of his favorite pupils; corresponded freely with him during the later years. One is practically driven to the conjecture that the old trouble between Smith and Commandant Burrows of the Marine Corps remained unforgotten, and that the sins of the fathers were being visited on the children.

Whatever it was, there it was. Burrows celebrated his return to the United States by obtaining a furlough from his captain for the specific purpose of waiting upon the Navy Department in Washington. Obviously, it did not do him much good; Mr. Lieutenant Burrows, still very junior on the list, next appears in the records as commanding officer of a gunboat, enforcing the Embargo on the Delaware. In that unpleasant assignment he remained for over two years, completely withdrawn from society, described as spending long hours in brooding. Then in 1809 Madison replaced Jefferson, and Paul Hamilton succeeded Secretary Smith; Burrows posted off to Washington again, laid his claim before the new head of the Department, and begged that if he could not be given his promotion he should be allowed to resign from the service that had been everything in life to him.

The resignation was refused. Instead Hamilton posted Burrows as Third Lieutenant of *President,* 44, the first ship to put to sea under the new policy of deep-water cruises, with William Bainbridge as captain. The pay was the same as before, but as Third Lieutenant of a heavy frigate he had moved well up the line. When the frigate returned, Bur-

William Burrows

rows was sent to *Hornet,* 18, as First Lieutenant. James Lawrence was in command, and the voyage was an adventurous one to Europe with dispatches. A gale of hurricane force struck the ship; the only record of the occurrence says she would certainly have been lost but for the seamanship of her First Lieutenant, but there is not a single detail of what he did or how.

At the close of the trip, Burrows told acquaintances—there was hardly anyone he could call a friend—that he was convinced the government would never get up backbone enough to do anything about the long-continued British aggressions. He applied for a furlough to make a commercial voyage. Bainbridge had just done the same thing, so the two former shipmates had probably talked matters over. But the results were very different. Burrows's billet was as first mate of the ship *Thomas Penrose,* for Canton with general merchandise. China was a long voyage, and while the ship was making her return trip the war that Burrows had never expected came at last, without anyone aboard having heard of it. Ranging up the South Atlantic, the ship was taken by a British cruiser and carried into Barbados, where Lieutenant William Burrows found himself a prisoner before he had a chance to fire a shot.

The British let him go home at once on parole, and by this date there were so many of their officers in American hands that there was no difficulty at all in finding an exchange for him. The confirmation came through early in 1813. Burrows, who was in Washington at the time, was immediately summoned to the Navy Department and informed that he had been named Lieutenant-Commandant of U.S.S. *Enterprise,* 12, then lying at Portsmouth. "He threw off a great deal of his habitual reserve, became urbane and attentive, and those who had lately looked upon him as a mere misanthrope were delighted with his manners."

Well might he show pleasure; for of all the ships of the navy none within reach of his rank bore any such reputation as this little brig. Built as a schooner for work among the West Indian islands during the French War, she made herself famous in that conflict for her wonderful speed and her still more wonderful good fortune; she had been famous in the Barbary War, where for the second time she saw more action than any other ship. The names of her past commanders were a roll of all the best and most successful captains in the service: Sterrett, Decatur, Isaac Hull, David Porter, Charles Stewart.

Like the other navy schooners she had fallen into the hands of Captain Thomas Tingey at the Washington Navy Yard during the Jefferson era. He was a traditionalist of British navy ideas, to whom the idea of mere speed in a small cruiser had small appeal beside the fact that a schooner could not be stopped or backed in action by the mere handling of her sails. Besides, he considered the brig rig more suitable for a warship, since the foot of a square sail is less in the way of gunners than is a boom; so he had all the schooners changed to brigs. Moreover, he changed their armament of twelve long 6-pounders for fourteen 18-pound carronades and two long 9s. The change of rig quite spoiled the sailing of vessels designed for a different set of stresses and pulls, and in addition the ships were now badly overweighted by their new armament. All the schooners warmed over into brigs had been run down and taken by 1813; that is, all but *Enterprise,* since no tinkering could ruin her luck.

She came around from New Orleans at the beginning of January 1813, right through the tightest of the blockade, and had taken a couple of prizes on the way. Since then, her operations were off the New England coast, defending the local traffic there against small privateers that came down from Nova Scotia under the British flag; took one of them, and drove the rest away. Burrows found her a happy ship; he cruised in her for two months offshore without sighting anything of importance until September 4, when he put out of Portland to the eastward in search of a couple of privateers that had been reported off Monhegan. Near Penguin Point a brig was sighted inshore, just getting under way and bearing every appearance of a man-o'-war. Any doubt as to her character was soon removed; she set British ensigns and came loping out to sea, firing a challenge gun.

In fact she was H.M.S. *Boxer,* of a force identical with *Enterprise* save that her long guns were 6s instead of 9s and she had a smaller crew. Her captain was Samuel Blyth, who had been in Halifax when the captured *Chesapeake* was brought in, and who acted as one of Lawrence's pall-bearers; he had nailed his colors to the mast, and now set everything that would draw in pursuit of *Enterprise* as she stood seaward.

Aboard the American brig, Burrows was busy having axmen enlarge the window of the poop cabin and hauling one of the long 9s aft to fire through the gap. The crew thought he intended to use the piece as a stern-chaser while running away, which shows that their service under him had not quite taught them what kind of man William Burrows was. They sent a delegation from the forecastle to say they wished to be laid alongside the Britisher. Burrows told them somewhat stiffly that they would soon have all the fighting they wanted, and held on to gain sea room; then at 3:00 P.M., shortened sail and swung toward his enemy.

The two brigs were now on opposite tacks; they kept away together along a broad reach, *Enterprise* to the weather, and opened fire not half a pistol-shot apart, both crews cheering. At the first discharge an 18-pound shot almost cut Captain Blyth in two; a moment later a canister ball struck Burrows in the leg as he braced against a bulwark, heaving on the tackle of a carronade that had lost some of its people. The missile went right through the limb and glanced into his body, a mortal wound.

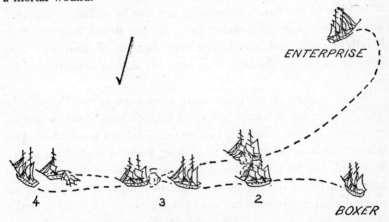

Enterprise—Boxer
(1) The approach; *Enterprise* gains her sea-room. (2–3) *Enterprise* forereaches; *Boxer* is raked. (4) *Boxer* raked again; loses her mainmast and surrenders.

He would not let the men carry him below, but lay on the quarter-deck, crying that the colors should never come down. There was little danger of such an outcome, for the American brig's accurate fire had cut so many of *Boxer's* ropes that the latter's sails spilled wind; *Enterprise* forged ahead, ported her helm, and raked her opponent heavily with the 9-pounder from the cabin window. The action had now been going on for fifteen minutes; the dying American commander allowed his opponent to come up on the starboard quarter and delivered a diagonal rake with another series of broadsides that brought down the Britisher's main-topmast. Now *Enterprise* gained again; shot up in the wind athwart *Boxer's* bow and raked her until somebody hailed from her deck to say she surrendered, but could not haul down her flag until firing had ceased, because it was nailed fast.

Enterprise had lost 2 killed and 10 wounded; the British ship had lost 3 killed and 17 wounded, and was reduced to an unmanageable wreck, with many guns dismounted and her bulwarks so beaten in that she was sold as of no use to her captors. Blyth's sword was brought to Burrows where he lay; he clasped it to his chest and murmured, "I am satisfied. I die contented," then did so.

He was buried at Portland, side by side with his late opponent. "The crew of the *Boxer*; enemies by law, but by gallantry, brothers," was the toast at a naval dinner later; for the British brig had been bravely fought, and was beaten only because of Burrows's forethought in placing the long 9 aft, and his skill in maneuvering his ship.

He left a green memory, especially among the sailors. Probably he was the strangest character among all Preble's boys, indrawn and introspective, the one least likely to have succeeded as a naval officer. This was not for want of wanting, to be sure; Burrows studied his profession hard. But his reserve, his touchiness, the glooms that came upon him when things did not go according to plan, were not exactly the psychological equipment that would strike one as ideal for a service in which men are, during long periods, thrown into association with fellows not of their own choosing and in which the very exigencies of the service produce injustices to the individual.

He had a little more than his share of injustices, and at first sight it is rather surprising that he did not resign from the navy, as so many officers did during the dark days of the second Jefferson administration. Rising prices had made a junior officer's pay inadequate, there was no prospect of the prize-money that was supposed to supplement pay, and the whole service was suffering under a load of public disapproval as the enforcer of the Embargo, as well as a deep sense of shame and distrust in itself, the result of the *Leopard-Chesapeake* affair.

But something happened to William Burrows under the walls of Tripoli. More than with any of the others, it stands recognizable as a key period in his career. Under Preble, he somehow learned the art of relaxation; learned that, having done all, one must stand and await the fullness of time. It looks like an idiosyncrasy that the form Burrows's relaxation took should be the establishment of closer relations with the enlisted seamen. But it was not this altogether; for concern over the common seaman was as much endemic among the veterans of that campaign as it was extraordinary beyond the limits of the group. They had studied under the man who taught himself how to keep people healthy in Eastern seas. "God bless him," the men said of Decatur; Bainbridge's people sent daily delegations to ask after the Captain's health when he was hit in the combat with *Java*; Porter's "principal care was the health of my people." Burrows employed a different method from any of these, but it had its origin in the same sources and it led to the same result.

THE SEA-RAIDERS

Chapter 10

The Carolina Student: Johnston Blakely

No more shall Blakely's thunders roar
   Upon the stormy deep;
Far distant from Columbia's shore
   His tombless ruins sleep;
But long Columbia's song shall tell
How Blakely fought, how Blakely fell.

Though long our foaming billows cast
   The battle's fury brav'd;
And still unsullied on the mast
   The starry banner wav'd,
Unconquer'd will Columbia be
While she can boast of sons like thee.

—Broadside ballad

IN APRIL 1814, A KEY POINT IN THE WAR OF 1812 HAD BEEN REACHED. It had now become reasonably clear that England was in possession of the formula for winning the contest, and would apply her pressures with increasing vigor until the United States chose to accept whatever terms she offered. To be sure, Lake Erie had been the scene of a stunning and quite irretrievable setback during the previous summer, but Erie was the most remote of the contested lakes, and nearly everywhere else the balance of the past fifteen months had swung to the cause of Britain.

Ontario lay across the line of communications to Erie, and on Lake Ontario British skill had come to the support of British valor by giving Commodore Yeo so considerable a naval superiority that the American fleet was blockaded in Sackett's Harbor. British soldiers were on their way across the lake to wrest the Niagara frontier from the Americans. The British squadron on Lake Champlain was momentarily inferior, but this would be redressed at an early date by the completion of a splendid new 36-gun frigate, whereupon it would be possible to send an army into the heart of New York State. The destruction of Napoleon's forces in Spain had made abundant troops available for the purpose, and the army was already en route—14,000 veteran soldiers, more men than the United States had under arms, all told. Another great expedition was already on the seas to chastise the Americans by destroying their capital and laying waste the shipyards of Baltimore, which had sent out so many of those annoying privateers. A smaller force would annex part of the Maine district in order to provide easy overland communications to Quebec; an expedition to capture New Orleans and the outlets of the Mississippi had reached the planning stage. It seemed unlikely that the Americans could make effective resistance to any of these.

On the ocean, the unexpected fighting power of the American heavy frigates and the utterly unexpected skill with which they were handled had provided a series of nasty shocks, but these shocks were now over. One of the frigates had been taken during the 15-month period, after an action that would ever redound to the credit of British arms, and with the capture of *Essex* in Valparaiso harbor the last of the large American cruisers had been driven from the sea.

The two hundred warships employed in the blockade of American ports made it unlikely that more American warships would get out, or, if they did, insured their capture. The blockade had become so severe that flour stood at $18 a barrel in Boston, because the normal supply from the Chesapeake Bay region could not be brought in. All the major centers of the country were practically isolated from each other. In the seaport towns—which meant every important place—there was grievous unemployment. The government was in financial difficulties, and could no longer console itself even with the triumph of its lighter vessels. Only the loss of the insignificant brig *Boxer* marred the British navy's record for the 15-month period. In return for her they had taken not only the frigates *Chesapeake* and *Essex,* but the *Frolic,* sloop-of-war, and the brig *Argus.*

This last capture was an indicator of the only difficulty that still offered any disturbance to the Lords in Admiralty. To be sure, *Argus* had been taken in a handsome manner by H.M.S. *Pelican,* of somewhat greater force (280 pounds weight of broadside metal to 210), after a combat whose fairness was not altered by the facts that *Argus'* powder was bad, most of her crew drunk, and some of them behaving in a cowardly manner. This was the type of performance Britons expected from Americans, above all when pressure was put upon them —the type of performance they had frequently given at sea during the War of the Revolution. The disturbing element of *Argus'* capture lay in the place where it had been made and in the events that preceded and followed it.

For the place was the English Channel, the home of British sea power, and also the boulevard along which the greatest mass of her commercial traffic moved, whether to the south coast ports or to the Pool of London. And before she was brought to book, *Argus* wrought dreadful havoc in that commercial traffic, having taken no fewer than 21 ships between mid-June and mid-August and burned them all but one, with a damage bill of £600,000. What followed was even worse, for *Argus* set up a beacon for those formidable American privateers which were now offering Britain such a problem as she had never yet faced on the sea.

Privateering was not new to the English, of course; the war commerce—*guerre de course,* or running war—had been the backbone of the French system on the sea, ever since Louis XIV found it too expensive to maintain a navy and rented his warships to commercial firms who wished to engage in military speculation. The rental system had long since passed and the privateering of the great war of Napoleon was truly a private enterprise—which started with a rush at the beginning of the war, as always in the contests between France and England, then had been brought under control as the British tightened their blockade and multiplied by four the number of their small cruising ships in service. The French privateers were mostly small and poorly armed; they stayed not far from their home ports and rarely offered resistance when approached by regular warships. Dealing with them was mainly a question of numbers. They had a few large cruiser-privateers which attempted the Indiamen, east and west, but these valuable vessels could be placed in convoy.

The American privateers that hurried to sea at the outbreak of war were of a disturbingly different pattern. Many were small indeed; but all were armed to the teeth and most fought like tigers,* so that the armaments with which British merchant ships were accustomed to keep French privateers at a distance became utterly inadequate. *Kemp* of Baltimore, for instance, attacked a convoy of seven armed Indiamen and took them all after a savage fight. *Saratoga* of New York captured the 18-gun mail-packet *Morgiana,* which had a navy crew. *Atlas* of Philadelphia fought an action on both broadsides with two heavy packets, each of more than her own force, and captured both. By April 1814 these unusual privateers had three times attacked ships of the Royal Navy and taken them—in one case after a whirlwind cutlass-and-pistol battle across the decks which saw a higher percentage of casualties than any regular cruiser fight of the war.

Moreover, these American privateers were manned by such a race of seamen as the world had rarely known. They were accustomed to deep-sea cruising; they knew the West Indies, the River Plate, and the North Atlantic runs, they provisioned themselves for long periods at sea and headed straight for such places. *Benjamin Franklin* of New York invaded a fortified harbor in the West Indies and shot things out with the fort, while her boats cut out a valuable prize. *Yankee* of Bristol sent landing parties ashore and laid towns under contribution. The Governor of Jamaica complained that the privateers had placed his island under blockade.

Seven months after the war began, it was reckoned that the American privateers had taken 500 British merchant ships, which was more than the great power of France had been able to do in a year. The Admiralty's defense was essentially the same as against France

---

* Not always, to be sure. Mahan and Roosevelt cite instances of tame surrender. But both these writers were concerned with demolishing a legend which had magnified a real achievement into something superhuman, and neither took the trouble to compare the performance of the American privateers with that of the French.

—a tight blockade, valuable ships in convoy, and plenty of small cruisers on patrol. For a time, in the early months of 1813, it seemed probable that this time-honored prescription would reduce American privateering to a mere nuisance. But with the coming of summer and the cruise of *Argus,* a flaw began to appear in the syllogism. The blockade had indeed put an end to commercial traffic, but in so doing had left the sailors with nothing to do but go privateering. They accepted the only employment open to them, and they approached the project with an emotion in which greed for profits was not the only element. This was their own war. "No Impressment," "Free trade and sailors' rights," read the banner over many a tavern where a privateer's recruiting office was opened.

There were thus plenty of men, and there began to be ships. The blockade was so close that the warmed-over commercial craft which began the privateering business were no longer valid, and British warships had become so numerous that it was not safe for privateers to operate off the banks of Newfoundland or in the Gulf Stream. To meet the first difficulty, the privateersmen turned to their own shipwrights; there began to slide from the ways those wonderful Baltimore topsail schooners and brigs, with steep-raking masts, some of the most beautiful and certainly the fastest ships that ever cruised deep water under sail; of such graceful lines that modern naval architects can do no better in spite of their towing tanks; flimsily built, but they were not expected to last long and lightness meant more speed; having 5 to 7 carriage guns a side with an 18-pounder Long Tom on a pivot between the masts. Even the earlier privateers had shown some notable turns of speed, but the new ones, designed for the service, were beyond anything the Royal Navy possessed or had seen. They could sift through a blockade like smoke, eat right into the wind's eye, and outrun anything. During the whole of 1813 not one of them was taken in a straightaway chase.

And after *Argus* had shown the way, they began to appear where British ships were thickest—in the waters around the home islands. *Yankee* of Bristol approached the coast of Ireland and took seven ships in the wine trade that summer. *Scourge* of New York and *Rattlesnake* of Philadelphia got into the North Sea, and between them took

18 prizes to the value of half a million sterling. *Lion* of Baltimore cruised the Bay of Biscay; *Sabine* of Baltimore attacked the Portugal wine ships and took one of the East India Company's best vessels, homeward bound from Bombay.

This was hard to bear for a nation weary with the 21-year struggle against France. Yet the key question of the war was not whether England would be willing to support her losses, but whether the United States could stand up under the British counterattack. The privateers, however they might rejoice the men of the seaport towns and provide for their doxies hair-ribbons woven of ten-dollar bills, could do but little to allay the general feeling of futility.

By April 1814 the army had suffered a series of peculiarly galling defeats on the northern frontier. From the force of the British effort, it seemed that more might be in store during the coming summer. And now the navy had apparently reached its limits. With the public cruisers destroyed or locked in harbor, it could not be long before the British hit upon some extension of the devices successful against privateering in the past.

This, then, was the overall picture of the war in that fateful month. But on May 1, 1814, U.S.S. *Wasp,* 20, broke through the blockade from Portsmouth, New Hampshire, and the situation exploded.

II

She was the second of the name, one of William Doughty's new ship-sloops, and her commander was Master-Commandant Johnston Blakely. At this time he was a small man of 32 with once-black hair that had become very nearly white; black, darting eyes; a man who walked like a cat, with an appearance of always being on tiptoe. He was Irish by birth, from Seaford in County Down, and Scotch-Irish Protestant by race, his first name being that of one of the local great families. At the close of the Revolution, when his father decided to migrate to the new lands beyond the sea, he was only two years old.

At this time the Scotch-Irish already had a strong foothold in the Carolinas, and the elder Blakely chose to join his compatriots in Charleston. It was an unfortunate selection, since he was hardly ashore before his wife died of a fever and with her an infant son, younger than Johnston. Conceiving a dislike for the city that had cost him so much, John Blakely removed to Wilmington, North Carolina, where he had an acquaintance named Edward Jones, who had come out from Seaford earlier and had done well in the legal profession. Jones met father and son at the dock, carrying young Johnston to his house. The senior Blakely had some money, with which he engaged in trade, investing his gains in buildings. But he found the climate insalubrious and decided to take no risks with his remaining child. When the boy was five or six, Blakely sent him to be placed in a well-known school at Flatbush, Long Island, a corresponding merchant named Mr. Hoope having agreed to watch over the lad.

Young Blakely made not infrequent visits to Wilmington, during which he spent most of his time with the Jones family at their country seat. There was a good deal of intellect among the Joneses. The father was to become solicitor-general of the state and all the children had brilliant careers. Conversations and amusements were on a fairly high plane during the visits, and young Blakely held up his end well. He had a reputation for high spirits and a remarkably melodious singing voice, but—quite unlike most of the young bucks around him—preferred books to outdoor sports, drank no more than his position as a gentleman required, and gambled not at all. In 1796 his father died, and he entered the University of North Carolina, where Jones (now his guardian) wished him to study for the law. Johnston Blakely's own bent was toward the sea, and so far as he was allowed the election of his courses he specialized in such subjects as mathematics applied to navigation, astronomy, and surveying.

The University of North Carolina was a fairly turbulent place in those days, with a long series of student riots, which eventually became so uncontrollable that Principal Professor Gillespie was forced to resign. Blakely took no part in the disturbances—it is related that he assembled some of his fellow-students and told them it was a matter of principle—and he was an honor student. But he had fallen under suspicion of "French doctrines," such as radicalism and atheism, because he read and quoted from Tom Paine's *The Age of Reason*. (In later years he used to say the book had done permanent injury to his mind.) Thus it came about that one evening Presiding Professor Caldwell appeared in Blakely's room to demand some information about a recent row. The young man denied any knowledge of it; Caldwell called him a liar, which remark was resented in terms that led the professor to suggest he might throw the student out the window.

"I beg, sir, that you will not attempt it," said young Blakely, "as it will necessitate my putting you out instead."

There was a momentary battle of wills; then the professor turned and stamped from the room without another word. Long later, when Blakely had become an officer in the navy, he journeyed back to the university to tell Professor Caldwell that he had learned what respect a junior owed to a senior and that he wished to offer an apology. The two were afterwards good friends, and wrote to each other frequently.

One must not think of such clashes as anything very unusual in that slightly perfervid atmosphere of an educational institution of the post-frontier, where learning was so greatly valued and so difficult to attain. As a student Blakely complains bitterly that the available books are inadequate, in both quality and quantity. He joins the Philosophical Society, which conducts debates on such subjects as "Is Luxury Always the Cause of the Downfall of Nations?" and is a leading debater in it, but is three times fined fifteen cents for laughing immoderately at the character of the questions propounded and the arguments advanced. Yet upon the whole Blakely's college career must have been an existence rather bright with intellectual excitements, a springtime of the world.

But it could no more last than any other springtime. In 1799 there was a big fire in Wilmington. The buildings left to Johnston Blakely by his father all went, and as they were uninsured, and the rents from them were the young man's only income, he was left penniless.

III

Counsellor Jones, as he could well afford to do, offered young Blakely a loan to continue his education. As one might expect, it was refused, but the student sought his patron's good offices in obtaining a midshipman's warrant in the new navy, of which such glowing accounts were beginning to come from the Caribbean. Of course, nobody dreamed of denying so prominent a man so small a request, but the pace of the age did not lend itself to speed; it was March of 1800 before news of his appointment reached Blakely. As Wilmington was not a naval port, it was nearly another year before the Department could make up its mind to keep him on the rolls of the peace establishment and assign him to a ship fitting for sea.

She was *President,* 44, Captain Richard Dale, for the Mediterranean on the first cruise against the Barbary pirates. Blakely later called his first captain "an excellent instructor of aspiring youth," but in view of the records of the two men it is not unreasonable to attribute the excellence of the instruction to the capacity of the student for absorbing what he got. Blakely certainly found himself in a very peculiar position aboard *President.* Probably he was the best-educated man in the ship, and something of an intellectual leader, as he could not help being because of the quality of his mind; yet he was completely ignorant of the practical detail of his profession. In addition, he was probably looked upon as a political pet, since all the other officers were veterans of the French War, who had survived the wave of dismissals on the basis of meritorious service, while Blakely's service had been at Mr. Jones's country seat.

However, if any feeling against him survived personal contact, the fact is not recorded in existing documents. Blakely's gaiety on social occasions doubtless had something to do with this; and so did the fact that the honor student of U.N.C. remained a student still, quickly respected for the assiduous humility with which he applied himself to his profession. To the young man himself this seemed the normal and natural way of becoming a naval officer. His letters do not even comment on the work; he is concerned with questions of valor, family, and good name. "I hope the last Blakely who exists," he writes, "will lay down his life ere he tarnish the reputation of those who have gone before him. My father's memory is very dear to me, and I trust his son will never cast a reproach on it."

President's cruise was uneventful, save for the accident in December 1801, when she ran on a rock at the entrance to Port Mahon, tearing off her forefoot and so damaging her keel that a quick run for

Toulon and a dockyard was necessary. There it was found that her crew owed their lives to the skill of the frigate's builders, William Doughty and Christopher Bergh. Instead of carrying the planks at the bow into a groove cut in the stem, as was the custom, they had led this planking into a joint formed by the junction of the stem itself with the apron-piece that braces its after end. The result was that when the stem went in the crash, the planking remained tight.

The French naval architects greatly praised the ingenuity of this device, and at the same time besought Commodore Dale's permission to take off the lines of his frigate, since the First Consul was building a large number of new warships and this was the finest model they had ever seen. The American officers were proud of the speed and grace of their ship, as true seamen always are; but this astounded them hugely, for French shipbuilders were considered the best in the world, and even at home and among Americans it was the custom to attribute *President's* sailing qualities to the "French moddle" to which most people thought she had been built.

Midshipman Johnston Blakely certainly listened to as much as he could of these discussions. The question of what makes a ship perform well was one of those scientific aspects of the naval business which interested him most deeply, and it is probable that he learned a good deal about it at Toulon. Almost as soon as he returned to the United States he was sent to sea again in *John Adams,* 28, Captain John Rodgers. This was in the cruise of Commodore Richard V. Morris, which accomplished so little and ended so badly; but Blakely did see one little spurt of fighting, during the operation when *Enterprise,* 12, drove the Tripolitan *Meshouda* into a bay and, with *John Adams'* help, cannonaded her till she blew up.

Rodgers liked the studious midshipman, and when both were back in the States asked for him aboard *Congress,* 38, which was fitting for the cruise of 1804–5, that following Preble's. Blakely was duly gazetted to the ship and did some recruiting duty for her, but was pulled out of it because the news of the loss of *Philadelphia* made it necessary to support Preble without delay. *John Adams* was to return to the Mediterranean at once, with a load of stores, ammunition, and other necessities. Isaac Chauncey was her captain; she arrived off Tripoli in the peak of the fighting and Blakely had an opportunity to see how a great commander led his men in action, as well as to learn from the old man's lips something of his method.

When Rodgers arrived on the station with *Congress,* he took Blakely aboard that ship and kept him there till 1805. Back in the United States again, he had a short period of service in *Hornet,* 18, on her trial cruise; then a billet at Norfolk Navy Yard until February 10, 1807, when he received his lieutenant's commission. The *Leopard-Chesapeake* affair had been followed by an embargo on all American shipping, by which means President Jefferson conceived he could bring Britain to terms, through shortages in the supplies she normally obtained on this side of the Atlantic.

Lieutenant Blakely was given the division of gunboats stationed off the Chesapeake capes to enforce the edict; one of the most important posts of all, in view of the width of the waters and the variety of the normal traffic. The duty was unpleasant and he considered it degrading that the weakness of the government with regard to British aggression should be visited on its own citizens, but he handled the unwieldy gunboats so well as to be spoken of as one of the coming men in the service.

With Madison as President and the navy ships cruising again, Blakely went to *Essex,* 32. He did so good a job there that when the commands were generally shifted in 1811 Secretary Hamilton gave him a ship of his own, the little brig *Enterprise,* 12, then lying at New Orleans. She bore the name of the luckiest vessel in the navy, but she had long been laid up, her guns were ashore, and men for her crew were very difficult to find, so Blakely had everything to do. Nor was his task lightened by the unfortunate series of alterations that had turned the beautiful little warship into one peculiarly crank and sluggish. Blakely spent months trying to bring her up to the mark, altering the arrangement of her guns—which was easy enough to do, since all these small cruisers were pierced for more cannon than they carried—and such details of her rigging as the hang of the top-gallant yards. All this time he was training her crew in the last details of handling ropes and artillery, till the men could go through their evolutions like so many watchworks. He expressed himself as much dissatisfied with the conduct of the government toward Britain, and discussed resigning his commission—an act from which he was withheld partly by his interest in the exacting task before him, partly by the evident growth of the war party in Congress.

The declaration found him with a ready ship. He cruised with *Enterprise* in the Gulf until toward the close of 1812, when he received orders to bring her around into the Atlantic, and sailed January 2, 1813. The new station was off the southern coast. The ship cruised out of St. Mary's and Savannah during most of the spring, but had no luck at all in making captures, the chases proving fruitless by reason of the vessel's poor speed.

The blockade was now very tight on all the northern ports, but Blakely turned toward New England, in the hope of winning some distinction at the mouth of danger, and he did have the satisfaction of making a couple of prizes before reaching Portsmouth, N. H. in June. His ship was rather too small and handy inshore to be kept in port by the blockaders along so incidented a coast, and was therefore employed in protecting the local trade against Canadian privateers. On August 20, Blakely decoyed a good-sized one under his guns and took her, reaching port to find a letter from the Department announcing that he had been promoted master-commandant. He was offered command of the new sloop-of-war *Wasp,* then building at Newburyport; *Enterprise* could be turned over to Lieutenant Burrows, who had been serving as her exec.

IV

Blakely accepted with no attempt whatever to disguise his pleasure in escaping from the ship he had made into a wonderfully efficient little fighting machine, but one which was outclassed by almost every vessel she was likely to encounter, and was besides too lacking in storage space for long-range cruising. He wanted distant raids and hot battle; close student as he was, he had by no means missed the lesson of *Argus'* cruise as to where both could be obtained. Convoys have to break up somewhere, so that the ships which compose them can be distributed to various ports, and the most important of the enemy's distribution areas was the Channel of England.

Johnston Blakely

That it was heavily patrolled against privateers by the British brig-sloops only increased Johnston Blakely's appetite as he contemplated the lines of the cruiser growing under the builders' hands. She was an improvement on the original *Wasp* class—longer, with slightly more drag to her keel; a full fish-head entrance that would let her stand hard driving; low bilges which would stiffen her for carrying sail in a seaway; a tremendous run to where the deadwood was cut away around the steeply raking rudder. Doughty had improved on the *President* design; this new ship should be as fast as a witch. Her twenty 32-pound carronades and two long 12s would make her almost as much superior to the lighter type of British brig-sloops as our 44s were to their 38s; and, as for the larger British sloops, dealing with those would depend on Johnston Blakely.

He began enlisting and training his crew as soon as the ship was in the water; mainly New Hampshire men. But there were to be two disappointments before the spring night when he tore out on the wings of a gale. Blakely would be far from grudging anything to anyone, but it was hard that only 16 days after he had given up *Enterprise* she should meet and take a vessel of her own class. He found it harder still that canvas, cables, anchors, the whole equipment of his warship, did not arrive. The situation was difficult, no doubt, with normal water traffic halted by the blockade and the overland routes so heavy after the beginning of the autumn rains. But it seemed to Blakely that there were quite inexcusable delays piled on the natural ones. In December he went down to New York to marry the daughter of his old school-day guardian, Mr. Hoope (now that he had a master-commandant's pay instead of a lieutenant's), and tried to get at the root of the trouble, without success.

"I shall ever view as one of the most unfortunate events of my life," he wrote, "having quitted the *Enterprise* when I did. Had I remained a fortnight longer, my name might be classed with those who stand so high. I cannot but consider it a mortifying circumstance that I left her but a few days before she fell in with the only enemy on this station with which she could have creditably contended. The *Peacock* has ere this spread her plumage to the winds and the *Frolic* will soon take her revels on the ocean, but the *Wasp* will, I fear, remain for some time a dull, harmless drone in the waters of her own country. Why this is, I am not permitted to inquire."

But at last came the night when *Wasp* burst free beneath a starless sky, and, as Blakely had said he would, he turned her straight for the Channel. If ever a ship had a hand-picked crew it was this one—175 New England men, not a foreigner on board, nor a landsman, a crew that knew when to do without orders, and when to wait. By the end of the first month they were on station and examining neutrals; on June 2, they took the brig *Neptune* and burned her, then in the next three weeks four more ships, one of them an Indiaman larger than *Wasp* herself, which was cut out of a convoy with a British battleship in plain sight, yet quite unable to come up with the American cruiser. All were burned or scuttled, for Blakely would risk no recaptures by trying to send ships in. He provisioned himself from the prizes.

Raiding work of this kind is about the sharpest test a crew can have, for whatever it is desirable to save from the flames and waters can obviously be looted. The consequence of this was clear in the case of *Argus,* which had taken a Portuguese wine-brig on the night before her last battle. *Wasp's* crew looted, certainly; the lieutenants were wrapped in shawls of the finest cashmere as they stood their watches, every midshipman had a pair of gold horologes, and the ordinary seamen slept under brocade. But with the sharp Blakely to lead them there was no relaxation in discipline or vigilance—as was made evident on the 28th of June, when the first light of a quarter after four in the morning showed two sail on the lee beam. The weather presented an aspect unusual for the Channel, overcast and warm, with a light wind and smooth sea. *Wasp* bore away in chase of the pair, but had hardly done so before another stranger came slanting down from windward.

In this region there was an excellent chance that any stranger might prove a man-o'-war; therefore to gain sea-room Blakely bore up for the latecomer, and at ten in the morning made her out clearly as a brig bearing British colors and showing a disposition to engage. She was H.M.S. *Reindeer,* a rated 18, actually mounting twenty 24-pound carronades instead of the 32s more normal to her class, with a shifting

12-pounder chase-gun forward. Her captain was William Manners, a younger son of the ducal house of Rutland; he had made his ship to be called "the pride of Portsmouth"; no officer in the Royal Navy was better beloved by his crew, and not even Broke of *Shannon* had spent more time in drilling them. He soon showed his own quality and theirs; for as the fast and weatherly *Wasp* came toward him, tacking rapidly to gain the windward position, he sheeted home his own tacks so sharp as to beat her at the maneuver.

The breeze was so light that the ships hardly heeled to it at all. At half-past one *Wasp's* crew was beat to quarters; Captain Blakely ordered the cook to bring up a tub of grog and serve it to the men at the guns. They drank mock toasts to Johnny Bull's agony when he felt the sting of the *Wasp,* swearing by Geeckus Crow and peering through the portholes to estimate the advance of the enemy ship. Blakely set his light sails to close, still trying to jockey himself into the weather position. In vain; at half-past two *Reindeer* made another tack, took in her staysails, and stood for the American. It was now clear to Blakely that he must be weathered; he furled his own kites and trotted off slowly on a reach, with the enemy coming up on his port quarter. At 3:17, the ships were only 60 yards apart; *Reindeer* opened with grapes and canister from her shifting gun. One—two—three—four—five times she fired it, with the utmost deliberation, a hard ordeal for the *Wasps,* who had not a gun that would bear to make a reply. There was blood in the sand along the American cruiser's deck; men set their teeth and muttered grimly, the gun-captains fondling their lanyards.

At the fifth shot, Blakely luffed his ship sharply, the guns opening fire from aft forward as they bore. *Reindeer* luffed with him, the ships ran side by side, firing into each other from 20 yards' distance in one continuous explosion. At maybe the third broadside a grapeshot went through both Manners' legs; he scrambled to his feet and, perceiving that *Wasp's* metal was far too heavy and too accurately used to be borne at this game of cannonade, put up his helm and ran her aboard on the quarter, calling for boarders.

They came storming forward valorously and there was a desperate hand-to-hand struggle through wreaths of smoke where the ships touched; but *Wasp's* men were as well-trained as *Reindeer's,* and the

English could not win an inch onto the American deck. A bullet through the body knocked Manners down again; he hauled himself into the rigging and, sword in hand, was cheering his men on, when still another bullet from an American marine went through his head. It was the moment; "Board!" cried Blakely, and, with their bugles shouting them on, the *Wasps* poured across the bulwarks in a wave tipped with steel and fire, and swept the enemy's deck from end to end.

The senior surviving officer made the formal surrender, and he was the captain's clerk; for *Reindeer* had been more desperately and skilfully fought than any other British vessel of the war. She had 33 killed and 34 wounded, nearly all severely, on a complement of only 118, and was smashed to pieces in a line with her ports, spare spars and boats all

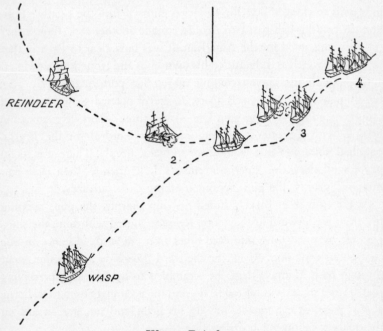

Wasp—Reindeer
(1) The approach; *Wasp* cannot gain the weather-gauge.
(2) *Reindeer* uses her shifting gun. (3) *Wasp* luffs; the
broadside action. (4) Boarders away.

gone, guns dismounted, ports themselves knocked into one yawning hole. Her foremast came down after the battle; there was nothing to do but take the shifting 12-pounder out and burn the rest. *Wasp* herself had 5 killed, 22 wounded, and a good many shot in her hull; she was simply too heavy for an opponent who in training and leadership was not far from her equal, the odds in weight of metal being 315 to 210 in favor of the American.

Now the damage must be repaired. Blakely made for L'Orient in friendly France, catching two more sail of British merchants on the way in. The Bourbons had just returned to their rule there and, although the Americans found themselves very popular as enemies of detested Albion, everything was so much at sixes and sevens that the repairs took a long time. Blakely growled about it in letters home, but he got to sea again on August 27, and three days later was back at his old haunt in the English Channel, taking a brig loaded with barley, which was scuttled. On the day following there was another prize, which had spoken of a big convoy farther to the westward. Blakely turned in that direction and on September 1 came up with them—ten sail of merchants and transports under guard of *Armada,* 74. The battleship gave chase; Blakely found *Wasp* could easily outrun her on any point of sailing, and managed to lead her far enough out so that he could circle back to the convoy first, taking a ship loaded with brass cannon and valuable military stores, which he put to the torch under the very eyes of the indignant escort.

The second pursuit drove *Wasp* so far to the south and west that the convoy was out of sight astern by early afternoon, and, being now in the normal trade lane between England and Gibraltar, Blakely merely held his course, running free. At half-past six, four sail were made out ahead, two on the starboard bow, two to port. The thought that one or more of them might be warships occurred to Blakely, but he did not care. He clapped on sail and ran for the starboardmost of the four, she being nearest the weather; by 7:00 she was visible as a man-o'-war brig, now making feverish signals with guns, lanterns, and rockets.

At 9:20, the enemy was on *Wasp's* lee bow. Blakely fired into her with the shifting 12, put his helm hard up, ran under her lee "to prevent her escaping," and opened fire. It had grown very dark,

with a strong wind that sent the ships rocking along at 10 knots, and a
high sea, across which one could only make out the winking gleam
of the enemy's battle-lights and the foam along her run. Against this
boil, *Wasp's* gunners aimed, and the action was close enough so they
could tell they were hitting her hard by the crash of shot against her
wood and the occasional scream that followed. Just before the clock
touched ten, one of the brig's masts was missing from its place against
the sky and her firing ceased. Blakely hailed to know if she had struck,
but she replied with a couple of shot, so he fired into her again until
a cry came across the heaving water to say stop it for God's sake, they
had struck and were sinking.

Just as a boat was being lowered to take possession, another brig
came into sight, coming up rapidly. *Wasp* had only 2 killed and 1
wounded, but her control-ropes were a good deal cut. Blakely let her
run free with working parties in the rigging, while his drums rolled to
quarters for the second battle in an hour, as the Britisher charged after
him. But now in the background still a third warship appeared, letting
off gun and rocket signals in a perfect passion of activity, and the
second antagonist, after throwing a few futile shot, turned back to join
her beside Blakely's prize.

The last was H.M.S. *Avon,* of eighteen 32-pound carronades, 280
points weight of broadside, Captain the Honourable James Arbuthnot
(Blakely had a strange penchant for contacts with the sons of noble
houses)—or rather she had been H.M.S. *Avon,* for she was now a
wreck, with 10 killed and 32 wounded, with tiller, foreyard, main-
boom, and all her shrouds shot away, 5 guns dismounted, magazine drowned, seven feet of water in her hold and leaks gaining so
rapidly that the rescue ships barely got her people out before she went
down. They were H.M.SS. *Castilian,* 18, and *Tartarus,* 20, and one of
them could have done all the work necessary; but they had seen what
Wasp's guns did to their consort, and neither quite cared to follow that
terrible raider into the dark alone.*

Now *Wasp* cruised southward, taking a prize on the 12th of Septem-

---

* *Castilian's* commander sent in a self-congratulatory report to the Admiralty,
saying *Wasp* had run away from him but that he could easily have taken her.
The shots he fired at the American sloop all missed.

ber, another on the 14th, and on the 21st an American-built brig, so valuable both for herself and her cargo that Blakely varied his procedure by putting a midshipman and some men in her and ordering her home. On October 9, near the Azores, *Wasp* spoke the Swedish brig *Adonis,* and took out of her a lieutenant and a master's mate who had been aboard *Essex* and had escaped from the British. After that, neither Captain Blakely nor his ship was ever heard of again.

v

All sorts or rumors and wild stories cropped up to explain the disappearance of the most effective light cruiser that ever flew the American flag. There is no substance to any of them; she simply was—and was not. The State of North Carolina voted to pay for the upbringing of Blakely's posthumous daughter, and Congress sent her a sword of honor and a gold medal; but the really important point was that the studious little North Carolina Captain and his ship had posed for the Royal Navy a problem quite insoluble in terms of this war. The close blockade of the American coast, though very expensive, did keep the American frigates from making trouble. But the blockade had demonstrated that it was incompetent to deal with vessels of the speed and handiness of the Doughty sloops-of-war.

After the *Wasp-Frolic* and *Hornet-Peacock* affairs, the British had, indeed, hastily knocked together a class of 18 vessels, especially intended to blockade the American sloops or deal with them on the ocean. They were heavy brigs, mounting twenty 32-pounder carronades and two long 9s: an armament not even so good as that of the Doughty sloops, and the British design proved to be so bad that some of the forward guns had to be landed to give the brigs stability, and it was found the tiller could not be used while the after guns were in their ports. The result was a vessel both clumsier and with less fire power than the standard 18-gun British brig.

The strategic solution as against the American privateers rested on the convoy system, combined with patrols by light warships along the trade lanes. *Wasp's* raid had furnished destructive criticism of both; she took ships right out of convoy, and sank one vessel of the patrol that was supposed to deal with her. When a vessel of her speed and hitting power was loose, the British must necessarily concentrate their fighting ships in larger units of force and some shipping would necessarily be abandoned to the privateers.

This was made clear in no uncertain manner when, on the heels of Blakely's campaign, it began to rain privateers in the regions sacred to British shipping. *Prince de Neufchâtel* of New York took 18 prizes in Biscay; *Harpy* of Baltimore hung between Liverpool and Dublin for weeks, cutting off all mail service between John Bull's two islands. *Mammoth* of Baltimore spent 17 days off Cape Clear, taking a ship a day. And a British captain out of Bristol for Spain sighted no fewer than ten sail of privateers during the voyage. It was the old privateering tradition of the Revolution; but now become adult, because backed by a genuine fighting navy, which not only graduated sailors familiar with the great guns into private ships, but also demonstrated in the most convincing manner that there was nothing sacred about cruisers that flew the cross of St. George.

The worst was yet to come; for while this was going on, *Globe* of Baltimore captured Levanters in the eastern Mediterranean, and *Rambler* and *Jacob Jones,* both of Boston, turned up in the China seas and sent prizes loaded with gold dust and opium into Canton and Macao. Off Lisbon Rock, *Leo* of Baltimore took a transport with the Duke of Wellington's paymaster and uniforms for his army; while *America* of New Haven—built, armed, and manned like a sloop-of-war—took no fewer than 24 ships, all the way from the West Indies to the coasts of Norway. That fall appeared the most dangerous of all: *Chasseur* of Baltimore, which captured 30 ships, with a bulk value of over a million pounds, and sent in a proclamation to be posted at Lloyd's to say that she had placed the British Isles under blockade. Half a dozen warships were sent out to look for her, and one of them, *St Lawrence,* 13, found her—with results dismaying from the Admiralty's point of view, for after a twenty-minute fight *Chasseur* captured the cruiser by boarding.

Tom Boyle, the privateer's captain, produced something more than a joke with his proclamation; for by an incredible reversal the privateers of blockaded America had actually placed Britain under blockade. The price of delicacies like sugar and coffee jumped 200 per cent; and when insurance on the short voyage from Liverpool to Dublin could be had at all, it was at rates between 13 and 15 per cent. Allowing for the profit the underwriters must have on the transaction, this meant that at least one ship in ten would be lost on the trip; and it is very difficult to conduct any business in which 10 per cent both of goods and of conveyance goes down the drain.

Mr. Croker of the Admiralty advised that it was not safe for ships even to run from Bristol to Plymouth without convoy. And the *Wasp's* nest still held unhatched eggs.

Chapter 11

Virginia Aristocrat: Lewis Warrington

1. Let us now praise famous men, and our fathers that begat us.
2. The Lord hath wrought great glory by them . . .
4. And some there be which no memorial; who are perished as though they never had been.

ECCLESIASTICUS, 44

ONE IS TEMPTED TO APPLY THE QUOTATION TO THE CASES OF LEWIS Warrington and John Smith. To be sure, Warrington has not been left utterly without memorial; three destroyers have been named after him, and several streets in the grounds of various navy yards. He even left an indentation on the body of precedent that constitutes international law, though nobody now recognizes it as his. But this is very little in comparison with the recognition received by the remainder of Preble's boys. The remainder, that is, with the exception of Smith. That captain is truly of the company that perished as though they had never been.

It is strange. Both men led full and useful lives, and Warrington's was a long and not uninfluential one. They were closely associated, not only in their personal careers, but also with respect to a curious absence of record about their personalities and even their doings. There are no anecdotes; neither Smith nor Warrington is involved in a sensational transaction of any kind; nobody mentions them in letters and their own letters are straightforward business documents. Everything about either man is stamped "official."

One must make a slight exception with regard to the first appearance of Warrington's name in writing, in 1791, when he was not quite nine years old. At this date he had a stepfather elsewhere described as a "dissipated wretch." The boy's name is mentioned in a letter from a Miss Pamela Davenport of Richmond to her friend Miss Elizabeth Pelham of New Kent City, some distance up the peninsula of Virginia from Williamsburg, where Lewis was born; and it is worth quoting for the light it throws on the background and character of the future naval officer:

"I was scarce ever more affected than I was a few moments ago—Little Lewis Warrington came up in the Stage from a long visit to his poor unhappy Mother, this morning, and agreed to stay this day with us—just now he called me privately to him, and while the tears streamed from his fine eyes, entreated me to write tomorrow to his dear Mama, to let her know of his safe arrival, and entreat to her from her son. Then taking from his pocket five biscuits, while tears almost chok'd his utterance, he beg'd I would send them to her with the letter—she gave them to him this morning (added he) but I don't want them and would much rather she should have them—I was much affected with his distress, but told him he had better keep them—and did not imagine his Mama wanted them—this last hint most sensibly increased his distress—and thrusting the biscuits into my hand—with a fresh gust of tears, he said I must send them for he wou'd not keep them—yet even then, such was his delicacy that he cou'd not plainly tell me she was in want tho' that was evidently his meaning—I took them at last from him, and hiding my face on the bed gave a loose for a few moments to emotions that may be felt but cannot be described—while L., pleased to have carried his point—dried his face and brightening into smiles, endeavour'd with the firmness of a Man to assume a cheerfulness—I am pretty certain he cou'd not feel."

Now this was in the age of sensibility, when delicate ladies set great store by anything that produced floods of tears without requiring remedial action on their part, so Miss Pamela was perhaps overdoing things a little. But the picture of an unhappy childhood and a little boy only occasionally able to visit the home where his mother lived with the dissipated wretch is unmistakable. One wonders (vainly, for there are no data) whom he did live with. Possibly there were relatives on the father's side; someone found the money to send him to William and Mary College at the age of thirteen.

He made a very good record there, not so good as Blakely was making in North Carolina, but well in the upper levels of his class, and was graduated in 1799. At this point comes the note that beats repeatedly through the stories of Preble's boys: he was intended for one of the professions, but expressed a desire to go to sea instead. After a gap of some months, during which one may imagine the young man's guardian trying to dissuade him, the ice went out of the river, and on January 6, 1800, Lewis Warrington received his midshipman's warrant aboard *Chesapeake,* 38, Captain Samuel Barron, who came from the same part of Virginia and was probably instrumental in opening the gates of the service.

The cruise, off the southern coast of the United States, and down to the Guadeloupe station, was not a particularly long one as cruises went in those days, and was devoid of exterior incident, save for the capture of the privateer *Jeune Créole,* run down among the islands on New Year's Day of 1801. Warrington presumably learned something about handling a ship from the thorough seaman who was his captain—also something he never forgot about handling a crew. Neither of the two Captains Barron was a very good disciplinarian, and when *Chesapeake* put into St. Kitts, shortly after taking her prize, things were in fairly bad shape aboard. The men had been enlisted in Norfolk, not a major seaport and already pretty well drained of sailors by other vessels before Barron's was ready. As a result he had to take what he could get, and drew "a most infamous set of rascals." In addition, they had been shipped for a year, as the custom then was, instead of for the cruise; and *Chesapeake* was so slow in fitting out that the year had run by with less than the ship's allotted service done. The infamous rascals clamored for their money and their discharge; were as disrespectful as they dared be, working slowly and badly. The climax was that one of them wrote a letter to the British colonial governor, offering to desert and to bring several companions with him.

Barron intercepted the letter, but apparently did not know quite what to do when he put into St. Kitts. There he found the squadron commander, Tom Truxtun, aboard *President,* 44. That forthright officer spent no time on doubts or alternatives; he ordered the author of the desertion letter to be given 39 lashes (three over the three dozen normal for serious crimes) and had him drummed ashore to heal his lacerated back at Danish St. Thomas, where he would find it hard enough to reach his British friends. *Chesapeake* he sent home to be paid off, but, as his own ship was at the end of her cruise, Truxtun sailed in company, so that if anything broke loose aboard Barron's ship there would be force enough at hand to throttle the disturbance.

The two ships arrived to find that the French War was over, and the orders for *President* were to go to the Mediterranean as flag of the squadron being sent out to put a term to the increasing demands of Barbary. Truxtun fell on a dispute with the government over rank and resigned his commission. His replacement was Captain Richard Dale of Virginia, who had James Barron as captain of his flagship, so it was natural that Mr. L. Warrington, also of Virginia, should be one of the mids retained on the peace establishment and taken aboard for the cruise.

The first halt was at Algiers, where the appearance of the powerful frigate, presently followed by two of her consorts, was described by the American consul as more salutary than the arrival of a dozen cargoes of the stores which the Dey had been getting as tribute. The old scoundrel became very amiable; Dale pushed on to Tunis, where he arrived just in time. A fire in the arsenal there had lately destroyed 50,000 stand of arms. The Bey informed our consul, who was the adventurous William Eaton, that his good friends would have the inestimable privilege of making good the loss, and the share of the United States would be 10,000 stand. His good friends the Americans had been paying tribute of some sort since President Washington's day, but Eaton never did like the idea and was aware that Jefferson's policy was against tribute in any form. He refused even to transmit the demand, and was just wondering whether the placing of guards at his door meant that he had not long to last, when *President* came drifting into the harbor, with the Stars and Stripes at her gaff.

This settled Tunis for the time being, but farther along the coast Tripoli had actually declared war on America, and Dale did not consider that he had the authority to fight unless physically attacked, so all he did was blockade the place for 18 days, make a circuit of the central Mediterranean, and sail for home. *President* had barely reached the States when James Barron was ordered to take *New York*, 36, out on the second cruise, that of Commodore Richard V. Morris; he carried his young Virginia protégé into the new command with him. The ship dropped at Algiers some supplies which were part of a tribute, and pushed on to Malta, where there was an advice from Morris that Secretary Smith had sent him new orders. For reasons nobody could ascertain, but which probably had something to do with economy (a word of great power in the first Jefferson administration), two of the squadron's frigates were to be sent home at once, one of them *Chesapeake*. Morris would transfer his flag and his acting captain, Isaac Chauncey, from that ship to *New York*. Barron to take *Chesapeake* home.

Of course Warrington followed Barron when the ships met each other at Gibraltar in April 1803, and the exchange of commanders was made. The young man then had a period of leave, which can have been of no long duration, for trans-Atlantic voyages normally took over a month, and already on June 7 he received new orders. The leave was apparently spent in Richmond, possibly with the friends or relatives who had brought him up. There is nothing further in the record about the former Mrs. Warrington or her dissipated wretch of a second husband.

II

Warrington's new commander was the shadowy John Smith, and his ship the schooner *Vixen*, 12, then completing at Baltimore. She was one of the four new light vessels constructed for close-in work at Tripoli after the outstanding performance of the schooner *Enterprise* had disclosed the utility of such craft. *Vixen* was intended to be an exact duplicate of *Enterprise,* an idea which had to be given up when it was discovered that the plans of the famous little schooner had somehow been lost. The Department therefore went to a Baltimore clipper-schooner designer named Benjamin Hutton, and told him to do the best he could. They never had any reason for disappointment, for if there was any ship in the Mediterranean that handled better or sailed faster than *Enterprise,* it was *Vixen.*

All hands were charmed with her by the time they reached Gibraltar in mid-September, just after the new Commodore, Edward Preble of Maine, who had come out in *Constitution,* 44. The Emperor of Morocco was making difficulties; Preble himself took the flag to Tangier to see what could be done, meanwhile sending *Vixen* up the Mediterranean, under the general orders of Captain William Bainbridge of *Philadelphia,* 38, for the Commodore was determined that neither weather nor any other condition should make him relax the blockade of Tripoli. When the two ships reached the place in early October 1803, Bainbridge met a vessel of the Austrian Empire, which gave him positive intelligence that two of the Tripolitan cruisers were out.

It seemed obvious they must have gone westward, since there was nothing to the east to attract them. Bainbridge himself remained before the pirate stronghold, sending Smith and his *Vixen* out to Cape Bon, to catch the rovers when they passed through the Strait of Sicily on their way in. It was a futile errand, for the Austrian report was a rumor and there were no corsairs; but exactly how futile, Smith only learned on November 1 when, putting into Malta for provision, he heard that *Philadelphia* had been taken by the Tripolitans. Without losing a moment he set sail to carry the news to Preble at Gibraltar. But the stormy season had now begun, and *Vixen* met nothing but heavy seas and contrary gales like those which so badgered Lord Nelson in his pursuit of the French through the same water eighteen months later. Provisions ran out, and the schooner was forced to turn back to Syracuse, where Preble had already arrived. *Vixen* was at once sent down the Mediterranean with dispatches.

This running about lasted until April, when Preble began to draw in all his light ships to tighten the blockade, spring being the season when the improvident Moors normally ran short of corn, so that it was possible to hurt them by cutting off the coastal trade. There were several little brushes with the forts and the Tripolitan gunboats as spring turned to summer, one fortification ashore receiving the name of "Vixen battery," because it discovered itself by firing into that ship; and in July came an incident of lasting effect. It is recorded quite simply in a letter from Lieutenant-Commandant Smith to Commodore Preble, informing the latter that Midshipman Warrington has been placed in arrest for "behaving in an insulting and disrespectful manner" to Lieutenant William Crane, second of the ship.

What lay behind this is lost; the important feature is what lay beyond it. Up to this time the 21-year-old mid has been personally referred to only as "studious." One may infer that he exhibited the touchy sense of honor, the desire for renown, the romanticism, that were normal for a Virginian and an officer in those days; if he had not, it would have caused remark. Assuredly Warrington belonged to the Barron wing of the navy, and although this had by no means become the well-marked group that it did later, there were certain differences in pattern of conduct and method of thought between Barron's school and the other nascent groupings in the service. Preble, who kept an extremely close eye on his young men, would be aware of this; and aware also that in normal circumstances an insulting and disrespectful manner would lead to a court-martial or a duel.

It came to neither in this case; instead, the old Commodore had Warrington into his cabin for a heart-to-heart talk. There is no record of what he said, but at the end of the interview Warrington was released from his arrest, and, in view of the fact that First Lieutenant Trippe was being placed in charge of one of the gunboats, Midshipman Warrington was made acting second of *Vixen*. This promoted him over the sailing master, placed him just under the insulted Crane, and gave him command of a watch.

However Preble's medicine was compounded, it took effect. No one in the squadron worked harder or to more purpose than Acting Lieutenant Warrington during the fighting off the harbor. After Preble's return to the United States had been followed by that of the ailing Commodore Samuel Barron, the young officer's temporary rank was confirmed in permanence by Commodore John Rodgers, not an easy man to please. This gave *Vixen* too many lieutenants, so Warrington was transferred to the brig *Siren,* 16, under Charles Stewart. In her he served nearly a year; at that point, the Barbary powers had become so tame that it was decided to reduce the Mediterranean cruise to three

ships, and all the officers who wished were allowed to go home. Warrington did not wish, and he had shown up so well that Rodgers
made him First Lieutenant of *Enterprise* under David Porter.

When he did return to the United States in the summer of 1807, he
had thus spent all but a few weeks out of seven years, nearly his whole
service career, in the Mediterranean. There is a portrait of him painted
at approximately this date: a square-faced man, tall, powerful, broad-
shouldered, and strikingly handsome. The judgment as to his good
looks is based not merely on a painter's flattery; the Virginia belles
thought so, too, and one of them, named Sally Kennon, wrote to her
gossip:

"I received a letter from George a few days ago who now resides in
Richmond. He says that the exquisite Lewis Warrington was in town,
oh, there I wish I was also; apropos of him, last night I tried my fortune, in which I importuned my invisible guardian to show me the
man whose rib I was to become, exactly in the dress he was to wear on
the day we were married, and upon my word I positively saw the be-
forementioned divinity dressed in the most elegant suit of new
uniforms; and I am positively convinced that I shall one day be Mrs.
Warrington."

Alas for romance! Warrington did not marry until 1817, and then it
was to a lady named Margaret King, of Norfolk.

III

He had come back to a United States far different from the one he
left, to a navy which had nothing but gunboat duty for him, and this
rendered tolerable only by the fact that the gunboats under his command were stationed at Norfolk, so that he could spend much time in
the society he enjoyed. The gunboat period extended over two years.
With the resumption of cruising by the navy, Warrington was named
First Lieutenant of *Siren* for a trip to Europe with diplomatic
dispatches; and, when he returned, it was to find that he had been
asked for as First Lieutenant of *Essex, 32.*

The captain who asked for him was John Smith, which demon-
strates that the incident of the arrest cannot have been too serious, and

also that Warrington had some capacity for making people like him, a point which was to be again proved later and in other ways. At this juncture it would be desirable to have a good deal more about Captain Smith, since he was the man who spoiled both the sailing and the fighting qualities of *Essex* by exchanging the long 12s on her gundeck for 32-pound carronades. Did Warrington have anything to do with this misbegotten inspiration? Perhaps; later in life he showed himself a fearless technical experimenter. But the only information is that the two men stayed in *Essex* for three years, or until nearly the outbreak of the war. At this date, Smith's seniority moved him up to the command of *Congress,* 38, and of course he asked Warrington to accompany him as First Lieutenant.

Congress was a ship whose passion for anonymity almost equaled that of her captain. She was a sister of the famous *Constellation*; that is, had a hull of the Humphreys form, but was slightly smaller than the 44s, originally intended to mount twenty-four long 24s on the gundeck instead of the thirty guns of that caliber carried by the heavier type of cruiser. When she and her sister put to sea in the French War, it was discovered that the big guns strained them; therefore long 18s were substituted for the 24s, which made the ships of this class very like the heavy frigates of other nations as to armament, though below they had somewhat finer lines, and aloft somewhat taller masts. The peculiarity of *Congress's* career was that whenever there was action in some place she managed to be somewhere else. She was dismasted on her first cruise and, after being rerigged, did not get to sea again until the French War was over; reached the Barbary coast three times, but always just too early or too late to take any part in the shooting. This was not the fault of her captains, for she had some very good ones, including John Rodgers and Decatur; merely the luck of the dice.

Her first wartime cruise in 1812 went in the ship's usual fashion. *Congress* was lying at New York, part of the squadron of Commodore Rodgers, when word of the declaration came, with permission for the ships to go out once. Rodgers immediately put to sea, having *President,* 44, *United States,* 44, *Hornet,* 18, and *Argus,* 16, under his command besides *Congress.* He headed westward and south in the hope of falling in with the immensely valuable plate fleet from

Jamaica, which was known to have sailed from Port Royal on 20 May. There was some fog on the ocean, and a passing American merchant thought the plate fleet had slipped past under that cover. Rodgers turned in pursuit; on the morning of June 23 a sail was sighted to the north, which was presently made out to be a British frigate, *Belvidera, 36.*

She fled eastward, down a wind fresh from the west, with the Americans tailing out in chase, *President* leading and gaining. At 4:30 in the afternoon, Rodgers's ship was near enough to open fire from the bow-chasers. The first three shots all went right in, causing casualties and obvious damage. But on the next discharge one of *President's* main-deck guns blew up, shattering the forecastle above and killing or wounding 16 men, including Rodgers himself, whose leg was broken. There was much confusion aboard (with the possibility of other guns' proving defective as well), and into this confusion *Belvidera* now fired her stern-chasers. *President,* whether on the injured Rodgers's orders or someone else's, began yawing repeatedly to fire broadsides in the hope that one of them would cripple the chase. Some damage was indeed done aboard *Belvidera,* but the British repaired it as fast as it occurred and the American frigate lost ground steadily by her deviation. *United States* was too slow for chase work, and Smith somehow could never bring *Congress* into the action; by midnight the British cruiser was safe.

So was the plate fleet. Rodgers had lost so much ground in the fruitless chase that all he ever found was a quantity of coconut shells and orange peel floating along the tide. On the 15th of July, being within 20 hours' sail of the English Channel, he turned disappointedly homeward, with nothing to show for the cruise of his squadron but six sail of British merchant ships. After a stop at Boston, he put out again with the same ships, but the results were not much better, amounting to only a single prize, though she was the mail packet *Swallow,* with $200,000 in cash aboard, enough to pay for a 44-gun frigate. Off the western islands Rodgers detached *Congress* to cruise independently, in the hope that she might make some captures the combined group would miss; but Smith's ship picked up only one prize before putting in to Portsmouth, N. H., in December.

Preble's Boys

There were letters waiting for Warrington. After *United States* took *Macedonian* in October, the former's First Lieutenant had been promoted out of the ship to a command of his own. Captain Decatur was therefore without such an officer—would Warrington care to join him? Naturally, he would, since this was a promotion, *United States* being the higher-rating ship. But this was 1813, the weary summer when Decatur's vessel and her consorts lay blockaded in Long Island Sound. Decatur, who was senior officer of the forces afloat in the New York area, was a man who liked to see things happening; he thought that even though the frigates could not work through the blockade, there would be a good chance for sloops-of-war, which could work out through less deep waters and make fast tacks. At this time there was a new one about to be laid down at New York—*Peacock,* 20, named after *Hornet's* prize of the previous year. Decatur suggested to the Department that Warrington be promoted to master-commandant of this ship and sent to New York to supervise her construction. Secretary Jones agreed.

The keel was laid on July 26th, to a design by William Doughty, just after Warrington received his new commission. There can have been little loitering in the building yard, for the ship was in the water before the end of September. Men were recruited at once, being employed in working on the rigging and internal arrangements of the ship. It would be some time in the winter when *Peacock* was complete, and moved down the bay to try her paces. No doubt she could have ridden through the blockaders on one of the winter gales, but Warrington wanted time to drill his crew into a unit and therefore kept his ship back until the equinoctial storms of mid-March—the dark March of 1814 when everything looked so evil for the American cause.

He slipped out at night. There was not even a shadow of pursuit, and *Peacock* had hardly been at sea for 12 hours when Warrington realized that he had one of the fastest warships afloat, particularly in blowing weather. He ran south for the Florida Strait, with the intention of cutting into the Europe-bound traffic from the West Indies, and reached station on April 14. But from that date to the 24th only one ship was sighted, and she was a neutral.

A boat was sent ashore to inquire about this singular absence of shipping. It brought back word that not a single "running ship" had come through from the Gulf that spring; the valuable vessels that might otherwise have tried it were all driven into Havana for fear of the Yankee privateers. They were waiting for the homeward-bound Jamaica plate fleet and its escort, which escort would consist of a 74, two frigates, and two sloops-of-war. They would sail from Jamaica soon after the first of May. Warrington had enough confidence in the speed and handiness of his own cruiser to believe he could do something with this convoy in spite of the guards, and therefore remained in the strait.

He was easing along off Cape Carnaveral at seven o'clock in the morning of April 28 when several sail were sighted easterly and to windward. All but one spread canvas in flight; this vessel came toward *Peacock,* revealing herself as a British brig-sloop. She was H.M.S. *Épervier,* 18, of sixteen 32-pound carronades (against *Peacock's* 20) and two 18-pound carronade chase-guns (against the American's two long 12s);* Captain Richard Wales; a new ship, built in 1812, and a very fine one. The papers recorded that as she dropped down London River on her first commission, bets were offered that she would return with an American sloop or a small frigate as a prize. In her hold were $118,000, placed there by merchants, who feared to use commercial craft because of the privateers.

As she approached, the wind veered round to southward, and she came in close-hauled on the port tack. Since *Peacock* was running free, they made the approach almost prow to prow. Warrington edged away in an effort to get in a rake, but the British ship followed his motion until 10:20, when *Épervier* suddenly rounded to, and both starboard broadsides let go together in a clap of thunder. The maneuvering position being what it was, each had fired high to cripple, and *Épervier* attained her object, for two round-shot completely disabled *Peacock's* foreyard, compelling her to run large before the wind.†

---

* The broadside weights of metal were *Peacock,* 315, *Épervier,* 274.

† From the loss of the fore-topsail, the only square sail set while under fighting canvas. With topsails on the other two masts, any attempt to run close-hauled or even on a reach would result in the ship's coming head to wind and being taken aback, because the sail pressure aft of the center of lateral resistance would drive her stern to leeward.

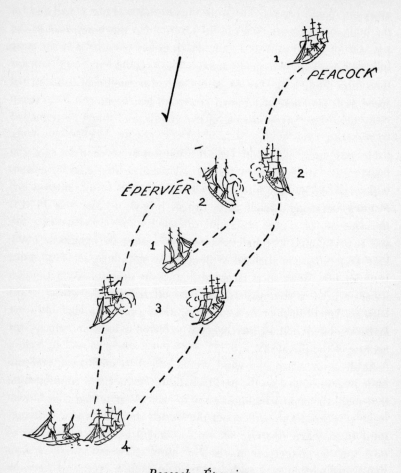

Peacock—Épervier

(1) The approach; *Peacock* edges away for a rake; *Épervier* follows. (2) The first broadside; *Peacock* loses her foreyard. (3) The broadside battle; *Épervier* hard hit. (4) *Épervier* gives up.

But the brig was also damaged aloft and could do no better than ease away into parallel battle. The word on *Peacock* was fire at will and for the hull; there was an even ripple of movement down the deck as the left arms of the gun-captains going up to indicate readiness to fire were followed by the pounce of the gun-crews, dragging the pieces back for reloading. One of the British lieutenants said afterward that he had never seen guns fired so fast or so accurately. *Épervier's* main-boom went, the bowsprit was hit, the carpenter ran aft through the shot that were tearing great holes in the bulwarks to say she had been hit along the waterline. With his ship melting round him and half his engaged battery out of action, Captain Wales ordered his helm up and the drum beat for boarders. But as the brig charged in, a perfectly dreadful hail of musketry fell among the gathering men from the American's tops; the British tars could not stand it, they threw down their cutlasses, shouting "She's too heavy for us!" and—as *Épervier's* maintopmast leaped over the side—her colors came down, half an hour from the first gun.

Peacock had only two wounded, and the lightest of damage to her rigging; the British sloop was a wreck, with 45 shot in her hull, her foremast almost cut in two, and 23 casualties, nearly a fifth of the crew. Warrington threw a heavy work-party into her and by sunset had his prize in condition to carry sail, after a terrific battle to keep her from sinking. He accompanied his capture toward the Georgia ports, and it was as well that he did so, for next morning, off Amelia Island, two frigates became visible to the north and leeward. Warrington immediately took everyone but Lieutenant J. B. Nicholson and 16 men out of *Épervier,* directing that officer to make for St. Mary's River, while he himself edged toward the frigates, certain that if he could draw them after *Peacock* there would be no real trouble.

So it fell out; the frigates chased *Peacock* all day, on a beat to southward, and were out of sight by the following morning. When Warrington turned back north, however, there they were again, and he had to give them another run until two in the afternoon of the second day, before they realized what they were up against. Warrington's ship was now full of prisoners and he needed a new foreyard, so he circled about and put into Savannah, finding that the brig had preceded him. Nicholson narrowly missed capture at that; halfway up to the Georgia port, he was becalmed in shoal water and one of the frigates (which had turned after him when they lost *Peacock*) hoisted out her boats for a close-in attack. But, as they approached, the lieutenant shouted through his speaking trumpet to yaw round and give them a broadside and they, assuming *Épervier* was heavily manned, pulled away.

By time Warrington had attended to the necessary business, it was June 4 and too late to think of the plate fleet, so he steered straight across the Atlantic to the region of the southern tip of Ireland. In July, when Blakely's *Wasp* was making torches of ships all along the English Channel, Warrington also began to destroy: five ships that month, some of them of great value, and three more in the first days of August.

It was a bad summer for the Admiralty, especially as the privateer *Surprise,* of Baltimore, was simultaneously making sad work between England and Ireland, *Mammoth* of Baltimore was off Belfast, and the formidable *Chasseur* in the North Sea. Every available frigate was sent out, with several patrols of two or three brig-sloops each. How it fared with one of these has been told in Blakely's story. Warrington shifted his cruising ground to the north of Ireland, where he made three more prizes, sent one in with a load of prisoners to advertise his presence, and then turned away to cruise off the capes of Spain. Another three vessels were taken and destroyed there before sea stores began to run short. Warrington made for home, picking up a big "running ship" on the way in, for a total of 14 captures during the cruise, nearly all of them valuable.

Peacock came up New York Harbor on October 29, 1814, and began fitting at once for another cruise. This was a planned squadron operation, Decatur to lead it in *President*; to the East Indies, where British trade was carried on in large and very rich ships, usually without much escort, since the Indiamen themselves were armed strongly enough to beat off local pirates and French privateers. Besides his own ship, Decatur was to have *Peacock, Hornet,* 18, and a store-ship rather oddly named *Tom Bowline.*

President ran out on the gale of January 14, damaged herself on the bar, and was taken by the British squadron. No news of this had reached the port by the 22nd, when the wind began to blow from the northwest, accompanied by gusts of snow; all three ships un-moored and ran. It was still daylight when they crossed the bar, under storm canvas through a wildly tumbling sea, the blockaders being plainly visible to the southward, trying to beat up. More snow came with dark; not an enemy was sighted nor a gun fired, all the way down the lanes of the Atlantic to Tristan d'Acunha, which had been set as the squadron rendezvous. *Peacock* reached the place on March 18, 1815, but was driven off by a gale, and could not return till the 23rd, when Warrington found *Hornet,* which had just destroyed a British sloop-of-war. The two ships cruised in the offing until April 13; then, deciding that *President* must have been captured, took the stores out of *Tom Bowline* and continued their voyage to the Indies.

They were not far round Good Hope, on the 27th, when a large ship was sighted to the northwestward, which both American com-manders took to be an Indiaman. They bore down, but discovered they were closing a line-of-battleship. It was easy for the speedy *Pea-cock* to outrun the danger, but her consort faded over the horizon of one of the emptiest oceans in the world with the liner in pursuit, and Warrington reasoned that it would be useless to attempt regaining contact. He held on alone across the Indian Ocean.

On June 13, approaching Java, the first prize was made, an India-man big enough to have a crew of 57. She was burned, and so were two others encountered during the fortnight. On June 30, in the Strait of Sunda, just off a fort at Anjier, *Peacock* met a war-brig, being the Honourable East India Company's ship *Nautilus,* 14, mainly 18-pounder carronades. This vessel hailed to say there was a peace. War-rington, estimating time, distance, and the fact that the brig was no match for his ship, considered this very probably a ruse to give the brig time to slide in under cover of the fort. In an answering hail, he told the brig that if there was indeed a peace, she should heave to, haul down her flag, and send a boat. *Nautilus* refused. "Fire!" said Warrington, and the brig received a broadside that showed there was little falling off in the skill of *Peacock's* gunners, for it left her totally disabled.

The British were very indignant about Warrington's conduct, ignoring the fact that in the *Leopard-Chesapeake* case and many others they themselves had behaved even worse, with less reason and no sign of remorse. At the same time they lodged a complaint against *Peacock's* captain for violating the customs of war, in that he had equipped his boarding parties with special helmets made of bear's fur and stiffened with steel bands. There is a faint note of amusement in the correspondence, which treats both complaints as merely silly. *Peacock* reached New York again on November 2, 1815, after the war with Algiers was over. Warrington had paid his crew and reprovisioned his ship with money and stores taken from the prizes; the men were entirely dressed in clothes made of goods secured in the same way. There was no sickness aboard.

IV

Warrington returned to find himself a captain, having been promoted while on the cruise to the Indies. He was almost immediately given command of *Macedonian,* 38, since Captain Jones of that ship was going on leave. In this frigate he made one trip to the Mediterranean, then took a leave himself to get married, and was appointed head of a board to look over Hampton Roads with a view to fortifying the place as a fleet anchorage. His report was favorable, and the result was Fortress Monroe, to become so famous during the Civil War. Then came two more Mediterranean cruises of a year's duration each, and a four-year tour of duty at Norfolk Navy Yard.

By this time, Warrington's reputation for getting people to like and work with him had moved well out beyond the stage of having captains ask for him as a First Lieutenant. In 1824 Commodore David Porter, in charge of the squadron for suppressing piracy in the West Indies, fell into difficulties with the Spanish authorities. The government's treatment of him was distinctly on the shabby side, but there was nothing wrong with their idea that an officer who used oil instead of blasting powder was needed down there, or with their choice of Warrington as the man for the post.

He went out in *John Adams,* 28, arriving on station in February 1825. The slightly stiff but very courtly Virginia courtesy of his background worked wonders; in no time at all he was on the most cordial basis, not only with the British commodore on station, but also with the Danish governor of the Virgins and the Spanish heads at Puerto Rico.

The results became apparent at once. On the first occasion when a piratical sloop was driven ashore by one of Warrington's squadron, there were Spanish soldiers waiting to receive the pirates as they jumped overboard. The Puerto Rican governor had them hanged and quartered, and a section of each was marched through all the seacoast villages behind drums. A little later a big hideout of picaroons was located at the Rio Sagua la Grande. Warrington did not have treaty rights to go in there, but the British did, so the American leader placed two of his small ships and a body of Marines under the British flag and technical command of one of their lieutenants, went in and cleaned the place out. At the same time the whole conduct of Caribbean operations was materially improved by changing the American base from Key West, which was haunted by yellow fever, up to Pensacola. Warrington liked the latter place, and rendered a report on it that led to the establishment of the naval base there. When he relinquished his command, piracy in the West Indies was practically done with.

That was his last sea duty. When he returned to the United States in 1826, he was named one of the three Navy Commissioners, and held that post until 1830. In the last year he rendered a report, sufficiently curious in the light of modern developments, recommending the abolition of the Marine Corps. It was an imitation of British practice (he said), but the more favorable conditions of enlistment in the American navy made Marines unnecessary as a seagoing police force to keep sailors in order. Norfolk Navy Yard had Warrington as its head again for the next ten years; Daniel Ammen, later famous as an admiral, reported to him there as a new midshipman, and remarked that old Commodore Warrington was a Tartar, "whose face did not express great benevolence, but officers are not paid for such traits, but for duties that cannot at all times make kindliness controlling."

In 1842 the administrative side of the navy was completely reorganized into the system of bureaus, and Warrington, who had come back to Washington as one of the commissioners, was named head of the Bureau of Yards and Docks. His most important activity of the period was extracurricular. Always a student himself, he had long been profoundly dissatisfied with the irregularity of education in the service, and had joined himself enthusiastically to the party headed by William Bainbridge, which sought the foundation of an accredited naval school. Several attempts were made to set up such an institution, but they always foundered on the theoretical objection of Jacksonian Democratic congressmen, that a naval school would lead to the establishment of a privileged caste, not consonant with American democracy.

Just before the general reorganization a chaplain named George Jones, also much interested in naval education, waited on Warrington and pointed out that no congressional action to found a school was really necessary. Professors for the instruction of midshipmen were already borne on the rolls of the navy, and it was within the competence of the department to order them to the places where the teaching was to be done. Why not order them all to one place, and that place ashore? The chaplain succeeded in convincing Warrington, and Warrington convinced Secretary A. P. Upshur. But, before the project could be put into operation, Upshur was killed by the explosion of a gun aboard U.S.S. *Princeton*. David Henshaw, who took over the portfolio, tried another line of approach to the school problem; and he was presently succeeded by John Y. Mason, who did not want any school at all, saying the midshipmen could not be spared from their duties afloat.

But the man who took *Peacock* halfway round the world was not easily discouraged. Mason failed to get along with President Tyler (most people did); when he resigned, Warrington himself was made ad interim Secretary of the Navy, and proceeded to a quiet series of machinations. There is no direct evidence that he was the man who made the deal with the army by which the latter service turned over Fort Severn at Annapolis; but the place was turned over and the school established in exactly the manner that Chaplain Jones had suggested. The historian George Bancroft did it, when he came in as Secretary under President Polk—but it is noteworthy that one of his first official acts was a trip of inspection to Fort Severn, on which he

Lewis Warrington

was accompanied by two persons, Secretary of War Marcy and Commodore Lewis Warrington.

Shore after this; the Commodore, now 66 years old, transferred from the Bureau of Yards and Docks to that of Ordnance. It was under his direction that John A. Dahlgren conducted the experiments which revolutionized naval artillery, by producing guns whose greatest strength was in the area of greatest pressure, thus making possible heavy powder charges and high muzzle velocities, and driving fighting ships apart to distances where the Warrington boarding-cap would never again be used.

The old man died quietly in 1851, much honored by all who knew him, though it is probable that a good many of them would have found it difficult to give a résumé of his services. He had a gift for staying out of the limelight, for taking no part in agitations; it was one of the reasons why he always got along with people. For example, there is no record that he even expressed an opinion on the Decatur-Barron duel. Indeed, he would have placed himself in a false position by expressing an opinion; for he belonged to both camps. It is probably not too much to say that the healing of the breach that this incident left in the service was in some respect due to the fact that the adroit, the conciliatory, the intelligent Warrington was so near the seats of power when it was necessary to have a man of his stamp there.

Chapter 12

The Millionaire:
James Biddle

"What *is* a Biddle?"
—The Prince of Wales, later Edward VII, during a
visit to Philadelphia (to the horror of his audience)

T HE FAMILY WAS A PROLIFIC ONE, AND ONE BOTH BY PERSONAL
taste and by its fortunate location at Philadelphia closely identified with that complex of finance, shipping, and governmental service
which Alexander Hamilton sought to establish as the dominant unify-
ing force of the new nation. The Biddles were, in fact, Hamiltonians
before Hamilton, and without benefit of economic or political theory.
Their minds worked along those lines in the most natural way in the
world. They thought in terms of a large, rather than a local, set of interests, trying to achieve an alliance between the business communities of
the North and the producing regions of the Carolinas. They were also
patriots, in no paltry sense of the word. One of them describes the taking off of his brother, who was a member of that Continental Congress
which was presently to fight the Revolution, in the following terms:

"The first day Congress sat, I rode out with my brother Edward. He
told me that, from the disposition of the members, he was sure much
blood would be spilt before the dispute was settled. He said that he
would give up his practice at the bar, and go into the army, as he had
been an officer in the Provincial Army, and was in the prime of life.
He would probably have been next in command to General Washington, but coming to Philadelphia in January, 1775, from Reading in a
boat, he fell overboard. We got him out immediately and went ashore
to a tavern that happened to be near. In order to prevent his taking

cold, he drank a great deal of wine, and stood before a large fire in his shirt, to dry it. The landlord being a Tory, and saying something about what Congress had done being improper, he beat him severely. He ordered a blanket to be brought, and would not change his shirt, but lay down in it damp before the fire. The next morning he was very ill, and in a few days broke out all over his body and face large blotches. He had one in the eye that deprived him of the sight of it. Although he lived nearly five years afterward, he had scarce a day of health."

The point worth remarking is Edward Biddle's calm acceptance of the possibilities of hostilities with the mother country, at a time when almost everyone but Sam Adams was being tentative about such an idea. It is quite true, incidentally, that good health would have given him a high command in the Continental Army; he had been at the taking of Fort Duquesne, and the provincial legislature thought his six years' service so valuable that it voted him 5,000 acres of land. Another brother was that Nicholas Biddle who was one of the best captains in the Continental navy, who was killed when his *Randolph*, 32, blew up in the midst of an action against the British *Yarmouth*, 64, while giving the battleship quite as much as she could handle. An uncle of Nicholas and Edward Biddle was named Charles; he engaged in the shipping trade at Beaufort, South Carolina, and was well and favorably known in that part of the country. Carolina looked on Nicholas Biddle as one of her own sons, and he refitted his frigate at Charleston.

The brother who wrote the memoir was also named Charles. He was the father of our James Biddle, and himself a very distinguished man who went to sea at 14, returned from it to go into banking, business, and shipping, and became vice-president of the Executive Council of Pennsylvania and one of the wealthiest men in the state. In spite of his Federalism, he was on intimate terms with Aaron Burr—who came to his house after the duel in which Hamilton was killed—and with Thomas Truxtun, after that celebrated captain made his home in Philadelphia.

Truxtun made this Charles Biddle his personal prize-agent during the French war, and since the captain's squadron made numerous cap-

tures, including the frigate *Insurgente*, there was much financial business for the agent to handle. He accomplished it with shrewdness,
honesty, and dispatch, and the friendship between the two men grew.
It was quite natural that when Truxtun came north at the close of 1799
to put into commission the fine new frigate *President*, 44, the prize-
agent should solicit from him midshipmen's warrants for his two
sons—Edward II and James.

At this time James Biddle was not quite 17, having been born in February 1783. It was said of him that he had a taste for literature and a
strong sense of humor, though no examples of the latter are cited. He
had already received his sheepskin from the University of Pennsylvania, *magna cum laude,* but, unlike the cases of other college-trained
young men who went into the navy, there was never any question that
the sea service was a correct and honorable profession for a Biddle.

President put to sea in September 1800, cruising down to the Guadeloupe station, where she spent six months without anything special
occurring, since the French were pretty well driven from West Indian
waters by this date. During the voyage young Edward Biddle died of
a fever, much regretted; he was the third of the family and the second of
the name to lose his life at sea, and had been considered the more
brilliant of the two brothers.

The peace establishment, which brought discharges to so many officers, could, of course, hardly affect anyone bearing the name of Biddle
and having Tom Truxtun's stamp of approval. Young James spent a
couple of months' leave at home, then was ordered to *Constellation*,
38, Captain Alexander Murray, for a voyage to the Mediterranean. This
was the rather disorganized cruise headed by Commodore Richard V.
Morris, during which Murray had so much trouble with his lieutenants.
One of those lieutenants was Jacob Jones; Biddle formed a friendship
with the ex-doctor which lasted throughout their lives and may have
had something to do with the fact that when *Constellation* returned to
the States the midshipman was transferred with Jones into *Philadelphia,* 38.

She sailed in June 1803, under Captain William Bainbridge, who had
the then unusual habit of making written reports on the capacity of his
officers. Of Biddle he said: "From his high sense of honor and talents

must one day be conspicuous in the service of his Country. I think qualified for an acting lieutenancy which, I hope, the Secretary will give him." In an appendix he lists Biddle as one of four officers whom he would like to have with him in any future command. This was high praise, but probably deserved; when the ship reached Gibraltar, Commodore Preble also placed himself on record with regard to the young officer's smartness and promise.

On 31 October, *Philadelphia* had her terrible accident off Tripoli. Biddle, with Lieutenant David Porter, was dispatched in a longboat toward the clustering Tripolitan gunboats with a message of surrender. No sooner had the Americans approached than from every side they were commanded in an almost incomprehensible gibberish, accompanied by gestures, to lay alongside this craft or that. An attempt to select the commander's boat brought yells and a series of shots, after which the Americans backed water. As one of the gunboats came alongside, Biddle offered his sword. Not the slightest attention was paid to this; instead some twenty of the ruffians leaped into the boat, brandishing weapons and gabbling. Two of them pulled off Biddle's coat and fought for it until, unable to decide possession, they gave it back to him. His cravats were violently torn from his neck, his waistcoat and shirt opened, his pockets emptied of everything he possessed, except twenty dollars in gold which he had had the forethought to conceal in his boots. When the prisoners were led on shore, the populace received them with hooting and insults.

This was a foretaste of what the 19 months of captivity would be like; a captivity relieved only by the boom of Preble's guns and the occasional crash of masonry and yellings when something in the town was struck. Biddle did some studying in the prison school established by Lieutenant Porter, and was the only officer besides Bainbridge himself who succeeded in getting letters out. With the financial backing he had, one may suspect that the Oriental practice of bribery was at work. The family funds were behind an offer that came through to ransom Biddle out of captivity as an individual; he refused, saying that he would share the fate of his companions, and they voted that this was a noble thing to do.

One series of special favors it was allowable for Biddle to accept. He had brought out letters of introduction from commercial men in Philadelphia to Sir Alexander Ball, the Governor of Malta; that gentleman sent to Tripoli packages of food and clothes, with instructions to the British consul at Tripoli to keep a special watch over the young man's well-being.

II

James Biddle reached home in September 1805, and found waiting not only the lieutenant's commission Bainbridge had asked for him, but also an active sea command, which was practically a miracle at that date. To be sure, the command was only that of gunboat *No. 1,* one of the most ridiculous vessels any navy ever had, which on her maiden voyage had encountered some wind and ended up in a cornfield in Georgia. Since that date, however, she had been officially pronounced "a safe vessel outside the bar," and the duty held some promise to an ambitious officer.

The St. Mary's River was then the southern boundary of the United States, and the authorities in Spanish Florida were lax, so that a nice little industry in piracy had grown up, conducted by small craft which operated out of the inlets against ships plying between New Orleans and the eastern states. President Jefferson, who had his doubts about naval force for other purposes, never hesitated to employ ships or anything else against pirates; such gentry produced in him an irritation which caused all theoretical questions to be laid aside. He ordered a patrol from the St. Mary's to St. George's Bank, and as far into the Gulf as necessary to protect commerce, assigning the light frigate *Adams,* 28, and the sloop *Hornet,* 18. *No. 1* was attached to these ships, partly as a tender, and partly to see how the gunboat type would stand sustained cruising. The home port was Charleston; Lieutenant Biddle, in view of his family, was readily received into the close-knit aristocratic society there.

The gunboat did not stand sustained cruising at all well, and although Biddle's superiors reported that he was "very attentive" and did everything of which his unhappy ship was capable, four months of the service were enough, and he asked for relief. Secretary Smith replied that "a gunboat expedition" was in prospect—where, he did not say—and requested that Lieutenant Biddle remain with *No. 1*. The Lieutenant did so for three months more, and, when no expedition developed or seemed likely to do so, sent in a really strongly worded request for a furlough, and went home to Philadelphia.

In the spring of 1807, he sailed to China as mate of a merchant ship. Like a good many other officers, he had come to believe that there was little future in the navy, either for the individual or for the service of the United States, and he talked a good deal about imitating the numerous officers who were resigning from the service. But during the Chinese voyage he argued things out with himself, and on his return agreed to accept any billet in which the department placed him.

It was gunboats again, of course, and this time the most thankless task he could have been given—that is, the enforcement of the Embargo in the Delaware, which meant holding back and arresting the ships of people most intimately connected with him by family and friendship. But he stuck it out until 1809 when the big ships were put into commission again. In that year Bainbridge was appointed to *President,* and promptly made good on his earlier desire to have Biddle with him again by asking the young man to come as his Second Lieutenant. This was the deep-sea cruise that lasted over a year; Biddle had no sooner returned from it than he was asked to take the brig *Siren,* 16 (whose commander was sick), down to Norfolk, leave her there, and himself join *Constitution.*

She was John Rodgers's ship but, on one run down the coast, that captain had found her to behave so badly that he exercised his privilege as ranking sea officer of the service, and exchanged ships with Isaac Hull, who had just refitted *President.* All the talk in the town was of how the *Chesapeake-Leopard* affair had been aggravated by the conduct of the British frigates along our coast, stopping ships and impressing men, even in the very mouths of the harbors. *President* was to make an offshore cruise, under orders which Rodgers left no doubt he would interpret into permission to open fire at the slightest sign of aggression from the British. Biddle asked to go with him, expressing the hope that they would meet a British frigate and there would be a fight.

He was eminently correct in the general idea, for *President* did find herself plunging through midnight waters alongside a warship which answered a hail by firing a shot which struck the American cruiser's mainmast—and was instantly repaid with crushing broadsides. But Biddle's timing was wrong; all this came a year later, in 1811, after *President* had made one uneventful cruise and laid over a winter in New London. In the meantime the impatient Biddle had left the ship, in despair of anything interesting turning up, and accepted a commission to carry dispatches to the American minister to France. It was winter when he arrived, and Napoleon was in residence. The Emperor's game at the time was to favor Americans, and he had the warmest of welcomes for a young man who was both an officer of the United States navy and a connection of the great Philadelphia house whose ships were so frequently in French ports. Biddle swam through an endless series of parties and balls at the Tuileries, and was retained at court until April 1812, when it was time for Napoleon to leave with his armies for the great war against Russia.

III

The Anglo-American war broke out soon after the Lieutenant returned to the States. He hurried to New York to try for a place aboard Commodore Rodgers's ship, but that officer had sailed with his squadron before Biddle arrived, and the only other navy vessel in port was *Essex,* 32. Her captain was Biddle's old chief and good friend, David Porter. He would have been delighted to take Biddle aboard, but then it was discovered that the Lieutenant had so much seniority that he could only be First Lieutenant of the ship, and the officers already aboard were unwilling to be pushed down, each a grade. Now Biddle took the stage back to Washington to press his suit for appointment to a ship. It was to no purpose; the answer was that every frigate had her full complement of lieutenants, and the only places open were in the gunboats.

He returned to Philadelphia in a mood described as of deepest despondency, which can hardly have been lifted by the thought that if he had stayed aboard *Constitution* he would now be a sharer in the victory which everyone was praising. But the despair lasted only until

James Biddle

Wasp, 18, came up the river with dispatches from France. Her commander was another old friend, Jacob Jones, and she lacked a First Lieutenant.

So at last James Biddle put to sea as an officer of a warship in time of war; and five days later he was in battle. When *Frolic's* bowsprit stabbed through *Wasp's* rigging, Biddle leaped to lead the boarders, but he was pulled back by a mid who grabbed his coattails, and so became only the second man to reach the British brig's nearly empty deck. After the battleship *Poictiers* took both *Wasp* and *Frolic,* he was carried to Bermuda with the other officers, and with them came back on parole in November. His return to Philadelphia was a triumph; Congress voted him a silver medal and the Pennsylvania legislature added a gold-mounted sword. A committee of citizens had a silver urn made for him, with a representation of the battle in high relief.

An anecdote accompanies these honors. The gold-mounted sword was so long in the making that by time it was ready another Pennsylvanian had earned one, Stephen Decatur. The captain of *United States* had a wonderful tongue in repartee and in extempore speaking, but his education was mostly of the quarterdeck, and he was nervous about the set oration required on accepting the sword. He therefore besought the aid of his friend, the *magna cum laude* man, Biddle. Biddle gravely helped in the preparation of the speech; but when the ceremony took place, he received his own sword first as the junior officer, and simply paralyzed Decatur by delivering, word for word, the oration the latter had intended to make.

Of course, as First Lieutenant of a victorious ship, he received a promotion—to master-commandant—and had to be given an independent command. For the time being, the command was no more than gunboats again, the flotilla in the Delaware. But on March 13, 1813, James Lawrence came home with *Hornet* and a victory over British *Peacock.* He was moved up to the frigate *Chesapeake,* and Biddle was given the sloop.

She lay at New York, being part of the squadron under Decatur. In her, Biddle accompanied *United States* and *Macedonian* in their effort to break out through Long Island Sound during the spring, and with the two frigates was blockaded in New London. During the summer, all sorts of challenges to individual battles flew back and forth, accompanied by debate on the terms of the duels. Biddle offered one challenge to the British sloop *Loup Cervier*, 18, which had slightly less than *Hornet's* broadside but a slightly larger crew. The British captain replied that he would be glad to accept, and would limit his crew to the same number as *Hornet's*, provided Biddle would tell him what that number was. Biddle was willing, but Decatur scented a trick, and would not permit an acceptance; he believed that the enemy would put a specially picked crew aboard their ship.

In the early part of 1814, *United States* and *Macedonian* were dismantled and laid up at New London. During nearly the whole of the year *Hornet* was kept in the Thames to protect the frigates against a landing or a cutting-out expedition. But toward the fall shore batteries were set up for that purpose, and Biddle learned that Decatur was planning a raid to the Indies with *President* and the new sloop-of-war *Peacock*. Permission was asked to bring *Hornet* through Hell Gate to be a part of this squadron. Granted; in November, Biddle sailed away from the blockaders in the Sound, and was ready for sea, after nearly 17 months of swinging at anchor.

Nevertheless, the period is not to be thought of as idle; there were drills, drills, drills, and more of them in the bay after the arrival at New York. Yet it was the night of January 22, 1815, before *Hornet* ran through the blockade on the wings of a storm-wind, accompanied by *Peacock* and the supply schooner *Tom Bowline*. They were to rendezvous with Decatur at Tristan d'Acunha; halfway down the Atlantic, *Hornet* separated from her consorts to chase a sail, which proved to be a valuable Indiaman, and accordingly did not reach the island until March 23. She was just preparing to anchor when a sail was made out to the southeast, steering west, quite evidently a brig-of-war. The land hid the stranger in an instant, but *Hornet* sheeted home the light sails that had already been let go, and ran around the projection of land. At this the Englishman, sighting Biddle's ship for the first time, came down toward her, rapidly.

It is possible that the British captain, whose name was James Dickenson, took *Hornet* for the vessel he was seeking, and to fight which he had been supplied at Cape Town with an extra complement of Marines—a heavy, ship-rigged privateer from Philadelphia, named *Young Wasp,* of 20 guns and 150 men, which had lately taken 8 big ships in the Cape and India trade. It is possible, but it would hardly have mattered to Dickenson, who was valiant in the tradition of his race and service, and had a new ship, *Penguin,* 18, all 32-pounder carronades, like *Hornet* herself, so that the weight of metal for the British ship was 274 pounds, for the American, 279—a difference so slight as to be meaningless.

Hornet hove to as *Penguin* came down; then filled and backed, filled and backed, wearing occasionally to keep way on, and to prevent her adversary from gaining a raking position, for the wind was stiff across a heavy sea, and the maneuvering rapid. At 1:40 *Penguin* hauled up to a reach, on the starboard tack, about a hundred yards distant, hoisted a white ensign and fired a challenge gun; *Hornet* luffed up at the same time, and the action began with broadsides fired from both sides, the ships on courses slightly converging.

From the first fire the American sloop had the better of it; every shot went home, one of them entering at a slight angle to take off six legs and dismount a gun before it passed out the opposite bulkhead. Twelve minutes, or enough for every gun to fire thrice; Captain Dickenson shouted to his Lieutenant MacDonald above the din: "That fellow is giving it to us like hell; we shall have to go on board!" The next moment a roundshot tore him all apart; MacDonald put the helm up and came charging in, with drum and bo'sun's pipe calling for boarders.

Penguin's bowsprit jagged into *Hornet's* mizzen rigging, but, as fast as the British seamen gathered to board, the American Marines shot them down. They could not, they dared not, press home in the face of that fire, they broke back across their own deck, the American seamen began shouting and climbing into the nettings to counterboard, as *Wasp's* had done in the earlier battle, but Biddle held them back to the guns, crying that they were cutting her to pieces.

At 1:57 *Penguin's* bowsprit ripped away *Hornet's* main-boom and in the same instant snapped off short; her foremast came tumbling down, and someone cried from her deck that she surrendered. Biddle called to cease fire, and leaped to the taffrail; a pair of English marines turned their muskets on him in rage and despair, and sent the American Captain tumbling to the deck with a bullet through his throat. They were instantly killed; *Hornet's* men ran back to their guns, shouting "No quarter!" and would very likely have sent the unfortunate brig to the bottom with every man aboard, had not Biddle raised himself and said he was not seriously hurt.

He had done almost as complete a job on an English ship of his own force as had the first *Wasp,* and in far less time; for *Penguin* had 14 killed and 28 wounded in a crew of 132, while *Hornet* had only

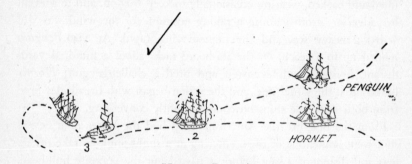

Hornet—Penguin
(1) Broadside action. (2) *Penguin* comes in to try boarding. (3) *Penguin* drops away, a wreck, and surrenders.

2 killed and 9 wounded. The brig was so smashed that she would clearly never be good for anything but firewood. Everything valuable was taken out of her and she was burned; while the process was going on, two more sail came over the horizon, and it looked like another battle, but they proved to be *Peacock* and *Tom Bowline.*

This was fortunate, for when, on April 12, Biddle and Warrington decided to continue their cruise to the Indies without waiting any longer for *President,* they could use the schooner as a cartel, and so disembarrass themselves of their prisoners. The ocean across which they progressed lay empty until April 27, when a sail was sighted eastward. *Peacock* and *Hornet* bore toward her through light airs, and ran that way all the afternoon and night. In the morning the chase was yet visible; both sloops put out their studding-sails and ran down, making her out to be a big Indiaman. On *Hornet's* deck they were just discussing what they would do with the silks when, at a little after three in the afternoon, *Peacock* made the signal that this was a ship of the line, and an enemy. A light vessel would stand little chance trying to run off the wind when pursued by a ship with so huge a spread of canvas; Biddle accordingly went about, close-hauled for a beat to windward.

At this time the Britisher, which was *Cornwallis*, 74, was eight miles distant, but as afternoon turned to evening, it became evident that she was not only very fast, but uncommonly weatherly for a battleship. At nine in the evening, Biddle perceived that she was gaining so fast it would be necessary to lighten ship, so he hove out 12 tons of ballast, some shot, and the spare spars, and cut away his sheet anchor with its cable. The enemy now gained less, but still gained, so that at daylight of the 29th, he was within gunshot; hoisted an admiral's flag, and began firing from his chasers. The shot went right over *Hornet*; Biddle cut away the remaining anchor, threw away the launch, hove overboard six of his guns and some more shot. At 9:00 A.M. his ship had pulled so far into the lead that *Cornwallis* stopped shooting, after having fired over 30 times without once hitting the American.

But the battleship's cessation of fire now improved her sailing. By 11:00 she was once more pulling up, and Biddle was forced to lighten still more, by throwing overboard all but one of his guns, with stores and every other heavy object that could be pried loose. In the meanwhile the battleship had again begun to fire steadily; Biddle thought it perfectly extraordinary that his ship was not reduced to kindling-wood, since *Cornwallis* was closer to him than *United States* had been to *Macedonian* when she slaughtered that ship. Yet only three shot came aboard, two striking the hull and one passing through the jib without casualties.

The only real effect of this fire was once more to deaden the battleship's wind, and just as this happened, the breeze began to freshen, which caused *Hornet* to gain, and rapidly. At sundown *Cornwallis* had dropped back to four miles astern, only occasionally visible through the squalls that were now sweeping the water. The chase continued through one more night, but by daylight of the 30th a good 12 miles separated the pair, and the battleship gave up. Neither in seamanship nor gunnery had her performance given the Royal Navy any occasion for pride.

Biddle now had to turn home; reached Bahia in June, where he learned of the peace, and New York at the end of July. The city voted him a public dinner; Philadelphia took up a subscription to buy him a service of plate. There had to be a court of inquiry on the loss of *Hornet's* guns during the pursuit; not only did it find Biddle guiltless, but added that of the two achievements his escape was better than the capture of *Penguin,* and recommended his promotion to captain which was promptly granted.

IV

Now came the new peace establishment, with the captains outnumbering the ships in commission. Biddle spent the first two years of this period in the wealthy society of Philadelphia, where he could well hold up his end, since in addition to the family funds he had prizemoney by Congressional grant for both *Frolic* and *Penguin*, no inconsiderable amount. The Monroe administration brought in John Quincy Adams as Secretary of State. That long-headed New Englander had helped write the Treaty of Ghent, which closed the War of 1812, and no one knew better than he that it provided for the restoration of all posts and territories taken during the conflict. Now among such posts and territories was Astoria, the fur settlement at the mouth of the Columbia River, anchor of the vast and rich wilderness called the Oregon. The British claimed that they had owned the place before the war, and their action during the conflict was only a recovery of property illegally occupied; but Adams saw a shrewd opportunity to obtain a formal recognition of the American view that the Oregon Country was part of the Louisiana Purchase, extending to the Pacific. He asked the Navy Department for a good warship and a captain who had the necessary background to act as a diplomat. The choice fell on Biddle; he sailed for the Pacific with the sloop-of-war *Ontario,* 20, one of *Peacock's* sister ships.

On the way out, early in 1818, *Ontario* reached Callao, and sent in her boat for water. At this time both the Argentine and the Chilean residencies had revolted against Spain, but Peru still held by the King, and an expedition was preparing in the south to take it for the revolutionists, who had realized that they could not maintain their independence unless they deprived the monarchy of its bases in the western world. American sympathy was rather obviously with the republicans, and the Spanish soldiers at Callao had become so exercised over this that when *Ontario's* boat put in, its crew were first hooted, then stoned, then set upon with weapons.

Fortunately, nobody was killed. Biddle instantly sent in another boat with a white flag and a request for explanations. No reply; the Captain waited a few hours, then sent in a third boat to announce that he would begin bombarding the place in twenty minutes unless satisfaction were given in the meanwhile. *Ontario* cleared for action and was just warping into position to get a good line on the viceroy's palace, when that worthy's barge came pulling out. It contained a number of men in manacles, and an interpreter, who said that these were the offending soldiers; His Excellency requested that the American Captain would give them a good naval flogging and then return them for court-martial. Biddle, whose only point was to obtain official respect for his flag, returned the men unflogged, with a request that they be punished no more. After this Callao was a friendly port for American ships for as long as the Spanish rule endured.

Along the Pacific coast of North America, Biddle found things in much confusion, with agents of the British, the Russian, and even the French governments deeply involved in a sport which became extremely popular during the century—that of playing position for a land-grab. The whaling industry, which Porter had done so much to save, had been virtually brought to a halt by a system of port regulations that nobody had ever heard of until some ship was confiscated for violating a new one. Biddle went to Oregon first, and, as John Quincy Adams had been so forehanded that there was no British force along the coast, gained Astoria at the price of some verbal indignation; then cruised back and forth for nearly a year, straightening matters out for the whaling captains.

The success of this quasi-diplomatic mission was so outstanding that, when it was decided to do something serious about West Indian piracy during 1821, Biddle was named commodore of a squadron to operate in the Caribbean. His flag was *Macedonian, 38*; in addition he was given the frigates *Congress, 38, Cyane, 32,* and *John Adams, 28;* the sloops *Hornet, 18,* and *Peacock, 20;* with six 12-gun light craft originally intended to be raiders in those very waters—*Spark, Enterprise, Alligator, Grampus, Shark,* and *Porpoise;* also three of the old gunboats, which might be useful for inshore work. The Commodore received some rather mysterious "special orders"; perhaps they had something to do with the long visit he made to Havana, where he tried to persuade the Governor of Cuba to co-operate in running down the pirates. The Spaniard promised everything and did practically nothing; moreover, he flatly refused to agree to the one American proposal that would have been effective—namely, allowing American landing-parties to go ashore in pursuit of the picaroons.

The mission was therefore a failure in the diplomatic sense. In action the squadron did better. *Enterprise* captured 8 piratical craft of varying sizes, *Grampus* took another after a really sharp action, and several pirate ships were driven ashore and burned. The report Biddle made, when he returned in the fall, led to the revision of the squadron that went out with David Porter in the following year, most of the frigates being eliminated and very small ships substituted for them.

Biddle himself was given *Congress, 38,* and another semidiplomatic mission, this time that of carrying ministers to Spain and to the new government at Buenos Aires. After this, brief periods of leave were alternated with a long cruise on the South American station and one as Commodore Mediterranean. During the last tour of duty, Biddle went to Constantinople, again as a naval diplomat, and arranged the commercial treaty for which Bainbridge had laid the foundation long before, the one that carried a proviso for Henry Eckford as chief constructor to the Turkish navy.

In 1838, a new chapter started, when Secretary of the Navy James K. Paulding appointed Biddle governor of the Naval Asylum at Philadelphia. The place was a kind of veterans' home, and the post was not normally one for an officer who possessed Biddle's background and activity of mind; but there was more in the arrangement than met the eye, for it was a perfectly legitimate maneuver by which the educated Biddle and the literary Paulding hoped to achieve a naval school. All previous efforts to obtain such a thing had foundered on objections from the Democratic side of Congress that a naval academy would produce a privileged caste, and, from the Whig side, that it would "degenerate, like West Point" into a nursery for wealthy young men, obtaining their education at the public expense. Biddle was one of the officers who agreed with Warrington that such objections were non-sense. Placing him at the Asylum, where he could take direct action on the school question, would give the project a nonpartisan aspect, since the appointment was made by a Democratic Secretary, while Biddle's own brother, Nicholas, was president of the Bank of the United States and one of the biggest Pooh-Bahs of the Whig Party.

As soon as Biddle was installed, things began to move, but cautiously, in such a way as not to stir up Congressmen. Paulding's first report to the legislature remarked that the provision for instruction afloat was not satisfactory. As Governor of the Asylum, Biddle was legally president of the Board of Examiners, which passed midshipmen up to junior lieutenancies. He now followed Paulding's report with a proposal that before the mids were examined they be given a brief period of instruction at the Asylum in the two most difficult subjects—mathematics and navigation. They would be free of the bustle of a ship while cramming on these subjects, and would have regular hours and, above all, identical instruction—a point which had caused much difficulty for the Board of Examiners.

There was nothing in this that Congress could grumble about, and no appropriation was entailed, so in November 1839 Paulding sent one professor and 15 midshipmen to the Asylum. The school session was a success for everyone but the mids, who were used to getting over-night liberties in all parts of the world, and now found themselves tied down by a 9:00 P.M. curfew and really made to work.

They called the place "Biddle's Nursery" and did not like it, but by 1842 several more professors had been added and the courses expanded into what was the real foundation of the Naval Academy. Biddle himself was not present to see the founding at Annapolis. Things were going badly with his brother, so when the navy was reorganized in 1842 he retired, looking forward to a peaceful twilight.

But by 1845, the China trade had grown to such proportions that it was felt that some kind of diplomatic representation there was needed. It was decided to send out a minister, and quite naturally the new Navy Secretary, George Bancroft, turned to the man who for nearly 30 years had been engaged in naval-diplomatic errands. Biddle received command of *Columbus,* 74, and took aboard A. H. Everitt as commissioner to China. That Everitt became so ill he had to leave the ship at Rio did not seem to Biddle any reason for discontinuing his mission; he pushed on to China, negotiated the treaty himself, and left a naval lieutenant in charge of the United States office before sailing for home.

The trip homeward was leisurely. As the custom was, Biddle followed the old route of the galleons to touch at the west coast ports of North America. He reached them early in 1847 and made the somewhat unexpected discovery that the United States was not only at war with Mexico, but in danger of being otherwise embroiled. The Oregon question with Britain remained unsettled; Commodore J. D. Sloat, who had the American squadron on the coast, reached San Francisco only just in time to hoist the American flag there, before a powerful British fleet came in with the intention of taking the place under protection. Now Sloat had proclaimed the whole coast down to Central America under blockade, and Her Majesty's officers were protesting. Biddle perceived at once that Sloat had given them an admirable opportunity for intervention. The American squadron was nowhere near big enough to cover every port; the British had only to sail a ship into some harbor where no American blockader was present, declare the blockade broken, and take the place (temporarily, but with an eye to permanence) under the British flag—later exchanging it against Oregon, or immediately using it as a *point d'appui* against that territory. As senior officer present, the old man assumed command of the American squadron, canceled the general blockade in favor of a specific one against the ports of Mazatlan and Guaymas, and sent ships to close these ports with all rigor.

It was his last service. In July he started around the Horn again, reached home after a voyage that had covered 63,000 miles, and died in the following year. He was 65 at the time, a figure universally respected for fairness, for intellect, for perception; and for what he had done to introduce that tradition of close co-operation between the navy and the overseas trading interest of the nation, which was of such importance during the middle years of the 19th century.

DECISION

Chapter 13

The Psychic Celt:
Charles Stewart

> We raked her again, and her flag came down—
> The haughtiest flag that floats—
> And the lime-juice dogs lay there like logs,
> With never a bark in their throats.
>
> —Broadsheet ballad: The *Constitution's* Last Fight

ROM A GROUP IN WHICH INDIVIDUALISM WAS SO PRONOUNCED AS among Preble's boys, it is almost impossible to select one as either completely representative or outstandingly a character. Indeed, such a selection is rather futile; but if it has to be made, the choice must undoubtedly fall on Charles Stewart. He began his career as a poor and almost illiterate tanner's apprentice; he ended it as the first admiral in the history of the American navy (the only one of Preble's boys who attained that rank), a wealthy man, and a writer of considerable grace and force. His first commanding officer thought him languid and his second thought him insubordinate; yet he shared with Bainbridge the saving of the navy in the dark opening hours of 1812, and only by his own choice did he miss becoming President of the United States. In his first action, he shot at a ship for four hours without killing a man aboard her; in his last, he fought two ships at once, and captured them both by a combination of some of the most skillful maneuvering and accurate gunnery ever seen on blue water. All Preble's boys who were not killed in action lived to a considerable age; but Stewart so much outdid the rest that he saw the inauguration of U. S. Grant, and his own grandson beginning a meteoric rise as one of the major political figures of the British Empire. He was a self-made and a self-educated man; and there is some reason to believe he was psychic.

The family was Irish, the father a merchant skipper who settled in Philadelphia, and who died there two years after Charles was born in July 1778, the youngest of eight children. To the difficulties that normally faced a widow with such a brood, there were added the special troubles attendant on the Revolutionary War. Whatever estate there was vanished like a puff of smoke, and Mrs. Stewart was hard put to it to keep the family together. One of the biographies says she not only succeeded, but also gave the children a good English education, which in Charles Stewart's case requires a rather special definition of the word "good." He did attend Dr. Abercrombie's academy for a time, and became one of the quadrumvirate that included Stephen Decatur, Richard Somers, and Richard Rush, but he certainly did not learn much there, and at 13 left the place forever.

His departure was due to a new shift in the family fortunes. Something like a year before, Mrs. Stewart married as her second husband one Captain Britton, member of the First Congress and close personal friend of George Washington. Britton presented young Charles to the President ("After that not one of the boys dared knock a chip off my shoulder," Stewart used to say in his old age), and took up seriously the question of the boy's career. Young Charles is described at this time as a "wild, courageous lad," who showed no taste whatever for learning the trade of the tanner whose apprentice he was in the intervals of his schooling. Captain Britton was interested in several vessels sailing out of Philadelphia; he found a cabin boy's billet for his stepson aboard the Indiaman *Loraine,* Captain Church.

In those days the merchant marine was not without certain dangers outside insurance policy coverage. Two years later, when *Loraine* put into one of the ports of what was to become the Republic of Haiti, the general in local command had himself rowed out to look over the ship—a general who was ultimately to make himself both famous and infamous as Henri Christophe, the black Emperor. Leaning over the rail, Stewart saw a boat being propelled with awkward, splashing strokes, carrying in its sternsheets a huge, very squat black man, whose lower teeth projected beyond his lips from a prognathous jaw. He was hung with medals and clad in the brilliant full-dress uniform of a French officer, all but his feet, which were perfectly bare. As the boat came alongside, this person shouted something that might have been an order to throw a rope. The strange gabble of Franco-Negro-English completed the effect of his appearance; the boy burst into laughter, shook the rope in the air, and replied in a mocking imitation of the General's gibberish.

He realized his mistake instantly, for the dark countenance writhed into a paroxysm of rage, and one of the sailors shouted, "Run!" Where? Not the cabin, it would surely be searched. An inspiration sent Stewart to the galley and the cubby by the side of the stove, where the cook kept his wood. It had a trapdoor with a ring on the inside. Stewart leaped in, thrust a stick through the ring, and curled up in palpitating silence. Outside, General Christophe and his henchmen had gained the deck with no help at all from those aboard, and the black leader was demanding that "the white-haired boy" should be delivered to him for immediate execution on the charge of having laughed at a dictator. Captain Church declared that Stewart had leaped overboard and swum to a French ship nearby; Christophe did not believe him, and ordered a search of the vessel, going so far as to have some of the cargo moved in the hold. The galley was not exempt; Christophe tried the trap of the wood-hole, found it held, and, deciding that breaking it open would hardly be worth the trouble, contented himself with thrusting his sword in all round the edges, luckily without touching the cabin-boy inside.

There is nothing more of importance in the record until 1798 and the organization of the new navy. To be sure, Stewart did rise in the interim to the command of a vessel, like Bainbridge at a similar age, but this may have been partly due to his stepfather's connection with the business. It is also true that he was commissioned into the service as a lieutenant, while most young men of his age were receiving midshipmen's warrants, but this is not so unusual either for the stepson of the friend of George Washington. Most of the officers who came to the navy from ship commands received lieutenancies in any case.

What is of special interest is the first recorded document bearing Stewart's signature. It is a letter to Captain John Barry of *United*

States, 44, in which both were to sail. Stewart has inspected the ship, and has made certain arrangements, which he describes in a handwriting barely legible, using an English almost incoherent and studded with such misspellings as "warter" for "water." Neither does he seem to have been a complete success as a naval officer at this time. *United States* was the flag of the squadron on the Windward Islands station until she came back home for a refit and a new crew in May 1799. Stewart had become her First Lieutenant by seniority when she went out again for a cruise along the coast of the southern states in the fall of that year, and Barry made no effort to exchange him for another officer, which would seem to indicate that his conduct gave satisfaction. But when, early in 1800, the schooner *Experiment,* 12, put in, accompanied by such disquieting reports about her commanding officer, Secretary Stoddert decided she needed a new captain, and asked Barry what he thought of Stewart for the post. The old man replied:

"I am perfectly satisfied with your appointment of Lieutenant Stewart I hope he will be more active when he com*ds* than when he is com*d*."

A portrait of the Lieutenant at this time shows him as a rather thin-faced young man, and handsome, with a big nose and mobile lips. He was five feet nine; his hair had become red. Whether a command of his own acted as a tonic, or whether he had a vessel of a type more suitable to the type of operations of which the French War mainly consisted, he was certainly a great deal more active. The first cruise was to Bermuda, then to the Guadeloupe station; off St. Bartholomew's on September 9, *Experiment* fell in with one of the more notorious French privateers, *Deux Amis,* of 8 guns and 40 men, which had taken many American merchantmen. *Experiment* easily ran her down and took her after a brief resistance; there are no details. She was the ship into which Stewart put Lieutenant David Porter with only four men, and which Porter had such difficulty in bringing to harbor after *Experiment* walked over the horizon on another chase.

Putting into Prince Rupert's Bay to join his prize, Stewart found himself in contact with the activities of the British press-gang. There were a pair of British brig-sloops in harbor. One of them had a seaman aboard named Seeley, who somehow managed to smuggle a letter to

Stewart, saying that he was a pressed American and wanted to be rescued. The Lieutenant waited on the British captain and somehow managed to persuade him to give up the man—probably the only time such a thing ever happened, though it must be remembered that the British were trying to behave well toward Americans at the time, both being enemies of the French.

Experiment's next contact was on the morning of October 1, when, leeward of St. Bartholomew's, Stewart made out two sail bearing down under English colors—a man-o'-war brig and a three-masted schooner. He set the British signal of the day; it was not answered, and as the pair closed in to nearly gunshot distance, with the brig showing 9 ports on a side and the schooner 7, it was clear they were enemies. Stewart set everything and ran to windward. It was soon clear that the fine Baltimore model of his ship gave her so much the advantage in sailing on this bearing that she could lose them when she chose, and toward noon the pursuers admitted it by firing in defiance to windward, then turning away.

But if *Experiment* was faster than either of the others, the three-sticker was also swifter than the brig, and had opened out about a league on her companion. In this Stewart saw an opportunity for business; he cleared for action, swung round, and became the pursuer in his turn, running downwind, wing and wing. The people of the schooner were soon observed heaving guns overboard to lighten ship; the brig had come round again in an effort to assist her consort, but she had a beat to windward to make through light airs, and was nowhere near in range, when *Experiment* reached position on the schooner's quarter and gave her a broadside which brought down her flag. She was named *Diana,* and now had only three guns left; to the intense joy of the Americans one of the people aboard her was Hyacinthe Rigaud, the mulatto general, "King of the Picaroons"—of all French nationals the man they would most have preferred to lay hands on. Tom Truxtun, who was commodore on the station, treated the fellow well but sourly, and used him in an exchange which brought home a number of American merchant seamen captured by the French.

This was a feather for Lieutenant Stewart's cap, but in the next transaction he did not show so well. It fell out at night, off Antigua, when

Experiment came alongside a heavily armed schooner she had been following through the evening. The chase refused to answer hails; when ordered to heave to so that Stewart could send a boat aboard for examination, she replied with a musket, whereupon he fired a shot into her, and an action commenced that lasted for four hours, or until the stranger struck. She proved to be not French but British, a privateer named *Louisa Bridger,* commanded by an obstinate and bad-tempered man named Eve, who had already enjoyed a brush with U.S.S. *Patapsco,* 20, for exactly the same reason.

Yet the main point about the affair is that in four hours of intermittent firing, Stewart's ship damaged the Britisher so little that she had not a single man killed and only a few wounded. It is true that at the time *Experiment* was heeling so far to a heavy-running sea that pieces of board had to be placed beneath the trucks of the gun-carriages to depress the muzzles sufficiently to fire at *Louisa Bridger's* hull; nevertheless, this sort of shooting did not redound much to the credit of the American ship or her commander.

Neither did some of the Lieutenant's other actions, according to Commodore Truxtun, who remarks in a letter home that Lieutenant Stewart has "made a point of keeping out of the way of the commander of the squadron he was sent out to join, as much as possible." There is none of Barry's complaint of a lack of activity in this, however, and the records show that *Experiment* was all over the Caribbean, retaking a couple of merchant vessels and running several convoys before being sent home in January, 1801, with the ship in bad condition and her crew's time expired.

On the way, off the island of Saona, near Santo Domingo, Stewart sighted a vessel on the reef, making signals of distress. There was a strong sea running, but he worked his ship in and took off 60 people, mostly women, wives and daughters of the local Spanish officials. They had been basely abandoned aboard the wreck by its captain and other officers, who had hid themselves on the mountain in the center of the island. Stewart sent a file of Marines after them, captured the scoundrels, and delivered them in irons to the Governor of Santo Domingo, who wrote a letter to the President of the United States with official thanks and a request that Stewart's merits should receive attention.

Charles Stewart

II

Lieutenant Charles Stewart thus brought home to the peace establishment a record which, if not the best in the service, was a long way above the worst, and quite good enough for him to be retained as the senior officer of his rank in the navy. His next assignment was to *Constellation,* 38, Captain Alexander Murray, for the Mediterranean cruise on which that skipper had so many of his lieutenants under arrest. There is no sign that Stewart took any part in the troubles. When the frigate reached home, he applied for a return to the Barbary Coast on active duty. Secretary Smith wrote him a letter, expressing gratification at such a spirit, and saying that Stewart should have a command of his own, the new brig *Siren,* 16, which he was to see through the last stages of construction and to furnish with a crew.

The correspondence became fairly voluminous when Stewart reported difficulties about shipping men, because merchant vessels had raised their wages above the navy figure, and also submitted a model of a new type of carriage for carronades, invented by himself. It was a slide arrangement, which turned out to be a genuine improvement, permitting much more accurate fire, and it was one of the reasons why American ships were to shoot so well in the War of 1812. But the focus of interest in this series of letters is the letters themselves. The Lieutenant who could hardly write at all in 1798 has by 1803 become a man who not only sets his words down in a neat fist, but also expresses himself without errors of spelling or grammar and with considerable ability in handling words. Eloquence, of course, is something innate, depending upon the quality of the mind which arranges expressions into patterns for more effective communication, and it seems to be something Stewart always possessed. But the improvement of the means employed must be due to some self-educative process to which there is not the slightest clue in any surviving document. Self-educative, because the Lieutenant had been at sea during practically all the five years in which he changed from a semi-illiterate merchant skipper into a very good writer indeed. Incidentally, like all converts, he became a lion of the new faith; none of Preble's boys, hardly any naval officer, wrote more frequently or more at length on more subjects during all the rest of his life.

He was also showing much evidence of energy. *Siren* was ready to sail only seven days after launching, and did sail on August 29, 1803, a day also marked by the ship's barber going insane. Gibraltar was reached on October 1, and there for the first time Stewart met Edward Preble, who was to become his very good friend and to mold into a firm pattern of conduct the parts of a character which had shown excellent qualities, but some traces of disorganization. The first transaction which found them together was characteristic of both men. Eight seamen had deserted from *Constitution*. Preble suspected they were aboard British ships in the harbor, but had no proof; Stewart organized a party in a tavern ashore with some officers of H.M.S. *Medusa,* 32, got the Englishmen drunk, and secured from them the necessary admissions, with the names of the men.

In spite of this the affair turned out badly. Preble requested the delivery of the deserters; the senior British officer replied that the men were claimed to be British, and the orders of his government were "on meeting with the Ships of any foreign Nation whatever to demand all such British Seamen that may happen to be on board them." He would not however, "distress the American commodore at present" by asking for the other Englishmen he understood to be aboard *Constitution*. Preble could only reply: "British commanders of course will not attempt to take by force our men unless they have orders from your government to commence hostilities against us"; commit his cause to the future, and make Syracuse his base instead of convenient but very British Malta.

He sent *Siren* with a convoy to Leghorn, where she picked up some American property for delivery to Algiers; then, after a rough passage, reached Syracuse at the end of the year. Stewart had the stepping of her mainmast shifted there, since she had proved distinctly slower than the other brig, *Argus*.

At Syracuse came an incident characteristic of Preble's methods. *Siren's* surgeon, S. R. Marshall, and her acting Second, Joseph Maxwell, did not get along at all well with Purser Nathan Baker. They filed charges against him—that he had wrongfully charged the wardroom mess with a barrel of beef, also some minor matters. Stewart held an inquiry which discovered that the surgeon and the lieutenant had had the beef opened for the wardroom, found it not up to the quality they expected, and sent it forward for the crew's mess. Of course, Baker was chargeable with the beef, since the storeroom was under his jurisdiction, and he had not issued it, so he charged it to the wardroom.

The papers now went to the Commodore; he found that the purser had acted perfectly correctly and the two officers from motives "by no means creditable"; but he only ordered that both should be transferred to other ships as soon as this could be done. Before the transfer took place, Maxwell was in trouble again, this time for sleeping on watch. Preble had Stewart write him a letter describing the offense, and replied with another saying that it was indeed a serious one, but as it was the first time and involved a very young man, there would be no punishment but having both letters read aloud to *Siren's* assembled crew. The old Commodore took a good deal of pains in straightening out his hard cases; whether he would have made something of Maxwell or not we shall never know, for that officer died in 1804.

As soon as *Siren* was ready, she went down to Tripoli as covering vessel for the bold expedition of Stewart's old friend Decatur into the harbor to burn the captured *Philadelphia*. Four of the brig's midshipmen—Anderson, Dorsey, De Krafft, and W. R. Nicholson—managed to secrete themselves aboard Decatur's ship and so to join the expedition; the odd feature of it was that De Krafft was to kill Nicholson in a duel a year later.

Through all the winter and spring gales, *Siren* was very busy on the blockade, since Stewart's position as second ranking officer to Preble made her the senior ship. He kept the brig close in to the fortress, on March 17 running in under fire from the batteries to capture a brig that was trying to slip out. She proved to be a valuable and useful prize, built as a small man-o'-war; Preble supplied her with 12 light guns and added her to the squadron as U.S.S. *Scourge*.

There was another prize during the same month; Stewart had to send her to Malta because she was Russian flag, and the British island held the nearest Admiralty court; H.M.S. *Narcissus,* 32, promptly impressed five men of the prize crew. In July a big provision-carrying galliot was observed, trying to work in; Stewart gave chase and the craft ran ashore some six miles from Tripoli, from which a number of people came out to protect the ship. Just as *Siren* was going in to shoot she lost her wind, so Stewart sent the launch, with a 12-pounder carronade, and a barge with a heavy swivel, the two working in close enough to beat the galliot to pieces with gunfire.

Now came August, the month of battles, with Stewart and his *Siren* in the thick of them, towing gunboats, shooting matters out with the batteries and behaving in a manner that led Preble to write that Captain Stewart would please accept his particular thanks. The news of more substantial reward came out with the relief squadron; on the strength of Preble's reports, Congress had decided to revive the grade of master-commandant, and Charles Stewart's name stood at the head of the list for the new rank. The same express brought tidings that Decatur had been jumped over all the masters-commandant to a captaincy for his feat in burning *Philadelphia,* but no one grudged him that.

III

With the fighting over, *Siren* was sent to cruise between Morocco and Gibraltar, which she did until January 1805, when the poor state of her masts, badly built of white pine, compelled her to go into Cadiz for major repairs. Stewart himself took over the frigate *Essex,* 32, vice her captain, who was going home. He was still in this ship, under John Rodgers's command, when the Tunisian difficulty arose in July. It came about this way: a Tunisian xebec had tried to run into Tripoli with two prizes she had captured, and, as Tripoli was under a legally notified blockade, all three ships were taken by the American squadron. The Bey of Tunis said that the laws of blockade did not apply to Barbary powers; he wanted the ships back and a supply of powder as indemnity. When the American consul refused, the Bey became very much excited, drove him from the presence, and threatened to order his cruisers out against our ships.

The uncertain-tempered barbarian was probably looking for an excuse to capture merchant ships, but he chose the wrong man to deal with in John Rodgers, who had plenty of force to back up his own very certain temper. He sailed at once, and appeared in Tunis harbor with a force consisting of *Constitution,* 44, *Constellation,* 38, *Congress,* 38, *Essex,* 32, *John Adams,* 28, *Siren,* 16, *Nautilus,* 12, *Enterprise* 12, *Hornet,* 10, and a train of eight new gunboats—one of the largest squadrons that ever entered a Barbary port. Decatur was sent ashore to negotiate. The Bey refused to receive him, whereupon Rodgers called a council of officers, whose approval he sought before opening fire, which he proposed to do. All the captains but one were in favor of doing so after giving the barbarian a few hours' grace. The exception was Stewart; under the Constitution, he said, only Congress had the power to declare war. If even the President could not do so, how much less the commander of a naval squadron? The right of defense against attack existed under international law, but that alone.

This reasoning convinced Rodgers that he would get into trouble if he went ahead with his plan, and he rather regretfully abandoned it for moral suasion which eventually brought the Bey to terms. But the occurrence did not endear Stewart to him, and there were a couple of rather stiff exchanges between the two men before Stewart sailed for home in mid-August, taking with him a hundred flower-pots and a pipe of wine for his old friend Preble. In Washington they took a somewhat different view; President Jefferson publicly announced his "high satisfaction at having an officer in the squadron who comprehended international law, the condition of his country, and the policy of his government," and promoted Stewart to his captaincy.

Nevertheless there was very little a junior captain could do in a navy that had run out into gunboats. After a few months spent in superintending the construction of these craft, Stewart obtained a furlough and went off on a series of commercial voyages that carried him to the East Indies, the Mediterranean, and the Adriatic. They seem to have been quite profitable; it was 1811, and the war already near, when he sought Washington again, in the hope of obtaining a sea command. The cruising ships all had commanders, however, and he was merely waiting out his time at the capital when the news came that the British impressments were at last to be paid out in blood. But there was also the other and appalling news that the navy would have no part in the struggle; the ships were to be laid up.

Stewart must have been one of the first to hear of this, since he was a prominent figure in the limited society the town afforded. He looked up Captain Bainbridge, who had recently arrived, and the two men went round to make their famous presentation of the navy's case. It resulted in the reluctant, half-hearted permission for the ships to make one cruise, and everyone knows how that turned out. Stewart himself was present when *Macedonian's* battle-flag was borne into the wildly applauding hall, and Secretary Hamilton cried across the music that the celebrants must never forget that it was to Bainbridge and Stewart that these victories were really due.

Even before this apotheosis, the red-headed captain had helped to set American naval thinking on a sound basis. Congress was in a giving mood after the sea victories, and Secretary Hamilton inquired of Stewart, as the officer most experienced and available, what ships would provide the best naval defense. Stewart replied in words that sound like those Mahan was to write three-quarters of a century later, that the United States needed four classes of warships—battleships, technically of 74 guns, but designed to be individually heavier than those of foreign powers; more of the heavy 44-gun frigates; a few light 32s, to act as scouts and signal-repeaters for the ships of the line; and 16-gun sloops-of-war.

Only on a basis of line-of-battleships (he says) can real defense be developed. Without them, an enemy can use his own battleships as individuals off our harbors, thus holding our frigates in port, while his smaller cruisers scour the seas. When we have even one squadron of ships-of-the-line as powerful proportionately as our frigates, the enemy will be forced to watch the harbor where they lie with something like double the number of his own 74s. This not only gives him a good opportunity to lose a major battle, if chance or marine accident brings the number of the blockaders down to where they can be dealt with. It also involves the enemy in a severe maintenance problem at the limits of the Atlantic, and creates an opportunity for our light cruisers to run free against both his commerce and his transports. A European power would find it very hard to spare enough liners to hold an American squadron of the same type in port and at the same time to post other battleships off each harbor that held a 44-gun frigate.

Stewart's reasoning convinced Congress; it voted four ships-of-the-line, six new 44s, and six of the sloops which turned out to be the wonderful *Peacock* class. But there was still no command for the Captain until the end of December; and, when there was one, it was a disappointment. He received *Constellation*, 38, which had been lying at Washington; Truxtun's old flagship, and regarded as one of the most fortunate frigates in the service. But fortune had left her this time; before she could repair and win beyond the Virginia capes, the topsails of a blockading squadron of four battleships and four frigates came over the horizon. Stewart kedged his *Constellation* up to Norfolk, landed some of her guns on Craney Island, and made preparations for burning the ship, in case the enemy came in in great force.

Eventually they did come in great force, and took a stunning repulse that cost them 92 men in killed and captured alone; but Stewart was not there to see it, for President Madison, anxious to do something for the man who had aided so greatly in saving the credit of his administration, sent the Captain up to Boston to take over *Constitution* from William Bainbridge. Stewart reached the place early in the summer of 1813, and found that the frigate needed repairs, which took a matter of months. Then there were blockaders off the harbor, and it was January 1, 1814, with a strong wind blowing, before he dropped Boston Light astern and was out to sea at last.

IV

He steered for the Carolina coast, found nothing, slanted over to the Bermudas and down to Guiana. There, within a single week of February, four merchant ships were taken, with the schooner-of-war *Pictou*, 14, which of course could offer no resistance to such an antagonist. Stewart now turned north again, and in the entrance to Mona Passage sighted a sail that was evidently a British frigate. She fired a gun to windward in challenge, backed a topsail, and waited for *Constitu-*

tion to close; but, while the American was still three miles off, changed her mind, set all, and ran.

She was H.M.S. *Pique,* 36, an 18-pounder frigate that in the early days of the war would have had no hesitation about fighting an opponent heavier than herself. But things had changed since then, and one of the changes was an order from H.M. Admiralty to all officers, that British 18-pounder frigates were to sail two in company and never again engage American 44s alone. *Constitution* bore in chase of *Pique;* gained steadily till eight in the evening, when thick weather came down which not only gave the Britisher good cover but tore two or three of the American's sails. Examination showed more of the sails in bad condition. Stewart was enough a perfectionist to feel uneasy about cruising an ocean swarming with enemies unless he had his own ship in the best possible running order. He turned for home, and when near there, fell in with a pair of British 38s, *Junon* and *Tenedos.* They chased him most of the day, but *Constitution* fairly outsailed them into Marblehead, and neither British captain liked the idea of going in after her, although the place was unfortified. A little later Stewart slipped into Boston without trouble.

There *Constitution* stayed through the summer. By the time she had secured her new suit of sails—and this was a matter that could not be hurried—the British were off Boston with a squadron particularly designed against the ship that, more than any other, they desired to bring to book. Sir George Collier was the commodore; he had *Acasta,* 40, an experimental frigate with 24-pounders on the gundeck, and two new ships, hastily built in pitch-pine to overmatch the American 44s, *Leander* and *Newcastle.* They were called "spar-deck frigates"—a euphemism, for they were really two-deckers, mounting thirty long 24s on the lower deck, and twenty-six 42-pound carronades and four long 24s on the upper, being rated as 50s. The scantling was made very light in an effort to give them speed, but this proved not quite the correct solution to the problem Joshua Humphreys had met in the 44s with fine lines and careful adjustment of masts and spars. Only off the wind were these spar-deck frigates really fast; their great topweight and light construction made them crank; they were outrageous rollers, and not at all weatherly.

Charles Stewart

In December of 1814, the event occurred which Stewart had predicted to Congress for the case of an enemy attempting to blockade American 74s. Sir George ran low on provision and had to send one of his big ships up to Halifax to bring it, since nothing less was safe from the infernal Yankee privateers. The other two blockaders were unequal to holding the gate with a westerly gale blowing; on the 17th December, *Constitution* sheeted home her jibs and ran out without being seen. The glory of her exploits and Stewart's own popularity had enabled him to pick and choose among men; he had all New Englanders, perhaps the finest crew of any ship in the war save Blakely's *Wasp*—"they were qualified to fight the ship without her officers."

Stewart bore for the Bermudas again, but found only one prize in that region—a brig loaded with fine wines and brandies. He swung across the Atlantic till the Rock of Lisbon rose over the horizon. A big ship was sighted in rather thick weather; *Constitution* bore in chase, but abandoned her pursuit for a somewhat nearer vessel, which was presently run down and found to be an Indiaman so valuable that in spite of the dangers the Captain decided to send her in. This ship reached port, and her cargo alone sold for $75,000; but the really fortunate event was that Stewart abandoned the other chase, for she turned out to be *Elizabeth,* 74, whose captain put out of Lisbon immediately, on learning there was an American frigate off the coast.

He missed her for a reason which Stewart himself could never explain with any logic, since he simply developed a desire to run off toward the Madeiras, not having heard any news. Now came a second strangeness. On the morning of February 19, with the ship's work in progress, her officers gathered at the starboard gangway to indulge in a little mild grousing over not having had any opportunity to distinguish themselves after so long a cruise. Stewart came up to the group unobserved. "Be content, gentlemen," said he. "I promise you that before tomorrow's sun goes down you will be engaged in battle with the enemy, and it will not be with a single ship."

The next morning he inexplicably gave the order to run the ship off to the southwestward, where there should have been an empty ocean; but at 1:00 in the afternoon a sail hove over the searim ahead, and by 2:00 a second was visible, both to leeward and close-hauled. They were clearly warships, which kept away, and Stewart reasoned that they were trying to hold off on their best point of sailing until night should give them cover. He had studding-sails set below and aloft.

There was some haze, and aboard *Constitution* a considerable puzzlement about the class of the nearer stranger, which seemed smallish but showed a double line of ports. The lieutenants thought she might be an old-fashioned frigate on two decks; actually, she was quite a new ship, a constructor's experiment, a heavy corvette or light frigate, H.M.S. *Cyane,* 32, Captain Gordon Falcon, mounting twenty-two 32-pounder carronades on her gundeck, and ten 18-pound carronades and two long 9s topside. Her consort was the ship-sloop *Levant,* 18, Captain the Honorable George Douglass, with eighteen 32-pound carronades, a 12-pounder carronade, and two long 9s. This gave the combined British ships 763 pounds of metal in the broadside against *Constitution's* 704. Yet for anything but very close action the advantage was with the American, for the thickness of her sides and the range of her artillery. Or put it this way: the forces were somewhat different in character, like those on Lake Ontario, and victory would be a matter of which could better use the tools.

The British captains really had no intention of avoiding combat; did not consider that the Admiralty's prohibition against fighting Americans of superior force applied in their case. *Cyane* had set all sail while *Levant* bore up and waited for her; at 5:30 they were near enough for Falcon and Douglass to communicate by voice, whereupon they agreed to delay the action till after dark, which in this thick weather would give the two ships an excellent opportunity to maneuver the one into position for disastrous rakes. In the meanwhile they remained close-hauled, but with everything set, hoping to weather *Constitution* and so gain the maneuvering advantage of engaging from windward. *Levant* was ahead of her consort by about 200 yards.

Although the air was light and the sea smooth, the American frigate came down too fast to be weathered upon, so both the British stripped to fighting canvas. While the juggling was going on, the sun went down and the mist suddenly blew clear; now, as a big moon leaped past islands of cloud, *Constitution* rounded to on the starboard beam of the pair, and heavy firing began at once, the range being 250 yards.

Charles Stewart

In this first exchange the American frigate was hurt hardly at all, while her heavy shot went smashing right through *Cyane's* sides; but soon the billowing smoke piled to a mountain under *Constitution's* lee, hiding her antagonists, who could mark her exact position by watching the tips of her taller upper spars. Fifteen minutes, and their fire died away; Stewart knew that the idea of their being crippled in so brief a time was too good to be true, and ordered his guns loaded but not again touched off.

The smoke whipped clear; *Levant* was broad abeam, but here astern of her was *Cyane,* just luffing to get under *Constitution's* stern for a rake. Stewart and his crew acted like lightning; a full broadside hit *Levant,* while under its smoke the frigate's main and mizzen topsails were flung aback and everything forward shaken loose. She checked; took sternway, and backed smoothly down on the starboard bow of the corvette, giving her a heavy diagonal rake and forcing her to fill away or take another rake from right under the bows. Now the two ships were very close, with all the topmen in action, and *Cyane* could not stand the treatment she was getting from the heavy frigate. Her fire almost died again, not this time from orders, but because the guns were being dismounted and the men who served them shot down.

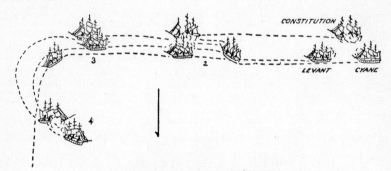

Constitution—Cyane—Levant

(1) The action begins. (2) Stewart discovers *Cyane's* maneuver and backs down on her. (3) Stewart catches *Levant* trying to wear; orders everything set and rakes her on the turn. (4) *Levant* out of action; *Cyane* tries to wear, but *Constitution* comes around faster.

But over the rolling smoke Stewart saw *Levant's* yards swing, and divined that she was wearing round to cross the sterns of both the other ships. He hastily filled all; *Constitution* leaped ahead like a rabbit past *Cyane's* bows and, catching *Levant* just on the turn with her stern exposed, raked her twice with such fury that the sloop was almost dismantled and forced to make sail out of the combat. Now *Cyane* in turn was discovered wearing round; but, with her Yankee crew moving like boxers, *Constitution* wore faster, inside the British ship's circle, and gave her a stern rake that completed the work of disorganization previously begun. The corvette fired a few more shots and surrendered, forty minutes after the first gun.

Down in the offing, Captain Douglass was repairing his damages. He was a brave man, not certain that *Cyane* had given up, and not willing to quit even if she had, for he knew that in battles of this sort the ship strongest at the beginning often becomes so crippled as to become incompetent before a weaker antagonist, as had happened in the case of *President*. By eight o'clock *Levant* had everything ready, and came back; she and *Constitution* passed close aboard on opposite tacks, and Douglass' ship took one mighty broadside which informed him that the American frigate was not in the least crippled. He turned in flight, but after an hour's chase was run down and could do nothing more but take in his flag. He had 23 killed, 16 wounded; *Cyane,* 27 killed, 26 wounded—proportions which show how the American Marines had been at work. *Constitution* lost 6 killed, 9 wounded.

Of all the frigate battles of the war, this was the most brilliantly fought; for years afterward there was talk about the wonderful skill of Stewart and the adroitness of his crew in so handling their heavy ship that two lighter and supposedly more nimble opponents were both raked repeatedly. Later, while the British captains were sitting in his cabin, a mid entered to ask Stewart if the men could have their issue of grog. It was long past the usual hour; Stewart asked if they had been given none. "No, sir," said the mid; "it was just ready for serving before the battle began, but the forecastle men said they didn't want any Dutch courage for such a fight and capsized the grog-tub in the scuppers."

Douglass and Falcon had never heard of sailors who refused their grog before a battle. They expressed their astonishment, then passed to reviewing the action, becoming somewhat heated as each blamed the other for not having made some maneuver that would have averted the double defeat. After hearing them go round in circles for a time, Stewart grew a little impatient. "Gentlemen," he said, "if you really want to find out what would happen under other conditions, I will place you aboard your ships and we can try it again."

That finished the British captains, but not the story. Stewart ran down to the Cape Verdes with his prizes, and put into Porto Praya, where David Porter had had such an odd encounter nearly three years before. Off the place a small merchant ship was hired, and was being fitted as a cartel for the prisoners, when on March 10, with heavy fog-banks on the water, the topsails of a large vessel were seen, standing in. Captain Stewart was in his cabin; to the lieutenant who reported the sighting, he remarked that she was probably a British frigate, and preparations should be made at once to go out and attack her. The people were summoned, but even before the ship could be cleared for action, the yards of two more vessels were seen behind the first, and from their size and squareness it was clear they were all large ships of war.

They were Sir George Collier, with *Leander, Newcastle,* and *Acasta,* which had flown across the Atlantic on the news that the devil-ship of the American navy was loose again. (Five sail of privateers ran out when they left Boston.) Stewart had no confidence in either the ability of the Portuguese to preserve the neutrality of their harbor, or the willingness of the British to respect it. He ordered all ships out to sea at once; and it is a proof of the quality of *Constitution's* crew that it took only ten minutes for all three to be in motion.

They were lost had they taken a minute longer; even as matters stood, *Constitution* and her prizes slanted out of the harbor only a gunshot from the nearest of the British, which was *Acasta.* Now *Constitution,* which had opened the war with a celebrated chase from a British squadron, was finishing it in the same way. Stewart cut adrift the two boats he had towing astern, but it speedily became apparent he could outsail all three of the enemy on this point, a beat nearly to windward on the port tack. *Acasta* weathered on him, it is true, so that he would be cut off if forced to change to the other tack, but the British frigate lost much ground in the process and was soon well astern. Nevertheless, all was not perfect; Collier's squadron began to gain on the prizes. At 1:10 in the afternoon *Cyane* had dropped so far back that Stewart signaled her to go about on the opposite tack. She did so, steering northwest, and, when the British neglected her to hold after the other two ships, was over the horizon in an hour, and in New York a month later. *Cyane* remained in the American navy for a long time and was a useful ship.

By 3:00 *Levant* had also lagged so far as to be in the position *Cyane* had occupied before. Stewart signaled her to tack, thinking once more to draw the British after his own larger ship, but to his infinite surprise all three of the enemy tacked after the sloop. The haze was in part responsible; Sir George explained afterwards that he took *Levant* to be *President* or *Congress*. If true, it is evidence of a poor seaman's eye on his part, and in any case there was no reason why he need send three ships after one. "The most blundering piece of business recorded in these six volumes," the historian of the British navy called it, without stopping to inquire about whether captains of H.M. navy had not grown a little nervous about taking any single ship into action with an American 44.

Levant was weathered upon, and put back into Porto Praya, where the British followed her, and quite justified Stewart's apprehensions by opening fire at once. After taking it for fifteen minutes, the prize-crew surrendered. They had not lost a man, which means that the British gunnery was bad enough to justify Sir George in not sending any single unit after *Constitution*. Congress later noted to pay Stewart and his crew the full value of the sloop as prize-money, and instructed our diplomats to collect from the Portuguese, which was done.

v

Constitution made across the Atlantic to Maranhao in Brazil, where she landed her prisoners and heard of the peace; then, with two tigers in a cage, turned up to New York, arriving a month after *Cyane*. The ship was recognized as she came up the harbor, and when Stewart

landed he was greeted by bonfires in the streets, with a delegation of
the Common Council to present him with the freedom of the city in a
gold box. Boston voted him a triumphal procession; the State of Pennsylvania, its thanks and a gold-hilted sword; Congress, a gold medal.

Neither did President Madison forget to whom he really owed those
victories; he summoned Stewart to Washington and offered him
a place in the Cabinet, which was refused on the typically Stewart
ground that he "was yet young, had rank, and all he desired
was glory." His prize-money had piled up to a very considerable sum;
he spent a good deal of it on a fine estate near Bordentown on the
Delaware, where he added a story to the house, planted a number of
trees, and began raising stock of fine imported breeds. Unlike David
Porter's agricultural venture, Stewart's was a great financial success;
he kept on making money out of it all the rest of his life, and there was
something like a fortune for his two children.

In the period after the war, there were many trips to Washington,
where Madison, and after him Monroe, used Stewart as a kind of unofficial secretary and general consultant on naval matters. One of the
questions with which he was concerned came to a head in 1817, when
there were rather disquieting reports from the Mediterranean, where
Isaac Chauncey was then Commodore. The old ruffling temper of
the days of the great war died hard, and seemed to be turning inward
now that the war itself was over. The report was that the junior officers
of the squadron had become so malcontent that they threatened to
draw their swords on their commanders. The situation was quite evidently beyond Chauncey's grip, and President Monroe decided to have
Stewart relieve him.

The flag of the new Commodore was *Franklin,* 74, which had just
gone into commission at Philadelphia, and on the trip out he had the
pleasure of carrying, as minister to England, his old schoolmate
Richard Rush. As to the matter of Mediterranean discipline, there
may have been minor unrecorded incidents, but things did not de-
velop until Stewart had been in command for a year. A Marine was
accused in a stabbing case. As Commodore, Stewart issued orders for
the court-martial, directing that it be held aboard *Guerrière,* 44. But the
place was Naples in the summer, the ship was hot, the judge-advocate

of the court was not feeling well, and the officers of the court would have a good deal of rowing back and forth from the frigate to do. They held their court in a hotel ashore, and found the man guilty.

Stewart disapproved the proceedings and released the prisoner on the perfectly sound ground that a court meeting anywhere except as specified by orders was illegal. This so incensed the members of the honorable court that they reconvened themselves and passed a series of indignant resolutions, requesting that they be sent to Washington. Stewart promptly placed every captain in the squadron under arrest— those who had signed the resolutions for doing so, and those who had not, for failing to restrain their juniors. Washington approved everything the Commodore had done, and as the recalcitrant officers had over a year more to live under Stewart's command, they subsided and made the best of it.

Franklin brought her commander home in mid-1820. By this date, the reports of Captain James Biddle on the situation along the Pacific coast of South America were in hand, exhibiting a state of affairs that invited more action than could be taken during the casual visit of a single sloop-of-war; and action that would need to be taken by some-one who understood international law.

The situation had grown out of the endemic state of war between Spain, which still held the Peruvian presidency, and her revolted colonies there. The "patriots" (as the colonists were called) could clearly not be ousted from what they had gained, but their armed forces were small, the distances were vast, and local geography permitted the Spaniards to made defensive concentrations which the patriot forces could not handle. It had thus become a war without progress on either side; but the coast was swarming with buccaneers, operating under privateering licenses from Spain. In reply to these gentry the patriot governments proclaimed blockades of all Spanish-held ports; but, as they had no naval strength to speak of, these blockades were paper of the flimsiest kind, rarely backed by a ship.

At least this was the technical position. Actually, both sides were out for plunder, but particularly the patriot governments, who were using their "blockade" as a pretext for seizing every ship whose manifest showed she had visited a harbor held by Spain. Most of these ships were

Charles Stewart

American, in the trade for guano and hides, or in the important whaling industry. Ordinary diplomatic action was difficult, since the question of what government the diplomats should be accredited to would involve the United States in matters of recognition or nonrecognition of new and possibly ephemeral governments.

Monroe accordingly decided to set up a cruise in those waters under an officer who could act on his own authority, and chose Stewart. He sailed aboard *Franklin* in the fall of 1821 and remained nearly three years, making Callao his base. The first step he took was with regard to the blockade; he used his battleship to convoy merchant vessels to Spanish-held ports, and capped this action with a long letter to Mariscal Sucre, the head of the patriot Peruvian government. The document is actually an essay on the rights and duties of neutrals and the doctrine of blockade. John Marshall, Chief Justice of the United States, no mean lawyer himself, thought it the ablest presentation of the subject ever written, and most of it is still good international law. It had its immediate effect, too; Sucre withdrew the blockade proclamation.

But there were a good many Americans interested financially or emotionally on the patriot side, and when Stewart returned to the United States after the Spanish regime collapsed in 1824, all these rose up against him and demanded his court-martial on four several charges. The first was that he had aided American, French, and British ships in carrying on an "illicit and contraband trade" with certain ports of Peru; the second, disobedience to orders in so doing, and in giving refuge aboard *Franklin* to certain Spanish officials; the third that he failed to exercise his crew at the guns (an odd charge indeed against one of Preble's boys!); the fourth, that he had visited cruel and unusual punishment upon a lieutenant named Joshua Sands.

This last was a parenthetical business, apparently brought up by the accusers in the hope of finding some stick to beat the old sea-dog with if the main charge failed. Sands was a turbulent character, who had been restricted to the ship for "violating the rules of society and decorum"; whereupon he got drunk, attacked one of the senior lieutenants, and broke his restriction to "go off on an expedition." Stewart sentenced him to stay in his cabin for six months, except as he might have to leave it for exercise or other necessities.

Preble's Boys

The court-martial was held in Washington before seven captains and five lieutenants. When it was over, they not only honorably acquitted the Commodore, but felt "compelled by a sense of duty to go further and to make unhesitatingly the declaration—that, so far from having violated his high duties of neutrality and respect for the law of nations; so far from having sacrificed the honor of the American flag, or tarnished his own fair fame, by acting upon any motive of a mercenary or sordid kind; so far from having neglected his duty, or betrayed that trust reposed in him by refusing proper protection to American citizens or property, or rendering such protection subservient to individual interests, no one circumstance has developed throughout the whole course of this minute investigation into the various occurrences of a three years' cruise, calculated to impair the confidence which the members of the court, the navy, and the nation, having long reposed in the honor, the talents, the patriotism of this distinguished officer, or to weaken in any manner the opinion which all who know him entertain of his humanity and disinterestedness. These virtues only glow with brighter lustre from this ordeal of trial, like the stars he triumphantly displayed when valor and skill achieved a new victory to adorn the annals of our naval glory."

It is a rather highfaluting appreciation, but distinctly necessary since the attackers were powerful and had started a whispering campaign; and it was followed by a splendid public dinner at Philadelphia. After this Stewart went to sea no more, but was constantly employed on various courts and boards until 1830, when President Jackson made him one of the three Navy Commissioners, a post he held for three years. There followed an interval at the Bordentown estate—which he called Montpelier, but which everyone else knew as "Old Ironsides"—before he was appointed to the Philadelphia Navy Yard in 1837.

This tour of duty was for the specific purpose of seeing to completion the giant four-decker line-of-battleship *Pennsylvania,* 120, the largest sailing warship ever built in America. She was designed by Samuel Humphreys, son of old Joshua. The problems of turning out so huge a vessel in wood are extremely serious, and Humphreys had to go back to the Spanish *Santissima Trinidad,* 110, of the Napoleonic

Wars, to find cognates for some of his design features, and even then it was felt that a captain of unusual experience and intelligence would be needed to superintend her. She was supposed to be a blockade-breaker; hardly fewer than four or five 74s would be required to keep her in port. Stewart made some changes in the design and saw to it that she was armed on the system originally intended for the *Independence* class, with 32-pounders throughout, carronades on the topmost deck, and long guns below. She turned out to be a very successful vessel, though captains who had grown up in frigates found her hard to handle at first, and for a long time she was the most powerful warship in the world.

With this task completed, the Commodore, getting to be quite an old gentleman now, went back to Bordentown, though it must not be imagined he lived in anything like retirement. He kept considerable state, entertained freely, and became quite famous as a story-teller, so that people came all the way from Missouri to see him—Thomas Hart Benton among others. His most famous yarn is still repeated in wardrooms, the one about the visit of the Empress of Austria aboard *Franklin* at Naples. One of the glittering officers of the Imperial suite mistook a windsail for a solid object, leaned against it and tumbled into the cockpit. Stewart inquired what the commotion was. "Oh, nothing, sir," an old quartermaster replied. "Just one of them damned kings has fallen down a hatch."

The Navy Department consulted Stewart freely, and usually took his advice, though not on the subject of a naval school, which he did not believe in, pronouncing that the best place to educate an officer was on the deck of a ship—perhaps not a remarkable view considering the manner in which Stewart had attained his own education.

All these social and governmental contacts came to a head in the spring of 1844. The Democratic Party was in bad shape for a candidate for the presidency that year. The record of the incumbent Whigs had been such that anyone on whom the Democrats could unite would probably win—but on whom could they unite? Martin Van Buren, ousted in the previous election, was the most nearly obvious choice, but he was personally opposed to the annexation of the independent republic of Texas, and any Democrat who wished to carry the southern states would have to be for Texas. Tyler, the President, was all right on principle, but he had been elected as a Whig, and the Democrats would have no more of him. General Lewis Cass was only the leader of a faction; he wanted Oregon, the other desirable of the expanding nation, but he was lukewarm on Texas. John C. Calhoun could carry the Deep South, but he had stood with the nullificationists, and his nomination would lose the influential wing of the party which still followed the leadership of Andrew Jackson. In fact, the Democrats had no candidate who could bring them together.

At this juncture someone—the precise origin of the idea is now beyond recovery—bethought himself of the old gentleman at Bordentown. He was 66, but younger than Harrison had been at his election, in much better health, lively and acute. His record in the War of 1812 and in the Pacific made him the perfect spearhead of a party which was expressing the belligerent expansionism of the age. He was immune to the political attacks that could be brought against Van Buren, Cass, and Calhoun, and to the personal objections that could be leveled against Tyler. He was an eloquent speaker, a good writer, and possessed of all the necessary social qualities; he was from Pennsylvania, a crucial state. An "Address to the Democratic Party" was issued, first in the quasi-official *Spirit of the Times* and then, as the demand for it spread, in 25,000 reprints. No fewer than 67 newspapers declared that they wanted Commodore Charles Stewart for President.

The only trouble was that the political promoters had neglected to consult Commodore Charles Stewart. When he began reading his name in print, "he became unusually nervous and fidgetty"; when they came to talk to him about it, he offered them a drink, but refused to discuss the matter. He would not issue statements; he told sea-yarns and simply dropped out of the conversation when it became political. The baffled promoters withdrew and settled for James K. Polk.

After this Stewart was not heard from publicly until the late '50s, when a special act of Congress gave him the title of "Senior Flag Officer" of the navy and he refused the commission on the ground that he already held that rank by seniority. When he was 83 the Confederates began shelling Fort Sumter; Stewart wrote to the department asking for active sea service at once. "I am as young as ever to fight for my country," he said in the letter, and he probably could have been used in some capacity, for he lived on with undiminished intellect until 1869— at the last with an admiral's commission, for when that grade was instituted by Congress in 1862 the first admiralcy almost automatically went to the navy's senior surviving officer. Stewart's last two or three years were full of pain, probably from cancer, but they were somewhat lightened by the long visit of the brilliant young grandson from Ireland who bore his name—Charles Stewart Parnell.

Probably few of Preble's boys contributed more directly to the American naval tradition. He was the exact opposite of Biddle: the poor boy who made good, the illiterate who became a literatus, the undisciplined young man who became an expert on discipline. He remained for long and long a living example of what a naval career could do for those who took it up. Nor was his influence one of example alone. The direct contributions he made to ship construction and armament have vanished with changing technologies; the contributions he made to naval regulation and international law have become part of the general body and are now beyond being isolated; but we must never forget that it was to Captains Stewart and Bainbridge that we really owed those victories.

Chapter 14

Leadership: Thomas Macdonough and Stephen Cassin

'Twas autumn, around me the leaves were descending,
    And lonely the wood-pecker peck'd on the tree;
While thousands their freedom and right were defending.
    The din of their arms sounded dismal to me;
For Sandy, my love, was engaged in the action,
His death would have ended my life in distraction;
Without him I valued this life not a fraction,
    As lonely I stray'd on the Banks of Champlain.

But soon an express all my sorrows suspended,
My thanks to the Father of Mercies ascended;
My shepherd was safe and my country defended,
    By freedom's brave sons on the Banks of Champlain.

      —Song sung by a young lady at a dinner in New York
      for Macdonough; Air, "Banks of the Dee"

O N FEBRUARY 9, 1799, OFF THE ISLAND OF NEVIS IN THE WEST INDIES, U.S.S. *Constellation*, 38, Captain Thomas Truxtun, fought and captured the French national ship *Insurgente*, 36. It was the first victory gained by the infant navy of the United States, and it was won in a style that set all the taverns ringing with toasts to the wooden walls of Columbia, for *Insurgente* was cut to pieces, with 70 casualties, while *Constellation* had but one man killed and three wounded. One of the latter was Midshipman James Macdonough, whom a cannon-ball deprived of a foot. He lay for a long time in hospital, and when he was brought home at the end of April it was determined that his injury was so serious as to render him incapable of obtaining a livelihood from the seafaring profession. He was awarded a half-pay pension for life, consisting of one-half ration per diem (or the commuted value thereof) and nine and a half dollars per month; and there was a family council.

James Macdonough was the eldest son in a family of ten children, who had been left in somewhat straitened circumstances on the death of their father, named Thomas, some four years previous. They lived at a place called The Trap, in New Castle, Delaware, a fine house built of bricks brought from England, and set up by the elder Macdonough, who lived too big and too fast to leave his children with anything but this property. He was a distinguished gentleman, who left his profession of physic to follow the drums of the Revolution in that famous Delaware regiment known as "The Blue Hen's Chickens"; was with them under the ramparts of Quebec, where fell his brother, James senior. Becoming commander of the regiment, the former Dr. Macdonough participated in the battles of Long Island and White Plains in a manner that earned him the personal commendation of General Washington. In the former of these contests he received so severe a wound as to be obliged to quit the profession of arms. Another brother, Micah, entered the service somewhat later and was involved in the unfortunate expedition of General St. Clair against the Indians beyond the Ohio.

As for Dr. (and Major) Macdonough, he was elected a member of the Privy Council, a body peculiar to the State of Delaware; when his term had expired he was repeatedly returned to the upper house of the legislative assembly until 1788; then resigned, to add a third title to his name by becoming justice of the Court of Common Pleas, an office he held until his death. In the course of his political career, he became a warm friend of the Honorable Caesar Rodney, who so opportunely arrived in Philadelphia to cast the deciding vote in favor of independence; he was also intimate with the equally celebrated George Latimer. It was through the influence of the latter that James Macdonough received his midshipman's warrant. When he returned as an invalid, the family made application to Latimer in favor of the next son of Judge (and Dr.) Thomas Macdonough, a boy of 16, also named Thomas.

The younger Thomas Macdonough was at this time tall for his age, with light hair and a long sharp nose over a long sharp chin. Nobody bothered to record his remarks or the details of his ideological equipment; he is described in general terms as modest, untalkative, sincerely religious, and patriotic in the post-Revolutionary fashion. Education was more by the ear than the eye in those days; the fireside tales on which Thomas Macdonough had been brought up were of bivouacs and marches, and the struggle for liberty against the huge power beyond the Atlantic, which found it so difficult to realize that Americans were not as much its subjects as were the people of Ireland or India. It seemed the most obvious thing in the world that at all times at least one member of the family should be bearing arms for the defense of the new nation, and quite as reasonable that, his brother having been crippled in the service, Thomas should be the next.

His warrant came through in February 1800, and three months later was followed by orders to proceed to New Castle and join *Ganges*, 24, Captain John Mullowney. She had been the first ship of the new navy to put to sea; an Indiaman converted to a corvette by the mounting of 26 long 9s, tubby, high-pooped, and a poor sailor; not well adapted to any station where serious enemy forces might be discovered. She was sent to the north coast of Cuba, where French privateers were using the friendly ports of Spain. Not long after her arrival one of these privateers was discovered at Matanzas—a schooner bearing the name of *Fortune*. She beat out during the night of July 28, and ran to windward; Mullowney handled his ship smartly enough to weather her, and was soon in range. *Ganges'* first three or four shots went over the chase; when she failed to heave to, a broadside was fired into her, whereupon she ran ashore, and those of her crew who had not been killed by the firing took to the beach.

Young Macdonough was in one of the boats that towed the corsair out. She was somewhat damaged in the spars, so that she had to be taken to a port for refitting before being sent anywhere. Havana was the only port available. As soon as he reached it, the American captain put half his crew aboard the prize as working parties, got her ready, and sent her out on the very night of his arrival, as he feared the pro-

French Spaniards would try to seize her. His estimate of the Dons' intentions was perfectly accurate; in the morning the Governor of Havana threw all the sentries of Morro Castle into prison for not having kept a better watch.

This governor was subsequently allowed a poor sort of revenge, since yellow fever boarded the American cruiser in his harbor, attacking five seamen, the surgeon's mate, and three mids, who had to be landed and sent to hospital. One of these was young Macdonough; he found the place like a filthy jail, in which there were no comforts and but little food. As fast as the patients died—and nearly all of them did— their bodies were bundled into carts and carried off to be thrown into pits. Macdonough himself, with the surgeon's mate and one of the other mids, recovered after a wasting illness. They found that the people of the hospital had looted all their effects, this being the custom since there were so few recoveries from yellow fever. John Morton of New York, the American consul at the port, supplied them with some shirts, nankeen trousers, a straw hat, and a pair of canvas shoes apiece, and arranged a passage for them on a ship bound for Philadelphia.

Their misfortunes were not yet done, however; off the Delaware capes a British cruiser halted the vessel for examination and sent her to Halifax as prize, on the ground that she had Spanish property aboard. Macdonough, being a naval officer, was permitted to transfer to another ship, which landed him penniless at Norfolk. The navy agent there furnished enough money to take him home; when he stepped off the stage at The Trap with his canvas shoes worn out, all the relatives and friends were astonished, since—though his death had not been notified—no one was expected to recover from yellow fever on the Havana.

His ship coming into the Delaware a few weeks later, Midshipman Macdonough rejoined her for a brief cruise to the Indies, sailing in January of 1801. He returned to find that through the intercession of the younger Caesar Rodney he was one of the officers to be retained on the peace establishment. There would have been small difficulty in any case, since the number of midshipmen kept in the service was quite out of proportion to the higher officers, Secretary Smith believing that the true foundation of a national marine lay in young men who had never known any other species of employment. Of course, this large retention meant that many of the mids were without ships, but Macdonough was fortunate enough to obtain an appointment to *Constellation* for the cruise of 1802.

She sailed in March, with Alexander Murray as captain, who made all his midshipmen keep journals in order to improve their calligraphy as well as to give them a proper sense of composition in English. The latter purpose was hardly achieved in Macdonough's case; he did nothing but copy the daily log, with records of winds, tides, currents, and anchorages. The cruise was quite uneventful for him, *Constellation* returning to Washington in the spring of 1803 to be laid up in ordinary. Macdonough remained aboard with the caretaking party until May, when he was furloughed to await call. Only three days later the call came—to *Philadelphia,* 38, Captain William Bainbridge, bound for the Mediterranean in Commodore Edward Preble's squadron. Macdonough was now 20 years old, the fourth ranking midshipman in the ship, and up to this point there had been nothing in the least remarkable about him. Bainbridge, who rendered careful reports on his other officers, never even mentions Midshipman Macdonough.

II

Now came a change. *Philadelphia* had hardly entered the Mediterranean before she discovered the Emperor of Morocco's cruiser *Mirboka,* 22, with an American brig she had taken. Of course Bainbridge captured the corsair; Macdonough was named junior prize officer, and so remained at Gibraltar when the parent frigate sailed up the Mediterranean to keep her appointment with destiny on the rocks off Tripoli harbor. When the captured cruiser was returned to Morocco, the Emperor was sufficiently impressed with Macdonough to offer him a lieutenancy in his own service, and without the usual proviso of a change of religion. But the midshipman was uninterested, especially as it would have meant sailing aboard a ship which Preble described as "such a miserable piece of naval architecture that I do not believe we

have a naval officer in our service that would be willing to cross the Atlantic in her for ten times her value." Macdonough went aboard *Constitution,* and was with her when she sailed up the Mediterranean to
meet the news of *Philadelphia's* capture.

Enterprise, 12, was the first of the light craft to join the flag. She
had been out for some time and, as several of her officers had gone home,
she lacked a mid. Preble sent Macdonough over as the senior officer
of that rank aboard the ship, now commanded by Stephen Decatur.
The two young men met for the first time, and suited each other perfectly; Decatur later described Macdonough as his "favorite midshipman." They were frequently aboard the flagship together, and still
more frequently was the old Commodore aboard their fast and handy
little craft, discussing and refining to the last detail the plan for taking
the ketch *Intrepid* in to burn *Philadelphia.*

On that expedition Macdonough with another midshipman and a detail of ten men had the duty of firing the forward berth-deck; he was
one of the last people to leave the burning frigate, but used to say afterward that the most serious danger he encountered was from the ver-
min left in the 'ketch by her former owners. He was one of the officers
who refused the two months' extra pay which Congress voted in reward to the participants in the expedition. Congress later rectified the
matter by voting the formal and correct prize-money for the capture of
a ship of superior force; but this was not done until 1836, and few of the
men who swarmed aboard *Philadelphia* on that wild night received
any benefit from the action.

It took another exploit to gain for Macdonough the kind of reward
he really wanted. When July brought the squadron down for the direct
attacks on Tripoli harbor, Decatur was placed in charge of a division
of three of the gunboats borrowed from the King of Naples, and he took
his favorite midshipman along as acting captain of gunboat *No. 4.* The
two were together in the fierce boarding action of August 3; Decatur
was the first man to board a Tripolitan gunboat and Macdonough was
the second. They were two of the eleven men who charged into the
second gunboat, the one in which Decatur's brother had been treacher-
ously shot. The center of her deck was all one hatch; Decatur led the

attack around one side of the gap, while Macdonough stormed first around the other. The midshipman's cutlass snapped off at the hilt as he dueled with a big Turk, just as the fellow was raising a pistol. With wonderful agility Macdonough flung himself on the man's arm, wrenched the weapon loose, and killed the pirate with his own weapon. It hung over the mantelpiece at The Trap for many years.

The reward came when Decatur's report said formally: "I now feel it is my duty to Assure you that nothing could surpass the zeal, courage and readiness of Mr. Thomas Macdonough." On his last day as squadron commander, Preble called the midshipman to his cabin and handed him a paper. It was as formal as the other: "You are hereby appointed lieutenant of the U.S. schooner *Enterprise*. Given under my hand on board the U.S. Ship *Constitution* off Tripoly." This was promotion for gallantry on the field of action, and it should have rated highly with the authorities back home, but the stingy Congress which confirmed the appointment only made Macdonough's what was called a "gunboat commission," bringing no increase in pay over that which he received as a mid.

Not all the fighting in the Mediterranean was done at Tripoli; Macdonough had hardly left the battles there when he was involved in an adventure at Syracuse, where the state of civilization is adequately pictured by the fact that the King was known as "Ferdinand the Burglar" because robbery and garroting were his favorite sports. One night late as the young lieutenant was about to go out to his ship, he noted that there were three men instead of the usual two in the hire-out boat at the wharf. He refused to get in; the three growled and leaped at him with long knives. Macdonough managed to get his back against a wall and laid about him so well with his sword that two of the three antagonists were soon stretched on the pavement. The third ran with the Lieutenant in pursuit, and clambered up the front of one of the galleried buildings. This was a mistake, for he had a man after him who was used to running the ratlines of ships. The robber had barely reached the flat roof of the building on one side before Macdonough came over the opposite edge with his sword in his teeth. Whether the scoundrel jumped or was driven is uncertain, but in any case down he went and broke his neck.

Thomas Macdonough, Stephen Cassin

Most of the other incidents of a tour of duty that lasted into the middle of 1806 were pleasant enough. *Enterprise* went up to Venice, where Macdonough enjoyed himself so thoroughly that a rumor he had formed a romantic attachment for a girl of the place reached a young lady in Delaware to whom he was supposed to be engaged, and she married another man. Later Macdonough went down to Ancona and was occupied with the fitting out of a pair of vessels known as trabaccolos, lugger-rigged and double-ended, with which it was desired to experiment as gunboats. Macdonough found them not at all suitable to American conditions, being unhandy craft which it was necessary to tow in all but the lightest airs.

In March of 1806, he was ready to go home when the reduction of the Mediterranean squadron made it possible for all officers who wished to do so. He exchanged with Lewis Warrington, who was first lieutenant of *Siren*, 16; and on the way in, had an experience which few American officers missed in the years before 1812—a clash with the British press-gang. It fell out in Gibraltar Bay, where *Siren* was anchored just astern of an American merchant brig, and Macdonough had the deck, Captain Smith being ashore. A British frigate was lying in the harbor; one of her boats boarded the brig and was seen to leave with one more man than it had carried before. Macdonough sent to the brig; yes, the British had pressed one of her men, although he carried a diplomatic "protection" as an American citizen.

Siren's gig was instantly manned by an armed crew and, with Macdonough in the sternsheets, pulled like mad in pursuit of the frigate's boat. He caught her up just as the bow-oar was raising his boathook at the side of the warship. There were a few moments of vivid argument, the Americans handled their weapons, and took the brig's man aboard.

Naturally, the matter was not allowed to rest at that point. The afternoon was not half over when the frigate's captain came aboard *Siren*, angrily demanding how Macdonough dared take a man out of one of His Majesty's boats; refused to come to the cabin to discuss matters, and ended with a threat to lay the frigate alongside *Siren* and take the man by force.

Macdonough: "I suppose your ship can sink the *Siren*; but as long as she can swim we will keep the man."

English Captain: "You are a very young man, and a very indiscreet young man. Suppose I had been in the boat. What would you have done?"

Macdonough: "I would have taken the man."

English Captain: "What, sir! Would you attempt to stop me, if I were to impress men from that brig?"

Macdonough: "I would, sir; and to convince yourself, you have only to make the attempt."

The Englishman stamped from the deck; presently a boat put out from the frigate's side. Macdonough called away *Siren's* longboat, had it filled with Marines and rowed to the brig; being nearer, he got there first. The British boat took a couple of turns around; then its officer, doubtless reflecting that this would be a poor way to die, rowed back to his own ship.

It had been three years since Macdonough left the United States. He came back a fairly well-finished product as an officer, but there was little for him to do except go up to Middletown, Connecticut, and assist Captain Isaac Hull in the construction of gunboats. The time was not altogether lost; in Middletown he met a lady named Lucy Ann Shaler, whom he later married, and received from Secretary Smith the honor of a silver replica of Preble's Tripoli medal.

In 1809, the mysterious Captain John Smith placed *Essex*, 32, in commission, and asked Macdonough to come with him as first lieutenant. He remained only until September of the same year, when, presumably in order to be nearer to the lady of his favors, he asked for and received command of the division of gunboats in Connecticut and Long Island.

At the moment he leaves the ship, there is one of those fascinating and fugitive glimpses of a man that come through the eyes of other people. The crew of the frigate took the extraordinary step of addressing him in a round-robin:

"Respected Sir: We, the warrant & Petty Officers, Seamen, ordinary seamen and Landsmen of the U.S. frigate *Essex,* do learn with heart-felt sorrow your intention of leaving the Ship. Permit us, Sir, before your departure to return you our most Sincere thanks and acknowledg-ment. We don't Wish to trouble you with a great Harangue. We can only assure you, Sir, that we all feel as one in the cause of Regret at your about to leave the Ship."

By the early part of 1810, Macdonough had obtained the consent of the charming Miss Shaler, but found his finances in no very good state to support marriage, and, with the policy of the government so apparently fixed on peace at any price, there seemed little prospect of advancement through action. Like many other officers, he applied for a furlough to make a commercial voyage; received it, and went to Cal-cutta in the brig *Gulliver*, holding a quarter share in the venture him-self. He brought back a cargo of silks and gall nuts, rope, hemp, can-vas, and shellac; an operation so successful that the merchants who backed it besought him to make another voyage. Macdonough some-what imprudently agreed before asking for an extension of his furlough. But it was now 1811; the Cabinet knew what few outside it realized, that there was little prospect of solving things with England except by means of the cannon. Secretary Hamilton wanted his officers at hand; he refused the furlough.

This placed Lieutenant Macdonough in a cruel dilemma. He had just been formally baptized into the Episcopal Church, of which he was to remain an ardent communicant all his life, and one of the reli-gious principles he believed in was dealing justly with all men. A month of thought and prayer brought him to the conclusion that there was only one honest thing to do. In October he wrote to the Secretary that unless the furlough could be granted so that he could keep his engage-ment with the merchants, this was his resignation from the service to which he had devoted his life.

The letter is still in existence in the Navy Department, en-dorsed "Resignation to be accepted," but after he had made the note Hamilton fell into conversation with someone who persuaded him that Macdonough was too valuable an officer to be let go;* the Secretary

* This could very well have been Charles Stewart, who was in Washington at the time, but there is no direct evidence.

changed his mind and allowed the furlough. It was not much use; by the time the necessary preliminaries of finding a ship, a crew, and a cargo had been carried through, it was April of 1812. The Non-Intercourse Act that was the immediate preliminary to war held Macdonough in port.

His request for active duty at the outbreak of hostilities was answered by an appointment as First Lieutenant of *Constellation, 38.* He hurried down to Washington, where the frigate was lying, but found her in such a state that it would be five or six months before she was ready for sea. This was intolerable; with the regretfully given permission of Bainbridge, who was captain of the ship, Macdonough asked for a transfer to a post which he believed would give him combat duty—command of the gunboat flotilla at Portland, Maine. He received it, but never had a chance to be disappointed, for less than a month after his arrival on station a new order came in, placing him in command of the naval forces on Lake Champlain. For $75, he hired a horse and chaise to take him over the mountains to Burlington, Vermont.

IV

The command could not have looked like anything but a pigeonhole to the Lieutenant, for his "forces" consisted of two one-gun gunboats, of a type similar to those employed in the ocean harbors. The army had six small transports on the lake, single-sticker sloops, of a little over 100 tons burden. Secretary of War Armstrong had already directed that they be turned over as the nucleus of a more effective naval force, since it was obvious, even from the distance of Washington, that command of Champlain would be the key factor in both attack and defense along the northern frontier.

The history of the place was inescapable. Champlain himself, Abercrombie, Montcalm, Amherst, Arnold, Burgoyne, had all ridden the tide along that river of war in one direction or the other, and always the result was fatal unless the attacker fully held command of the lake. Delay to clear the forts that covered the lake had lamed the offensives of Abercrombie and Montcalm; delay to fight down the small American squadron had left Burgoyne marooned in woods swarming with

Thomas Macdonough, Stephen Cassin

Continental riflemen. There was a reason for this—logistics. The route by the Richelieu River-Champlain-Lake George-the Hudson was the shortest one from the key centers of Canada to the key centers of the United States, but even in an age where practically all heavy traffic went by water, marine transportation was at a premium in this region. North of Albany the country was all wooded and very rough; there were no roads that would bear the weight of artillery or a wagon-train sufficient to support an army.

Macdonough hurried over to Plattsburg to visit General Henry Dearborn, the army departmental commander, and received a shock. Dearborn had been a dashing captain in the Revolution; now he was a fat old man, tired, cranky, and confused, who fussed venomously about the order to turn over the six transports for naval operation—how could he move his troops? He eventually yielded on five, but the best one, *President,* he flatly refused to give up unless President Madison ordered him to do so in a personal letter.

Very brief inspection showed that three of the five were in so rotten a state that their decks could not possibly stand the recoil of cannon. The remaining two, *Hunter* and *Bull Dog,* Macdonough took down to Whitehall at the southern end of the lake to fit for campaigning. In reply to his request, Captain Hull of the New York station said that stores would be sent up at once, but as for sailors, there were not enough for the ships fitting out at New York, "and men are not to be got." Soldiers detailed from the army filled the gap temporarily, but rather badly; few of them knew how to handle ropes and there were no quartermasters.

Still, such as it was, the "poor, forlorn squadron" was ready by early November, *Bull Dog* armed with four 6-pounders, *Hunter* with two 12s, four 6s, and a long 18 on a pivot. Accompanied by the gunboats, these ships covered the flank of Dearborn's army as it moved down the lake on the 16th to invade Canada. Just beyond the boundary a quite insignificant force of Canadians was posted. With the courage and address that distinguished every American land commander in the war until Jacob Brown appeared on the scene, Dearborn fired a few shots at the enemy and decided to go home.

But the General now did give up *President,* and on February 15,

1813, ship-carpenters arrived from New York. With their help Macdonough took off the short quarterdecks of *Hunter* and *Bull Dog,* which lightened them so that each could carry five guns a side, plus an 18-pounder chaser. Each was given five 6s and as many 18-pound carronades; their names were changed to *Growler* and *Eagle. President,* a more important craft, received eight 18-pound carronades and four long 12s. In mid-April, it became possible to leave winter quarters, and Macdonough ran down to Plattsburg, complaining by letter both to Hull at New York and to Commodore Chauncey at Sackett's Harbor that he could get "neither good officers nor men, as there are none on the station." His unhappiness was quite justified; some of the incompetents ran *President* aground on the last day of May, and she had to be hove out for repairs.

This led indirectly to an event of almost fatal consequences. Down the Richelieu River, the British had worked up a squadron of four galley gunboats, each armed with a long 24 and a 32-pound carronade. It was the custom of these vessels to come up the lake now and then to annoy the American positions. On June 2 a report ran in that they were out; Macdonough sent *Growler* and *Eagle* down, under Lieutenant Sidney Smith, to drive the British back to their own lines. Smith sighted his quarry late in the afternoon, and under winds light from the southward, pursued them into the river for a distance of about six miles, to a place called Île aux Noix. It fell calm; he anchored for the night, putting out a guard-boat farther downstream.

At 6:00 in the morning the airs were still light and from the south, and, with a strong current running against him in a river whose channel was nowhere more than 300 yards wide, Lieutenant Smith began to realize he might have trouble. He was perfectly correct. Fifteen minutes later, as he was hoisting sail to beat back to the lake, the guardboat arrived with word that the enemy were coming, and at 6:30 the gunboats were close enough to open fire.

The British remained at long range, using their 24s; the sloops' guns could not carry the distance, and they could make little headway against wind and current. As they tacked back and forth, they presently began to receive showers of musketry from troops who had advanced along both sides of the stream. This was replied to with grape from the 6-pounders, and did not do much damage, but there was no real return to the fire of the gunboats, and at 11:00, just as the sloops were preparing for a desperate attempt to run down and attack the enemy by boarding, a 24-pound shot hit *Eagle* under the port quarter, went right through her, and ripped out three planks on the opposite side. She sank at once in shoal water. Fifteen minutes later *Growler* lost her main-boom and forestay. With nothing that would carry sail, she ran aground and was captured.

Macdonough was furious at his lieutenant's stupidity, but there was no avoiding the fact that the British now had command of the water. As soon as the two sloops were repaired for their own service, on July 31, they came up the lake with three gunboats and 1,000 troops. The men landed at Plattsburg and burned all the barracks and stores, while the naval contingent slid across to Burlington, where Macdonough had established his base. General Wade Hampton was in the town, having come north to lead a new projected invasion of Canada. He had enough troops with him to make Burlington safe against amphibious attack, while Macdonough had hastily mounted some guns to protect the roadstead and shipping. The enemy tried one long-range bombardment; the only result was that a ball came through the window of the house where Macdonough was shaving and hit his dressing table. He went on shaving; the British hauled off into the central lake, where they cruised back and forth, prohibiting American movements and covering the gathering of supplies from the Vermont farmers who thought more of their pocketbooks than of their patriotism. Their behavior doubtless had some influence with British strategists who thought that New England might readily be detached from the Union.

In Washington, the loss of *Growler* and *Eagle* provided a much-needed shock. The new Navy Secretary, William Jones, ordered New York to send up a number of ship-carpenters, guns, and a large detachment of seamen and officers. The ship-carpenters came easily enough, since it was a matter of hiring, but seamen were almost impossible to find for the thankless service of the lakes. It was August 19 before any arrived, and then there were only 50, barely enough to man a sloop; 200 more, with some officers, did come in September, but most of them were a fairly sorry lot.

By this date, Macdonough was ready to claim control of the lake again. His carpenters had taken the masts out of the old gunboats and fitted them as galleys for work down the Richelieu, where Sidney Smith's defeat had demonstrated the failings of sailing ships. Two more of the class were built; so were two new sloops, named *Preble* and *Montgomery,* the former armed with seven long 12s, the latter with seven long 9s, and each with two 18-pounder columbiads. These last were a new and experimental type of gun invented at New York, midway between a carronade and a long gun in weight, and so cast that the shot fitted the barrel more closely than in either, which gave a high muzzle velocity with only a medium powder-charge. Probably they were the only pieces immediately available when Jones's rush order for cannon came. *President* was rearmed with the same type of artillery.

On September 6 the American fleet sailed; the British retreated into the Richelieu. General Hampton now wanted Macdonough to make an unsupported water-borne attack on Île aux Noix, where the British had set up their base, but the naval commander refused on the quite reasonable ground that the only ships he dared take down the river were his gunboats, which mounted a single 12-pounder each and were quite incompetent to deal with the heavy fortifications the enemy had set up. The General, who like Dearborn was a warmed-over relic of the Revolution, wrote peevish letters to the War Department about this, but finally got moving under his own power on September 19, with the ships supporting his right flank, the artillery train moving in transports behind. The invasion resulted in as dismal a failure as Dearborn's when the army got itself caught in an ambush well short of Île aux Noix, and everybody fled in a panic, headed by Hampton.

This ended operations for the year. Macdonough put his fleet into winter quarters at Vergennes, Vermont, up Otter Creek, principally because he expected to do some building, and Vergennes more nearly met the requirements of a construction base than any place on the lake. It had a good road to Boston and another running south; some quantity of local industry, as a blast furnace, eight forges, and a rolling mill.

Thomas Macdonough, Stephen Cassin

There was good access to the lake by Otter Creek, which is narrow and crooked but deep, so that quite large ships could be warped down, but an enemy coming up would have difficulty unless he first gained control of the banks.

v

Early in February there was word that the British were building a 20-gun corvette at Île aux Noix, with more galleys. Macdonough sent this report to Washington, with a survey of local conditions, by the hand and voice of his new second in command, Lieutenant Stephen Cassin.

This Cassin was another of Preble's boys, one who had been held back up to this time by misfortune. His father was John Cassin, who had the decidedly peculiar record of having served with distinction in both the British and the American navies. In the old wars before the Revolution, he had a corvette on convoy duty to the Americas; beat off French corsairs in a manner that won him a service of plate from the London underwriters, and then emigrated to the colonies, where he became a personal friend of George Washington. (It is odd how many times friendship with the first President turns up in this tale.) There is no record of Cassin's having served in the Revolution, but he was certainly settled in Philadelphia at the close of it, for Stephen Cassin was born there in 1782.

When the U.S. navy was re-established in '99, John Cassin went into it as a lieutenant aboard the frigate *Philadelphia*, and later spent several years at the Washington Navy Yard, before being elected to Congress from Pennsylvania. He procured a midshipman's warrant for Stephen, who passed the last year of the French War aboard his father's ship. The younger Cassin was to have gone to the Mediterranean in the same vessel under Bainbridge in 1803, but at the last moment the schooner *Nautilus*, 12, was found to be short a midshipman, and as her commander was Richard Somers, who had known the Cassin family in Philadelphia, he took the young man under his wing.

In *Nautilus*, Stephen Cassin fought through the Tripoli campaign, and did well enough to be appointed sailing master of the ship over

· 359 ·

the hand of Preble himself. Like many others, he found naval prospects so poor on his return to the States that he obtained a furlough to make a merchant voyage. It nearly finished him; the voyage was to the west coast of South America, where the Spanish presidency of Callao confiscated his ship on the ground that she carried contraband, and threw Cassin into prison for two years. This cost him much seniority on the navy list, and it was as a very junior lieutenant that he made a pre-war cruise under Isaac Hull in *Constitution*. Since then he had been on shore duty; Hull sent him up to Champlain as a place where a junior officer stood some chance of making progress.

After Secretary Jones had heard Cassin's report, he authorized Macdonough to take over an unfinished vessel lying at Vergennes, which had been intended as a steamboat, and also to build at 24-gun corvette. Henry Eckford from Lake Ontario furnished the design for the corvette; Noah Brown, one of the famous brothers from New York, brought a work-gang up to build her. He and Macdonough got along capitally from the start; they had the same type of fire in their vitals. The ship was a bluff-bowed vessel, quite without sheer, on the very plain lines necessary for rapid construction, shallow in the hull. Brown launched her out in 40 days from cutting timber, on April 11. Macdonough called her *Saratoga*, a name of great memories in that region, and armed her with whatever guns he could get from New York, which happened to be eight long 24s, six 42-pound carronades, and twelve 32-pound carronades. Six new galleys were also added, of a heavier model than the earlier four, each mounting an 18-pound carronade and a long 24. The prospective steamer was completed as the schooner *Ticonderoga,* with eight long 12s, four long 18s, and five 32-pound carronades. Cassin received command of her.

In the meanwhile the British had been milling around at the lower end of the lake, their gunboats appearing frequently around Rouse's Point during March, when the lake became navigable much earlier than usual. Information as to their exact strength and purposes was very hard to obtain, but it finally became clear that they were in possession of a heavy brig, and would be coming up the lake with her before Macdonough could get his *Saratoga* ready. The naval commander wanted General James Wilkinson (now in command at Plattsburg) to set up some batteries at Rouse's Point to hold the enemy in the Riche-lieu, but the army man said it could not be done, without giving any reason. As the British were reported loading barges with stone, it occurred to Macdonough that they might come down to block him in Otter Creek, so he set up some batteries at its outlet, and asked the Governor of Vermont to call out the militia to prevent a landing, which was willingly done.

On May 9, the British did appear, with a 16-gun brig named *Linnet*, 5 sloops, and 13 galley-gunboats. They looked in at Burlington, came up to the mouth of Otter Creek, and after an indecisive cannon-ade went back to the Richelieu. It was not until May 20 that Mac-donough could put out with the American squadron, and then only because the army lent him 400 soldiers to make good his burning need of crews. Wilkinson probably would not have made the loan, but that marplot had fortunately now vanished from the scene and been replaced by an officer who really knew his business, General Alexander Macomb.

Macomb was very anxious that the lake be held, having received quite reliable intelligence that the British were building at Île aux Noix a vessel of at least *Saratoga's* force, as well as making preparations ashore that indicated a major invasion. The first part of this news seemed confirmed when one of the American galleys captured a huge spar under tow in the Richelieu, the size of the timber indicating that it might be the mainmast of a frigate. Macdonough appealed to Wash-ington, and Washington replied by sending Noah Brown and his workmen back to Vergennes to build another ship in the greatest haste. Within the time available, they could do no better than a stout brig; she was named *Eagle* and equipped with eight long 18s and twelve 32-pound carronades.

As a matter of fact Macomb and Macdonough would have been even more deeply troubled had they known the full extent of the storm-cloud building up below Lake Champlain. It was the major British effort of the war, with 14,000 troops of Wellington's veterans of the Pen-insula in it, commanded by Sir George Prevost in person—a greater army than Burgoyne or Cornwallis had had, the largest invading force ever launched against America, while at Plattsburg Macomb had but

1500 men. The new British ship was named *Confiance*: a rated 36, but actually nearly as heavy as the American 44s, mounting thirty long 24s on her gundeck, with six 42-pound carronades and a 24 on a pivot topside, and equipped with a furnace for heating shot. She was alone nearly equal to the whole American squadron. Her captain, and the commodore of the fleet, was named George Downie. The ship had been completed only a week when Sir George insisted that she put out, because the season was growing late and it was essential that the lake be cleared for carrying supplies before winter came on the army in the woods north of Albany.

Downie sailed out of the Richelieu then, on September 11, and came up the lake with a fair breeze from the northeast; five days before, the British army had advanced, and was now facing the Americans at Plattsburg, with the Saranac River between. Behind the big frigate were *Linnet,* 16, Captain Daniel Pring, with the sloops *Chubb* and *Finch* (which had been *Growler* and *Eagle*), the former now mounting ten 18-pound carronades and a long 6, the latter seven 18-pound carronades and four long 6s; also twelve of the galley-gunboats, variously armed, but mainly with heavy weapons—92 guns all told, 1192 pounds weight of metal in the broadside.

On paper this was almost an equality with the American squadron, which had been joined by *Eagle* only the day before the British reached Plattsburg, with Master-Commandant Robert Henley in command. This gave Macdonough, who had ten gunboats and the sloop *Preble,* 88 guns and a broadside weight of metal of 1194 pounds. But the figures are deceptive; they take no account of the great force of *Confiance* and her thick scantling, or of the fact that most of the British weight was from long guns and big guns, far more effective than carronades, especially if the British could choose their distance. And if *Confiance* was hurried into action, so was *Eagle*, and aboard *Ticonderoga* there were no matches for the guns.

Say that the actual odds were something like five to three for England. Macdonough set out to reduce them by his arrangements. On this lake the winds blow commonly from north or south, and the ships, being of shallow draft, had little capacity for making tacks to work to windward. Therefore the American commander anchored in Plattsburg Bay, with his ships' heads pointing northward from Crab Island, *Eagle, Saratoga, Ticonderoga, Preble,* in that order, with the gunboats behind the two ends of the line. The whole formation lay somewhat behind the high peninsula of Cumberland Head. The enemy would be forced to attack; if they came up the lake on a favorable northerly wind, they would have to beat against it in rounding the Head. They would hardly dare wait for a southerly breeze in the narrow lake, for it might come in the form of one of the gales that are common at this season and wreck their whole squadron.

Even with a favoring wind, they must pass down the length of Macdonough's line; could not double upon its stern because *Preble* at that end lay so close to the shoal of Crab Island; and could not take position altogether beyond range of the American carronades, because Macdonough's line was too close to Cumberland Head. One thing more: the young Commodore, in command of a fleet at 28, had studied carefully the accounts of the three battles in the great European war where fleets received attacks at anchor—the Nile, Algeciras, Copenhagen. In two of these the defenders were beaten piecemeal because they did not possess even the most limited mobility; but at Algeciras, the French merely turned their ships at the crisis of the battle, and so defeated a far superior British force.

The waters of Plattsburg Bay were too narrow and the likelihood of losing spars was too great to count on moving with sails; but sails are not the only means by which a ship may be moved. Macdonough put springs on his cables; that is, from each of the anchors to which his ships swung by the bows, led a line to their quarters, which lines, being windlassed in, would move the ships. Now it occurred to him that if his ship's spars and rigging might be cut by shot, so might these springs. He put down an extra kedge anchor off each bow and carried the lines to *Saratoga's* quarter hanging in bights under the water. Now one final preparation: as eight bells struck on the morning of September 11 and the British sails became visible round Cumberland Head, Macdonough knelt on the quarterdeck with his officers around him and offered prayer to heaven.

On they came, almost in line abreast. Downie's plan was to have *Confiance* lead in, give *Eagle* a broadside, then drop down and devote her undivided attention to *Saratoga,* for he believed that if he got rid of the major American ship the rest would be easy. *Linnet* and *Chubb* together should attack *Eagle*; she would be somewhat reduced in strength by the effect of the frigate's first broadside. All these ships were to take position at a range as long as possible, to discount the effect of the American carronades. *Finch* would lead the whole gunboat squadron to close action with *Ticonderoga* and *Preble,* driving these ships out of position, and then raking *Saratoga* from astern.

On they came. *Eagle* let go with her long 18s, but the shot fell short. *Linnet,* a little ahead of the other British, fired her long 12s at *Saratoga*; these shots were also short, all but one, which struck a chicken-coop on the American corvette's deck. Out leaped a gamecock to the slide of a carronade, flapped his wings, and crowed lustily.

The men all laughed and cheered; at the same moment Macdonough himself sighted one of his long 24s against *Confiance*. The shot went right in a hawse-hole and ranged the length of the British frigate's deck, killing or wounding half a dozen men. All the long guns in the American squadron followed, and they were better laid than Downie had estimated in advance, for *Confiance* had two anchors shot away and was so much hurt about the spars that it was clear she could not attain her purpose of smashing *Eagle* before taking on *Saratoga*. The British commodore rounded to, 350 yards from *Saratoga's* beam, cool and collected as became a veteran of Trafalgar; not firing a shot until all was secure, then letting go one tremendous double-shotted broadside, carefully aimed.

In that smooth water, not a shot missed. *Saratoga* trembled all over as though she had been struck by a gigantic hammer, a cloud of splinters leaped through the smoke, and full half the corvette's crew were stretched on the deck, some merely stunned, but so many killed and wounded that the hatch-covers were taken off in order to hurry the casualties to the cockpit. The range was so long that her carronades had to be elevated before each shot, which not only slowed her fire but also offered many chances of error in the passion of fighting, with things crashing around, men shouting, screaming, and dying. But the men stood well to their work, and under the smoke the two big ships pounded each other with cannon-balls as fast as the guns could be

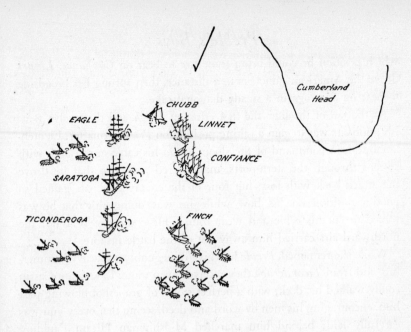

Lake Champlain—I
The British attack; firing becomes general.

loaded, survivors leaping to take the places of those who were carried below.

At the head of the line, *Chubb* came early into action against *Eagle* and four of the American gunboats. Their fire carried away so much of her top-hamper that the one-sticker was crippled and drifted helplessly down between the lines to near *Saratoga,* which gave her a shot from a heavy gun. She struck and was taken into possession by a mid, who towed her inshore. In revenge for this, *Eagle* soon found she had more than she could do to bear up against the full broadside of *Linnet,* with some of *Confiance's* forecastle guns; Henley cut his cables, sheeted home his topsails, and ran down *Saratoga's* unengaged side, to take station between and behind her and *Ticonderoga,* from

• 365 •

which position he could bring some fire to bear on *Confiance*. *Linnet* drove the American gunboats to a distance, then sprung her broadside to bear on *Saratoga* in a steady diagonal rake.

At the tail of the line, the first effort of *Finch* and the twelve British gunboats was to gain a raking position on *Preble's* quarter. Lieutenant Budd, in command of the sloop, let go his cable-spring and, with sweeps through the stern-ports, maneuvered round so that he drove the attack back with loss; but four of the enemy gunboats gained so good a position on his bow while he was doing this that he was forced to cut his cable and wear round. He could not beat up; the northward airs carried him away out of the battle inshore.

While she remained, *Preble* had given the gunboats a heavy hammering, and from *Ticonderoga* they received even more. Lieutenant Cassin coolly walked his deck, with a perfect storm of grapeshot blowing past him, encouraging his men by word and deed, seeing that every gun was carefully laid; behind him marched Midshipman Hiram Paulding (who would live to be an admiral one day), touching off the guns by flashing his pistols at the priming. They shot so accurately that an hour after the battle began, *Finch* was crippled as *Chubb* had been, and drifted down to Crab Island. It was occupied by an army hospital which had a single gun. Some of the convalescents fired this piece at the sloop until she struck. Only four of the enemy gunboats now remained capable of offensive action. Three times they charged in on *Ticonderoga,* firing the heavy pieces over their bows, and pushing within a boat's length, with their men already rising from the oars to board, before they were beaten back.

Thus the small craft of both sides at both ends of the line were practically eliminated, with some slight advantage to the Americans. In the main battle, *Linnet* still had her raking fire on *Saratoga,* but it had become quite weak, since the brig had taken a bad beating from the gunboats and the occasional piece *Saratoga* turned on her. She had water in her hold. *Confiance* was in even worse case; Captain Downie had been killed by maybe the second fire and, without his supervision, the men overloaded the guns in their excitement, doing things like putting in two shot and no powder, or a wad below the shot, or two powder charges and no shot at all. Many more guns had been disabled by the American fire; there was not a single piece in action.

On the other side, *Eagle* was still shooting, but only at about the same rate as *Linnet*. After that first jarring broadside from the enemy, *Saratoga* had suffered less, because the quoins of *Confiance's* guns worked loose and, not being replaced, let the shot go high; but enough of them had come aboard the corvette to do frightful damage. The ship had twice been set afire by hot shot; her spanker was almost completely burned. Another shot had severed the spanker-boom, which dropped with stunning force on Macdonough's head; and he was no sooner on his feet again than he was knocked senseless clean across the deck by a ball that took off the head of a gun-captain and dashed it in his face. The Second Lieutenant was dead, and 28 men with him; the Marines had laid down their muskets to work at the guns, but these were gradually disabled until only a single carronade remained. Macdonough fired it himself; on the recoil the navel-bolt burst and the piece rumbled backward down the hatch, leaving the ship without a single piece in action. The battle was a draw, or worse.

Or would have been but for Macdonough's forethought; for now he let go a stream anchor that had been suspended under *Saratoga's* stern. The whole crew now roused on the cable that had been hanging under water to the starboard kedge forward; the cable to the stream anchor was payed out. Round and round the ship slowly came until her stern was over the kedge. But there she hung, stern toward *Linnet,* taking a slow, accurate raking fire from that ship. Macdonough sent his men forward to be protected as much as possible, and hauled in on the line to the stream anchor; it brought the ship round a few degrees more until the aftermost maindeck gun in the new broadside would just bear on *Confiance*.

The piece was instantly manned and began to shoot; but now the ship lay stern to whatever wind there was, and no further effort with those two cables would shift her more. There remained, however, the other kedge, the one that had been off the port bow and was now near the starboard quarter. Macdonough had the line led forward under the prow of the ship, then back inboard, and, with everyone waltzing

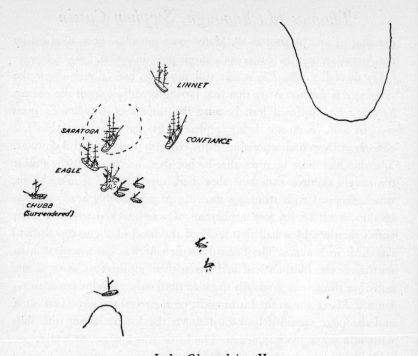

LINNET

SARATOGA

CONFIANCE

EAGLE

CHUBB
(Surrendered)

Lake Champlain—II
The crisis of the battle; last attack of the British gunboats; *Saratoga* begins to wind round.

around the windlass, by main force dragged the ship in the loop of rope. All her broadside bore; cheering madly for revenge and victory, the American sailors flung themselves to the guns and poured into *Confiance* the fire of a wholly fresh ship. The British had tried to wind their ship round when they saw *Saratoga* beginning to move, but being without Macdonough's careful preparations, and having lost two of their anchors, they could not make it. *Confiance* hung; took the American's battering for a minute or two, and then hauled down her flag.

Now *Saratoga* was winded round again, until her fresh battery bore on *Linnet*. Brave Captain Pring, who had fought as plucky and clever a battle as any man in the two squadrons, stood the fire for fifteen minutes, until the water was a foot over his gundeck. Then he too surrendered and the battle was over. The British galleys moved off slowly and with many oars missing, and Macdonough could not have his own pursue them, for their crews were desperately needed to keep not only the prizes but also his own ships from sinking.

VI

He bowed when the surviving British officers came aboard with their caps in their hands, and said: "Gentlemen, return your swords into your scabbards and wear them. You are worthy of them." He could afford to be generous, for he had just won the most murderous naval battle of the war, one of the most murderous in any war, so that Britishers who had been at Trafalgar said that was child's play to this. The American squadron had nearly 200 casualties in 882 men, a little less than one in four, and *Saratoga* had 55 shot in her hull. Aboard the British ships there were 300 casualties in 937, nearly one in three. *Confiance* had been hit in the hull 105 times, and hardly resembled a ship any more, her rudder shot away, her stout bulwarks beaten in, "her masts bundles of match-sticks, her sails bundles of rags," her decks so slippery with blood that a man could hardly stand upright.

It was also one of the most decisive battles. It decided that the United States would not be invaded from the north. Sir George Prevost fired a few shots into Macomb's lines, then turned back into Canada, in spite of being nearly ten to one of the land forces opposing him. In London there was some dissatisfaction over his retreat, but he was probably right. He could not take the American positions without a fight, for Macomb's men were regulars and well dug-in. Then the British would have their wounded, and a long, hard march to make up the lake, with the only road exposed to the fire of ships all the way, until they should reach Ticonderoga, where there was a well-armed fortress; and beyond that forests, through which it would be impossible to move guns or wagons, with the fall rains already begun.

The proof of Prevost's judgment came when the British Cabinet asked the great Duke of Wellington to take over the Canadian command, offering him whatever was necessary to turn the movement southward into a success. The great Duke looked over the maps and documents, and replied that what was really needed was not troops or supplies, but naval victories on the lakes; if the Cabinet could furnish him with these, he would be glad to accept the charge.

They could not do that now or ever. For the second time in a year, which was the second time in history, a British fleet had been wiped out beyond recovery. On the American side there was a lively appreciation of what the victory meant. Congress voted Macdonough the gold medal usual for victories, and by legislative action jumped him to the permanent rank of captain, seniority from September 11, 1814. Vermont State bought the whole of Cumberland Head for him as a present, and New York gave him a thousand acres of land. Half the cities of the State sent up gold boxes or deeds of gift. After the battle, Macdonough was granted a short leave with his family in Middletown; the journey thither was a triumphal procession of balls, dinners, illuminations.

During the winter he was ordered to leave Champlain in charge of Cassin, and go down to New York to take command of the steam blockade-breaking ship *Demologos,* or *Fulton the First,* as she was renamed after her inventor's death. He did not like the craft, and his health was far from good, so he asked for a command that would take him to a warmer climate, and was assigned to *Guerrière,* 44, for a voyage on which he would carry a minister to Russia, then join the Mediterranean squadron. *Guerrière* sailed in July 1818, made a good passage, and, after the usual entertainments and visits at Kronstadt, went on down to Naples.

There Macdonough fell afoul of Commodore Charles Stewart over the matter of a court-martial, which the Commodore had ordered held aboard *Guerrière,* and which the members of the court, for reasons that seemed adequate to them, held on shore instead. Stewart, who had been sent out to check a growing spirit of insubordination in the squadron, disapproved the court's findings and released the prisoner. Macdonough, as senior officer of the court, convoked it again by signal, and it passed resolutions of protest, whereupon Stewart suspended the Captain from command of his ship and sent him home.

Here was the making of a fine quarrel, or at least of some bitterness, but Macdonough was not made of the stuff that harbors grudges.

Thomas Macdonough, Stephen Cassin

He consulted a lawyer when he got home; was told that Stewart's position was perfectly correct legally; at once went to see the Secretary, confessed himself in the wrong and asked to be returned to the Mediterranean under Stewart's command. The request was granted, but Macdonough's health was so poor that he could not take the appointment after all. What the nature of the illness was is not clear; probably something connected with the tuberculosis that killed both him and his wife within a few weeks of each other in 1825. They left five children.

He was the first of Preble's boys to go, excepting those killed in the war, and according to Theodore Roosevelt was "the greatest figure in our naval history down to the Civil War." The judgment is somewhat excited, since greatness is hardly to be predicated on any single event, however intelligently prepared and boldly and skillfully carried through. Yet Macdonough certainly did something accomplished by no other American naval officer in the War of 1812: handled his fleet as a fleet, not as a collection of individual units, and got the most out of everything he had. The British squadron was greatly superior, but its biggest ships used only half their guns, while Macdonough brought every gun he had into action, and so won his battle. Neither was this accident; he arranged things that way. He was also a not unimportant influence on the younger generation of officers. In the years after the war the Department employed him constantly on boards of examination for promotions; and of the midshipmen who cruised with him in *Guerrière* no fewer than five ultimately became admirals, an extraordinary proportion.

That is, like his old teacher, Preble, he was himself a teacher. Of what? Perhaps of leadership. Nothing stands so much at the root of the victory on Lake Champlain as the leadership on the American side. Forethought provided the means for victory, but it was Macdonough's leadership that saw they were properly used. Twice knocked senseless, he still walked the deck, seeing that *Saratoga's* guns were not overloaded like those of *Confiance*, and that they were properly laid as those of *Confiance* were not. It was Macdonough who gave the orders at just the proper moment to use the kedge anchors, and Macdonough who, when the ship would not swing further, thought of a way around that difficulty as well.

This was leadership on the plane of personal supervision in action, and it made the difference between a 26-gun corvette and a 36-gun frigate. But there is also evidence that Macdonough exercised a great deal of the other, educational type of leadership. He transformed the rather motley assemblage of men he received from New York and from the army into a fighting unit that on the day of battle showed not only skill, but a rather wonderful degree of steadiness as well. The losses taken by the British before they surrendered were simply appalling; but this should not conceal the fact that the American ships suffered a proportionate loss such as had been held to justify the surrender of more than one ship during the war. The men of *Saratoga* not only bore up under this bludgeoning; in the midst of it, suffering from a raking fire to which they could make no reply, they went through the complex maneuvers involved in winding the ship. The details of how Macdonough built this co-operation into his men are not now to be recovered. It was done by word of mouth, and nobody took down the words; the only thing clear is that he did it, and that he transmitted some of the skill of doing it to younger officers.

VII

Cassin contributed only less to the victory than Macdonough himself, also by means of leadership. He received a duplicate of Macdonough's gold medal, and also his promotion to master-commandant. After the war he was placed in command of *Peacock*, 20, for service against the West Indian pirates in Biddle's squadron of 1822. He captured one piratical craft near Havana in September of that year, and a few days later met a small schooner of the British cruise off the coast, which said she had been fired into by a pirate that then escaped among the keys. The schooner lacked the force to go in after this marauder, but Cassin readily consented to send the larger boats of his own ship in, under the British flag. They brought off not one but four piratical craft, with a number of prisoners who (as it was officially a British expedition) were sent to Jamaica to have their necks lengthened.

In the following year, under David Porter, Cassin took two more pirate ships, but does not seem to have seen much sea service thereafter, spending most of his time in Washington on administrative tasks. He made a romantic marriage with a Miss Abernethy, daughter of a British officer who had disappeared somewhere in the Northwest during the War of 1812; she had come to Washington, searching for some record of him. Cassin died in 1857, 74 years old.

Chapter 15
Patterson at New Orleans

I N 1803 THERE WAS AN EPIDEMIC OF YELLOW FEVER AT NEW YORK. MR.
Edward Livingston, who combined the offices of Mayor of the city
and Federal District Attorney, greatly distinguished himself by his
courage and humanity until he fell a victim of the disease. After his recovery, it was found that a rascally confidential clerk had embezzled
considerable sums of money, for which Mr. Livingston was officially
responsible. He promptly resigned both his offices and emigrated to the
newly acquired territory of Louisiana, where he engaged in the practice of the law so successfully that in a comparatively brief time he had
not only restored to the government all the losses caused by his clerk,
but had also become one of the most distinguished men in the territory,
the author of its organic law, and a major personal factor in its integra-
tion with the general fabric of American life.

He was an indefatigable correspondent, and the letters in which he
described the virtues of New Orleans to his family had much to do with
the establishment in the Creole city of a collateral relative, Daniel Todd
Patterson, a fellow-New Yorker and a lieutenant in the navy. Patterson was to contribute hardly less than Livingston himself to the history
of his adoptive state. Not so much is known about the early life of
this navy man, except that his father was a former collector of customs
who married into the Livingston clan and settled down on Long Island, where Daniel T. was born in 1786. There is no explanation of
why the boy was sent to sea at the age of 13, well below the legal age
limit for the navy, in one of the earliest vessels to put out during the
French War.

His rank was "acting midshipman"; she was a ship called *Delaware,*
which had been purchased out of the North Atlantic packet service and
armed as a light corvette of 20 guns rate, with sixteen long 9s on the gun-

deck and eight long 6s above—an armament which shows that except for a few fanatics like Joshua Humphreys, American naval planners were still doing their thinking in the days of the Revolution. Even this light armament made her a slow and clumsy cruiser. Her original captain had been the senior Stephen Decatur, who had been one of the cleverest privateersmen of the Revolution. He left a ship with a good reputation for efficiency and luck in making captures when he was moved up to one of the new frigates and *Delaware* passed into the hands of one Thomas Baker.

The cruise was an unfortunate one, down to the Curaçao station, where so many of the ship's men took the fevers that she could not be handled and had to lie in port for a long time. When she returned to the States, Patterson received his midshipman's warrant and went out with her again, this time to the Guadeloupe station. He reached home for the second time to learn that he was one of the midshipmen retained under the peace establishment; but, instead of seeking active duty, he abandoned the sea to take two years of schooling. It would be worth a good deal to learn what his schoolfellows thought of this lad of fifteen, a naval officer on the active list, who had seen two years of wartime service. But the only information we have is that his studies were almost exclusively concerned with navigational subjects until he was ordered to sea again, this time in *Constellation,* 38, Captain Alexander Murray, for the second Mediterranean cruise.

Patterson seems to have been an apt pupil under the rather hard hand of Murray, for when his next voyage out placed him in *Philadelphia,* 38, Captain William Bainbridge reported that he was "fully qualified to receive his lieutenant's commission" though he had only just turned 17. Secretary Smith took cognizance of this approval in a letter of instruction to Commodore Samuel Barron when the latter went out with the squadron in the fall of 1804, authorizing him to give Patterson an examination and then to commission the young man a lieutenant if he passed. This would have made him one of the youngest lieutenants the service ever had; but of course the examination could not take place, since at the time of Barron's arrival Patterson was in Tripoli prison with the other officers of the captured frigate, and he stayed there many months more.

His time was not altogether wasted. The energetic Lieutenant David Porter was one of the prisoners, and he set up a home university for the young officers, teaching such subjects as theoretical navigation, tactics, literature, and languages. Patterson was one of the star pupils; he used to say afterward that Tripoli was where he really obtained his education. He also formed a friendship with Porter which lasted all their lives.

The knowledge of French and Spanish acquired in Tripoli, together with the letters of his kinsman, Edward Livingston, explains Patterson's request for assignment to the New Orleans station when he returned to the United States. It was a request readily granted, since few others wanted anything to do with the task there, which was one of handling the smuggling and incipient piracy along the Gulf Coast, with no chance of renown. The resources of the station consisted of 12 badly found gunboats, short of crews and stores, while much of commercial New Orleans was on the side of the lawbreakers. Midshipman Patterson found he was too low in rank to accomplish anything, for, though he had passed his examination on emerging from Tripoli, the niggardly Secretary Smith refused to give him his lieutenant's commission, with its advance in pay, until the Senate concurred.

By this date Edward Livingston had become an influential man in New Orleans. It is possible to see his young relative seeking him out with information which the legislator could only too well confirm from personal knowledge; something to the effect that the law was being held in defiance, the navy in disrespect, and things would never go better until a more energetic man was found than the incumbent station commander, Captain John Shaw, who had been a dashing ship's officer but was not the man for this post.

At all events, this is what happened: in the summer of 1807 Patterson married a New Orleans girl and obtained leave for a honeymoon in the north; visited in Washington for some time; received his lieutenancy; took a brief further leave in New York; and returned to New Orleans to find Lieutenant David Porter commandant of the station. That eupeptic person set things moving at once, and it was a well-ordered naval command that he turned over to the control of Lieutenant Patterson in 1811, when he himself went north to take charge of a frigate.

Daniel Todd Patterson

There was only one cruising ship on the station at this time, the brig *Enterprise*, 12, and she was laid up in ordinary for lack of crew and maintenance money. But the peacetime work of the navy at New Orleans was either in the mouths of the river itself or among the shallow waters east and west of the delta, and for this purpose the gunboat squadron was reasonably adequate. There were now 11, mainly craft of a design prepared by James Barron, about 70 feet long, and with a "dandy" rig, which is a topsail-sloop with a small lug sail on a tiny pole mast right in the sternsheets. The boats mounted either one or two heavy guns, 24s, and two or three light pieces for grape, not much heavier than hand swivels. When the war came, they were augmented for defense of the river by a fine schooner purchased in Charleston, named *Carolina* and armed with 12 12-pound carronades; and by a ship purchased at New Orleans itself, furnished with 16 long 24s, and called *Louisiana*.

The real difficulties of Patterson, Livingston, and Governor William C.C.Claiborne, as it seemed to them in 1812–13, were not those of defense, for it struck no one as likely that the British would enter the Gulf in strength. Those troubles can be summed up under the name of Jean Lafitte. This gentleman was at the time, and has been since, freely called a pirate. This is not true; many of the men under Jean Lafitte were pirates, but he himself was a perfectly honorable business entrepreneur, whose own trouble was that he could not understand Anglo-Saxon objections to the Latin system of taxation by corruption.

His first appearance at New Orleans was in 1804, when he came up the river as commander of a French privateer in need of supplies, and apparently decided that the Gulf was a good center for future operations. Before 1809 he and his brother Pierre were operating a large blacksmith shop, which was supposed (though without any legal evidence one could hang a dog on) to be a depot for smuggled goods and stolen slaves.

In 1810 a new and beautiful horizon opened before the brothers

Lafitte. That singular adventurer, Francesco Miranda, landed on the coast of what is now Colombia, got part of the region under control, proclaimed the Republic of Cartagena, and began issuing commissions to privateers. At the time, a war was in progress over who really was King of Spain; but being in "insurrection" against any King, the Cartagenan privateers could take the ships and goods of both sides alike without much danger from either. They could do more: under the English doctrine that the goods polluted the vessel, they could capture and seize any ship that was judged to have Spanish property aboard. Pierre Lafitte remained in New Orleans as salesman and general business manager; Jean took out a Cartagenan privateer's license, and moved down to Barataria Bay, just west of the Mississippi mouths, where on an island called Grande Terre there had been for some time a settlement of various gentry of the coast.

Jean Lafitte had no little ability as a leader and, with the good connections established during the smuggling period, became prince of Barataria at once, with half a dozen fast light ships operating against Spanish commerce all around the Gulf and into the West Indies. It is to be noted that the Gulf was then a Spanish lake, and the Caribbean nearly so; a large proportion of the shipping present, and a still higher one of the goods carried, were Spanish in title. The profits of the Lafitte business were enormous, since the only expenses were for guns and powder, while the property could be whisked to New Orleans and sold at prices which far undercut the regular market for similar goods. And the beauty of it all was that it was perfectly legal.

To Governor William Claiborne, it did not seem in the least legal or desirable. For one thing, the Baratarians were not at all nice in their methods: their prizes were condemned not before any recognized admiralty courts, but by judges of their own at Grande Terre who had no international standing; and, if they wanted a ship or cargo, they found the property Spanish without inquiring too deeply into the evidence. It was even reported that American ships had been condemned; and in any case the American doctrine was that the flag covered the goods. In the second place, many of the cargoes consisted of slaves, and the importation of slaves into the United States had been absolutely forbidden since 1808. In the third place, the goods that came into

New Orleans up the back stairs from Barataria paid no duty; it was Claiborne's job and most especially Patterson's to enforce customs regulations.

On this matter of customs dues, Claiborne succeeded in making himself completely incomprehensible, not only to the Lafittes, but also to the whole of Creole society. They were quite willing to pay the Governor his share of the profits, and even to conduct the slaving part of the business in a decently clandestine manner, and they found it difficult to believe that these Northerners really wanted to stand by the letter of the law. There was a more or less silent tug-of-war between the conflicting philosophies until toward the end of 1813, when Claiborne lost his temper and issued a proclamation against the Lafittes and anyone dealing with them. "Emboldened by the impunity of past trespasses," it read, "the Baratarians no longer conceal themselves, but setting the government at defiance in broad daylight, carry on their infamous traffic." It ended by offering a reward of $500 for the apprehension of Jean Lafitte. Lafitte replied by posting a reward of $50,000 for the apprehension of Governor William Claiborne and went on about his business, laughing heartily.

Now Claiborne was forced to take drastic action. He empaneled a hand-picked grand jury to study the matter. They labored long and hard, and brought forth a presentment to the effect that piracy existed; that it was very deplorable; but that it would be difficult to obtain convictions "even where the strongest presentations of guilt are offered." This would not seem to have given the Governor too much of a free hand, but he accepted it as a call to action. Pierre Lafitte was thrown into jail, together with all the other Baratarians discoverable in New Orleans; Master-Commandant Patterson and Colonel Ross of the army were instructed to prepare an expedition against the pirate stronghold. Dominic You, Lafitte's most important lieutenant, was one of those taken.

But the date had now run to September 1814, and a new thread was added to the pattern. On the 3rd of that month the brig *Sophie,* 18, hove to off Grande Terre, fired a gun, and hoisted a flag of truce. Captain Lockyer of the Royal Navy came ashore. He was given a dinner which he remembered in his memoirs for the delicacy of the food and the splendor of the plate on which it was served, after which he presented certain papers. One was a letter from Colonel Nicolls, military head of the British post at Pensacola, offering Lafitte a commission in His Majesty's service; another was a confirming letter from the British admiral on the Jamaica station; and still a third announced the impending arrival off the Mississippi of a British force for the capture of New Orleans, powerful enough to crush any opposition.

III

The orders had gone out as early as July. Major-General Ross, commander of the British land forces then in the Chesapeake Bay area, was directed, as soon as he had completed the destruction of Washington and Baltimore, to proceed to Negril Bay, Jamaica, where he would rendezvous with another force being sent out from England. About November 19 or 20, the combined bodies, to the number of nearly 10,000 troops, would sail. Ross was to choose whether to attack New Orleans directly or to cut it off from the rear by the capture of Mobile and a campaign conducted with the help of the Creek Indians, who were fighting so desperate a war with the Americans on their own. The inhabitants of Louisiana were to be encouraged to declare themselves under the Spanish crown, or to announce their independence under British protection.

In October news reached London that Ross had been defeated and killed under the ramparts of Baltimore, but this altered the plan only by increasing its intensity. The new commander was Sir Edward Pakenham, Wellington's brother-in-law and his ablest lieutenant during the Peninsular War. He was to come on with reinforcements from the Gironde, where he was commanding part of the army occupying France.

Yet the plan was altered from the outside and, in the essential feature of timing, by one of those intolerable Yankee privateers. Captain Robert Lloyd, commanding *Plantagenet,* 74, was on his way to Jamaica, accompanied by *Rota,* 38, and *Carnation,* 18, the three carrying some of the troops and most of the artillery for the expedition, when they put into Fayal in the Azores on the afternoon of October 26. They saw a large brig lying in the inner harbor, which by her lines looked American; and she certainly was, being *General Armstrong* of New York, one of a famous pair of sister-ships that between them had taken 39 British vessels, five of them right out of convoys under the eyes of the infuriated escorts. At this time she was commanded by Captain Samuel Reid, a broad-faced man in a plug hat, who was subsequently to invent lightships and the arrangement of the stars in the American flag.

General Armstrong had only 90 men aboard, the other 60 having been sent in with prizes. Reid doubted whether the Portuguese would or could do much about preserving the neutrality of their port, and warped his ship close inshore, under the castle, where she could not be got at from all sides. The task was completed only just in time; about eight o'clock in the evening, four boatloads of armed men from the British frigate began to approach, and the Portuguese governor came out and settled himself on the wall of the castle to watch the fun. Reid hailed the boats several times, telling them to keep off; they came right on to reaching distance, when he gave the order to fire, and his people let loose a volley that sent the boats backing out again with 7 dead.

This made Captain Lloyd very angry indeed. He ordered away all the major boats of his squadron, 12 in number, with a carronade in each, carrying a total of some 400 men. At midnight, they came pulling in; the news had spread through the town, the whole population was out on rooftops and the waterfront blazing with fires. Captain Reid himself sighted the Long Tom for the opening shot; as the barges spread to attack *General Armstrong* from every possible angle together, the boats' guns replied and the brig's broadside came into action, throwing long tails of sparks across the dark water. There were hits among the boats and men killed in them, but cheering heartily and shouting "No quarter!" the British tars pulled through the flame and smoke and, after maybe two discharges, were bumping the privateer's side.

Now came a nightmare hand-to-hand struggle, in which men moved by reflex, the British climbing up the chains, slashing at the boarding nettings with cutlasses, the pistols of both sides firing and boarding-pikes stabbing through. On the brig's quarter, the attackers were slaughteringly beaten back, and the yelling privateersmen pursued them right into the barges. "The Americans fought more like bloodthirsty savages than anything else," said a survivor. "They rushed into the boats sword in hand put every soul to death"—having heard that cry of "No quarter!" they gave none. Seventeen men escaped by swimming from one boat and ran ashore so far that they were not picked up till three days later; in another a midshipman was the only survivor. Someone brought Captain Reid word that both his lieutenants on the forecastle were down and the enemy gaining. With a speaking trumpet in one hand and a cutlass in the other, he rallied the after division and led them forward. There was a brief torrid struggle around the base of the bowsprit; then the last of the attackers were expelled, and the remaining boats were pulling slowly away, full of moaning men.

The remaining boats; for the privateersmen had taken possession of two, manned only by dead and dying. Later, they found another under the stern, and two more drifted ashore. It was 12:40 and the British had suffered one of the bloodiest defeats of the war. According to Captain Lloyd's report (which the Admiralty suppressed) they lost 63 killed, 110 wounded, or as many as *Guerrière* and *Macedonian* together; and there is some reason to believe that the Captain was not entirely frank.

At three in the morning Reid had a note from the American consul, and went ashore to learn that Lloyd, in a fury that made his earlier rage pale by comparison, had sworn to take the privateer and her crew at any cost. If the Portuguese allowed the Americans to destroy their ship (he said), he would consider himself in an enemy port and bombard the place. Reid went back to his ship, where they had been working with the Long Tom, which had been knocked from its pivot. He clearly could not save his ship, but there were still a few words to be spoken, so he supervised the transfer ashore of the 2 dead and 7 wounded who were his only casualties, with the personal effects of the men, the booty from the prizes, and supplies of powder and shot for the hand weapons; then waited.

At dawn *Carnation* came drifting in with the day breeze. Reid opened on her with the Long Tom, and soon sent her out again, with her bowsprit shot through, her fore-topmast smashed, and more casualties. But she repaired, warped in again, and springing her broadside to bear on the privateer opened a slow fire, while *Plantagenet* also started to move. There was nothing more to be gained by standing up to this; Reid scuttled his brig and joined his men ashore. Captain Lloyd demanded that the Americans be surrendered to him, but they retired to an "old Gothic castle" behind Fayal, hauled up the drawbridge, and suggested that the British come and get them.

The British did not try, and after they went away the Americans went back to the wreck of their ship, dredged up the wooden likeness of General Armstrong that had been its figurehead, and set it at the door of the American consulate, where it stood for nearly a century, known locally as "O Sao Americano," and every October 26 received votive offerings of flowers from the populace. But the important thing is what happened before the British left. Lloyd had to spend a week in finding and burying the dead who were washing in the surf, and even then could not leave at once, since *Rota* had lost all her lieutenants and *Plantagenet* three of her five, while all the ships were desperately short-handed. He had to wait for replacements; was late at the rendezvous in Negril Bay; and, as a consequence, the expedition for New Orleans was a good week behind its proper time for sailing.

IV

Over the cigars and cordials, Jean Lafitte assured Captain Lockyer that the offer of His Majesty's officers was most generous, most gracious, and if they would give him a fortnight to put his affairs in order he would be entirely at their disposal. They retired, much pleased with themselves, but would have been considerably less so had they known that as soon as the brig's topsails were hoisted, the letters they brought and a précis of the British plan of invasion had been forwarded to Edward Livingston, who had been retained to defend brother Pierre. With it went a letter in stilted Franco-English to "Son Excellence William C. C. Clayborne:—I offer to return to the State many Citizens who perhaps have lost to your eyes that sacred title. I offer their Efforts for the Defense of the country."

Livingston laid the letters before Claiborne. Claiborne hastily summoned a council, at which were present Colonel Ross and Patterson— the latter now being a neat, compact man, full of energy and confidence, somewhat haughty, rather splendid in appearance. It was a stormy gathering. Claiborne was so impressed by the documents as to be converted. He pointed out that New Orleans was almost defenseless, having only a single regiment of regular troops to support the militia. General Andrew Jackson, the military commander of the district, was convinced that the British meant to strike through Mobile and the Indian country, and nearly all his forces were concentrated out there, away eastward. The pirates, who understood arms and were not afraid to use them, would make a valuable, almost an essential, reinforcement.

Ross and Patterson violently disagreed. They pronounced the British letters forgeries and the whole business a maneuver by the Lafittes to outwit justice; and, even if it were not, the law must be upheld against the Baratarians. They presented their case with so much vigor that Claiborne felt himself compelled to let their expedition sail as planned. It put out the next morning, with the gunboats, *Carolina,* and the troops; but during the night Pierre Lafitte mysteriously disappeared from the prison in which he had been confined.

The expedition had to move tortuously down the mouth of the Mississippi, only reaching Barataria on September 16, when it found ten sail of vessels in line off the bar, some of them prizes, some the Baratarians' own craft, all flying Cartagenan colors with white flags. As the American ships approached, the pirates fled in all directions in their boats. There was no resistance on sea or shore; Ross's men landed, burned the village, which consisted chiefly of shacks of the most miserable type, and carried off goods to the value of half a million dollars. (There was a not very creditable lawsuit between Patterson and Ross later over who was entitled to the larger share of the plunder-money.) The Lafittes were nowhere to be found; their men disappeared likewise.

All this time the storm-cloud was gathering at Negril Bay. On December 11, when Jackson reached New Orleans, at last having come to believe that this was the enemy's main objective, the main British convoy, with Pakenham and the troops, cast anchor at the entrance to Lake Borgne. This is not really a lake, but a long inlet of the Gulf, which cuts near the city from the east. By means of a bayou, it leads to a point on the levee and solid riverbank only six miles below New Orleans.

If the army could have gone in at once, New Orleans were an easy prize, for at this date Jackson had only about 1,000 wholly untrained militia and two regiments of regulars, numbering less than 800 men between them. His best troops, the Tennessee riflemen who had daunted down the Creeks, were several marches away at Baton Rouge. Kentucky riflemen also were coming, but they were still farther away, and the General absolutely refused to listen to Livingston's plea that he use the Baratarians. They were "hellish banditti," he said, and he wanted none of them, despite the fact that Patterson now gave fullest support to Livingston's plan. He pointed out that Lafitte's men were sailors and trained artillerists, the very men of whom the defense stood in most need, for although *Carolina* had reached the station with a good crew of New England seamen, *Louisiana* was so far short of her complement that she could not even be taken into action.

But the British could not cross Lake Borgne at once, for it held a squadron of five little gunboats, under command of Lieutenant Thomas Ap Catesby Jones. An expedition had to be organized to brush them from the path. It was the night of December 13 when it started, and noon of the 14th before it came up with the gunboats, consisting of some 45 barges, most of them specially built for the invasion. They carried 42 guns, all the way up to 24-pounders, and 1,200 men all told. The American crews totaled 182 men; only a miracle could have saved them, and rather the reverse of miracles was the order of the day, for it fell flat calm where the gunboats were, near Malheureux Island at the north rim of the lake, so that their formation was somewhat disordered by the set of the tide.

The first attack fell on Jones's personal command, gunboat *No. 156,* a little isolated from the rest. It was repulsed, and two of the three barges that made it were sunk. The second attack was made by four boats and was again beaten back, but Jones was wounded this time, and at the third try the British carried his boat by boarding. Her guns were turned on *No. 163* and she was taken, then the others in turn, *Nos. 162, 5,* and *23;* but they held out for nearly two hours against all that force, and their very presence gained precious days for the defense of New Orleans, since the British barges now had to go back and re-load before they could begin to take troops through the bayou.

The enemy reached the Mississippi bank on December 23, with a van-guard of 1,800 men, at a place called the Villeré Plantation, and were seen there by Major Latour, a French-trained officer who was the American Chief of Engineers. Now Andrew Jackson, who had made not a few errors of judgment in estimating the situation, showed his real quality. His Tennesseans had just arrived; he decided to attack and destroy that vanguard without a moment's delay, and to make the attack at night—one of the most difficult of military enterprises, but one of the most stunning when it succeeds.

On that very evening, the 23rd, the British were making comfort around their cook-fires under the falling twilight when they saw a black schooner drifting down the stream without a flag. Some of them gath-ered curiously at the levee to watch her; an anchor suddenly let go, the starry banner went to her masthead, Patterson's voice shouted, "Now give them this for the honor of America!" and the camp was swept with grape. Everything was confusion at once, for the British artillery had not yet come; in that confusion the sun dipped down, and the Tennessee riflemen burst from the cypress swamp upon the British flank, while Jackson with the regulars came charging down the levee.

The British were Wellington's veterans of the Peninsular War, who had stood up under the attacks of Napoleon; they did not panic, but collected in little knots around their officers, bayonets outward like the spines of hedgehogs, somewhat protected from *Carolina's* fire by an old levee that ran parallel to the new. Two regiments opportunely arrived from Lake Borgne to aid them; they held, and Jackson, seeing he could gain no more, had a recall sounded and retired, thoroughly dissatisfied. He need not have been; he had inflicted 247 casualties, many more than he took, and when Pakenham arrived with the bulk of the forces on Christmas Day the report he had of the fierce and sudden American onset made him take counsel of caution and resolve to advance slowly and in form. Jackson was granted more time; he used it to dig deeper and to supply with parapets an old dry canal, the Rodriguez, which ran across the thousand yards of dry ground between the cypress swamp and the Mississippi.

Daniel Todd Patterson

During all this time the reinforcements gathered. The first of the Kentuckians arrived, the wild men in coonskin caps, whom the Indians called Long Knives; a battalion of refugee blacks from Santo Domingo, and, most important of all, the Baratarians. Nearly everyone in New Orleans had been working on the General to accept them, but he held out until Judge Dominick Hall of the Federal Court obtained from the legislature a resolution suspending proceedings against Lafitte and his men. Dominic You was turned out of jail; Jean Lafitte himself appeared in the streets, and went to call on Jackson. *Louisiana's* complement filled up by magic, and swarthy men with rings in their ears filed into the gun-positions along the Rodriguez Canal, and into a three-gun battery thrown forward on the west bank to enfilade any force that attacked the main American position.

The batteries were under army command, but they were principally Patterson's, mounting naval guns. After the night attack, the Commodore kept his two ships in the stream to annoy the left flank of the British. Pakenham felt he could not advance without getting rid of them, so had some artillery brought through and established a masked battery under the edge of the levee with furnaces for heating shot. At dawn of the 27th, this battery, nine guns and two howitzers, opened suddenly on *Carolina*. Current and an unfavorable wind held her in position; in half an hour she was so badly afire that she had to be abandoned. But *Louisiana* escaped, and when, on December 28, Pakenham tried a tentative forward movement, the sloop-of-war poured so heavy a fire into the British columns that they must halt and take cover.

This decided the British general; he must keep *Louisiana* out of it, and set up artillery preparation before he made his assault. With enormous labor more guns were dragged through the bayous and placed in position; 7 heavy pieces facing the river to keep *Louisiana* off and to deal with Patterson's west-bank battery; some 23 others to bear on the incomplete parapets along the Rodriguez Canal, all revetted in with hogsheads of sugar. When the American guns had been beaten to silence, the infantry were to make their assault.

Behind Jackson's line there were 12 pieces only; but three of them were 24s, one a 32, and one an 18, and all were served by the cud-chewing Yankee gunners from *Carolina* and the Baratarians who followed Dominic You. To these men, accustomed to shooting from heaving decks, this fixed-position work was child's play. When the British opened with a shower of rockets and the fire of all their artillery on New Year's Day of 1815, the American gunners answered at first "faintly and with seeming difficulty," according to the British Canon Gleig, who saw it all. "By and by, however, the enemy's salutation became more spirited, till it gradually surpassed our own, both in rapidity and precision. We were a good deal alarmed by this and the more, that a rumour got abroad that our batteries were not proof against the American shot. Our fire slacked every minute; that of the Americans became every moment more terrible, dismounting our guns and killing our artillerymen in the very centre of the works." By one o'clock it was over; the British gunners abandoned whatever pieces were still capable of being fired, and the infantry assault was canceled.

At this date Pakenham had 5,000 troops in line and Jackson less than half that many, but the British commander decided to wait for his reserves, and Jackson's men assembled faster than his. Now the plan was for a simultaneous attack against Patterson's west-bank battery and a general assault on the Rodriguez Canal. Twelve hundred men were assigned to the former task; the guns that had been knocked from their mountings in the artillery duel were replaced, and by daylight on January 8, a bright and chilly morning, with hoarfrost covering the Chalmette plain, all was ready. The bugles blew and the command was forward.

The main force came on in two columns, to break down the American wings. They entered the fire of those batteries which the artillerists had been unable to put down, and they suffered from them; but these were the British grenadiers, they took their losses, and pressed on grimly into musketry range. Then the Louisianans, the Santo Domingo blacks, the United States Marines, the regulars, the pirates, and the frontier riflemen—all stood up, laid their guns on the parapet, and began to shoot. Aim for the officers, they had been told, and officers went down by dozens at the head of their men. Whole files collapsed under that blast; they could not stand it, they halted and began to go back. Word was brought to Pakenham that the general commanding one column was dead and the leader of the other mortally wounded. He ordered in the reserve, and rode forward himself to make a rally, with his hat on the point of a sword; he was instantly killed, the reserve was cut to pieces, and the last remnants of the assault force broke back to their own lines, leaving over 2000 men on the Chalmette plain. Five of the best regiments in the British army were practically wiped out, having but 200 men left among them; and of those who remained, most did not know where to gather or what officers were left to command. It hardly mattered that the west-bank force overran Patterson's battery after the repulse, for there was nothing for the survivors to do but get back to their boats, and the War of 1812 was over.

v

Afterward President Madison sent down a general pardon to the Baratarians for whatever they had done before the defense of New Orleans. Dominic You moved to the city and became a respected citizen, but Jean Lafitte set up his headquarters at Galveston, over the Mexican border, and went into business again on the old basis. He disappeared in 1825—killed in a brawl in Yucatan, it is said.

Patterson received the especial thanks of Congress, with his step to a captaincy, and something more than the special thanks of Andrew Jackson, one of whose most engaging qualities was a particularly lively sense of gratitude. The Commodore remained on the New Orleans station until 1824, most occupied with suppressing nests of small-time pirates—not gentlemen like Lafitte, but real buccaneers, who established themselves in haunts along the coast and plundered whatever ships were small or weak enough for them to handle. After this service, Patterson was made captain of *Constitution,* 44, and sent to the Mediterranean in a squadron commanded by John Rodgers. It was a long cruise; when he returned to the United States, Andrew Jackson was President, and at once made his old comrade-in-arms one of the three Navy Commissioners.

In 1832 Patterson expressed a desire to go to sea again, and Jackson gave him command of the Mediterranean squadron, with his flag in *Delaware,* one of the Doughty battleships, technically a 74, but actually an 86, and an uncommonly fine specimen of her class. In this command, he performed one of the cleverest feats of American naval diplomacy, the famous collecting of the Neapolitan debt. The debt came about as the result of the spoliation of American citizens during the Napoleonic wars by the Kingdom of Naples and Sicily. Diplomacy had accomplished its part in the collection; the Neapolitans acknowledged that the claim was just and agreed on the amount. But that fantastic tyrant, King Bomba, then ruler of the dual monarchy, simply did not pay. In fact, he said he had no intention of paying.

Andrew Jackson was not the sort of man to let a thing like that go by default. He told Patterson to get the money. Now this was a far from easy assignment, since force or the threat of force would be resented by Bomba to the point of declaring the obligation canceled, and the Neapolitans would assuredly be supported by France and Spain, against whom there were other spoliation claims which the debtors were finding it inconvenient to pay.

Therefore, Patterson used mystery as his tool, beginning by sending the *Brandywine* frigate to Naples with Captain M. C. Perry with a request for the money. The Neapolitans said No; Perry bowed graciously and returned to his ship in the harbor, but he did not sail. Four days later *United States,* 44, put into Naples and anchored astern of *Brandywine;* Perry went ashore again, asked for the money, took his refusal very amiably, and invited the court chamberlain to dine aboard the ship. The chamberlain observed that *Brandywine's* decks were not cumbered with gear, as is usual with a frigate in time of peace, but very nearly cleared for action. Another four days, and *Concord,* 22, one of the new sloops-of-war, dropped into Naples, anchoring in line with the other two. When Perry made the usual request, he found the town full of activity, new guns being mounted in the forts.

He affected to notice nothing; the refusal to pay was as usual and so was his courteous withdrawal, but two days later another new sloop, *John Adams,* 22, formed line with the rest. Perry went ashore with a request for payment. He was turned down; this time only one day elapsed before the arrival of a third sloop, *Boston,* 22; and the day after that, *Delaware* herself, with Patterson aboard, brought the total of American guns in Naples harbor up to over 250 pieces. Not an in-

Daniel Todd Patterson

temperate word was spoken, but when the Commodore sailed, it was with the money.

Patterson remained on the station until 1836, taking over the Washington Navy Yard on his return to America, and remaining in charge there until his rather sudden death in 1839. His two sons both became naval officers, but one of them left the service for the Coast Survey, worked to the head of it, and enlarged its work to make it a general coast and geodetic survey of the country.

Patterson was the only one of Preble's boys who did not hold a sea command during the war, but he ranks with Macdonough as a junior officer in a post which was considered of minor importance but which became one of the key points of the whole conflict through enemy action. A strict man; and one at just the place where strictness was needed, for nothing is easier than to let a command go downhill on a remote station, with little help from the central government, surrounded by official lassitude and occasional stupidity. The gunboats under Patterson's command on Lake Borgne were the only ones in over 200 belonging to the service that did anything important or even creditable during the war, and Patterson must have a part of this credit. A strict man, who believed in enforcing the law as it stood, but who, when it was enforced, would not press matters further to gain a mere dialectic victory.

Chapter 16

Edward Preble

THESE, THEN, WERE THE MEN WHO WON THE WAR OF 1812.
The word "won" is used prepense, and advisedly. It has become
the custom among historians to deny that the United States won the
war or gained anything out of it. This viewpoint is supported by com-
paring the Treaty of Ghent with Henry Clay's flamboyant pre-war toot-
ings about the capture of Canada; and by mentioning the destruction of
Washington, the exhaustion of the government, and the crushing effects of the British blockade. It is well to take these things into consideration; they form a useful corrective to the Fourth-of-July oratory of the
1880s and 1890s, when people used to talk about "beating the British
lion to his knees." It is perfectly true that the peace treaty mentioned
none of the causes of the dispute and, in effect, only gave the United
States a draw. Which is to say that on the basis of the documents the
war was no doubt futile.

But beg pardon, the War of 1812 was not fought on paper. It was not
fought even for things that could readily be expressed on paper. The
effort of Mr. Madison and his colleagues to put intangibles into words
produced much of the confusion, both at the time and among those who
have examined the results subsequently. The fourth President talked
about Indians and about the Orders in Council which placed such
severe restrictions on American trade, and Henry Clay talked about the
expansion of America to its natural limits.

The average seaman who carried the burden of the conflict was ignorant of these matters and uninterested in them. He knew perfectly well
why he was fighting: it was to preserve his goods from confiscation
and his body from impressment—that is, from involuntary servi-
tude. The archetype of that seaman is Jack Lang, clambering over

Frolic's bowsprit in spite of his Captain's orders; he had spent a couple of years in one of those British hell-ships, and he meant to let them know what he thought about it, with the edge of a cutlass. "Remember the *Chesapeake!*" shouted *Constitution's* gunners as they slammed 24-pound cannonballs into *Cyane*; and they were not remembering *Chesapeake* under Lawrence's command, either.

There was more to it than this, however. At the close of the Revolution, Benjamin Franklin remarked that this struggle had been won, but that the War of Independence remained to be fought. The War of 1812 was the battle for independence that he foresaw. This is sufficiently demonstrated by the tone in which semi-official Britain approached the peace negotiations that began in the summer of 1814, and by the instructions which official Britain gave to its peace commissioners. As the negotiators went forth, the *Times* of London remarked: "Having disposed of our enemies in Europe, let us have no cant of moderation. There is no public feeling in the country stronger than that of indignation against the Americans. As we urged the principle No Peace with Bonaparte! so we must maintain the doctrine of No Peace with James Madison! Our demands may be couched in a single word—Submission."

The British commissioners carried from their government as a *sine qua non,* or starting point for discussion, a demand for the establishment of a forever inviolable Indian Territory, or buffer state in the Northwest, with the Ohio River as its boundary amd Great Britain as its recognized protector; the Americans already beyond the Ohio (there were about 100,000) "must shift for themselves." In addition the eastern half of Maine was demanded to provide an overland communication between Halifax and Quebec; both sides of the Niagara frontier were to be British; there was to be a "rectification" of the Canadian boundary, bringing it down along a line from Sackett's Harbor to Plattsburg, and thence across the northern parts of Vermont, New Hampshire, and Maine. Americans were to be forbidden to maintain either forts or naval vessels on the lakes; and if, as confidently expected, New Orleans and Mobile were taken before the treaty was executed, these also were to fall to Britain.

When the American commissioners heard these terms, they prepared to pack for home, but, fortunately for them, the British instructions had been written in the late spring, and H. M. commissioners were bidden to delay matters until the big military expeditions of the summer should have given England an even more favorable negotiating position. They did delay; and in the meanwhile *Wasp, Peacock,* and *Hornet* broke loose, and the privateers began to make their presence felt around the British Isles.

The really serious part of these raids was the fact that the rest of the world was now at peace, and as the clock ticked, cargoes showed a distinct tendency to seek neutral bottoms. Now the people worst hurt by both the direct and the indirect losses were precisely the India merchants and the shipping men, who were the mainstay of the ruling Tory party and who had pushed that party to the Proclamation of Impressment and the Orders in Council. The summer deepened; it became evident that instead of obtaining relief from the privateers, they were going to have an intensification of the attacks, and the merchants began to grow restive. While Mr. Croker of the Admiralty was advising that it was not safe to sail from Bristol to Plymouth without convoy, the merchants of Liverpool held an indignation meeting, protested that their port was under actual blockade, and presented a strong address to the crown.

Glasgow was still more vehement. Under the presidency of the Lord Provost, the assembled shipping men and underwriters voted:

"That the number of American privateers with which our channels have been infested, the audacity with which they have approached our coasts, and the success with which their enterprise has been attended, have proved injurious to our commerce, humbling to our pride, and discreditable to the directors of the naval power of the British nation.

"That there is reason to believe, in the short space of twenty-four months, above 800 vessels have been captured by that power whose maritime strength we have hitherto impolitically held in contempt."

This left the British government somewhat unsure of holding its strength at home and hence its Parliamentary majority. The tone at Ghent began to moderate. The Indian Territory idea moved from a *sine qua non* to an interesting subject for discussion; and soon afterward even the discussion was dropped. The territorial demands stood until mid-October; then there arrived the news that the British army on the Niagara frontier had been bloodily beaten, that Macdonough had taken the whole British fleet on Lake Champlain, and that Sir George Prevost was in full retreat to Canada. This whittled the territorial demands down to one for a piece of Maine and a treaty on the basis of *uti possedetis,* or hold what you have at the close of hostilities, which was supposed to result in permanent British possession of the expected capture at New Orleans. Meanwhile, there were more privateers than ever, better armed, attacking more valuable ships; they were evidently going to make a winter campaign.

The American commissioners flatly rejected the modified terms, and now in November, when the British government dared not tell its public what terms had been turned down, it stood revealed that Britain had in fact lost the naval war. The situation on the lakes requires no comment. The British position on the ocean had also become perfectly intolerable in three different dimensions. In spite of the extremely expensive blockade, no method had been discovered of keeping the privateers in port, or of restraining their activities once they were at sea. During that fall, three such craft, *Reindeer, Avon,* and *Blakely,* were built on an inlet near Boston in 35 working days, and all three were out by November. While the British were in the Chesapeake with an enormous fleet, landing troops for the burning of Washington, the Baltimore privateer *Midas* slipped right through their formations, and off the capes captured the British admiral's tender with all his uniforms and his paychest. Lord Eldon pointed out that on its current basis, the sea war could well continue forever; the Americans were paying for their new cruisers out of the profits from their captures.

With time and money the British could possibly have put a stop to this sort of business. But the people who had the money were the shipping men, and they were not willing to wait. They were going bankrupt; they preferred peace; and even they did not yet know about the raiding squadrons fitting out under Porter and Perry.

In the second place, there had been found no method of handling the *Peacock* class sloops-of-war. They went to sea when they pleased; they hit too hard for the British light cruisers and were too fast for the heavies; and they were even more destructive than the privateers. Once again, time and intelligence might have found a way, but time was the lacking element, and the Admiralty's efforts to find an answer for the *Peacocks* had thus far shown no remarkable intelligence. In fact, American ship construction and handling were, on the whole, improving faster than the British. Moreover the two 1814 raids of *Constitution* showed that even the heavy cruisers could not always be held in.

Behind this was the problem of the American battleships, which promised to be well-nigh insoluble. It is doubtful whether any English naval officer or government official thought much about the Fulton steam battery; but many men in both categories were perfectly well aware of three American line-of-battleships building in as many ports, and of the meaning of that construction. Charles Stewart was perfectly right: outgunning the normal British 74s as they did, these ships each required at least two British battleships off the ports where they lay. (It is noteworthy that Sir George Collier's squadron, consisting of two 50-gun ships especially built to handle an American 44 and another cruiser of about *Constitution's* own force, had been unable to keep that ship in port.) Two 74s constantly on station off each of the three ports meant a minimum of three assigned to the task, to allow for accidents or absences; say nine or ten all told. Britain could doubtless afford this; she had afforded more during the war with France. But the war with France was for national existence and this was a point of pride; it was cheaper to make peace.

These were the physical manifestations. There was also an intangible, which the British needed time to think out. Preble's boys had really introduced something new in naval warfare, at least in the combats and operations of cruisers. Contacts of such ships were very common in the general European war; the pair fought until one became disabled and surrendered—something that usually happened when the losing party lost about a fifth of his crew. The ship then passed into the navy of the victor. It had always been that way; in the American Revolution, for instance, the light frigate *Fox* was taken by the Americans, retaken by the British, and then by the French. The Americans of 1812 struck with a speed and vindictive efficiency that made nonsense of the amenities; they did not take, they destroyed. In the whole war only *Épervier, Cyane,* and *Levant* were really in shape to be brought home. It took the most heroic efforts to keep *Macedonian* afloat, and the Lake Champlain fleet would have sunk anywhere but in perfectly still water. *Guerrière, Java, Alert, Frolic, Peacock, Boxer, Reindeer, Avon,* and *Penguin* sank in action or were not worth keeping afloat.

It was the same with the merchant captures; instead of trying to send them into port, as the French did, the American cruisers took out everything of value and burned or scuttled the prize. Toward the close of 1814, when they were more and more getting in among ships with cargoes of small bulk and high value, the privateers displayed a distressing tendency to imitate this procedure.

The British government, faced with American refusal to accept even its scaled-down terms, asked an opinion from the Duke of Wellington. It can hardly have made pleasant reading. "I confess," said Britain's leading military expert, "that I think you have no right, from the state of the war, to demand any concession of territory from the Americans. You have not been able to carry it into the enemy territory, notwithstanding your undoubted military superiority, and you have not even cleared your own territory on the point of attack. You cannot on any principle of equality in negotiation claim a cession of territory excepting in exchange for other advantages which you have in your power. You can get no territory; indeed, the state of your military operations, however creditable, does not entitle you to demand any."

So the peace was signed, and the announcement of its terms produced in England a dissatisfaction even more profound than it has among the recent generation of American historians. The London newspapers complained bitterly that it was nothing but an armistice, that the real war remained to be fought. The complaints lasted until early in March, when three pieces of news, arriving almost simultaneously, put them to silence forever. *Constitution* had taken two more British ships in a single action; there was an American cruiser loose in the East Indies; and instead of the anticipated capture of New Orleans, the expedition to that place had resulted in one of the most frightful defeats in English history.

The end of this part of the story can be dated 1829. In that year

England fell on a dispute with the United States. Two members were overheard conversing as they left the House of Commons:

"We had better yield a point or two rather than go to war with the Americans."

"Yes. We shall get nothing but hard knocks there."

II

These were the men who won the war. What did they have in common?

In temperament, practically nothing. No strain runs all the way through. There is as little resemblance as there could be among such characters as the ardent Decatur, the almost manic-depressive character of Burrows, the New England calm of Isaac Hull, and the cold intelligence of Stewart. In many of the group there is an early longing for the sea, but Biddle and Porter had it only by association, while Jacob Jones, Burrows, Stewart, Macdonough, and Patterson exhibit no such predisposition, all having been brought to naval careers by circumstance.

There is a general strain of taste for adventure, but there is no sign of it in Hull, Bainbridge, Chauncey, Cassin, or Patterson; not that they failed to seek reputation at the cannon's mouth, but they are visibly removed from the high romantic excitements of Decatur and Porter. Most of them were reasonably gregarious, after the manner of naval officers, whose profession requires them to get along well with companions not of their own choosing; and Decatur, Bainbridge, Chauncey, and Stewart were distinct social successes. But against these may be set the morose Burrows, the withdrawing Hull, and the quiet, almost pietistic Macdonough.

In intellectual and educational equipment, there is an equal diversity. Blakely and Biddle were not only college graduates, but honor graduates; Warrington and Jones had good educations. Hull, Bainbridge, Porter, and Stewart educated themselves, and the last three displayed considerable capacity for absorbing whatever culture they could lay their hands on. Beyond education there is a good deal of intellectual capacity in the group; Decatur was a wit and his studies in oceanography were a real contribution; Biddle and Warrington were able administrators; Stewart thought well on several subjects, including strategy. But no one ever noticed any particular intellectual attainments in Jones, Cassin, or Patterson.

In social background the group runs the full list of diversity from Biddle with all that money, Blakely and Patterson, brought up in homes where there was never any question of money, down to Stewart, the tanner's apprentice, and Warrington, the poverty-stricken son of decayed gentility. Porter made a great deal of money and spent it rapidly; Stewart showed uncommon capacity in financial affairs, and Decatur was almost as good; but Hull, Bainbridge, and probably Cassin always had to pinch a little.

Perhaps nearest to a common background is the geographical one. A compass with its point at Philadelphia and its radius reaching to Baltimore would describe a circle that took in the majority of Preble's boys.* But this is a large circle in the first place; Hull, Chauncey, and Patterson lie outside it to the north, Warrington and Blakely to the south; and if Porter is brought into it by taste and upbringing, Macdonough is driven out of it in the same way.

In fact, the general pattern is so intricate as not to be a pattern; and so we come to the one thing they all certainly and identifiably had in common—that they were Preble's boys.

It is hard to get away from the statistical record. With the single exception of the Battle of Lake Erie, every victory in the War of 1812 was won by one of Preble's boys. With three exceptions, every one of Preble's boys who had a command in 1812 brought home at least one British battle-flag. These exceptions were Joseph Bainbridge, on whom Preble's indoctrination somehow failed to bite, the mysterious John Smith, and Charles Morris.

This last officer was Hull's first lieutenant in *Constitution* when she took *Guerrière;* received his promotion for his part in that triumph,

---

* In this connection it is worth noting that although all the privateers were called "Yankees" and New England furnished some sensational examples, it was the city of Baltimore that really fought the war. In spite of the British blockade in the Chesapeake, that town sent out more privateers than any other city, almost as many as any other two; and the Baltimore-built ships were generally the best.

and went down to Washington to take command of *Adams,* 28.*
She was a peculiar ship, having been built by two contractors, each
working on one side, and as one of them was a little sparing in his
materials, she was shorter on that side than on the other.

When Morris arrived, she was in to have this deficiency made good.
At the same time, since the 28-gun frigate was a little light for the
conditions of this war, her quarterdeck and forecastle were taken off,
and she was turned into a flush-deck corvette of 24. As such, Morris
took her to sea in January 1814, cruised across to the coast of Africa,
came back to Savannah for stores in April, then made up toward
Ireland.

As a corvette, *Adams* was exceptionally fast; was several times pursued by frigates which got nowhere near her, and ran down everything she chased, for a total of ten ships. Toward the end of July,
scurvy made its appearance aboard; Morris turned back to the United
States, making for the Maine ports. In thick and heavy weather on
August 17, the ship ran aground on the island of Haute. Morris lightened her, got her off, and took her up the Penobscot, several miles
above Castine, to be hove down for repairs. It was his hard luck that
this should be just the time when the British arrived off the mouth
of the river with an expedition for the conquest of Maine. They came
up after *Adams* with 1500 men. The militia who had been called out
to defend the corvette all ran away, leaving Morris with only his own
men, who had but 150 muskets among them, so he burned his ship,
an act for which he was fully acquitted by the court-martial.

Of the total of Preble's boys who commanded during the War of
1812, then, Morris, Joseph Bainbridge, Smith, Chauncey, and Patterson won no sea victories, though the last did more than his share at
New Orleans, and there is something to be said for the services of
Chauncey. Thirteen of the group had triumphs to their credit. The
score for all the rest of the navy list put together was one victory.

This is by no means because all the fighting ships were commanded by graduates of the 40 days before Tripoli, for Preble's boys
accounted for but one-third of the officers of command rank by 1812,

---

* Which must not be confused with *John Adams* of the same rate, quite a different ship.

the total ship commands being 17 for Preble's boys as against 35 for the rest of the service. On the negative side, Decatur, Lawrence, Porter, and Patterson lost ships in action*, and Joseph Bainbridge lost one after a chase. The total losses by other commanders were 14 —though at this point the statistic lacks realism, since nearly all the 14 were insignificant little watermice of the lakes, like *Julia* and *Growler* on Ontario, and *Growler* and *Eagle* on Champlain.

The chances that such a statistical record could come about fortuitously are remote to an astronomical degree. Repeat: it cuts both ways—Preble's boys won all the victories but one, and nearly all Preble's boys won victories. The fact of the victories itself is, of course, enough to make worth while an investigation into common characteristics—just as it might be worth while inquiring into similarities among English admirals who won battles from the French, or mathematicians who made major discoveries in the theory of numbers. And if there is any common background factor in this group besides service under Preble, it fails to meet the eye.

Nor does it detract from the old Commodore's influence to point out that in some cases the service with him was brief, or the personal connection tenuous. The veterans of the Tripoli campaign formed themselves into a tight little association that was none the less real for being unofficial. It included even Patterson, whose direct connection with Preble was probably the least of any. (Biddle also had little immediate connection, but corresponded with Preble later about gunboats and other matters.) They all called themselves Preble's boys and were proud of their membership.

Moreover, doctrines and ideas are not contagious diseases that require physical contact for transmission. They penetrate; even the officers who had little personal touch with Preble were thoroughly exposed to his concepts of the way a navy should be run by association with the others during the years between 1804 and 1812. The fact that he influenced them in various specific ways can be traced without difficulty by anyone who takes the time. For example—one case

---

* The loss of Patterson's *Carolina* represented no real gain to the enemy; the ship's gunners merely moved ashore, where they played a major part in the New Year's Day artillery duel.

where the evidence follows a clear line: we know the care Preble gave to the well-being of his men during the long voyage to the East Indies in the French War and later aboard *Constitution,* and we know how the men felt toward him. Now this mutual relationship between captain and crew was not altogether unheard of among other captains and in other services. Broke and Manners of the Royal Navy, whom the Americans encountered during the war, were of mold similar to Preble's. But it is so unusual as to be phenomenal that every member of a specialized group should exhibit the same care for the men and win the same appreciation. "God bless him," the men said of Decatur; Porter's "principle care was the health of my people"; Burrows mingled with the men ashore; Blakely and Stewart had so many applicants for enlistment that they could choose their crews at a time when even the privateers were finding it difficult to obtain sailors; the enlisted write a testimonial to Lieutenant Macdonough when he leaves the ship; and the stern disciplinarian Biddle's men wanted to kill everybody aboard *Penguin* when their beloved captain was hurt.

There remains the possibility that the association of Preble's boys was arranged, that his Mediterranean command contained the pick of the service. In favor of this is the fact that Secretary Smith believed that the hope of the navy lay in its junior officers, the young mids who had known no other master. There is also the genuine love-affair between Preble himself and the Jeffersonian democracy. He believed in its principles—partly from a professional point of view, for he quite agreed with Jefferson's attitude that any tribute to the Barbary powers was morally wrong, and that resistance to them was not only patriotic, but in the long run wise. All his later years, while he lay dying, were spent in trying to make Jefferson's gunboat program work; in turning out model after model, corresponding with gunboat commanders and builders, suggesting improvements in gun-mountings, rig, and handling. There is nothing to suggest that this was because Preble was enamored of gunboats in themselves; but Jefferson wanted them, and that was sufficient for Edward Preble.

Yet there is no evidence that any process of selection for merit was applied to the officers who went out in 1803. Rather the reverse. He took out the smallest of all the Mediterranean squadrons, and he himself was so junior on the list that the big ships and better-known officers could not be sent with him. He had hardly even met a single one of the lieutenants in his command. Lieutenants and midshipmen together, they comprised one-seventh of the navy list, and a highly random seventh.

But he succeeded in integrating them into the service; in making it important to them, and, through them, to the nation. It will not do to call this an accidental effect, for Preble was perfectly conscious of what he was doing. In one of his farewell letters, he makes it a point of pride that during his tenure of the Mediterranean command, there had not been a single duel or court-martial in the squadron; and it has been noted that he went to some length in avoiding duels and court-martials. He made them comrades, and—what is a good deal more important—stamped his wing of the service with a pattern of conduct that became of infinite benefit to the whole.

Among the influences that determine the procedures of men of action, not enough attention is given to conduct patterns. At moments of crisis people do comparatively little thinking; or rather, they think with minds already fixed in certain paths by conditioned reflexes. At the time of the *United States-Macedonian* battle, there was much comment on the originality of Decatur's concept of pure gunnery action. It was only a logical extrapolation of Preble under the guns of Tripoli, using *Constitution's* fire as both attack and protection. Porter training *Essex's* men in the use of hand-weapons, Macdonough putting out extra anchors with cables looped under water, were in fact copying Preble when he employed his frigate against Tripoli castles while his light craft tackled the gunboats. Having decided on battle, the sole question for these men became one of getting the most out of the available materials.

There is another aspect of the Preble training here—"having decided on battle." Among the ideas brought to action-point by Preble and the young men he trained there is visible a conviction that wars are won by fighting. The old man expected that his squadron would suffer very much when he went in against Tripoli—but he went. Bainbridge and Stewart expected that "we may be captured and probably shall be," but wanted to put to sea anyway. Isaac Hull made for that part of the sea where he would be most likely to encounter British cruisers. Blakely had three enemy ships in sight, each of a force equal to *Wasp's* own, and unhesitatingly attacked one of them. That is, if a somewhat disproportionate number of contacts with enemy men-o'-war fell to Preble's boys in 1812, it is because they deliberately made those contacts. They took the offensive, went looking for trouble.

Yet this offensive spirit itself is perhaps only tangential to what was the most valuable feature of the Preble tradition—which, as it was developed by the officers he trained, became a part of the thinking of the later navy. This feature may be defined as the reason behind both the offensive spirit and the matter of best employing the available material to make the offensive stick. It is that old question of considering a given situation in the light of its own content and of nothing else.

A. A. Gallatin was a great man, and in his own field, which was finance, he did this; but it took Bainbridge and Stewart to show him that it could be done with regard to the navy. They looked past the reputation of the British navy and the supposed lack of experience of the American, and talked about gunsights, methods of enlistment, the trailing of artillerists, long 24s on the maindeck, and the speed of the Humphreys frigates.

Yet Bainbridge and Stewart were not exceptional among Preble's boys in this respect. One runs into the same thing in various forms all through the story. This is true even on the negative side. The few failures Preble's boys made were made when they did not consider a situation purely in its own terms. Lawrence failed when he let honor force him into a battle while in command of a ship and crew which he had not yet made thoroughly his own. Chauncey failed at the Burlington Races by not accepting the fact that, if his own ships were badly damaged, the British would be worse. On the other side, Porter heading for the Pacific, Stewart actually backing down in the midst of an action, Hull putting out without orders, Warrington drawing the two British frigates after *Peacock*—all considered nothing but what their surroundings had to tell them; and so considering, succeeded; and succeeding, left a legacy to future generations.

Index

General Index

For Index of Ships, see page 415

General Index

General Index

General Index

General Index

General Index

General Index

General Index

Trant, James, 187
Treaty of Ghent, 308, 392-97
tribute to Barbary pirates, 8, 9, 23, 27, 31, 37, 107, 108, 122, 140, 173, 279, 402
Tripoli, *see* Barbary states
Tripoli, attack on, 34-38
Trippe, Lieutenant, 96, 282
Trumbull, John, 15
Truxtun, Thomas, 24, 25, 28, 69, 70, 71, 120, 170-73, 201, 202-204, 208, 278-79, 297-98, 321, 322, 329, 344
Tunis, *see* Barbary states
Turkey, 122-24, 195-96
Two Sicilies, 32, 33, 96 (*see also* Naples and Sicily)
Tyler, John, 294, 342
Tyng, Colonel, 20

University of North Carolina, 261-62
University of Pennsylvania, 298
Upshur, A. P., 294

Van Buren, Martin, 341, 342

Waldron, Captain, 115

Wales, Richard, 287, 289
Warrington, Lewis, 5, 276-95, 306, 351, 398, 399, 404
Warrington, Mrs. Lewis (Margaret King), 283
Warrington, Mrs. (mother of Lewis), 277, 280
Washington, George, 9, 11-12, 74, 107, 279, 296, 318, 319, 345, 359
Washington, D. C., burning of, 132n., 395
Wellington, Duke of, 137, 274, 361, 369-70, 380, 386, 397
whalers, Pacific, 224, 227-28, 309
Wheeler, Susan, *see* Decatur, Mrs. Stephen
Whinyates, Thomas, 77
Wilkinson, General James, 185, 188, 191, 360-61
William and Mary College, 278
Wilmer, Lieutenant, 228
Wilson, Lieutenant, 228
Woolsey, Melancthon, 179, 180, 181, 192-93

Yeo, Sir James Lucas, 81-82, 133, 183, 185-95, 197, 224, 256
You, Dominic, 379, 387, 388

Index of Ships

Index of Ships

Index of Ships

Index of Ships

Index of Ships

Volontaire, 120

Washington, 64, 107

Wasp, 74-79, 138, 165, 176, 260, 266, 267-73, 290, 303, 305, 306, 331, 394, 404

Winthrop, 20-21

Wolfe, 184-89, 192

Yankee, 258, 259

Yarmouth, 297

Young Wasp, 305